The Divine Comedy

DANTE ALIGHIERI
The Divine Comedy

TRANSLATED BY HENRY FRANCIS CARY

ILLUSTRATED BY UMBERTO ROMANO

The PROGRAMMED CLASSICS

Illustrations
Copyright, 1946, by Doubleday & Company, Inc.
Printed in the United States of America

CONTENTS

PART I
Hell 3

PART II
Purgatory 149

PART III
Paradise 293

Notes 431

Hell

CANTO I

The writer is met by Virgil, who promises to show him the punishments of Hell and Purgatory and to lead him to Beatrice, who will conduct him into Paradise.

IN the midway of this our mortal life,
I found me in a gloomy wood, astray
Gone from the path direct: and e'en to tell,
It were no easy task, how savage wild
That forest, how robust and rough its growth,
Which to remember only, my dismay
Renews, in bitterness not far from death.
Yet, to discourse of what there good befell,
All else will I relate discover'd there.

How first I enter'd it I scarce can say,
Such sleepy dulness in that instant weigh'd
My senses down, when the true path I left;
But when a mountain's foot I reach'd, where closed
The valley that had pierced my heart with dread,
I look'd aloft, and saw his shoulders broad
Already vested with that planet's beam,
Who leads all wanderers safe through every way.

Then was a little respite to the fear,
That in my heart's recesses deep had lain
All of that night, so pitifully past:
And as a man, with difficult short breath,
Forespent with toiling, 'scaped from sea to shore,

Turns to the perilous wide waste, and stands
At gaze; e'en so my spirit, that yet fail'd,
Struggling with terror, turn'd to view the straits
That none hath passed and lived. My weary frame
After short pause recomforted, again
I journey'd on over that lonely steep,
The hinder foot still firmer. Scarce the ascent
Began, when, lo! a panther, nimble, light,
And cover'd with a speckled skin, appear'd;
Nor, when it saw me, vanish'd; rather strove
To check my onward going; that ofttimes,
With purpose to retrace my steps, I turn'd.

The hour was morning's prime, and on his way
Aloft the sun ascended with those stars,
That with him rose when Love divine first moved
Those its fair works: so that with joyous hope
All things conspired to fill me, the gay skin
Of that swift animal, the matin dawn,
And the sweet season. Soon that joy was chased,
And by new dread succeeded, when in view
A lion came, 'gainst me as it appear'd,
With his head held aloft and hunger-mad,
That e'en the air was fear-struck. A she-wolf
Was at his heels, who in her leanness seem'd
Full of all wants, and many a land hath made
Disconsolate ere now. She with such fear
O'erwhelm'd me, at the sight of her appall'd,
That of the height all hope I lost. As one,
Who, with his gain elated, sees the time
When all unawares is gone, he inwardly
Mourns with heart-griping anguish; such was I,
Haunted by that fell beast, never at peace,
Who coming o'er against me, by degrees
Impell'd me where the sun in silence rests.

While to the lower space with backward step
I fell, my ken discern'd the form of one
Whose voice seem'd faint through long disuse of speech.
When him in that great desert I espied,

HELL

"Have mercy on me," cried I out aloud,
"Spirit! or living man! whate'er thou be."

He answered: "Now not man, man once I was,
And born of Lombard parents, Mantuans both
By country, when the power of Julius yet
Was scarcely firm. At Rome my life was past,
Beneath the mild Augustus, in the time
Of fabled deities and false. A bard
Was I, and made Anchises' upright son
The subject of my song, who came from Troy,
When the flames prey'd on Ilium's haughty towers.
But thou, say wherefore to such perils past
Return'st thou? wherefore not this pleasant mount
Ascendest, cause and source of all delight?"
"And art thou then that Virgil, that well-spring,
From which such copious floods of eloquence
Have issued?" I with front abash'd replied.
"Glory and light of all the tuneful train!
May it avail me, that I long with zeal
Have sought thy volume, and with love immense
Have conn'd it o'er. My master thou, and guide!
Thou he from whom alone I have derived
That style, which for its beauty into fame
Exalts me. See the beast, from whom I fled.
O save me from her, thou illustrious sage!
For every vein and pulse throughout my frame
She hath made tremble." He, soon as he saw
That I was weeping, answer'd, "Thou must needs
Another way pursue, if thou wouldst 'scape
From out that savage wilderness. This beast,
At whom thou criest, her way will suffer none
To pass, and no less hindrance makes than death:
So bad and so accursed in her kind,
That never sated is her ravenous will,
Still after food more craving than before.
To many an animal in wedlock vile
She fastens, and shall yet to many more,
Until that greyhound come, who shall destroy
Her with sharp pain. He will not life support

THE DIVINE COMEDY

By earth nor its base metals, but by love,
Wisdom, and virtue; and his land shall be
The land 'twixt either Feltro. In his might
Shall safety to Italia's plains arise,
For whose fair realm, Camilla, virgin pure,
Nisus, Euryalus, and Turnus fell.
He, with incessant chase, through every town
Shall worry, until he to hell at length
Restore her, thence by envy first let loose.
I, for thy profit pondering, now devise
That thou mayst follow me; and I, thy guide,
Will lead thee hence through an eternal space,
Where thou shalt hear despairing shrieks, and see
Spirits of old tormented, who invoke
A second death; and those next view, who dwell
Content in fire, for that they hope to come,
Whene'er the time may be, among the blest,
Into whose regions if thou then desire
To ascend, a spirit worthier than I
Must lead thee, in whose charge, when I depart,
Thou shalt be left: for that Almighty King,
Who reigns above, a rebel to his law
Adjudges me; and therefore hath decreed
That, to his city, none through me should come.
He in all parts hath sway; there rules, there holds
His citadel and throne. O happy those,
Whom there he chuses!" I to him in few:
"Bard! by that God, whom thou didst not adore,
I do beseech thee (that this ill and worse
I may escape) to lead me where thou said'st,
That I Saint Peter's gate may view, and those
Who, as thou tell'st, are in such dismal plight."

Onward he moved, I close his steps pursued.

CANTO II

Dante doubts whether his strength suffices for the journey, but he takes courage and follows Virgil.

Now was the day departing, and the air,
Imbrown'd with shadows, from their toils released
All animals on earth; and I alone
Prepared myself the conflict to sustain,
Both of sad pity, and that perilous road,
Which my unerring memory shall retrace.

O Muses! O high genius! now vouchsafe
Your aid. O mind! that all I saw hast kept
Safe in a written record, here thy worth
And eminent endowments come to proof.

I thus began: "Bard! thou who art my guide,
Consider well, if virtue be in me
Sufficient, ere to this high enterprise
Thou trust me. Thou hast told that Silvius' sire,
Yet clothed in corruptible flesh, among
The immortal tribes had entrance, and was there
Sensibly present. Yet if heaven's great Lord,
Almighty foe to ill, such favor show'd
In contemplation of the high effect,
Both what and who from him should issue forth,
It seems in reason's judgment well deserved;
Sith he of Rome and of Rome's empire wide,
In heaven's empyreal height was chosen sire:
Both which, if truth be spoken, were ordain'd
And stablish'd for the holy place, where sits
Who to great Peter's sacred chair succeeds.
He from this journey, in thy song renown'd,
Learn'd things, that to his victory gave rise
And to the papal robe. In after-times
The chosen vessel also travel'd there,
To bring us back assurance in that faith

THE DIVINE COMEDY

Which is the entrance to salvation's way.
But I, why should I there presume? or who
Permits it? not Æneas I, nor Paul.
Myself I deem not worthy, and none else
Will deem me. I, if on this voyage then
I venture, fear it will in folly end.
Thou, who art wise, better my meaning know'st,
Than I can speak." As one, who unresolves
What he hath late resolved, and with new thoughts
Changes his purpose, from his first intent
Removed; e'en such was I on that dun coast,
Wasting in thought my enterprise, at first
So eagerly embraced. "If right thy words
I scan," replied that shade magnanimous,
"Thy soul is by vile fear assail'd, which oft
So overcasts a man, that he recoils
From noblest resolution, like a beast
At some false semblance in the twilight gloom.
That from this terror thou mayst free thyself,
I will instruct thee why I came, and what
I heard in that same instant, when for thee
Grief touch'd me first. I was among the tribe,
Who rest suspended, when a dame, so blest
And lovely I besought her to command,
Call'd me; her eyes were brighter than the star
Of day; and she, with gentle voice and soft,
Angelically tuned, her speech address'd:
'O courteous shade of Mantua! thou whose fame
Yet lives, and shall live long as nature lasts!
A friend, not of my fortune but myself,
On the wide desert in his road has met
Hindrance so great, that he through fear has turn'd.
Now much I dread lest he past help have stray'd,
And I be risen too late for his relief,
From what in heaven of him I heard. Speed now,
And by thy eloquent persuasive tongue,
And by all means for his deliverance meet,
Assist him. So to me will comfort spring.
I, who now bid thee on this errand forth,
Am Beatrice; from a place I come

HELL

Revisited with joy. Love brought me thence,
Who prompts my speech. When in my Master's sight
I stand, thy praise to him I oft will tell.'

"She then was silent, and I thus began:
'O Lady! by whose influence alone
Mankind excels whatever is contain'd
Within that heaven which hath the smallest orb,
So thy command delights me, that to obey,
If it were done already, would seem late.
No need hast thou further to speak thy will:
Yet tell the reason, why thou art not loth
To leave that ample space, where to return
Thou burnest, for this centre here beneath.'

"She then: 'Since thou so deeply wouldst inquire,
I will instruct thee briefly why no dread
Hinders my entrance here. Those things alone
Are to be fear'd whence evil may proceed;
None else, for none are terrible beside.
I am so framed by God, thanks to his grace!
That any sufferance of your misery
Touches me not, nor flame of that fierce fire
Assails me. In high heaven a blessed dame
Resides, who mourns with such effectual grief
That hindrance, which I send thee to remove,
That God's stern judgment to her will inclines.
To Lucia, calling, her she thus bespake:
"Now doth thy faithful servant need thy aid,
And I commend him to thee." At her word
Sped Lucia, of all cruelty the foe,
And coming to the place, where I abode
Seated with Rachel, her of ancient days,
She thus address'd me: "Thou true praise of God!
Beatrice! why is not thy succor lent
To him, who so much loved thee, as to leave
For thy sake all the multitude admires?
Dost thou not hear how pitiful his wail,
Nor mark the death, which in the torrent flood,
Swol'n mightier than a sea, him struggling holds?"

THE DIVINE COMEDY

Ne'er among men did any with such speed
Haste to their profit, flee from their annoy,
As, when these words were spoken, I came here,
Down from my blessed seat, trusting the force
Of thy pure eloquence, which thee, and all
Who well have mark'd it, into honor bring.'

"When she had ended, her bright beaming eyes
Tearful she turn'd aside; whereat I felt
Redoubled zeal to serve thee. As she will'd,
Thus am I come: I saved thee from the beast,
Who thy near way across the goodly mount
Prevented. What is this comes o'er thee then?
Why, why dost thou hang back? why in thy breast
Harbor vile fear? why hast not courage there,
And noble daring; since three maids, so blest,
Thy safety plan, e'en in the court of heaven;
And so much certain good my words forebode?"

As florets, by the frosty air of night
Bent down and closed, when day has blanch'd their leaves,
Rise all unfolded on their spiry stems;
So was my fainting vigor new restored,
And to my heart such kindly courage ran,
That I as one undaunted soon replied:
"O full of pity she, who undertook
My succor! and thou kind, who didst perform
So soon her true behest! With such desire
Thou hast disposed me to renew my voyage,
That my first purpose fully is resumed.
Lead on: one only will is in us both.
Thou art my guide, my master thou, and lord."

So spake I; and when he had onward moved,
I enter'd on the deep and woody way.

HELL

CANTO III

Dante and Virgil come to the gate of Hell where those were punished who spent their time on earth in apathy and indifference to good and evil.

"THROUGH me you pass into the city of woe:
Through me you pass into eternal pain:
Through me among the people lost for aye.
Justice the founder of my fabric moved:
To rear me was the task of power divine,
Supremest wisdom, and primeval love.
Before me things create were none, save things
Eternal, and eternal I endure.
All hope abandon, ye who enter here."

   Such characters, in color dim, I mark'd
Over a portal's lofty arch inscribed.
Whereat I thus: "Master, these words import
Hard meaning." He as one prepared replied:
"Here thou must all distrust behind thee leave;
Here be vile fear extinguish'd. We are come
Where I have told thee we shall see the souls
To misery doom'd, who intellectual good
Have lost." And when his hand he had stretch'd forth
To mine, with pleasant looks, whence I was cheer'd,
Into that secret place he led me on.

   Here sighs, with lamentations and loud moans,
Resounded through the air pierced by no star,
That e'en I wept at entering. Various tongues,
Horrible languages, outcries of woe,
Accents of anger, voices deep and hoarse,
With hands together smote that swell'd the sounds,
Made up a tumult, that forever whirls
Round through that air with solid darkness stain'd,
Like to the sand that in the whirlwind flies.

THE DIVINE COMEDY

I then, with error yet encompast, cried:
"O master! what is this I hear? what race
Are these, who seem so overcome with woe?"

He thus to me: "This miserable fate
Suffer the wretched souls of those, who lived
Without or praise or blame, with that ill band
Of angels mix'd, who nor rebellious proved,
Nor yet were true to God, but for themselves
Were only. From his bounds Heaven drove them forth
Not to impair his lustre; nor the depth
Of Hell receives them, lest the accursed tribe
Should glory thence with exultation vain."

I then: "Master! what doth aggrieve them thus,
That they lament so loud?" He straight replied:
"That will I tell thee briefly. These of death
No hope may entertain: and their blind life
So meanly passes, that all other lots
They envy. Fame of them the world hath none,
Nor suffers; mercy and justice scorn them both.
Speak not of them, but look, and pass them by."

And I, who straightway look'd, beheld a flag,
Which whirling ran around so rapidly,
That it no pause obtain'd: and following came
Such a long train of spirits, I should ne'er
Have thought that death so many had despoil'd.

When some of these I recognized, I saw
And knew the shade of him, who to base fear
Yielding, abjured his high estate. Forthwith
I understood, for certain, this the tribe
Of those ill spirits both to God displeasing
And to his foes. These wretches, who ne'er lived,
Went on in nakedness, and sorely stung
By wasps and hornets, which bedew'd their cheeks
With blood, that, mix'd with tears, dropp'd to their feet,
And by disgustful worms was gather'd there.

HELL

Then looking further onward, I beheld
A throng upon the shore of a great stream:
Whereat I thus: "Sir! grant me now to know
Whom here we view, and whence impell'd they seem
So eager to pass o'er, as I discern
Through the blear light?" He thus to me in few:
"This shalt thou know, soon as our steps arrive
Beside the woful tide of Acheron."

Then with eyes downward cast, and fill'd with shame,
Fearing my words offensive to his ear,
Till we had reach'd the river, I from speech
Abstain'd. And lo! toward us in a bark
Comes on an old man, hoary white with eld,
Crying, "Woe to you, wicked spirits! hope not
Ever to see the sky again. I come
To take you to the other shore across,
Into eternal darkness, there to dwell
In fierce heat and in ice. And thou, who there
Standest, live spirit! get thee hence, and leave
These who are dead." But soon as he beheld
I left them not, "By other way," said he,
"By other haven shalt thou come to shore,
Not by this passage; thee a nimbler boat
Must carry." Then to him thus spake my guide:
"Charon! thyself torment not: so 'tis will'd,
Where will and power are one: ask thou no more."

Straightway in silence fell the shaggy cheeks
Of him, the boatman o'er the livid lake,
Around whose eyes glared wheeling flames. Meanwhile
Those spirits, faint and naked, color changed,
And gnash'd their teeth, soon as the cruel words
They heard. God and their parents they blasphemed,
The human kind, the place, the time, and seed,
That did engender them and give them birth.

Then all together sorely wailing drew
To the curst strand, that every man must pass
Who fears not God, Charon, demoniac form,

HELL

With eyes of burning coal, collects them all,
Beckoning, and each, that lingers, with his oar
Strikes. As fall off the light autumnal leaves,
One still another following, till the bough
Strews all its honors on the earth beneath;
E'en in like manner Adam's evil brood
Cast themselves, one by one, down from the shore,
Each at a beck, as falcon at his call.

Thus go they over through the umber'd wave;
And ever they on the opposing bank
Be landed, on this side another throng
Still gathers. "Son," thus spake the courteous guide,
"Those who die subject to the wrath of God
All here together come from every clime
And to o'erpass the river are not loth:
For so Heaven's justice goads them on, that fear
Is turn'd into desire. Hence ne'er hath past
Good spirit. If of thee Charon complain,
Now mayst thou know the import of his words."

This said, the gloomy region trembling shook
So terribly, that yet with clammy dews
Fear chills my brow. The sad earth gave a blast,
That, lightening, shot forth a vermilion flame,
Which all my senses conquer'd quite, and I
Down dropp'd, as one with sudden slumber seized.

CANTO IV

The poet descends into Limbo where he finds those who have lived virtuously, but through lack of baptism do not merit the bliss of Paradise.

BROKE the deep slumber in my brain a crash
Of heavy thunder, that I shook myself,
As one by main force roused. Risen upright,
My rested eyes I moved around, and search'd

THE DIVINE COMEDY

With fixed ken, to know what place it was
Wherein I stood. For certain, on the brink
I found me of the lamentable vale,
The dread abyss, that joins a thundrous sound
Of plaints innumerable. Dark and deep,
And thick with clouds o'erspread, mine eye in vain
Explored its bottom, nor could aught discern.

"Now let us to the blind world there beneath
Descend," the bard began, all pale of look:
"I go the first, and thou shalt follow next."

Then I, his alter'd hue perceiving, thus:
"How may I speed, if thou yieldest to dread,
Who still art wont to comfort me in doubt?"

He then: "The anguish of that race below
With pity stains my cheek, which thou for fear
Mistakest. Let us on. Our length of way
Urges to haste." Onward, this said, he moved;
And entering led me with him, on the bounds
Of the first circle that surrounds the abyss.

Here, as mine ear could note, no plaint was heard
Except of sighs, that made the eternal air
Tremble, not caused by tortures, but from grief
Felt by those multitudes, many and vast,
Of men, women, and infants. Then to me
The gentle guide: "Inquirest thou not what spirits
Are these which thou beholdest? Ere thou pass
Farther, I would thou know, that these of sin
Were blameless; and if aught they merited,
It profits not, since baptism was not theirs,
The portal to thy faith. If they before
The Gospel lived, they served not God aright;
And among such am I. For these defects,
And for no other evil, we are lost;
Only so far afflicted, that we live
Desiring without hope." Sore grief assail'd
My heart at hearing this, for well I knew

HELL

Suspended in that Limbo many a soul
Of mighty worth. "O tell me, sire revered!
Tell me, my master!" I began, through wish
Of full assurance in that holy faith
Which vanquishes all error; "say, did e'er
Any, or through his own or other's merit,
Come forth from thence, who afterward was blest?"

Piercing the secret purport of my speech,
He answer'd: "I was new to that estate
When I beheld a puissant one arrive
Amongst us, with victorious trophy crown'd.
He forth the shade of our first parent drew,
Abel his child, and Noah righteous man,
Of Moses lawgiver for faith approved,
Of patriarch Abraham, and David king,
Israel with his sire and with his sons,
Nor without Rachel whom so hard he won,
And others many more, whom he to bliss
Exalted. Before these, be thou assured,
No spirit of human kind was ever saved."

We, while he spake, ceased not our onward road,
Still passing through the wood; for so I name
Those spirits thick beset. We were not far
On this side from the summit, when I kenn'd
A flame, that o'er the darken'd hemisphere
Prevailing shined. Yet we a little space
Were distant, not so far but I in part
Discover'd that a tribe in honor high
That place possess'd. "O thou, who every art
And science valuest! who are these, that boast
Such honor, separate from all the rest?"

He answer'd: "The renown of their great names,
That echoes through your world above, acquires
Favor in Heaven, which holds them thus advanced."
Meantime a voice I heard: "Honor the bard
Sublime! his shade returns, that left us late!"
No sooner ceased the sound, than I beheld

THE DIVINE COMEDY

Four mighty spirits toward us bend their steps,
Of semblance neither sorrowful nor glad.

When thus my master kind began: "Mark him,
Who in his right hand bears that falchion keen,
The other three preceding, as their lord.
This is that Homer, of all bards supreme:
Flaccus the next, in satire's vein excelling;
The third is Naso; Lucan is the last.
Because they all that appellation own,
With which the voice singly accosted me,
Honoring they greet me thus, and well they judge."

So I beheld united the bright school
Of him the monarch of sublimest song,
That o'er the others like an eagle soars.

When they together short discourse had held,
They turn'd to me, with salutation kind
Beckoning me; at the which my master smiled:
Nor was this all; but greater honor still
They gave me, for they made me of their tribe;
And I was sixth amid so learn'd a band.

Far as the luminous beacon on we pass'd,
Speaking of matters, then befitting well
To speak, now fitter left untold. At foot
Of a magnificent castle we arrived,
Seven times with lofty walls begirt, and round
Defended by a pleasant stream. O'er this
As o'er dry land we pass'd. Next, through seven gates,
I with those sages enter'd, and we came
Into a mead with lively verdure fresh.

There dwelt a race, who slow their eyes around
Majestically moved, and in their port
Bore eminent authority: they spake
Seldom, but all their words were tuneful sweet.

We to one side retired, into a place

HELL

Open and bright and lofty, whence each one
Stood manifest to view. Incontinent,
There on the green enamel of the plain
Were shown me the great spirits, by whose sight
I am exalted in my own esteem.

Electra there I saw accompanied
By many, among whom Hector I knew,
Anchises' pious son, and with hawk's eye
Cæsar all arm'd, and by Camilla there
Penthesilea. On the other side,
Old king Latinus seated by his child
Lavinia, and that Brutus I beheld
Who Tarquin chased, Lucretia, Cato's wife
Marcia, with Julia and Cornelia there;
And sole apart retired, the Soldan fierce.

Then when a little more I raised my brow,
I spied the master of the sapient throng,
Seated amid the philosophic train.
Him all admire, all pay him reverence due.
There Socrates and Plato both I mark'd
Nearest to him in rank, Democritus,
Who sets the world at chance, Diogenes,
With Heraclitus, and Empedocles,
And Anaxagoras, and Thales sage,
Zeno, and Dioscorides well read
In nature's secret lore. Orpheus I mark'd
And Linus, Tully and moral Seneca,
Euclid and Ptolemy, Hippocrates,
Galenus, Avicen, and him who made
The commentary vast, Averroes.

Of all to speak at full were vain attempt;
For my wide theme so urges, that ofttimes
My words fall short of what bechanced. In two
The six associates part. Another way
My sage guide leads me, from that air serene,
Into a climate ever vex'd with storms:
And to a part I come, where no light shines.

CANTO V

In the second circle of Hell, Dante beholds Minos, the Infernal Judge, and witnesses the punishment of carnal sinners.

FROM the first circle I descended thus
Down to the second, which, a lesser space
Embracing, so much more of grief contains,
Provoking bitter moans. There Minos stands,
Grinning with ghastly feature: he, of all
Who enter, strict examining the crimes,
Gives sentence, and dismisses them beneath,
According as he foldeth him around:
For when before him comes the ill-fated soul,
It all confesses; and that judge severe
Of sins, considering what place in Hell
Suits the transgression, with his tail so oft
Himself encircles, as degrees beneath
He dooms it to descend. Before him stand
Always a numerous throng; and in his turn
Each one to judgment passing, speaks, and hears
His fate, thence downward to his dwelling hurl'd.
"O thou! who to this residence of woe
Approachest!" when he saw me coming, cried
Minos, relinquishing his dread employ,
"Look how thou enter here; beware in whom
Thou place thy trust; let not the entrance broad
Deceive thee to thy harm." To him my guide:
"Wherefore exclaimest? Hinder not his way
By destiny appointed; so 'tis will'd,
Where will and power are one. Ask thou no more."

Now 'gin the rueful wailings to be heard.
Now am I come where many a plaining voice
Smites on mine ear. Into a place I came
Where light was silent all. Bellowing there groan'd

HELL

A noise, as of a sea in tempest torn
By warring winds. The stormy blast of Hell
With restless fury drives the spirits on,
Whirl'd round and dash'd amain with sore annoy.
When they arrive before the ruinous sweep,
There shrieks are heard, there lamentations, moans,
And blasphemies 'gainst the good Power in Heaven.
I understood, that to this torment sad
The carnal sinners are condemn'd, in whom
Reason by lust is sway'd. As, in large troops
And multitudinous, when winter reigns,
The starlings on their wings are borne abroad;
So bears the tyrannous gust those evil souls.
On this side and on that, above, below,
It drives them: hope of rest to solace them
Is none, nor e'en of milder pang. As cranes,
Chanting their dolorous notes, traverse the sky,
Stretch'd out in long array; so I beheld
Spirits, who came loud wailing, hurried on
By their dire doom. Then I: "Instructor! who
Are these, by the black air so scourged?" "The first
'Mong those, of whom thou question'st," he replied,
"O'er many tongues was empress. She in vice
Of luxury was so shameless, that she made
Liking be lawful by promulged decree,
To clear the blame she had herself incurr'd.
This is Semiramis, of whom 'tis writ,
That she succeeded Ninus her espoused;
And held the land, which now the Soldan rules.
The next in amorous fury slew herself,
And to Sichæus' ashes broke her faith:
Then follows Cleopatra, lustful queen."

There mark'd I Helen, for whose sake so long
The time was fraught with evil; there the great
Achilles, who with love fought to the end.
Paris I saw, and Tristan; and beside,
A thousand more he show'd me, and by name
Pointed them out, whom love bereaved of life.

THE DIVINE COMEDY

When I had heard my sage instructor name
Those dames and knights of antique days, o'erpower'd
By pity, well-nigh in amaze my mind
Was lost; and I began: "Bard! willingly
I would address those two together coming,
Which seem so light before the wind." He thus:
"Note thou, when nearer they to us approach.
Then by that love which carries them along,
Entreat; and they will come." Soon as the wind
Sway'd them toward us, I thus framed my speech:
"O wearied spirits! come, and hold discourse
With us, if by none else restrain'd." As doves
By fond desire invited, on wide wings
And firm, to their sweet nest returning home,
Cleave the air, wafted by their will along;
Thus issued, from that troop where Dido ranks,
They, through the ill air speeding: with such force
My cry prevail'd, by strong affection urged.

"O gracious creature and benign! who go'st
Visiting, through this element obscure,
Us, who the world with bloody stain imbrued;
If, for a friend, the King of all, we own'd,
Our prayer to him should for thy peace arise,
Since thou hast pity on our evil plight.
Of whatsoe'er to hear or to discourse
It pleases thee, that will we hear, of that
Freely with thee discourse, while e'er the wind,
As now, is mute. The land, that gave me birth,
Is situate on the coast, where Po descends
To rest in ocean with his sequent streams.

"Love, that in gentle heart is quickly learnt,
Entangled him by that fair form, from me
Ta'en in such cruel sort, as grieves me still:
Love, that denial takes from none beloved,
Caught me with pleasing him so passing well,
That, as thou seest, he yet deserts me not.
Love brought us to one death: Caïna waits
The soul, who spilt our life." Such were their words;

At hearing which, downward I bent my looks,
And held them there so long, that the bard cried:
"What art thou pondering?" I in answer thus:
"Alas! by what sweet thoughts, what fond desire
Must they at length to that ill pass have reach'd!"

   Then turning, I to them my speech address'd,
And thus began: "Francesca! your sad fate
Even to tears my grief and pity moves.
But tell me; in the time of your sweet sighs,
By what, and how Love granted, that ye knew
Your yet uncertain wishes?" She replied:
"No greater grief than to remember days
Of joy, when misery is at hand. That kens
Thy learn'd instructor. Yet so eagerly
If thou art bent to know the primal root,
From whence our love gat being, I will do
As one, who weeps and tells his tale. One day,
For our delight we read of Lancelot,
How him love thrall'd. Alone we were, and no
Suspicion near us. Ofttimes by that reading
Our eyes were drawn together, and the hue
Fled from our alter'd cheek. But at one point
Alone we fell. When of that smile we read,
The wished smile so rapturously kiss'd
By one so deep in love, then he, who ne'er
From me shall separate, at once my lips
All trembling kiss'd. The book and writer both
Were love's purveyors. In its leaves that day
We read no more." While thus one spirit spake,
The other wail'd so sorely, that heart-struck
I, through compassion fainting, seem'd not far
From death, and like a corse fell to the ground.

CANTO VI

The poet finds himself in the third circle where he sees the punishment of the gluttonous, one of whom foretells the coming agitations in Florence.

My sense reviving, that erewhile had droop'd
With pity for the kindred shades, whence grief
O'ercame me wholly, straight around I see
New torments, new tormented souls, which way
Soe'er I move, or turn, or bend my sight.
In the third circle I arrive, of showers
Ceaseless, accursed, heavy and cold, unchanged
Forever, both in kind and in degree.
Large hail, discolor'd water, sleety flaw
Through the dun midnight air stream'd down amain:
Stank all the land whereon that tempest fell.

Cerberus, cruel monster, fierce and strange,
Through his wide threefold throat, barks as a dog
Over the multitude immersed beneath.
His eyes glare crimson, black his unctuous beard,
His belly large, and claw'd the hands, with which
He tears the spirits, flays them, and their limbs
Piecemeal disparts. Howling there spread, as curs,
Under the rainy deluge, with one side
The other screening, oft they roll them round,
A wretched, godless crew. When that great worm
Descried us, savage Cerberus, he oped
His jaws, and the fangs show'd us; not a limb
Of him but trembled. Then my guide, his palms
Expanding on the ground, thence fill'd with earth
Raised them, and cast it in his ravenous maw.
E'en as a dog, that yelling bays for food
His keeper, when the morsel comes, lets fall
His fury, bent alone with eager haste
To swallow it; so dropp'd the loathsome cheeks

HELL

Of demon Cerberus, who thundering stuns
The spirits, that they for deafness wish in vain.

    We, o'er the shades thrown prostrate by the brunt
Of the heavy tempest passing, set our feet
Upon their emptiness, that substance seem'd.

    They all along the earth extended lay,
Save one, that sudden raised himself to sit,
Soon as that way he saw us pass. "O thou!"
He cried, "who through the infernal shades art led,
Own, if again thou know'st me. Thou wast framed
Or ere my frame was broken." I replied:
"The anguish thou endurest perchance so takes
Thy form from my remembrance, that it seems
As if I saw thee never. But inform
Me who thou art, that in a place so sad
Art set, and in such torment, that although
Other be greater, none disgusteth more."
He thus in answer to my words rejoin'd:
"Thy city, heap'd with envy to the brim,
Aye, that the measure overflows its bounds,
Held me in brighter days. Ye citizens
Were wont to name me Ciacco. For the sin
Of gluttony, damned vice, beneath this rain,
E'en as thou seest, I with fatigue am worn:
Nor I sole spirit in this woe: all these
Have by like crime incurr'd like punishment."

    No more he said, and I my speech resumed:
"Ciacco! thy dire affliction grieves me much,
Even to tears. But tell me, if thou know'st,
What shall at length befall the citizens
Of the divided city; whether any
Just one inhabit there: and tell the cause,
Whence jarring Discord hath assail'd it thus."

    He then: "After long striving they will come
To blood; and the wild party from the woods

THE DIVINE COMEDY

Will chase the other with much injury forth.
Then it behoves that this must fall, within
Three solar circles; and the other rise
By borrow'd force of one, who under shore
Now rests. It shall a long space hold aloof
Its forehead, keeping under heavy weight
The other opprest, indignant at the load,
And grieving sore. The just are two in number,
But they neglected. Avarice, envy, pride,
Three fatal sparks, have set the hearts of all
On fire." Here ceased the lamentable sound;
And I continued thus: "Still would I learn
More from thee, further parley still entreat.
Of Farinata and Tegghiaio say,
They who so well deserved; of Giacopo,
Arrigo, Mosca, and the rest, who bent
Their minds on working good. Oh! tell me where
They bide, and to their knowledge let me come.
For I am prest with keen desire to hear
If heaven's sweet cup, or poisonous drug of Hell,
Be to their lip assign'd." He answer'd straight:
"These are yet blacker spirits. Various crimes
Have sunk them deeper in the dark abyss.
If thou so far descendest, thou mayst see them.
But to the pleasant world, when thou return'st,
Of me make mention, I entreat thee, there.
No more I tell thee, answer thee no more."

This said, his fixed eyes he turn'd askance,
A little eyed me, then bent down his head,
And 'midst his blind companions with it fell.

When thus my guide: "No more his bed he leaves,
Ere the last angel-trumpet blow. The Power
Adverse to these shall then in glory come,
Each one forthwith to his sad tomb repair,
Resume his fleshly vesture and his form,
And hear the eternal doom re-echoing rend
The vault." So pass'd we through that mixture foul
Of spirits and rain, with tardy steps; meanwhile

Touching, though slightly, on the life to come.
For thus I question'd: "Shall these tortures, Sir!
When the great sentence passes, be increased,
Or mitigated, or as now severe?"

He then: "Consult thy knowledge; that decides,
That, as each thing to more perfection grows,
It feels more sensibly both good and pain.
Though ne'er to true perfection may arrive
This race accurst, yet nearer then, than now,
They shall approach it." Compassing that path,
Circuitous we journey'd; and discourse,
Much more than I relate, between us pass'd:
Till at the point, whence the steps led below,
Arrived, there Plutus, the great foe, we found.

CANTO VII

In the fourth circle, he sees Plutus and the torments of the prodigal and avaricious; in the fifth circle, the wrathful and gloomy are punished in the Stygian lake.

"AH me! O Satan! Satan!" loud exclaim'd
Plutus, in accent hoarse of wild alarm:
And the kind sage, whom no event surprised,
To comfort me thus spake: "Let not thy fear
Harm thee, for power in him, be sure, is none
To hinder down this rock thy safe descent."
Then to that swol'n lip turning, "Peace!" he cried,
"Curst wolf! thy fury inward on thyself
Prey, and consume thee! Through the dark profound,
Not without cause, he passes. So 'tis will'd
On high, there where the great Archangel pour'd
Heaven's vengeance on the first adulterer proud."

As sails, full spread and bellying with the wind,
Drop suddenly collapsed, if the mast split;
So to the ground down dropp'd the cruel fiend.

THE DIVINE COMEDY

Thus we, descending to the fourth steep ledge,
Gain'd on the dismal shore, that all the woe
Hems in of all the universe. Ah me!
Almighty Justice! in what store thou heap'st
New pains, new troubles, as I here beheld.
Wherefore doth fault of ours bring us to this?

E'en as a billow, on Charybdis rising,
Against encounter'd billow dashing breaks;
Such is the dance this wretched race must lead,
Whom more than elsewhere numerous here I found.
From one side and the other, with loud voice,
Both roll'd on weights, by main force of their breasts,
Then smote together, and each one forthwith
Roll'd them back voluble, turning again;

Exclaiming these, "Why holdest thou so fast?"
Those answering, "And why castest thou away?"
So, still repeating their despiteful song,
They to the opposite point, on either hand,
Traversed the horrid circle; then arrived,
Both turn'd them round, and through the middle space
Conflicting met again. At sight whereof
I, stung with grief, thus spake: "O say, my guide!
What race is this. Were these, whose heads are shorn,
On our left hand, all separate to the church?"

He straight replied: "In their first life, these all
In mind were so distorted, that they made,
According to due measure, of their wealth
No use. This clearly from their words collect,
Which they howl forth, at each extremity
Arriving of the circle, where their crime
Contrary in kind disparts them. To the church
Were separate those, that with no hairy cowls
Are crown'd, both popes and cardinals, o'er whom
Avarice dominion absolute maintains."

I then: " 'Mid such as these some needs must be,
Whom I shall recognize, that with the blot

THE DIVINE COMEDY

Of these foul sins were stain'd." He answering thus:
"Vain thought conceivest thou. That ignoble life,
Which made them vile before, now makes them dark,
And to all knowledge indiscernible.
Forever they shall meet in this rude shock:
These from the tomb with clenched grasp shall rise,
Those with close-shaven locks. That ill they gave,
And ill they kept, hath of the beauteous world
Deprived, and set them at this strife, which needs
No labor'd phrase of mine to set it off.
Now mayst thou see, my son! how brief, how vain,
The goods committed into Fortune's hands,
For which the human race keep such a coil!
Not all the gold that is beneath the moon,
Or ever hath been, of these toil-worn souls
Might purchase rest for one." I thus rejoin'd:
"My guide! of these this also would I learn;
This Fortune, that thou speak'st of, what it is,
Whose talons grasp the blessings of the world."

He thus: "O beings blind! what ignorance
Besets you! Now my judgment hear and mark.
He, whose transcendent wisdom passes all,
The heavens creating, gave them ruling powers
To guide them; so that each part shines to each,
Their light in equal distribution pour'd.
By similar appointment he ordain'd,
Over the world's bright images to rule,
Superintendence of a guiding hand
And general minister, which, at due time,
May change the empty vantages of life
From race to race, from one to other's blood,
Beyond prevention of man's wisest care:
Wherefore one nation rises into sway,
Another languishes, e'en as her will
Decrees, from us conceal'd, as in the grass
The serpent train. Against her nought avails
Your utmost wisdom. She with foresight plans,
Judges, and carries on her reign, as theirs
The other powers divine. Her changes know

HELL

None intermission: by necessity
She is made swift, so frequent come who claim
Succession in her favors. This is she,
So execrated e'en by those whose debt
To her is rather praise: they wrongfully
With blame requite her, and with evil word;
But she is blessed, and for that recks not:
Amidst the other primal beings glad
Rolls on her sphere, and in her bliss exults.
Now on our way pass we, to heavier woe
Descending: for each star is falling now,
That mounted at our entrance, and forbids
Too long our tarrying." We the circle cross'd
To the next steep, arriving at a well,
That boiling pours itself down to a foss
Sluiced from its source. Far murkier was the wave
Than sablest grain: and we in company
Of the inky waters, journeying by their side,
Enter'd, though by a different track, beneath.
Into a lake, the Stygian named, expands
The dismal stream, when it hath reach'd the foot
Of the gray wither'd cliffs. Intent I stood
To gaze, and in the marish sunk descried
A miry tribe, all naked, and with looks
Betokening rage. They with their hands alone
Struck not, but with the head, the breast, the feet,
Cutting each other piecemeal with their fangs.

The good instructor spake: "Now seest thou, son!
The souls of those, whom anger overcame.
This too for certain know, that underneath
The water dwells a multitude, whose sighs
Into these bubbles make the surface heave,
As thine eye tells thee wheresoe'er it turn.
Fix'd in the slime, they say: 'Sad once were we,
In the sweet air made gladsome by the sun,
Carrying a foul and lazy mist within:
Now in these murky settlings are we sad.'
Such dolorous strain they gurgle in their throats,
But word distinct can utter none." Our route

Thus compass'd we, a segment widely stretch'd
Between the dry embankment, and the core
Of the loath'd pool, turning meanwhile our eyes
Downward on those who gulp'd its muddy lees;
Nor stopp'd, till to a tower's low base we came.

CANTO VIII

*Phlegyas, the ferryman of the lake, conveys Dante
and Virgil to the city of Dis where the portals
are closed against them by Demons.*

My theme pursuing, I relate, that ere
We reach'd the lofty turret's base, our eyes
Its height ascended, where we mark'd uphung
Two cressets, and another saw from far
Return the signal, so remote, that scarce
The eye could catch its beam. I, turning round
To the deep source of knowledge, thus inquired:
"Say what this means; and what, that other light
In answer set: what agency doth this?"

"There on the filthy waters," he replied,
"E'en now what next awaits us mayst thou see,
If the marsh-gendered fog conceal it not."

Never was arrow from the cord dismiss'd,
That ran its way so nimbly through the air,
As a small bark, that through the waves I spied
Toward us coming, under the sole sway
Of one that ferried it, who cried aloud:
"Art thou arrived, fell spirit?"—"Phlegyas, Phlegyas,
This time thou criest in vain," my lord replied;
"No longer shalt thou have us, but while o'er
The slimy pool we pass." As one who hears
Of some great wrong he hath sustain'd, whereat
Inly he pines: so Phlegyas inly pined
In his fierce ire. My guide, descending, stepp'd

[32]

HELL

Into the skiff, and bade me enter next,
Close at his side; nor, till my entrance, seem'd
The vessel freighted. Soon as both embark'd,
Cutting the waves, goes on the ancient prow,
More deeply than with others it is wont.

While we our course o'er the dead channel held,
One drench'd in mire before me came, and said:
"Who art thou, that thus comest ere thine hour?"

I answer'd: "Though I come, I tarry not:
But who art thou, that art become so foul?"

"One, as thou seest, who mourn": he straight replied.

To which I thus: "In mourning and in woe,
Curst spirit! tarry thou. I know thee well,
E'en thus in filth disguised." Then stretch'd he forth
Hands to the bark; whereof my teacher sage
Aware, thrusting him back: "Away! down there
To the other dogs!" then, with his arms my neck
Encircling, kiss'd my cheek, and spake: "O soul,
Justly disdainful! blest was she in whom
Thou wast conceived. He in the world was one
For arrogance noted: to his memory
No virtue lends its lustre; even so
Here is his shadow furious. There above,
How many now hold themselves mighty kings,
Who here like swine shall wallow in the mire,
Leaving behind them horrible dispraise."

I then: "Master! him fain would I behold
Whelm'd in these dregs, before we quit the lake."

He thus: "Or ever to thy view the shore
Be offer'd, satisfied shall be that wish,
Which well deserves completion." Scarce his words
Were ended, when I saw the miry tribes
Set on him with such violence, that yet
For that render I thanks to God, and praise.

[33]

THE DIVINE COMEDY

"To Filippo Argenti!" cried they all:
And on himself the moody Florentine
Turn'd his avenging fangs. Him here we left,
Nor speak I of him more. But on mine ear
Sudden a sound of lamentation smote,
Whereat mine eye unbarr'd I sent abroad.

And thus the good instructor: "Now, my son
Draws near the city, that of Dis is named,
With its grave denizens, a mighty throng."

I thus: "The minarets already, Sir!
There, certes, in the valley I descry,
Gleaming vermilion, as if they from fire
Had issued." He replied: "Eternal fire,
That inward burns, shows them with ruddy flame
Illumed; as in this nether Hell thou seest."

We came within the fosses deep, that moat
This region comfortless. The walls appear'd
As they were framed of iron. We had made
Wide circuit, ere a place we reach'd, where loud
The mariner cried vehement: "Go forth:
The entrance is here." Upon the gates I spied
More than a thousand, who of old from heaven
Were shower'd. With ireful gestures, "Who is this,"
They cried, "that, without death first felt, goes through
The regions of the dead?" My sapient guide
Made sign that he for secret parley wish'd;
Whereat their angry scorn abating, thus
They spake: "Come thou alone; and let him go,
Who hath so hardily enter'd this realm.
Alone return he by his witless way;
If well he knew it, let him prove. For thee,
Here shalt thou tarry, who through clime so dark
Hast been his escort." Now bethink thee, reader!
What cheer was mine at sound of those curst words.
I did believe I never should return.

HELL

"O my loved guide! who more than seven times
Security hast render'd me, and drawn
From peril deep, whereto I stood exposed,
Desert me not," I cried, "in this extreme.
And, if our onward going be denied,
Together trace we back our steps with speed."

My liege, who thither had conducted me,
Replied: "Fear not: for of our passage none
Hath power to disappoint us, by such high
Authority permitted. But do thou
Expect me here; meanwhile, thy wearied spirit
Comfort, and feed with kindly hope, assured
I will not leave thee in this lower world."
This said, departs the sire benevolent,
And quits me. Hesitating I remain
At war, 'twixt will and will not, in my thoughts.

I could not hear what terms he offer'd them,
But they conferr'd not long, for all at once
Pellmell rush'd back within. Closed were the gates,
By those our adversaries, on the breast
Of my liege lord: excluded, he return'd
To me with tardy steps. Upon the ground
His eyes were bent, and from his brow erased
All confidence, while thus in sighs he spake:
"Who hath denied me these abodes of woe?"
Then thus to me: "That I am anger'd, think
No ground of terror: in this trial I
Shall vanquish, use what arts they may within
For hindrance. This their insolence, not new,
Erewhile at gate less secret they display'd,
Which still is without bolt; upon its arch
Thou saw'st the deadly scroll: and even now,
On this side of its entrance, down the steep,
Passing the circles, unescorted, comes
One whose strong might can open us this land."

THE DIVINE COMEDY

CANTO IX

The poet enters the city of Dis where he discovers heretics are punished in tombs burning with intense fire.

THE hue, which coward dread on my pale cheeks
Imprinted when I saw my guide turn back,
Chased that from his which newly they had worn,
And inwardly restrain'd it. He, as one
Who listens, stood attentive: for his eye
Not far could lead him through the sable air,
And the thick-gathering cloud. "It yet behoves
We win this fight"; thus he began: "if not,
Such aid to us is offer'd—Oh! how long
Me seems it, ere the promised help arrive."

I noted, how the sequel of his words
Cloked their beginning; for the last he spake
Agreed not with the first. But not the less
My fear was at his saying; sith I drew
To import worse, perchance, than that he held,
His mutilated speech. "Doth ever any
Into this rueful concave's extreme depth
Descend, out of the first degree, whose pain
Is deprivation merely of sweet hope?"

Thus I inquiring. "Rarely," he replied,
"It chances, that among us any makes
This journey, which I wend. Erewhile, 'tis true,
Once came I here beneath, conjured by fell
Erictho, sorceress, who compell'd the shades
Back to their bodies. No long space my flesh
Was naked of me, when within these walls
She made me enter, to draw forth a spirit
From out of Judas' circle. Lowest place
Is that of all, obscurest, and removed
Furthest from heaven's all-circling orb. The road
Full well I know: thou therefore rest secure.

HELL

That lake, the noisome stench exhaling, round
The city of grief encompasses, which now
We may not enter without rage." Yet more
He added: but I hold it not in mind,
For that mine eye toward the lofty tower
Had drawn me wholly, to its burning top;
Where, in an instant, I beheld uprisen
At once three hellish furies stain'd with blood.
In limb and motion feminine they seem'd;
Around them greenest hydras twisting roll'd
Their volumes; adders and cerastes crept
Instead of hair, and their fierce temples bound.

   He, knowing well the miserable hags
Who tend the queen of endless woe, thus spake:
"Mark thou each dire Erynnis. To the left,
This is Megæra; on the right hand, she
Who wails, Alecto; and Tisiphone
I' th' midst." This said, in silence he remain'd.
Their breast they each one clawing tore; themselves
Smote with their palms, and such shrill clamor raised,
That to the bard I clung, suspicion-bound.
"Hasten Medusa: so to adamant
Him shall we change"; all looking down exclaim'd:
"E'en when by Theseus' might assail'd, we took
No ill revenge." "Turn thyself round and keep
Thy countenance hid; for if the Gorgon dire
Be shown, and thou shouldst view it, thy return
Upwards would be for ever lost." This said,
Himself, my gentle master, turn'd me round;
Nor trusted he my hands, but with his own
He also hid me. Ye of intellect
Sound and entire, mark well the lore conceal'd
Under close texture of the mystic strain.

   And now there came o'er the perturbed waves
Loud-crashing, terrible, a sound that made
Either shore tremble, as if of a wind
Impetuous, from conflicting vapors sprung,
That 'gainst some forest driving all his might,

[37]

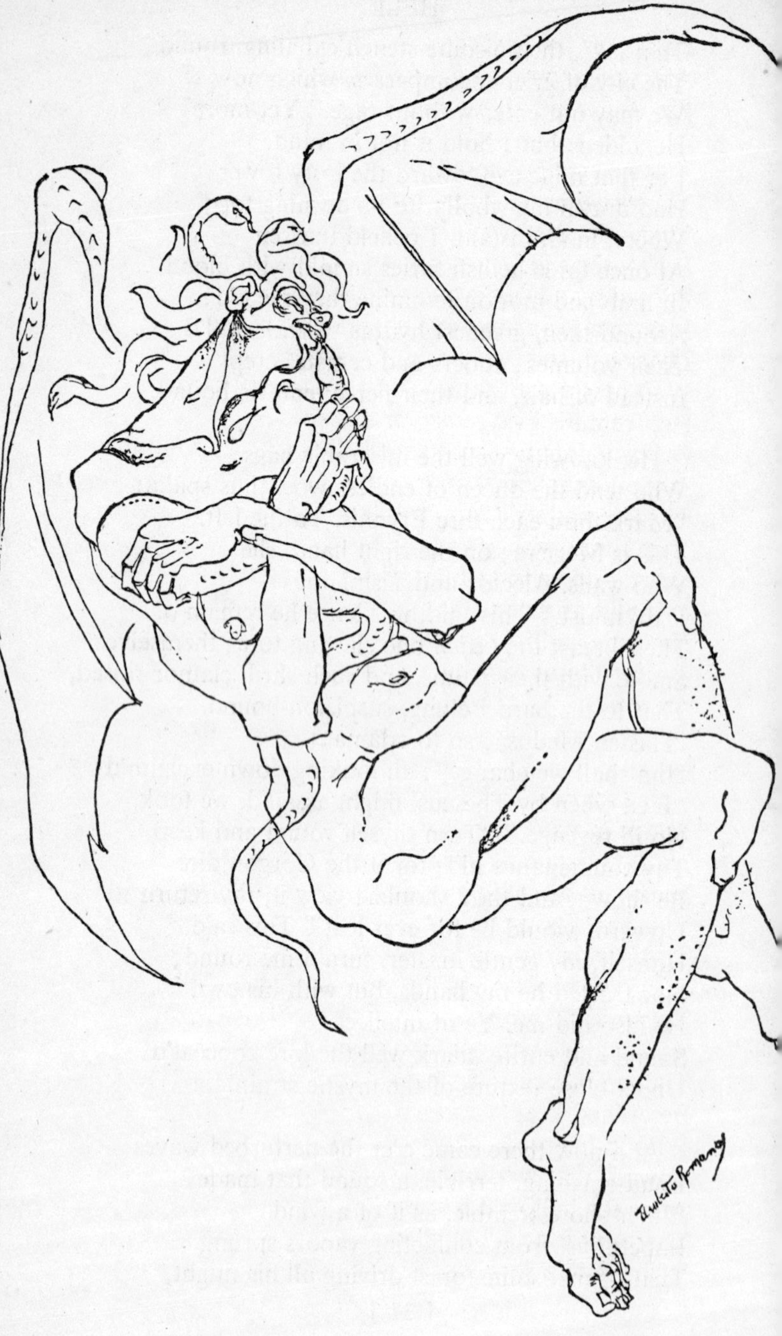

Plucks off the branches, beats them down, and hurls
Afar; then, onward passing, proudly sweeps
His whirlwind rage, while beasts and shepherds fly.

   Mine eyes he loosed, and spake: "And now direct
Thy visual nerve along that ancient foam,
There, thickest where the smoke ascends." As frogs
Before their foe the serpent, through the wave
Ply swiftly all, till at the ground each one
Lies on a heap; more than a thousand spirits
Destroy'd, so saw I fleeing before one
Who pass'd with unwet feet the Stygian sound.
He, from his face removing the gross air,
Oft his left hand forth stretch'd, and seem'd alone
By that annoyance wearied. I perceived
That he was sent from heaven; and to my guide
Turn'd me, who signal made, that I should stand
Quiet, and bend to him. Ah me! how full
Of noble anger seem'd he. To the gate
He came, and with his wand touch'd it, whereat
Open without impediment it flew.

   "Outcasts of heaven! O abject race, and scorn'd!"
Began he, on the horrid grunsel standing,
"Whence doth this wild excess of insolence
Lodge in you? wherefore kick you 'gainst that will
Ne'er frustrate of its end, and which so oft
Hath laid on you enforcement of your pangs?
What profits, at the fates to butt the horn?
Your Cerberus, if ye remember, hence
Bears still, peel'd of their hair, his throat and maw."
This said, he turn'd back o'er the filthy way,
And syllable to us spake none; but wore
The semblance of a man by other care
Beset, and keenly prest, than thought of him
Who in his presence stands. Then we our steps
Toward that territory moved, secure
After the hallow'd words. We, unopposed,
There enter'd; and, my mind eager to learn
What state a fortress like to that might hold,

THE DIVINE COMEDY

I, soon as enter'd, throw mine eye around,
And see, on every part, wide-stretching space,
Replete with bitter pain and torment ill.

 As where Rhone stagnates on the plains of Arles,
Or as at Pola, near Quarnaro's gulf,
That closes Italy and laves her bounds,
The place is all thick spread with sepulchres;
So was it here, save what in horror here
Excell'd: for 'midst the graves were scattered flames,
Wherewith intensely all throughout they burn'd,
That iron for no craft there hotter needs.

 Their lids all hung suspended; and beneath,
From them forth issued lamentable moans,
Such as the sad and tortured well might raise.

 I thus: "Master! say who are these, interr'd
Within these vaults, of whom distinct we hear
The dolorous sighs." He answer thus return'd:
"The arch-heretics are here, accompanied
By every sect their followers; and much more,
Than thou believest, the tombs are freighted: like
With like is buried; and the monuments
Are different in degrees of heat." This said,
He to the right hand turning, on we pass'd
Betwixt the afflicted and the ramparts high.

CANTO X

*Dante discourses with Farinata degli Uberti and
Cavalcante Cavalcanti, the first of whom predicts
the poet's exile from Florence.*

Now by a secret pathway we proceed,
Between the walls, that hem the region round,
And the tormented souls: my master first,
I close behind his steps. "Virtue supreme!"

[40]

HELL

I thus began: "Who through these ample orbs
In circuit lead'st me, even as thou will'st;
Speak thou, and satisfy my wish. May those,
Who lie within these sepulchres, be seen?
Already all the lids are raised, and none
O'er them keeps watch." He thus in answer spake:
"They shall be closed all, what-time they here
From Josaphat return'd shall come, and bring
Their bodies, which above they now have left.
The cemetery on this part obtain,
With Epicurus, all his followers,
Who with the body make the spirit die.
Here therefore satisfaction shall be soon,
Both to the question ask'd, and to the wish
Which thou conceal'st in silence." I replied:
"I keep not, guide beloved! from thee my heart
Secreted, but to shun vain length of words;
A lesson erewhile taught me by thyself."

"O Tuscan! thou, who through the city of fire
Alive art passing, so discreet of speech:
Here, please thee, stay awhile. Thy utterance
Declares the place of thy nativity
To be that noble land, with which perchance
I too severely dealt." Sudden that sound
Forth issued from a vault, whereat, in fear,
I somewhat closer to my leader's side
Approaching, he thus spake: "What dost thou? Turn:
Lo! Farinata there, who hath himself
Uplifted: from his girdle upwards, all
Exposed, behold him." On his face was mine
Already fix'd: his breast and forehead there
Erecting, seem'd as in high scorn he held
E'en Hell. Between the sepulchres, to him
My guide thrust me, with fearless hands and prompt;
This warning added: "See thy words be clear."

He, soon as there I stood at the tomb's foot,
Eyed me a space; then in disdainful mood
Address'd me: "Say what ancestors were thine."

I, willing to obey him, straight reveal'd
The whole, nor kept back aught: whence he, his brow
Somewhat uplifting, cried: "Fiercely were they
Adverse to me, my party, and the blood
From whence I sprang: twice, therefore, I abroad
Scatter'd them." "Though driven out, yet they each time
From all parts," answer'd I, "return'd; an art
Which yours have shown they are not skill'd to learn."

Then, peering forth from the unclosed jaw,
Rose from his side a shade, high as the chin,
Leaning, methought, upon its knees upraised.
It look'd around, as eager to explore
If there were other with me; but perceiving
That fond imagination quench'd, with tears
Thus spake: "If thou through this blind prison go'st,
Led by thy lofty genius and profound,
Where is my son? and wherefore not with thee?"
I straight replied: "Not of myself I come;
By him, who there expects me, through this clime
Conducted, whom perchance Guido thy son
Had in contempt." Already had his words
And mode of punishment read me his name,
Whence I so fully answer'd. He at once
Exclaim'd, up starting, "How! said'st thou, he *had*?
No longer lives he? Strikes not on his eye
The blessed daylight?" Then, of some delay
I made ere my reply, aware, down fell
Supine, nor after forth appear'd he more.

Meanwhile the other, great of soul, near whom
I yet was station'd, changed not countenance stern,
Nor moved the neck, nor bent his ribbed side.
"And if," continuing the first discourse,
"They in this art," he cried, "small skill have shown;
That doth torment me more e'en than this bed.
But not yet fifty times shall be relumed
Her aspect, who reigns here queen of this realm,
Ere thou shalt know the full weight of that art.

HELL

So to the pleasant world mayst thou return,
As thou shalt tell me why, in all their laws,
Against my kin this people is so fell."

"The slaughter and great havoc," I replied,
"That color'd Arbia's flood with crimson stain—
To these impute, that in our hallow'd dome
Such orisons ascend." Sighing he shook
The head, then thus resumed: "In that affray
I stood not singly, nor, without just cause,
Assuredly, should with the rest have stirr'd;
But singly there I stood, when, by consent
Of all, Florence had to the ground been razed,
The one who openly forbade the deed."

"So may thy lineage find at last repose,"
I thus adjured him, "as thou solve this knot,
Which now involves my mind. If right I hear,
Ye seem to view beforehand that which time
Leads with him, of the present uninform'd."

"We view, as one who hath an evil sight,"
He answer'd, "plainly, objects far remote;
So much of his large splendor yet imparts
The Almighty Ruler: but when they approach,
Or actually exist, our intellect
Then wholly fails; nor of your human state,
Except what others bring us, know we aught.
Hence therefore mayst thou understand, that all
Our knowledge in that instant shall expire,
When on futurity the portals close."

Then conscious of my fault, and by remorse
Smitten, I added thus: "Now shalt thou say
To him there fallen, that his offspring still
Is to the living join'd; and bid him know,
That if from answer, silent, I abstain'd,
'Twas that my thought was occupied, intent
Upon that error, which thy help hath solved."

THE DIVINE COMEDY

But now my master summoning me back
I heard, and with more eager haste besought
The spirit to inform me, who with him
Partook his lot. He answer thus return'd:
"More than a thousand with me here are laid.
Within is Frederick, second of that name,
And the Lord Cardinal, and of the rest
I speak not." He, this said, from sight withdrew.
But I my steps toward the ancient bard
Reverting, ruminated on the words
Betokening me such ill. Onward he moved,
And thus, in going, question'd: "Whence the amaze
That holds thy senses wrapt?" I satisfied
The inquiry, and the sage enjoin'd me straight:
"Let thy safe memory store what thou hast heard
To thee importing harm; and note thou this,"
With his raised finger bidding me take heed,
"When thou shalt stand before her gracious beam,
Whose bright eye all surveys, she of thy life
The future tenor will to thee unfold."

Forthwith he to the left hand turn'd his feet:
We left the wall, and toward the middle space
Went by a path that to a valley strikes,
Which e'en thus high exhaled its noisome steam.

CANTO XI

*At the seventh circle, he is instructed by Virgil concerning
the three following circles and why certain sinners
do not suffer within the city of Dis.*

UPON the utmost verge of a high bank,
By craggy rocks environ'd round, we came,
Where woes beneath, more cruel yet, were stow'd:
And here, to shun the horrible excess
Of fetid exhalation upward cast
From the profound abyss, behind the lid
Of a great monument we stood retired,

HELL

Whereon this scroll I mark'd: "I have in charge
Pope Anastastius, whom Photinus drew
From the right path." "Ere our descent, behoves
We make delay, that somewhat first the sense,
To the dire breath accustom'd, afterward
Regard it not." My master thus; to whom
Answering I spake: "Some compensation find,
That the time pass not wholly lost." He then:
"Lo! how my thoughts e'en to thy wishes tend.
My son! within these rocks," he thus began,
"Are three close circles in gradation placed,
As these which now thou leavest. Each one is full
Of spirits accurst; but that the sight alone
Hereafter may suffice thee, listen how
And for what cause in durance they abide.

"Of all malicious act abhorr'd in heaven,
The end is injury; and all such end
Either by force or fraud works other's woe.
But fraud, because of man's peculiar evil,
To God is more displeasing; and beneath,
The fraudulent are therefore doom'd to endure
Severer pang. The violent occupy
All the first circle; and because, to force,
Three persons are obnoxious, in three rounds,
Each within other separate, is it framed.
To God, his neighbor, and himself, by man
Force may be offer'd; to himself I say,
And his possessions, as thou soon shalt hear
At full. Death, violent death, and painful wounds
Upon his neighbor he inflicts; and wastes,
By devastation, pillage, and the flames,
His substance. Slayers, and each one that smites
In malice, plunderers, and all robbers, hence
The torment undergo of the first round,
In different herds. Man can do violence
To himself and his own blessings: and for this,
He in the second round must aye deplore
With unavailing penitence his crime.
Whoe'er deprives himself of life and light,

In reckless lavishment his talent wastes,
And sorrows there where he should dwell in joy.
To God may force be offer'd, in the heart
Denying and blaspheming his high power,
And Nature with her kindly law contemning.
And thence the inmost round marks with its seal
Sodom, and Cahors, and all such as speak
Contemptuously of the Godhead in their hearts.

"Fraud, that in every conscience leaves a sting,
May be by man employ'd on one, whose trust
He wins, or on another who withholds
Strict confidence. Seems as the latter way
Broke but the bond of love which Nature makes.
Whence in the second circle have their nest,
Dissimulation, witchcraft, flatteries,
Theft, falsehood, simony, all who seduce
To lust, or set their honesty at pawn,
With such vile scum as these. The other way
Forgets both Nature's general love, and that
Which thereto added afterward gives birth
To special faith. Whence in the lesser circle,
Point of the universe, dread seat of Dis,
The traitor is eternally consumed."

I thus: "Instructor, clearly thy discourse
Proceeds, distinguishing the hideous chasm
And its inhabitants with skill exact.
But tell me this: they of the dull, fat pool,
Whom the rain beats, or whom the tempest drives,
Or who with tongues so fierce conflicting meet,
Wherefore within the city fire-illumed
Are not these punish'd, if God's wrath be on them?
And if it be not, wherefore in such guise
Are they condemn'd?" He answer thus return'd:
"Wherefore in dotage wanders thus thy mind,
Not so accustom'd? or what other thoughts
Possess it? Dwell not in thy memory
The words, wherein thy ethic page describes
Three dispositions adverse to Heaven's will,

HELL

Incontinence, malice, and mad brutishness,
And how incontinence the least offends
God, and least guilt incurs? If well thou note
This judgment, and remember who they are,
Without these walls to vain repentance doom'd,
Thou shalt discern why they apart are placed
From these fell spirits, and less wreakful pours
Justice divine on them its vengeance down."

"O sun! who healest all imperfect sight,
Thou so content'st me, when thou solvest my doubt,
That ignorance not less than knowledge charms.
Yet somewhat turn thee back," I in these words
Continued, "where thou said'st, that usury
Offends celestial Goodness; and this knot
Perplex'd unravel." He thus made reply:
"Philosophy, to an attentive ear,
Clearly points out, not in one part alone,
How imitative Nature takes her course
From the celestial mind, and from its art:
And where her laws the Stagirite unfolds,
Not many leaves scann'd o'er, observing well
Thou shalt discover, that your art on her
Obsequious follows, as the learner treads
In his instructor's step; so that your art
Deserves the name of second in descent
From God. These two, if thou recall to mind
Creation's holy book, from the beginning
Were the right source of life and excellence
To human kind. But in another path
The usurer walks; and Nature in herself
And in her follower thus he sets at naught,
Placing elsewhere his hope. But follow now
My steps on forward journey bent; for now
The Pisces play with undulating glance
Along the horizon, and the Wain lies all
O'er the northwest; and onward there a space
Is our steep passage down the rocky height."

[47]

CANTO XII

Dante and his leader find the Minotaur on guard and descry a river of blood, patrolled by Centaurs, which is the torment of those who committed violence against their neighbors.

The place, where to descend the precipice
We came, was rough as Alp; and on its verge
Such object lay, as every eye would shun.

As is that ruin, which Adice's stream
On this side Trento struck, shouldering the wave,
Or loosed by earthquake or for lack of prop;
For from the mountain's summit, whence it moved
To the low level, so the headlong rock
Is shiver'd, that some passage it might give
To him who from above would pass; e'en such
Into the chasm was that descent: and there
At point of the disparted ridge lay stretch'd
The infamy of Crete, detested brood
Of the feign'd heifer: and at sight of us
It gnaw'd itself, as one with rage distract.
To him my guide exclaim'd: "Perchance thou deem'st
The King of Athens here, who, in the world
Above, thy death contrived. Monster! avaunt!
He comes not tutor'd by thy sister's art,
But to behold your torments is he come."

Like to a bull, that with impetuous spring
Darts, at the moment when the fatal blow
Hath struck him, but unable to proceed
Plunges on either side; so saw I plunge
The Minotaur; whereat the sage exclaim'd:
"Run to the passage! while he storms, 'tis well
That thou descend." Thus down our road we took
Through those dilapidated crags, that oft
Moved underneath my feet, to weight like theirs
Unused. I pondering went, and thus he spake:

HELL

"Perhaps thy thoughts are of this ruin'd steep,
Guarded by the brute violence, which I
Have vanquish'd now. Know then, that when I erst
Hither descended to the nether Hell,
This rock was not yet fallen. But past doubt,
(If well I mark) not long ere He arrived,
Who carried off from Dis the mighty spoil
Of the highest circle, then through all its bounds
Such trembling seized the deep concave and foul,
I thought the universe was thrill'd with love,
Whereby, there are who deem, the world hath oft
Been into chaos turn'd: and in that point,
Here, and elsewhere, that old rock toppled down.
But fix thine eyes beneath: the river of blood
Approaches, in the which all those are steep'd,
Who have by violence injured." O blind lust!
O foolish wrath! who so dost goad us on
In the brief life, and in the eternal then
Thus miserably o'erwhelm us. I beheld
An ample foss, that in a bow was bent,
As circling all the plain; for so my guide
Had told. Between it and the rampart's base,
On trail ran Centaurs, with keen arrows arm'd,
As to the chase they on the earth were wont.

At seeing us descend they each one stood;
And issuing from the troop, three sped with bows
And missile weapons chosen first; of whom
One cried from far: "Say, to what pain ye come
Condemn'd, who down this steep have journey'd. Speak
From whence ye stand, or else the bow I draw."

To whom my guide: "Our answer shall be made
To Chiron, there, when nearer him we come.
Ill was thy mind, thus ever quick and rash."
Then me he touch'd and spake: "Nessus is this,
Who for the fair Deïanira died,
And wrought himself revenge for his own fate.
He in the midst, that on his breast looks down,
Is the great Chiron who Achilles nursed;

THE DIVINE COMEDY

That other, Pholus, prone to wrath." Around
The foss these go by thousands, aiming shafts
At whatsoever spirit dares emerge
From out the blood, more than his guilt allows.

We to those beasts, that rapid strode along,
Drew near; when Chiron took an arrow forth,
And with the notch push'd back his shaggy beard
To the cheek-bone, then, his great mouth to view
Exposing, to his fellows thus exclaim'd:
"Are ye aware, that he who comes behind
Moves what he touches? The feet of the dead
Are not so wont." My trusty guide, who now
Stood near his breast, where the two natures join,
Thus made reply: "He is indeed alive,
And solitary so must needs by me
Be shown the gloomy vale, thereto induced
By strict necessity, not by delight.
She left her joyful harpings in the sky,
Who this new office to my care consign'd.
He is no robber, no dark spirit I.
But by that virtue, which empowers my step
To tread so wild a path, grant us, I pray,
One of thy band, whom we may trust secure,
Who to the ford may lead us, and convey
Across, him mounted on his back; for he
Is not a spirit that may walk the air."

Then on his right breast turning, Chiron thus
To Nessus spake: "Return, and be their guide.
And if ye chance to cross another troop,
Command them keep aloof." Onward we moved,
The faithful escort by our side, along
The border of the crimson-seething flood,
Whence, from those steep'd within, loud shrieks arose.

Some there I mark'd, as high as to their brow
Immersed, of whom the mighty Centaur thus:
"These are the souls of tyrants, who were given
To blood and rapine. Here they wail aloud

[50]

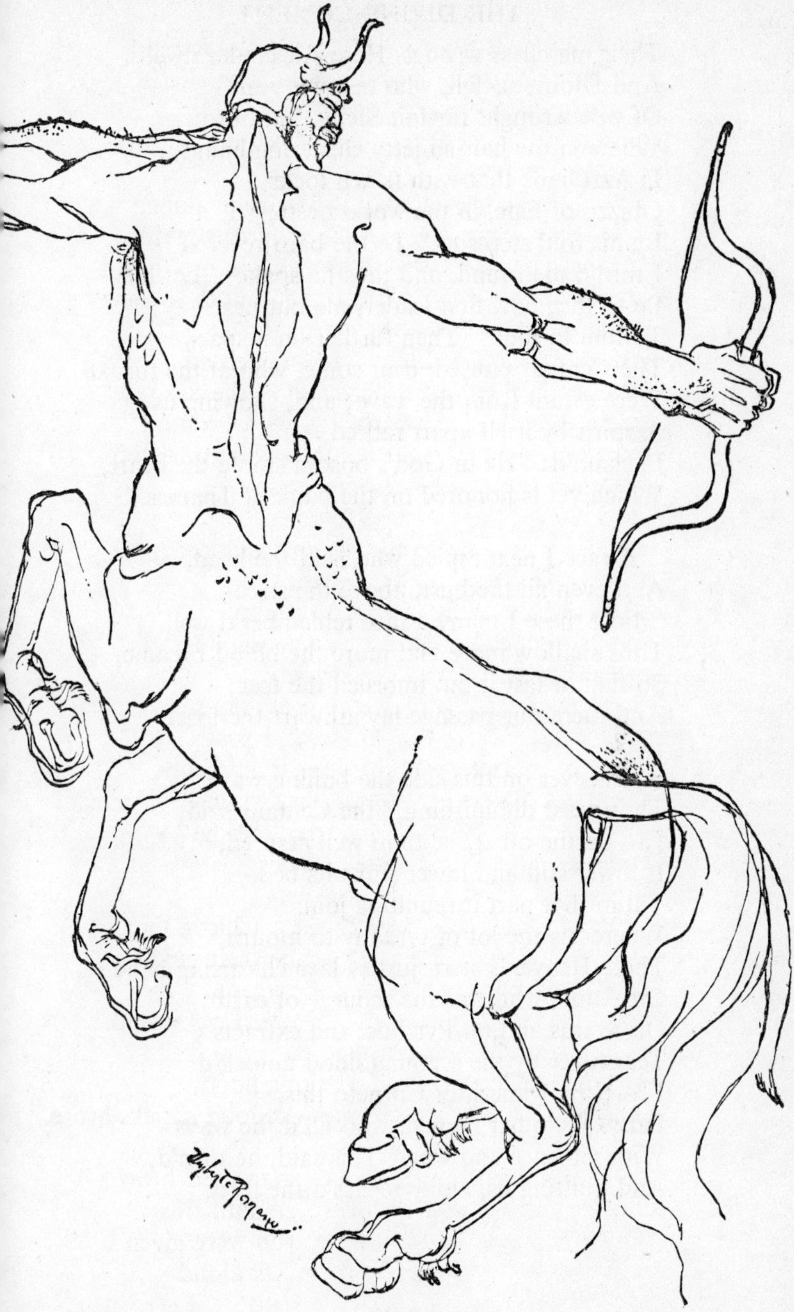

Their merciless wrongs. Here Alexander dwells,
And Dionysius fell, who many a year
Of woe wrought for fair Sicily. That brow,
Whereon the hair so jetty clustering hangs,
Is Azzolino; that with flaxen locks
Obizzo of Este, in the world destroy'd
By his foul step-son." To the bard revered
I turn'd me round, and thus he spake: "Let him
Be to thee now first leader, me but next
To him in rank." Then further on a space
The Centaur paused, near some, who at the throat
Were extant from the wave; and, showing us
A spirit by itself apart retired,
Exclaim'd: "He in God's bosom smote the heart,
Which yet is honored on the bank of Thames."

    A race I next espied who held the head,
And even all the bust, above the stream.
'Midst these I many a face remember'd well.
Thus shallow more and more the blood became,
So that at last it but imbrued the feet;
And there our passage lay athwart the foss.

    "As ever on this side the boiling wave
Thou seest diminishing," the Centaur said,
"So on the other, be thou well assured,
It lower still and lower sinks its bed,
Till in that part it reuniting join,
Where 'tis the lot of tyranny to mourn.
There Heaven's stern justice lays chastising hand
On Attila, who was the scourge of earth,
On Sextus and on Pyrrhus, and extracts
Tears ever by the seething flood unlock'd
From the Rinieri, of Corneto this,
Pazzo the other named, who fill'd the ways
With violence and war." This said, he turn'd,
And quitting us, alone repass'd the ford.

HELL

CANTO XIII

*Dante enters the second compartment of the seventh circle
which contains those who have done violence to their
own persons or have violently consumed their goods.*

ERE Nessus yet had reach'd the other bank,
We enter'd on a forest, where no track
Of steps had worn a way. Not verdant there
The foliage, but of dusky hue; not light
The boughs and tapering, but with knares deform'd
And matted thick: fruits there were none, but thorns
Instead, with venom fill'd. Less sharp than these,
Less intricate the brakes, wherein abide
Those animals, that hate the cultured fields,
Betwixt Corneto and Cecina's stream.

Here the brute harpies make their nest, the same
Who from the Strophades the Trojan band
Drove with dire boding of their future woe.
Broad are their pennons, of the human form
Their neck and countenance, arm'd with talons keen
The feet, and the huge belly fledge with wings.
These sit and wail on the drear mystic wood.

The kind instructor in these words began:
"Ere further thou proceed, know thou art now
I' th' second round, and shalt be, till thou come
Upon the horrid sand: look therefore well
Around thee, and such things thou shalt behold,
As would my speech discredit." On all sides
I heard sad plainings breathe, and none could see
From whom they might have issued. In amaze
Fast bound I stood. He, as it seem'd, believed
That I had thought so many voices came
From some amid those thickets close conceal'd,
And thus his speech resum'd: "If thou lop off

THE DIVINE COMEDY

A single twig from one of those ill plants,
The thought thou hast conceived shall vanish quite."

Thereat a little stretching forth my hand,
From a great wilding gather'd I a branch,
And straight the trunk exclaim'd: "Why pluck'st thou me?"
Then, as the dark blood trickled down its side,
These words it added: "Wherefore tear'st me thus?
Is there no touch of mercy in thy breast?
Men once were we, that now are rooted here.
Thy hand might well have spared us, had we been
The souls of serpents." As a brand yet green,
That burning at one end from the other sends
A groaning sound, and hisses with the wind
That forces out its way, so burst at once
Forth from the broken splinter words and blood.

I, letting fall the bough, remain'd as one
Assail'd by terror; and the sage replied:
"If he, O injured spirit! could have believed
What he hath seen but in my verse described,
He never against thee had stretch'd his hand.
But I, because the thing surpass'd belief,
Prompted him to this deed, which even now
Myself I rue. But tell me, who thou wast;
That, for this wrong to do thee some amends,
In the upper world (for thither to return
Is granted him) thy fame he may revive."
"That pleasant word of thine," the trunk replied,
"Hath so inveigled me, that I from speech
Cannot refrain, wherein if I indulge
A little longer, in the snare detain'd,
Count it not grievous. I it was, who held
Both keys to Frederick's heart, and turn'd the wards,
Opening and shutting, with a skill so sweet,
That besides me, into his inmost breast
Scarce any other could admittance find.
The faith I bore to my high charge was such,
It cost me the life-blood that warm'd my veins.
The harlot, who ne'er turn'd her gloating eyes

[54]

HELL

From Cæsar's household, common vice and pest
Of courts, 'gainst me inflamed the minds of all;
And to Augustus they so spread the flame,
That my glad honors changed to bitter woes.
My soul, disdainful and disgusted, sought
Refuge in death from scorn, and I became,
Just as I was, unjust toward myself.
By the new roots, which fix this stem, I swear,
That never faith I broke to my liege lord,
Who merited such honor; and of you,
If any to the world indeed return,
Clear he from wrong my memory, that lies
Yet prostrate under envy's cruel blow."

    First somewhat pausing, till the mournful words
Were ended, then to me the bard began:
"Lose not the time; but speak, and of him ask,
If more thou wish to learn." Whence I replied:
"Question thou him again of whatsoe'er
Will, as thou think'st, content me; for no power
Have I to ask, such pity is at my heart."

    He thus resumed: "So may he do for thee
Freely what thou entreatest, as thou yet
Be pleased, imprison'd spirit! to declare,
How in these gnarled joints the soul is tied;
And whether any ever from such frame
Be loosen'd, if thou canst, that also tell."

    Thereat the trunk breathed hard, and the wind soon
Changed into sounds articulate like these:
"Briefly ye shall be answer'd. When departs
The fierce soul from the body, by itself
Thence torn asunder, to the seventh gulf
By Minos doom'd, into the wood it falls,
No place assign'd, but wheresoever chance
Hurls it; there sprouting, as a grain of spelt,
It rises to a sapling, growing thence
A savage plant. The harpies, on its leaves
Then feeding, cause both pain, and for the pain

THE DIVINE COMEDY

A vent to grief. We, as the rest, shall come
For our own spoils, yet not so that with them
We may again be clad; for what a man
Takes from himself it is not just he have.
Here we perforce shall drag them; and throughout
The dismal glade our bodies shall be hung,
Each on the wild thorn of his wretched shade."

Attentive yet to listen to the trunk
We stood, expecting further speech, when us
A noise surprised; as when a man perceives
The wild boar and the hunt approach his place
Of station'd watch, who of the beasts and boughs
Loud rustling round him hears. And lo! there came
Two naked, torn with briers, in headlong flight,
That they before them broke each fan o' th' wood.
"Haste now," the foremost cried, "now haste thee, death!"
The other, as seem'd, impatient of delay,
Exclaiming, "Lano! not so bent for speed
Thy sinews, in the lists of Toppo's field."
And then, for that perchance no longer breath
Sufficed him, of himself and of a bush
One group he made. Behind them was the wood
Full of black female mastiffs, gaunt and fleet,
As greyhounds that have newly slipt the leash.
On him, who squatted down, they stuck their fangs,
And having rent him piecemeal bore away
The tortured limbs. My guide then seized my hand,
And led me to the thicket, which in vain
Mourn'd through its bleeding wounds: "O Giacomo
Of Sant' Andrea! what avails it thee,"
It cried, "that of me thou hast made thy screen?
For thy ill life, what blame on me recoils?"

When o'er it he had paused, my master spake:
"Say who wast thou, that at so many points
Breathest out with blood thy lamentable speech?"

He answer'd: "O ye spirits! arrived in time
To spy the shameful havoc that from me

[56]

My leaves hath sever'd thus, gather them up,
And at the foot of their sad parent-tree
Carefully lay them. In that city I dwelt,
Who for the Baptist her first patron changed,
Whence he for this shall cease not with his art
To work her woe: and if there still remain'd not
On Arno's passage some faint glimpse of him,
Those citizens, who rear'd once more her walls
Upon the ashes left by Attila,
Had labor'd without profit of their toil.
I slung the fatal noose from my own roof."

CANTO XIV

They arrive at the third compartment where violence against God, Nature, and Art is punished.

Soon as the charity of native land
Wrought in my bosom, I the scatter'd leaves
Collected, and to him restored, who now
Was hoarse with utterance. To the limit thence
We came, which from the third the second round
Divides, and where of justice is display'd
Contrivance horrible. Things then first seen
Clearlier to manifest, I tell how next
A plain we reach'd, that from its sterile bed
Each plant repell'd. The mournful wood waves round
Its garland on all sides, as round the wood
Spreads the sad foss. There, on the very edge,
Our steps we stay'd. It was an area wide
Of arid sand and thick, resembling most
The soil that erst by Cato's foot was trod.

Vengeance of heaven! Oh! how shouldst thou be fear'd
By all, who read what here mine eyes beheld.

Of naked spirits many a flock I saw,
All weeping piteously, to different laws

THE DIVINE COMEDY

Subjected; for on the earth some lay supine,
Some crouching close were seated, others paced
Incessantly around; the latter tribe
More numerous, those fewer who beneath
The torment lay, but louder in their grief.

O'er all the sand fell slowly wafting down
Dilated flakes of fire, as flakes of snow
On Alpine summit, when the wind is hush'd.
As, in the torrid Indian clime, the son
Of Ammon saw, upon his warrior band
Descending, solid flames, that to the ground
Came down; whence he bethought him with his troop
To trample on the soil; for easier thus
The vapor was extinguish'd, while alone:
So fell the eternal fiery flood, wherewith
The marle glow'd underneath, as under stove
The viands, doubly to augment the pain.
Unceasing was the play of wretched hands,
Now this, now that way glancing, to shake off
The heat, still falling fresh. I thus began:
"Instructor! thou who all things overcomest,
Except the hardy demons that rush'd forth
To stop our entrance at the gate, say who
Is yon huge spirit, that, as seems, heeds not
The burning, but lies writhen in proud scorn,
As by the sultry tempest immatured?"

Straight he himself, who was aware I ask'd
My guide of him, exclaim'd: "Such as I was
When living, dead such now I am. If Jove
Weary his workman out, from whom in ire
He snatch'd the lightnings, that at my last day
Transfix'd me; if the rest he weary out,
At their black smithy laboring by turns,
In Mongibello, while he cries aloud,
'Help, help, good Mulciber!' as erst he cried
In the Phlegræan warfare; and the bolts
Launch he, full aim'd at me, with all his might;
He never should enjoy a sweet revenge."

HELL

Then thus my guide, in accent higher raised
Than I before had heard him: "Capaneus!
Thou art more punish'd, in that this thy pride
Lives yet unquench'd: no torment, save thy rage,
Were to thy fury pain proportion'd full."

Next turning round to me, with milder lip
He spake: "This of the seven kings was one,
Who girt the Theban walls with siege, and held,
As still he seems to hold, God in disdain,
And sets his high omnipotence at naught.
But, as I told him, his despiteful mood
In ornament well suits the breast that wears it.
Follow me now; and look thou set not yet
Thy foot in the hot sand, but to the wood
Keep ever close." Silently on we pass'd
To where there gushes from the forest's bound
A little brook, whose crimson'd wave yet lifts
My hair with horror. As the rill, that runs
From Bulicame, to be portion'd out
Among the sinful women, so ran this
Down through the sand; its bottom and each bank
Stone-built, and either margin at its side,
Whereon I straight perceived our passage lay.

"Of all that I have shown thee, since that gate
We enter'd first, whose threshold is to none
Denied, naught else so worthy of regard,
As is this river, has thine eye discern'd,
O'er which the flaming volley all is quench'd."

So spake my guide; and I him thence besought,
That having given me appetite to know,
The food he too would give, that hunger craved.

"In midst of ocean," forthwith he began,
"A desolate country lies, which Crete is named;
Under whose monarch, in old times, the world
Lived pure and chaste. A mountain rises there,
Call'd Ida, joyous once with leaves and streams,

[59]

THE DIVINE COMEDY

Deserted now like a forbidden thing.
It was the spot which Rhea, Saturn's spouse,
Chose for the secret cradle of her son;
And better to conceal him, drown'd in shouts
His infant cries. Within the mount, upright
An ancient form there stands, and huge, that turns
His shoulders toward Damiata; and at Rome,
As in his mirror, looks. Of finest gold
His head is shaped, pure silver are the breast
And arms, thence to the middle is of brass,
And downward all beneath well-temper'd steel,
Save the right foot of potter's clay, on which
Than on the other more erect he stands.
Each part, except the gold, is rent throughout;
And from the fissure tears distil, which join'd
Penetrate to that cave. They in their course,
Thus far precipitated down the rock,
Form Acheron, and Styx, and Phlegethon;
Then by this straiten'd channel passing hence
Beneath e'en to the lowest depth of all,
Form there Cocytus, of whose lake (thyself
Shalt see it) I here give thee no account."

Then I to him: "If from our world this sluice
Be thus derived; wherefore to us but now
Appears it at this edge?" He straight replied:
"The place, thou know'st, is round: and though great part
Thou have already past, still to the left
Descending to the nethermost, not yet
Hast thou the circuit made of the whole orb.
Wherefore, if aught of new to us appear,
It needs not bring up wonder in thy looks."

Then I again inquired: "Where flow the streams
Of Phlegethon and Lethe? for of one
Thou tell'st not; and the other, of that shower,
Thou say'st, is form'd." He answer thus return'd:
"Doubtless thy questions all well pleased I hear.
Yet the red seething wave might have resolved
One thou proposest. Lethe thou shalt see,

HELL

But not within this hollow, in the place
Whither, to lave themselves, the spirits go,
Whose blame hath been by penitence removed."
He added: "Time is now we quit the wood.
Look thou my steps pursue: the margins give
Safe passage, unimpeded by the flames;
For over them all vapor is extinct."

CANTO XV

They meet a troop of spirits that have done great violence to nature, and Dante distinguishes Brunetto Latini, his former master.

ONE of the solid margins bears us now
Envelop'd in the mist, that, from the stream
Arising, hovers o'er, and saves from fire
Both piers and water. As the Flemings rear
Their mound, 'twixt Ghent and Bruges, to chase back
The ocean, fearing his tumultuous tide
That drives toward them; or the Paduans theirs
Along the Brenta, to defend their towns
And castles, ere the genial warmth be felt
On Chiarentana's top; such were the mounds,
So framed, though not in height or bulk to these
Made equal, by the master, whosoe'er
He was, that raised them here. We from the wood
Were now so far removed, that turning round
I might not have discern'd it, when we met
A troop of spirits, who came beside the pier.

They each one eyed us, as at eventide
One eyes another under a new moon;
And toward us sharpen'd their sight, as keen
As an old tailor at his needle's eye.

Thus narrowly explored by all the tribe,
I was agnized of one, who by the skirt
Caught me, and cried, "What wonder have we here?"

[61]

THE DIVINE COMEDY

And I, when he to me outstretch'd his arm,
Intently fix'd my ken on his parch'd looks,
That, although smirch'd with fire, they hinder'd not
But I remember'd him; and toward his face
My hand inclining, answer'd: "Ser Brunetto!
And are ye here?" He thus to me: "My son!
Oh let it not displease thee, if Brunetto
Latini but a little space with thee
Turn back, and leave his fellows to proceed."

I thus to him replied: "Much as I can,
I thereto pray thee; and if thou be willing
That I here seat me with thee, I consent;
His leave, with whom I journey, first obtain'd."

"O son!" said he, "whoever of this throng
One instant stops, lies then a hundred years,
No fan to ventilate him, when the fire
Smites sorest. Pass thou therefore on. I close
Will at thy garments walk, and then rejoin
My troop, who go mourning their endless doom."

I dared not from the path descend to tread
On equal ground with him, but held my head
Bent down, as one who walks in reverent guise.

"What chance or destiny," thus he began,
"Ere the last day, conducts thee here below?
And who is this that shows to thee the way?"

"There up aloft," I answer'd, "in the life
Serene, I wander'd in a valley lost,
Before mine age had to its fulness reach'd.
But yester-morn I left it: then once more
Into that vale returning, him I met;
And by this path homeward he leads me back."

"If thou," he answer'd, "follow but thy star,
Thou canst not miss at last a glorious haven;

HELL

Unless in fairer days my judgment err'd.
And if my fate so early had not chanced,
Seeing the heavens thus bounteous to thee, I
Had gladly given thee comfort in thy work.
But that ungrateful and malignant race,
Who in old times came down from Fesole,
Ay and still smack of their rough mountain-flint,
Will for thy good deeds show thee enmity.
Nor wonder; for amongst ill-savor'd crabs
It suits not the sweet fig-tree lay her fruit.
Old fame reports them in the world for blind,
Covetous, envious, proud. Look to it well:
Take heed thou cleanse thee of their ways. For thee,
Thy fortune hath such honor in reserve,
That thou by either party shalt be craved
With hunger keen: but be the fresh herb far
From the goat's tooth. The herd of Fesole
May of themselves make litter, not touch the plant,
If any such yet spring on their rank bed,
In which the holy seed revives, transmitted
From those true Romans, who still there remain'd,
When it was made the nest of so much ill."

"Were all my wish fulfill'd," I straight replied,
"Thou from the confines of man's nature yet
Hadst not been driven forth; for in my mind
Is fix'd, and now strikes full upon my heart,
The dear, benign, paternal image, such
As thine was, when so lately thou didst teach me
The way for man to win eternity:
And how I prized the lesson, it behoves,
That, long as life endures, my tongue should speak.
What of my fate thou tell'st, that write I down;
And, with another text to comment on,
For her I keep it, the celestial dame,
Who will know all, if I to her arrive.
This only would I have thee clearly note:
That, so my conscience have no plea against me,
Do Fortune as she list, I stand prepared.

[63]

THE DIVINE COMEDY

Not new or strange such earnest to mine ear.
Speed Fortune then her wheel, as likes her best;
The clown his mattock; all things have their course."

Thereat my sapient guide upon his right
Turn'd himself back, then looked at me, and spake:
"He listens to good purpose who takes note."

I not the less still on my way proceed,
Discoursing with Brunetto, and inquire
Who are most known and chief among his tribe.

"To know of some is well;" he thus replied,
"But of the rest silence may best beseem.
Time would not serve us for report so long.
In brief I tell thee, that all these were clerks,
Men of great learning and no less renown,
By one same sin polluted in the world.
With them is Priscian; and Accorso's son,
Francesco, herds among the wretched throng:
And, if the wish of so impure a blotch
Possess'd thee, him thou also mightst have seen,
Who by the servants' servant was transferr'd
From Arno's seat to Bacchiglione, where
His ill-strain'd nerves he left. I more would add,
But must from further speech and onward way
Alike desist; for yonder I behold
A mist new-arisen on the sandy plain.
A company, with whom I may not sort,
Approaches. I commend my *Treasure* to thee,
Wherein I yet survive; my sole request."

This said, he turn'd, and seem'd as one of those
Who o'er Verona's champaign try their speed
For the green mantle; and of them he seem'd,
Not he who loses but who gains the prize.

HELL

CANTO XVI

They meet the spirits of three military men, and then reach the place where the water descends to the eighth circle.

Now came I where the water's din was heard
As down it fell into the other round,
Resounding like the hum of swarming bees:
When forth together issued from a troop,
That pass'd beneath the fierce tormenting storm,
Three spirits, running swift. They toward us came,
And each one cried aloud, "Oh! do thou stay,
Whom, by the fashion of thy garb, we deem
To be some inmate of our evil land."

Ah, me! what wounds I mark'd upon their limbs,
Recent and old, inflicted by the flames.
E'en the remembrance of them grieves me yet.

Attentive to their cry, my teacher paused,
And turned to me his visage, and then spake:
"Wait now: our courtesy these merit well:
And were't not for the nature of the place,
Whence glide the fiery darts, I should have said,
That haste had better suited thee than them."

They, when we stopp'd, resumed their ancient wail,
And, soon as they had reach'd us, all the three
Whirl'd round together in one restless wheel.
As naked champions, smear'd with slippery oil
Are wont, intent, to watch their place of hold
And vantage, ere in closer strife they meet;
Thus each one, as he wheel'd, his countenance
At me directed, so that opposite
The neck moved ever to the twinkling feet.

"If woe of this unsound and dreary waste,"
Thus one began, "added to our sad cheer

[65]

THE DIVINE COMEDY

Thus peel'd with flame, do call forth scorn on us
And our entreaties, let our great renown
Incline thee to inform us who thou art,
That dost imprint, with living feet unharm'd,
The soil of Hell. He, in whose track thou seest
My steps pursuing, naked though he be
And reft of all, was of more high estate
Than thou believest; grandchild of the chaste
Gualdrada, him they Guidoguerra call'd,
Who in his lifetime many a noble act
Achieved, both by his wisdom and his sword.
The other, next to me that beats the sand,
Is Aldobrandi, name deserving well,
In the upper world, of honor; and myself,
Who in this torment do partake with them,
Am Rusticucci, whom, past doubt, my wife,
Of savage temper, more than aught beside
Hath to this evil brought." If from the fire
I had been shelter'd, down amidst them straight
I then had cast me; nor my guide, I deem,
Would have restrain'd my going: but that fear
Of the dire burning vanquish'd the desire,
Which made me eager of their wish'd embrace.

I then began: "Not scorn, but grief much more,
Such as long time alone can cure, your doom
Fix'd deep within me, soon as this my lord
Spake words, whose tenor taught me to expect
That such a race, as ye are, was at hand.
I am a countryman of yours, who still
Affectionate have utter'd, and have heard
Your deeds and names renown'd. Leaving the gall,
For the sweet fruit I go, that a sure guide
Hath promised to me. But behoves, that far
As to the centre first I downward tend."

"So may long space thy spirit guide thy limbs,"
He answer straight return'd; "and so thy fame
Shine bright when thou art gone, as thou shalt tell,
If courtesy and valor, as they wont,

Dwell in our city, or have vanish'd clean:
For one amidst us late condemn'd to wail,
Borsiere, yonder walking with his peers,
Grieves us no little by the news he brings."

"An upstart multitude and sudden gains,
Pride and excess, O Florence! have in thee
Engender'd, so that now in tears thou mourn'st!"

Thus cried I, with my face upraised, and they
All three, who for an answer took my words,
Look'd at each other, as men look when truth
Comes to their ear. "If at so little cost,"
They all at once rejoin'd, "thou satisfy
Others who question thee, O happy thou!
Gifted with words so apt to speak thy thought.
Wherefore, if thou escape this darksome clime,
Returning to behold the radiant stars,
When thou with pleasure shalt retrace the past,
See that of us thou speak among mankind."

This said, they broke the circle, and so swift
Fled, that as pinions seem'd their nimble feet.

Not in so short a time might one have said
"Amen," as they had vanish'd. Straight my guide
Pursued his track. I follow'd: and small space
Had we past onward, when the water's sound
Was now so near at hand, that we had scarce
Heard one another's speech for the loud din.

E'en as the river, that first holds its course
Unmingled from the Mount of Vesulo,
On the left side of Apennine, toward
The east, which Acquacheta higher up
They call, ere it descend into the vale,
At Forli, by that name no longer known,
Rebellows o'er Saint Benedict, roll'd on
From the Alpine summit down a precipice,
Where space enough to lodge a thousand spreads;

THE DIVINE COMEDY

Thus downward from a craggy steep we found
That this dark wave resounded, roaring loud,
So that the ear its clamor soon had stunn'd.

I had a cord that braced my girdle round,
Wherewith I erst had thought fast bound to take
The painted leopard. This when I had all
Unloosen'd from me (so my master bade)
I gather'd up, and stretch'd it forth to him.
Then to the right he turn'd, and from the brink
Standing few paces distant, cast it down
Into the deep abyss. "And somewhat strange,"
Thus to myself I spake, "signal so strange
Betokens, which my guide with earnest eye
Thus follows." Ah! what caution must men use
With those who look not at the deed alone,
But spy into the thoughts with subtle skill.

"Quickly shall come," he said, "what I expect;
Thine eye discover quickly that, whereof
Thy thought is dreaming." Ever to that truth,
Which but the semblance of a falsehood wears,
A man, if possible, should bar his lip;
Since, although blameless, he incurs reproach.
But silence here were vain; and by these notes,
Which now I sing, reader, I swear to thee,
So may they favor find to latest times!
That through the gross and murky air I spied
A shape come swimming up, that might have quell'd
The stoutest heart with wonder; in such guise
As one returns, who hath been down to loose
An anchor grappled fast against some rock,
Or to aught else that in the salt wave lies,
Who, upward springing, close draws in his feet.

CANTO XVII

The monster Geryon is described. By permission, Dante gets a closer view of those who have done violence to Art.

"Lo! the fell monster with the deadly sting,
Who passes mountains, breaks through fenced walls
And firm embattled spears, and with his filth
Taints all the world." Thus me my guide address'd,
And beckon'd him, that he should come to shore,
Near to the stony causeway's utmost edge.

Forthwith that image vile of Fraud appear'd,
His head and upper part exposed on land,
But laid not on the shore his bestial train.
His face the semblance of a just man's wore,
So kind and gracious was its outward cheer;
The rest was serpent all: two shaggy claws
Reach'd to the arm-pits; and the back and breast,
And either side, were painted o'er with nodes
And orbits. Colors variegated more
Nor Turks nor Tartars e'er on cloth of state
With interchangeable embroidery wove,
Nor spread Arachne o'er her curious loom.
As ofttimes a light skiff, moor'd to the shore,
Stands part in water, part upon the land;
Or, as where dwells the greedy German boor,
The beaver settles, watching for his prey;
So on the rim, that fenced the sand with rock,
Sat perch'd the fiend of evil. In the void
Glancing, his tail upturn'd its venomous fork,
With sting like scorpion's arm'd. Then thus my guide,
"Now need our way must turn few steps apart,
Far as to that ill beast, who couches there."

Thereat, toward the right our downward course
We shaped, and, better to escape the flame

THE DIVINE COMEDY

And burning marle, ten paces on the verge
Proceeded. Soon as we to him arrive,
A little further on mine eye beholds
A tribe of spirits, seated on the sand
Near to the void. Forthwith my master spake:
"That to the full thy knowledge may extend
Of all this round contains, go now, and mark
The mien these wear: but hold not long discourse.
Till thou returnest, I with him meantime
Will parley, that to us he may vouchsafe
The aid of his strong shoulders." Thus alone,
Yet forward on the extremity I paced
Of that seventh circle, where the mournful tribe
Were seated. At the eyes forth gush'd their pangs,
Against the vapors and the torrid soil
Alternately their shifting hands they plied.
Thus use the dogs in summer still to ply
Their jaws and feet by turns, when bitten sore
By gnats, or flies, or gadflies swarming round.

Noting the visages of some, who lay
Beneath the pelting of that dolorous fire,
One of them all I knew not; but perceived,
That pendent from his neck each bore a pouch
With colors and with emblems various mark'd,
On which it seem'd as if their eye did feed.

And when, amongst them, looking round I came,
A yellow purse I saw with azure wrought,
That wore a lion's countenance and port.
Then, still my sight pursuing its career,
Another I beheld, than blood more red,
A goose display of whiter wing than curd.
And one, who bore a fat and azure swine
Pictured on his white scrip, address'd me thus:
"What dost thou in this deep? Go now and know,
Since yet thou livest, that my neighbor here
Vitaliano on my left shall sit.
A Paduan with these Florentines am I.

HELL

Ofttimes they thunder in mine ears, exclaiming,
'Oh! haste that noble knight, he who the pouch
With the three goats will bring.' " This said, he writhed
The mouth, and loll'd the tongue out, like an ox
That licks his nostrils. I, lest longer stay
He ill might brook, who bade me stay not long,
Backward my steps from those sad spirits turn'd.

My guide already seated on the haunch
Of the fierce animal I found; and thus
He me encouraged. "Be thou stout: be bold.
Down such a steep flight must we now descend.
Mount thou before: for, that no power the tail
May have to harm thee, I will be i' th' midst."

As one, who hath an ague fit so near,
His nails already are turn'd blue, and he
Quivers all o'er, if he but eye the shade;
Such was my cheer at hearing of his words.
But shame soon interposed her threat, who makes
The servant bold in presence of his lord.

I settled me upon those shoulders huge,
And would have said, but that the words to aid
My purpose came not, "Look thou clasp me firm."

But he whose succor then not first I proved,
Soon as I mounted, in his arms aloft,
Embracing, held me up; and thus he spake:
"Geryon! now move thee: be thy wheeling gyres
Of ample circuit, easy thy descent.
Think on the unusual burden thou sustain'st."

As a small vessel, backening out from land,
Her station quits; so thence the monster loosed,
And, when he felt himself at large, turn'd round
There, where the breast had been, his forked tail.
Thus, like an eel, outstretch'd at length he steer'd,
Gathering the air up with retractile claws.

THE DIVINE COMEDY

Not greater was the dread, when Phaëton
The reins let drop at random, whence high heaven,
Whereof signs yet appear, was wrapt in flames;
Nor when ill-fated Icarus perceived,
By liquefaction of the scalded wax,
The trusted pennons loosen'd from his loins,
His sire exclaiming loud, "Ill way thou keep'st,"
Than was my dread, when round me on each part
The air I view'd, and other object none
Save the fell beast. He, slowly sailing, wheels
His downward motion, unobserved of me,
But that the wind, arising to my face,
Breathes on me from below. Now on our right
I heard the cataract beneath us leap
With hideous crash; whence bending down to explore,
New terror I conceived at the steep plunge;
For flames I saw, and wailings smote mine ear:
So that, all trembling, close I crouch'd my limbs,
And then distinguish'd, unperceived before,
By the dread torments that on every side
Drew nearer, how our downward course we wound.

As falcon, that hath long been on the wing,
But lure nor bird hath seen, while in despair
The falconer cries, "Ah me! thou stoop'st to earth,"
Wearied descends, whence nimbly he arose
In many an airy wheel, and lighting sits
At distance from his lord in angry mood;
So Geryon lighting places us on foot
Low down at base of the deep-furrow'd rock,
And, of his burden there discharged, forthwith
Sprang forward, like an arrow from the string.

CANTO XVIII

The poet describes the eighth circle divided into ten gulfs of fraudulent sinners, but treats only those who have seduced any woman from her duty and the flatterers.

THERE is a place within the depths of Hell
Call'd Malebolge, all of rock dark-stain'd
With hue ferruginous, e'en as the steep
That round it circling winds. Right in the midst
Of that abominable region yawns
A spacious gulf profound, whereof the frame
Due time shall tell. The circle, that remains,
Throughout its round, between the gulf and base
Of the high craggy banks, successive forms
Ten bastions, in its hollow bottom raised.

As where, to guard the walls, full many a foss
Begirds some stately castle, sure defence
Affording to the space within; so here
Were model'd these: and as like fortresses,
E'en from their threshold to the brink without,
Are flank'd with bridges; from the rock's low base
Thus flinty paths advanced, that 'cross the moles
And dykes struck onward far as to the gulf,
That in one bound collected cuts them off.
Such was the place, wherein we found ourselves
From Geryon's back dislodged. The bard to left
Held on his way, and I behind him moved.

On our right hand new misery I saw,
New pains, new executioners of wrath,
That swarming peopled the first chasm. Below
Were naked sinners. Hitherward they came,
Meeting our faces, from the middle point;
With us beyond, but with a larger stride.
E'en thus the Romans, when the year returns
Of Jubilee, with better speed to rid

THE DIVINE COMEDY

The thronging multitudes, their means devise
For such as pass the bridge; that on one side
All front toward the castle, and approach
Saint Peter's fane, on the other toward the mount.

Each diverse way, along the grisly rock,
Horn'd demons I beheld, with lashes huge,
That on their back unmercifully smote.
Ah! how they made them bound at the first stripe!
None for the second waited, nor the third.

Meantime, as on I pass'd, one met my sight,
Whom soon as view'd, "Of him," cried I, "not yet
Mine eye hath had his fill." I therefore stay'd
My feet to scan him, and the teacher kind
Paused with me, and consented I should walk
Backward a space; and the tormented spirit,
Who thought to hide him, bent his visage down.
But it avail'd him naught; for I exclaim'd:
"Thou who dost cast thine eye upon the ground,
Unless thy features do belie thee much,
Venedico art thou. But what brings thee
Into this bitter seasoning?" He replied:
"Unwillingly I answer to thy words.
But thy clear speech, that to my mind recalls
The world I once inhabited, constrains me.
Know then 'twas I who led fair Ghisola
To do the Marquis' will, however fame
The shameful tale have bruited. Nor alone
Bologna hither sendeth me to mourn.
Rather with us the place is so o'erthrong'd,
That not so many tongues this day are taught,
Betwixt the Reno and Savena's stream,
To answer Sipa in their country's phrase.
And if of that securer proof thou need,
Remember but our craving thirst for gold."

Him speaking thus, a demon with his thong
Struck and exclaim'd, "Away, corrupter! here

HELL

Women are none for sale." Forthwith I join'd
My escort, and few paces thence we came
To where a rock forth issued from the bank.
That easily ascended, to the right
Upon its splinter turning, we depart
From those eternal barriers. When arrived
Where, underneath, the gaping arch lets pass
The scourged souls: "Pause here," the teacher said,
"And let these others miserable now
Strike on thy ken; faces not yet beheld,
For that together they with us have walk'd."

From the old bridge we eyed the pack, who came
From the other side toward us, like the rest,
Excoriate from the lash. My gentle guide,
By me unquestion'd, thus his speech resumed:
"Behold that lofty shade, who this way tends,
And seems too woe-begone to drop a tear.
How yet the regal aspect he retains!
Jason is he, whose skill and prowess won
The ram from Colchos. To the Lemnian isle
His passage thither led him, when those bold
And pitiless women had slain all their males.
There he with tokens and fair witching words
Hypsipyle beguiled, a virgin young,
Who first had all the rest herself beguiled.
Impregnated, he left her there forlorn.
Such is the guilt condemns him to this pain.
Here too Medea's injuries are avenged.
All bear him company, who like deceit
To his have practised. And thus much to know
Of the first vale suffice thee, and of those
Whom its keen torments urge." Now had we come
Where, crossing the next pier, the straiten'd path
Bestrides its shoulders to another arch.

Hence, in the second chasm we heard the ghosts,
Who gibber in low melancholy sounds,
With wide-stretch'd nostrils snort, and on themselves

[75]

THE DIVINE COMEDY

Smite with their palms. Upon the banks a scurf,
From the foul steam condensed, encrusting hung,
That held sharp combat with the sight and smell.

So hollow is the depth, that from no part,
Save on the summit of the rocky span,
Could I distinguish aught. Thus far we came;
And thence I saw, within the foss below,
A crowd immersed in ordure, that appear'd
Draff of the human body. There beneath
Searching with eye inquisitive, I mark'd
One with his head so grimed, 'twere hard to deem
If he were clerk or layman. Loud he cried:
"Why greedily thus bendest more on me,
Than on these other filthy ones, thy ken?"

"Because, if true my memory," I replied,
"I heretofore have seen thee with dry locks;
And thou Alessio art, of Lucca sprung.
Therefore than all the rest I scan thee more."

Then beating on his brain, these words he spake:
"Me thus low down my flatteries have sunk,
Wherewith I ne'er enough could glut my tongue."

My leader thus: "A little further stretch
Thy face, that thou the visage well mayst note
Of that besotted, sluttish courtesan,
Who there doth rend her with defiled nails,
Now crouching down, now risen on her feet.
Thaïs is this, the harlot, whose false lip
Answer'd her doting paramour that ask'd,
'Thankest me much!'—'Say rather, wondrously,'
And, seeing this, here satiate be our view."

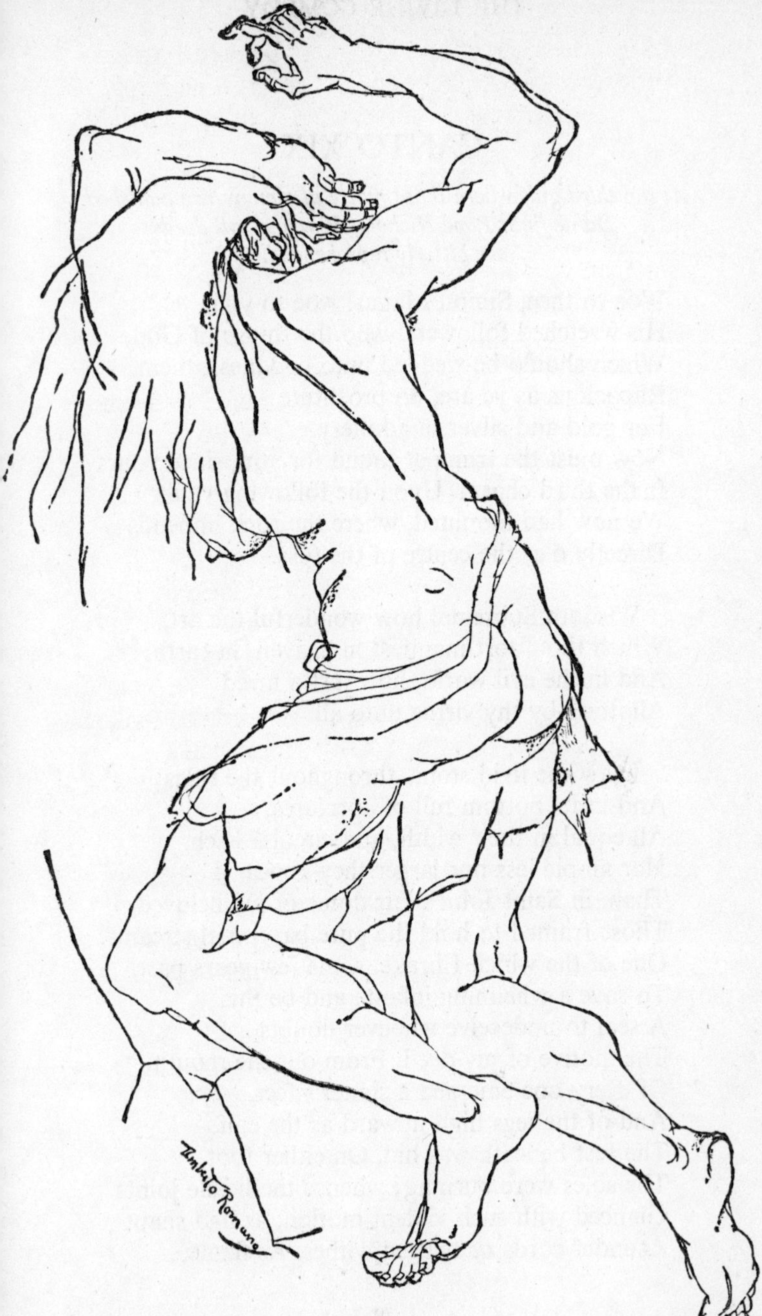
Umberto Romano

CANTO XIX

At the third gulf where those guilty of simony are punished, Dante finds Pope Nicholas V whose evil deeds are bitterly reprehended.

WOE to thee, Simon Magus! woe to you,
His wretched followers! who the things of God,
Which should be wedded unto goodness, them,
Rapacious as ye are, do prostitute
For gold and silver in adultery.
Now must the trumpet sound for you, since yours
Is the third chasm. Upon the following vault
We now had mounted, where the rock impends
Directly o'er the centre of the foss.

Wisdom Supreme! how wonderful the art,
Which thou dost manifest in heaven, in earth,
And in the evil world, how just a meed
Allotting by thy virtue unto all.

I saw the livid stone, throughout the sides
And in its bottom full of apertures,
All equal in their width, and circular each.
Nor ample less nor larger they appear'd
Than, in Saint John's fair dome of me beloved,
Those framed to hold the pure baptismal streams,
One of the which I brake, some few years past,
To save a whelming infant: and be this
A seal to undeceive whoever doubts
The motive of my deed. From out the mouth
Of every one emerged a sinner's feet,
And of the legs high upward as the calf.
The rest beneath was hid. On either foot
The soles were burning; whence the flexile joints
Glanced with such violent motion, as had snapt
Asunder cords or twisted withes. As flame,

HELL

Feeding on unctuous matter, glides along
The surface, scarcely touching where it moves;
So here, from heel to point, glided the flames.

"Master! say who is he, than all the rest
Glancing in fiercer agony, on whom
A ruddier flame doth prey?" I thus inquired.

"If thou be willing," he replied, "that I
Carry thee down, where least the slope bank falls,
He of himself shall tell thee, and his wrongs."

I then: "As pleases thee, to me is best.
Thou art my lord; and know'st that ne'er I quit
Thy will: what silence hides, that knowest thou."

Thereat on the fourth pier we came, we turn'd
And on our left descended to the depth,
A narrow strait, and perforated close.
Nor from his side my leader set me down,
Till to his orifice he brought, whose limb
Quivering express'd his pang. "Whoe'er thou art,
Sad spirit! thus reversed, and as a stake
Driven in the soil," I in these words began;
"If thou be able, utter forth thy voice."

There stood I like the friar, that doth shrive
A wretch for murder doom'd, who, e'en when fix'd,
Calleth him back, whence death awhile delays.

He shouted: "Ha! already standest there?
Already standest there, O Boniface!
By many a year the writing play'd me false.
So early dost thou surfeit with the wealth,
For which thou fearedst not in guile to take
The lovely lady, and then mangle her?"

I felt as those who, piercing not the drift
Of answer made them, stand as if exposed

[79]

In mockery, nor know what to reply;
When Virgil thus admonish'd: "Tell him quick,
'I am not he, not he whom thou believest.'"

And I, as was enjoin'd me, straight replied.

That heard, the spirit all did wrench his feet,
And, sighing, next in woful accent spake:
"What then of me requirest? If to know
So much imports thee, who I am, that thou
Hast therefore down the bank descended, learn
That in the mighty mantle I was robed,
And of a she-bear was indeed the son,
So eager to advance my whelps, that there
My having in my purse above I stow'd,
And here myself. Under my head are dragg'd
The rest, my predecessors in the guilt
Of simony. Stretch'd at their length, they lie
Along an opening in the rock. 'Midst them
I also low shall fall, soon as he comes,
For whom I took thee, when so hastily
I question'd. But already longer time
Hath past, since my soles kindled, and I thus
Upturn'd have stood, than is his doom to stand
Planted with fiery feet. For after him,
One yet of deeds more ugly shall arrive,
From forth the west, a shepherd without law,
Fated to cover both his form and mine.
He a new Jason shall be call'd, of whom
In Maccabees we read; and favor such
As to that priest his King indulgent show'd,
Shall be of France's monarch shown to him."

I know not if I here too far presumed,
But in this strain I answer'd: "Tell me now
What treasures from Saint Peter at the first
Our Lord demanded, when he put the keys
Into his charge? Surely he ask'd no more
But 'Follow me!' Nor Peter, nor the rest,
Or gold or silver of Matthias took,

When lots were cast upon the forfeit place
Of the condemned soul. Abide thou then;
Thy punishment of right is merited:
And look thou well to that ill-gotten coin,
Which against Charles thy hardihood inspired.
If reverence of the keys restrain'd me not,
Which thou in happier time didst hold, I yet
Severer speech might use. Your avarice
O'ercasts the world with mourning, under foot
Treading the good, and raising bad men up.
Of shepherds like to you, the Evangelist
Was ware, when her, who sits upon the waves,
With kings in filthy whoredom he beheld;
She who with seven heads tower'd at her birth,
And from ten horns her proof of glory drew,
Long as her spouse in virtue took delight.
Of gold and silver ye have made your god,
Differing wherein from the idolater,
But that he worships one, a hundred ye?
Ah, Constantine! to how much ill gave birth,
Not thy conversion, but that plenteous dower,
Which the first wealthy Father gain'd from thee."

Meanwhile, as thus I sung, he, whether wrath
Or conscience smote him, violent upsprang
Spinning on either sole. I do believe
My teacher well was pleased, with so composed
A lip he listen'd ever to the sound
Of the true words I utter'd. In both arms
He caught, and, to his bosom lifting me,
Upward retraced the way of his descent.

Nor weary of his weight, he press'd me close,
Till to the summit of the rock we came,
Our passage from the fourth to the fifth pier.
His cherish'd burden there gently he placed
Upon the rugged rock and steep, a path
Not easy for the clambering goat to mount.
Thence to my view another vale appear'd.

CANTO XX

The poet relates the punishment of those who presumed to predict future events while still living.

And now the verse proceeds to torments new,
Fit argument of this the twentieth strain
Of the first song, whose awful theme records
The spirits whelm'd in woe. Earnest I look'd
Into the depth, that open'd to my view,
Moisten'd with tears of anguish, and beheld
A tribe, that came along the hollow vale,
In silence weeping: such their step as walk
Quires, chanting solemn litanies, on earth.

As on them more direct mine eye descends,
Each wondrously seem'd to be reversed
At the neck-bone, so that the countenance
Was from the reins averted; and because
None might before him look, they were compell'd
To advance with backward gait. Thus one perhaps
Hath been by force of palsy clean transposed,
But I ne'er saw it nor believe it so.

Now, reader! think within thyself, so God
Fruit of thy reading give thee! how I long
Could keep my visage dry, when I beheld
Near me our form distorted in such guise,
That on the hinder parts fallen from the face
The tears down-streaming roll'd. Against a rock
I leant and wept, so that my guide exclaim'd:
"What, and art thou, too, witless as the rest?
Here pity most doth show herself alive,
When she is dead. What guilt exceedeth his,
Who with Heaven's judgment in his passion strives?
Raise up thy head, raise up, and see the man
Before whose eyes earth gaped in Thebes, when all
Cried out 'Amphiaraüs, whither rushest?

HELL

Why leavest thou the war?' He not the less
Fell ruining far as to Minos down,
Whose grapple none eludes. Lo! how he makes
The breast his shoulders; and who once too far
Before him wish'd to see, now backward looks,
And treads reverse his path. Tiresias note,
Who semblance changed, when woman he became
Of male, through every limb transform'd; and then
Once more behoved him with his rod to strike
The two entwining serpents, ere the plumes,
That mark'd the better sex, might shoot again.

"Aruns, with rere his belly facing, comes.
On Luni's mountains 'midst the marbles white,
Where delves Carrara's hind, who once beneath,
A cavern was his dwelling, whence the stars
And main-sea wide in boundless view he held.

"The next, whose loosen'd tresses overspread
Her bosom, which thou seest not (for each hair
On that side grows) was Manto, she who search'd
Through many regions, and at length her seat
Fix'd in my native land: whence a short space
My words detain thy audience. When her sire
From life departed, and in servitude
The city dedicate to Bacchus mourn'd,
Long time she went a wanderer through the world.
Aloft in Italy's delightful land
A lake there lies, at foot of that proud Alp
That o'er the Tyrol locks Germania in,
Its name Benacus, from whose ample breast
A thousand springs, methinks, and more, between
Camonica and Garda, issuing forth,
Water the Apennine. There is a spot
At midway of that lake, where he who bears
Of Trento's flock the pastoral staff, with him
Of Brescia, and the Veronese, might each
Passing that way his benediction give.
A garrison of goodly site and strong
Peschiera stands, to awe with front opposed

[83]

THE DIVINE COMEDY

The Bergamese and Brescian, whence the shore
More slope each way descends. There, whatsoe'er
Benacus' bosom holds not, tumbling o'er
Down falls, and winds a river flood beneath
Through the green pastures. Soon as in his course
The stream makes head, Benacus then no more
They call the name, but Mincius, till at last
Reaching Governo, into Po he falls.
Not far his course hath run, when a wide flat
It finds, which overstretching as a marsh
It covers, pestilent in summer oft.
Hence journeying, the savage maiden saw
Midst of the fen a territory waste
And naked of inhabitants. To shun
All human converse, here she with her slaves,
Plying her arts, remain'd, and liv'd, and left
Her body tenantless. Thenceforth the tribes,
Who round were scatter'd, gathering to that place,
Assembled; for its strength was great, enclosed
On all parts by the fen. On those dead bones
They rear'd themselves a city, for her sake
Calling it Mantua, who first chose the spot,
Nor ask'd another omen for the name;
Wherein more numerous the people dwelt,
Ere Casalodi's madness by deceit
Was wronged of Pinamonte. If thou hear
Henceforth another origin assign'd
Of that my country, I forewarn thee now,
That falsehood none beguile thee of the truth."

I answer'd, "Teacher, I conclude thy words
So certain, that all else shall be to me
As embers lacking life. But now of these,
Who here proceed, instruct me, if thou see
Any that merit more especial note.
For thereon is my mind alone intent."

He straight replied: "That spirit, from whose cheek
The beard sweeps o'er his shoulders brown, what time

[84]

HELL

Græcia was emptied of her males, that scarce
The cradles were supplied, the seer was he
In Aulis, who with Calchas gave the sign
When first to cut the cable. Him they named
Eurypilus: so sings my tragic strain,
In which majestic measure well thou know'st,
Who know'st it all. That other, round the loins
So slender of his shape, was Michael Scot,
Practised in every slight of magic wile.

"Guido Bonatti see: Asdente mark,
Who now were willing he had tended still
The thread and cordwain, and too late repents.

"See next the wretches, who the needle left,
The shuttle and the spindle, and became
Diviners: baneful witcheries they wrought
With images and herbs. But onward now:
For now doth Cain with fork of thorns confine
On either hemisphere, touching the wave
Beneath the towers of Seville. Yesternight
The moon was round. Thou mayst remember well:
For she good service did thee in the gloom
Of the deep wood." This said, both onward moved.

CANTO XXI

*They look down upon the barterers or public peculators
who are plunged in a lake of boiling pitch
and guarded by Demons.*

THUS we from bridge to bridge, with other talk,
The which my drama cares not to rehearse,
Pass'd on; and to the summit reaching, stood
To view another gap, within the round
Of Malebolge, other bootless pangs.

Marvellous darkness shadow'd o'er the place.

THE DIVINE COMEDY

In the Venetians' arsenal as boils
Through wintry months tenacious pitch, to smear
Their unsound vessels; for the inclement time
Seafaring men restrains, and in that while
His bark one builds anew, another stops
The ribs of his that hath made many a voyage,
One hammers at the prow, one at the poop,
This shapeth oars, that other cables twirls,
The mizzen one repairs, and main-sail rent;
So, not by force of fire but art divine,
Boil'd here a glutinous thick mass, that round
Limed all the shore beneath. I that beheld,
But herein naught distinguish'd, save the bubbles
Raised by the boiling, and one mighty swell
Heave, and by turns subsiding fall. While there
I fix'd my ken below, "Mark! mark!" my guide
Exclaiming, drew me toward him from the place
Wherein I stood. I turn'd myself, as one
Impatient to behold that which beheld
He needs must shun, whom sudden fear unmans,
That he his flight delays not for the view.
Behind me I discern'd a devil black,
That running up advanced along the rock.
Ah! what fierce cruelty his look bespake.
In act how bitter did he seem, with wings
Buoyant outstretch'd and feet of nimblest tread.
His shoulder, proudly eminent and sharp,
Was with a sinner charged; by either haunch
He held him, the foot's sinew griping fast.

"Ye of our bridge!" he cried, "keen-talon'd fiends!
Lo! one of Santa Zita's elders. Him
Whelm ye beneath, while I return for more.
That land hath store of such. All men are there,
Except Bonturo, barterers: of 'no'
For lucre there an 'ay' is quickly made."

Him dashing down, o'er the rough rock he turn'd;
Nor ever after thief a mastiff loosed

HELL

Sped with like eager haste. That other sank,
And forthwith writhing to the surface rose.
But those dark demons, shrouded by the bridge,
Cried, "Here the hallow'd visage saves not: here
Is other swimming than in Serchio's wave,
Wherefore, if thou desire we rend thee not,
Take heed thou mount not o'er the pitch." This said,
They grappled him with more than hundred hooks,
And shouted: "Cover'd thou must sport thee here;
So, if thou canst, in secret mayst thou filch."
E'en thus the cook bestirs him, with his grooms,
To thrust the flesh into the caldron down
With flesh-hooks, that it float not on the top.

Me then my guide bespake: "Lest they descry
That thou art here, behind a craggy rock
Bend low and screen thee: and whate'er of force
Be offer'd me, or insult, fear thou not;
For I am well advised, who have been erst
In the like fray." Beyond the bridge's head
Therewith he pass'd; and reaching the sixth pier,
Behoved him then a forehead terror-proof.

With storm and fury, as when dogs rush forth
Upon the poor man's back, who suddenly
From whence he standeth makes his suit; so rush'd
Those from beneath the arch, and against him
Their weapons all they pointed. He, aloud:
"Be none of you outrageous: ere your time
Dare seize me, come forth from amongst you one,
Who have heard my words, decide he then
If he shall tear these limbs." They shouted loud,
"Go, Malacoda!" Whereat one advanced,
The others standing firm, and as he came,
"What may this turn avail him?" he exclaim'd.

"Believest thou, Malacoda! I had come
Thus far from all your skirmishing secure,"
My teacher answer'd, "without will divine

[87]

THE DIVINE COMEDY

And destiny propitious? Pass we then;
For so Heaven's pleasure is, that I should lead
Another through this savage wilderness."

Forthwith so fell his pride, that he let drop
The instrument of torture at his feet,
And to the rest exclaim'd: "We have no power
To strike him." Then to me my guide: "O thou!
Who on the bridge among the crags dost sit
Low crouching, safely now to me return."

I rose, and toward him moved with speed; the fiends
Meantime all forward drew: me terror seized,
Lest they should break the compact they had made.
Thus issuing from Caprona, once I saw
The infantry, dreading lest his covenant
The foe should break; so close he hemm'd them round.

I to my leader's side adhered, mine eyes
With fixt and motionless observance bent
On their unkindly visage. They their hooks
Protruding, one the other thus bespake:
"Wilt thou I touch him on the hip?" To whom
Was answer'd: "Even so; nor miss thy aim."

But he, who was in conference with my guide,
Turn'd rapid round; and thus the demon spake:
"Stay, stay thee, Scarmiglione!" Then to us
He added: "Further footing to your step
This rock affords not, shiver'd to the base
Of the sixth arch. But would ye still proceed,
Up by this cavern go: not distant far,
Another rock will yield you passage safe.
Yesterday, later by five hours than now,
Twelve hundred threescore years and six had fill'd
The circuit of their course, since here the way
Was broken. Thitherward I straight despatch
Certain of these my scouts, who shall espy
If any on the surface bask. With them
Go ye: for ye shall find them nothing fell.

Come, Alichino, forth," with that he cried,
"And Calcabrina, and Cagnazzo thou!
The troop of ten let Barbariccia lead.
With Libicocco, Draghinazzo haste,
Fang'd Ciratta, Graffiacane fierce,
And Farfarello, and mad Rubicant.
Search ye around the bubbling tar. For these,
In safety lead them, where the other crag
Uninterrupted traverses the dens."

I then: "O master! what a sight is there.
Ah! without escort, journey we alone,
Which, if thou know the way, I covet not.
Unless thy prudence fail thee, dost not mark
How they do gnarl upon us, and their scowl
Threatens us present tortures?" He replied:
"I charge thee, fear not: let them, as they will,
Gnarl on: 'tis but in token of their spite
Against the souls who mourn in torment steep'd."

To leftward o'er the pier they turn'd; but each
Had first between his teeth prest close the tongue,
Toward their leader for a signal looking,
Which he with sound obscene triumphant gave.

CANTO XXII

Accompanied by the Demons, they see other sinners of the same description.

IT hath been heretofore my chance to see
Horsemen with martial order shifting camp,
To onset sallying, or in muster ranged,
Or in retreat sometimes outstretch'd for flight:
Light-armed squadrons and fleet foragers
Scouring thy plains, Arezzo! have I seen,
And clashing tournaments, and tilting jousts,
Now with the sound of trumpets, now of bells,

Tabors, or signals made from castled heights,
And with inventions multiform, our own,
Or introduced from foreign land; but ne'er
To such a strange recorder I beheld,
In evolution moving, horse nor foot,
Nor ship, that tack'd by sign from land or star.

   With the ten Demons on our way we went;
Ah, fearful company! but in the Church
With saints, with gluttons at the tavern's mess.

   Still earnest on the pitch I gazed, to mark
All things whate'er the chasm contain'd, and those
Who burn'd within. As dolphins that, in sign
To mariners, heave high their arched backs,
That thence forewarn'd they may advise to save
Their threaten'd vessel; so, at intervals,
To ease the pain, his back some sinner show'd,
Then hid more nimbly than the lightning-glance.

   E'en as the frogs, that of a watery moat
Stand at the brink, with the jaws only out,
Their feet and of the trunk all else conceal'd,
Thus on each part the sinners stood; but soon
As Barbariccia was at hand, so they
Drew back under the wave. I saw, and yet
My heart doth stagger, one, that waited thus,
As it befalls that oft one frog remains,
While the next springs away: and Graffiacan,
Who of the fiends was nearest, grappling seized
His clotted locks, and dragg'd him sprawling up,
That he appear'd to me an otter. Each
Already by their names I knew, so well
When they were chosen I observed, and mark'd
How one the other call'd. "O Rubicant!
See that his hide thou with thy talons flay,"
Shouted together all the cursed crew.

   Then I: "Inform thee, Master! if thou may,
What wretched soul is this, on whom their hands

His foes have laid." My leader to his side
Approach'd, and whence he came inquired; to whom
Was answer'd thus: "Born in Navarre's domain,
My mother placed me in a lord's retinue;
For she had borne me to a losel vile,
A spendthrift of his substance and himself.
The good King Thibault after that I served:
To peculating here my thoughts were turn'd,
Whereof I give account in this dire heat."

   Straight Ciratto, from whose mouth a tusk
Issued on either side, as from a boar,
Ripp'd him with one of these. 'Twixt evil claws
The mouse had fallen: but Barbariccia cried,
Seizing him with both arms: "Stand thou apart
While I do fix him on my prong transpierced."
Then added, turning to my guide his face,
"Inquire of him, if more thou wish to learn,
Ere he again be rent." My leader thus:
"Then tell us of the partners in thy guilt;
Knowest thou any sprung of Latin land
Under the tar?" "I parted," he replied,
"But now from one, who sojourn'd not far thence;
So were I under shelter now with him,
Nor hook nor talon then should scare me more."

   "Too long we suffer," Libicocco cried;
Then, darting forth a prong, seized on his arm,
And mangled bore away the sinewy part.
Him Draghinazzo by his thighs beneath
Would next have caught; whence angrily their chief,
Turning on all sides round, with threatening brow
Restrain'd them. When their strife a little ceased,
Of him, who yet was gazing on his wound,
My teacher thus without delay inquired:
"Who was the spirit, from whom by evil hap
Parting, as thou hast told, thou camest to shore?"

   "It was the friar Gomita," he rejoin'd,
"He of Gallura, vessel of all guile,

THE DIVINE COMEDY

Who had his master's enemies in hand,
And used them so that they commend him well.
Money he took, and them at large dismiss'd;
So he reports; and in each other charge
Committed to his keeping play'd the part
Of barterer to the height. With him doth herd
The chief of Logodoro, Michel Zanche.
Sardinia is a theme whereof their tongue
Is never weary. Out! alas! behold
That other, how he grins. More would I say,
But tremble lest he mean to maul me sore."

Their captain then to Farfarello turning,
Who roll'd his moony eyes in act to strike,
Rebuked him thus: "Off, cursed bird! avaunt!"

"If ye desire to see or hear," he thus
Quaking with dread resumed, "or Tuscan spirits
Or Lombard, I will cause them to appear.
Meantime let these ill talons bate their fury,
So that no vengeance they may fear from them,
And I, remaining in this self-same place,
Will, for myself but one, make seven appear,
When my shrill whistle shall be heard; for so
Our custom is to call each other up."

Cagnazzo at that word deriding grinn'd,
Then wagg'd the head and spake: "Hear his device,
Mischievous as he is, to plunge him down."

Whereto he thus, who fail'd not in rich store
Of nice-wove toils: "Mischief, forsooth, extreme!
Meant only to procure myself more woe."

No longer Alichino then refrain'd,
But thus, the rest gainsaying, him bespake:
"If thou do cast thee down, I not on foot
Will chase thee, but above the pitch will beat
My plumes. Quit we the vantage ground, and let

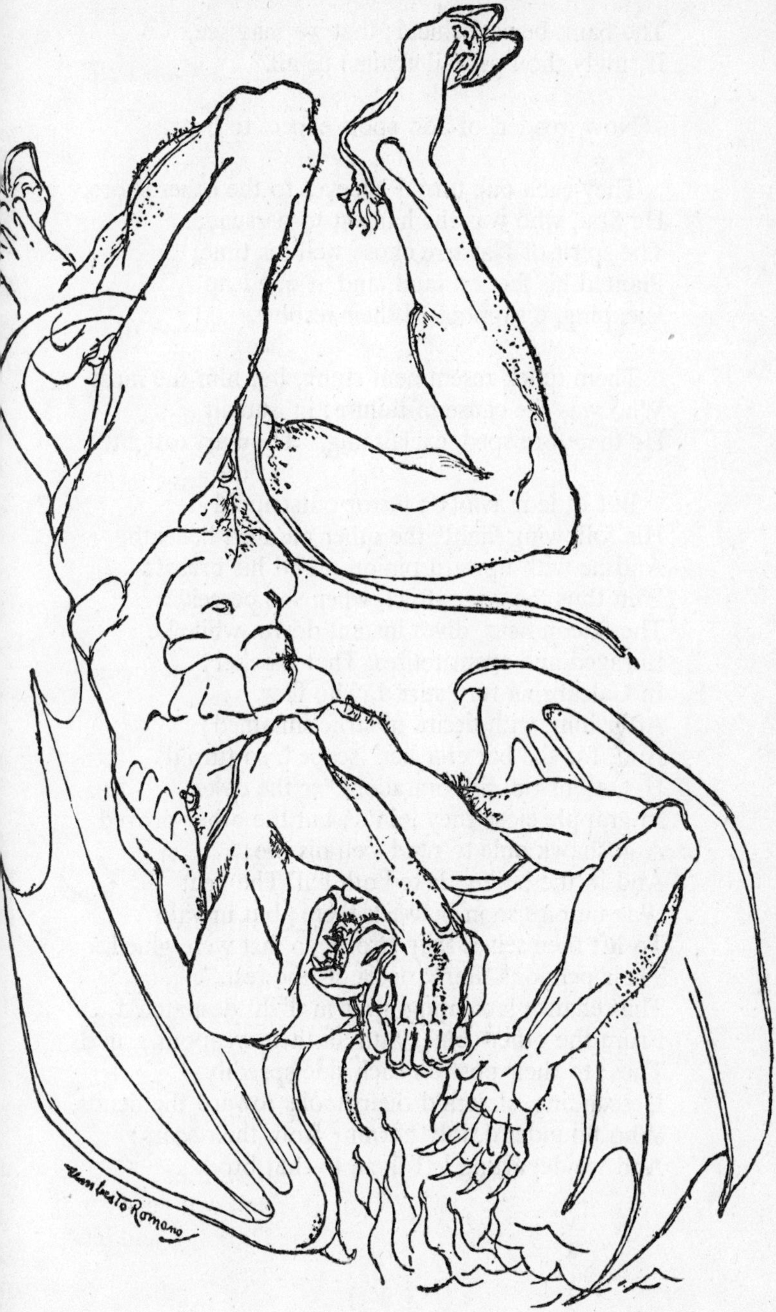
Umberto Romano

THE DIVINE COMEDY

The bank be as a shield; that we may see,
If singly thou prevail against us all."

Now, reader, of new sport expect to hear.

They each one turn'd his eyes to the other shore,
He first, who was the hardest to persuade.
The spirit of Navarre chose well his time,
Planted his feet on land, and at one leap
Escaping, disappointed their resolve.

Them quick resentment stung, but him the most
Who was the cause of failure: in pursuit
He therefore sped, exclaiming, "Thou art caught."

But little it avail'd; terror outstripp'd
His following flight; the other plunged beneath,
And he with upward pinion raised his breast:
E'en thus the water-fowl, when she perceives
The falcon near, dives instant down, while he
Enraged and spent retires. That mockery
In Calcabrina fury stirr'd, who flew
After him, with desire of strife inflamed;
And, for the barterer had 'scaped, so turn'd
His talons on his comrade. O'er the dyke
In grapple close they join'd; but the other proved
A goshawk able to rend well his foe;
And in the boiling lake both fell. The heat
Was umpire soon between them; but in vain
To lift themselves they strove, so fast were glued
Their pennons. Barbariccia, as the rest,
That chance lamenting, four in flight despatch'd
From the other coast, with all their weapons arm'd.
They, to their post on each side speedily
Descending, stretch'd their hooks toward the fiends,
Who flounder'd, inly burning from their scars:
And we departing left them to that broil.

[94]

CANTO XXIII

The enraged Demons pursue Dante, but he is preserved from them by Virgil. At the sixth gulf, Dante beholds the punishment of the hypocrites.

In silence and in solitude we went,
One first, the other following his steps,
As minor friars journeying on their road.

The present fray had turn'd my thoughts to muse
Upon old Æsop's fable, where he told
What fate unto the mouse and frog befell;
For language hath not sounds more like in sense,
Than are these chances, if the origin
And end of each be heedfully compared.
And as one thought bursts from another forth,
So afterward from that another sprang,
Which added doubly to my former fear.
For thus I reason'd: "These through us have been
So foil'd, with loss and mockery so complete,
As needs must sting them sore. If anger then
Be to their evil will conjoin'd, more fell
They shall pursue us, than the savage hound
Snatches the leveret panting 'twixt his jaws."

Already I perceived my hair stand all
On end with terror, and look'd eager back.

"Teacher," I thus began, "if speedily
Thyself and me thou hide not, much I dread
Those evil talons. Even now behind
They urge us: quick imagination works
So forcibly, that I already feel them."

He answer'd: "Were I form'd of leaded glass,
I should not sooner draw unto myself
Thy outward image, than I now imprint

[95]

THE DIVINE COMEDY

That from within. This moment came thy thoughts
Presented before mine, with similar act
And countenance similar, so that from both
I one design have framed. If the right coast
Incline so much, that we may thence descend
Into the other chasm, we shall escape
Secure from this imagined pursuit."

He had not spoke his purpose to the end,
When I from far beheld them with spread wings
Approach to take us. Suddenly my guide
Caught me, even as a mother that from sleep
Is by the noise aroused, and near her sees
The climbing fires, who snatches up her babe
And flies ne'er pausing, careful more of him
Than of herself, that but a single vest
Clings round her limbs. Down from the jutting beach
Supine he cast him to that pendent rock,
Which closes on one part the other chasm.

Never ran water with such hurrying pace
Adown the tube to turn a land-mill's wheel,
When nearest it approaches to the spokes,
As then along that edge my master ran,
Carrying me in his bosom, as a child,
Not a companion. Scarcely had his feet
Reach'd to the lowest of the bed beneath,
When over us the steep they reach'd: but fear
In him was none; for that high Providence,
Which placed them ministers of the fifth foss,
Power of departing thence took from them all.

There in the depth we saw a painted tribe,
Who paced with tardy steps around, and wept,
Faint in appearance and o'ercome with toil.
Caps had they on, with hoods, that fell low down
Before their eyes, in fashion like to those
Worn by the monks in Cologne. Their outside
Was overlaid with gold, dazzling to view,
But leaden all within, and of such weight,

HELL

That Frederick's compared to these were straw.
Oh, everlasting wearisome attire!

   We yet once more with them together turn'd
To leftward, on their dismal moan intent.
But by the weight opprest, so slowly came
The fainting people, that our company
Was changed, at every movement of the step.

   Whence I my guide address'd: "See that thou find
Some spirit, whose name may by his deeds be known;
And to that end look round thee as thou go'st."

   Then one, who understood the Tuscan voice,
Cried after us aloud: "Hold in your feet,
Ye who so swiftly speed through the dusk air.
Perchance from me thou shalt obtain thy wish."

   Whereat my leader, turning, me bespake:
"Pause, and then onward at their pace proceed."

   I staid, and saw two spirits in whose look
Impatient eagerness of mind was mark'd
To overtake me; but the load they bare
And narrow path retarded their approach.

   Soon as arrived, they with an eye askance
Perused me, but spake not: then turning, each
To other thus conferring said: "This one
Seems, by the action of his throat, alive;
And, be they dead, what privilege allows
They walk unmantled by the cumbrous stole?"

   Then thus to me: "Tuscan, who visitest
The college of the mourning hypocrites,
Disdain not to instruct us who thou art."

   "By Arno's pleasant stream," I thus replied,
"In the great city I was bred and grew,
And wear the body I have ever worn.

But who are ye, from whom such mighty grief,
As now I witness, courseth down your cheeks?
What torment breaks forth in this bitter woe?"

"Our bonnets gleaming bright with orange hue,"
One of them answer'd, "are so leaden gross,
That with their weight they make the balances
To crack beneath them. Joyous friars we were,
Bologna's natives; Catalano I,
He Loderingo named; and by thy land
Together taken, as men use to take
A single and indifferent arbiter,
To reconcile their strifes. How there we sped,
Gardingo's vicinage can best declare."

"O friars!" I began, "your miseries—"
But there brake off, for one had caught mine eye,
Fix'd to a cross with three stakes on the ground:
He, when he saw me, writhed himself, throughout
Distorted, ruffling with deep sighs his beard.
And Catalano, who thereof was 'ware,
Thus spake: "That pierced spirit, whom intent
Thou view'st, was he who gave the Pharisees
Counsel, that it were fitting for one man
To suffer for the people. He doth lie
Transverse; nor any passes, but him first
Behoves make feeling trial how each weighs.
In straits like this along the foss are placed
The father of his consort, and the rest
Partakers in that council, seed of ill
And sorrow to the Jews." I noted then,
How Virgil gazed with wonder upon him,
Thus abjectly extended on the cross
In banishment eternal. To the friar
He next his words address'd: "We pray ye tell,
If so be lawful, whether on our right
Lies any opening in the rock, whereby
We both may issue hence, without constraint
On the dark angels, that compell'd they come
To lead us from this depth." He thus replied:

"Nearer than thou dost hope, there is a rock
From the great circle moving, which o'ersteps
Each vale of horror, save that here his cope
Is shatter'd. By the ruin ye may mount:
For on the side it slants, and most the height
Rises below." With head bent down awhile
My leader stood; then spake: "He warn'd us ill,
Who yonder hangs the sinners on his hook."

To whom the friar: "At Bologna erst
I many voices of the devil heard;
Among the rest was said, 'He is a liar,
And the father of lies!' " When he had spoke,
My leader with large strides proceeded on,
Somewhat disturb'd with anger in his look.

I therefore left the spirits heavy laden,
And, following, his beloved footsteps mark'd.

CANTO XXIV

In the seventh gulf, Dante sees the robbers tormented by venomous and pestilent serpents.

In the year's early nonage, when the sun
Tempers his tresses in Aquarius' urn,
And now toward equal day the nights recede;
When as the rime upon the earth puts on
Her dazzling sister's image, but not long
Her milder sway endures; then riseth up
The village hind, whom fails his wintry store,
And looking out beholds the plain around
All whiten'd; whence impatiently he smites
His thighs, and to his hut returning in,
There paces to and fro, wailing his lot,
As a discomfited and helpless man;
Then comes he forth again, and feels new hope
Spring in his bosom, finding e'en thus soon

THE DIVINE COMEDY

The world hath changed its countenance, grasps his crook,
And forth to pasture drives his little flock:
So me my guide dishearten'd, when I saw
His troubled forehead; and so speedily
That ill was cured; for at the fallen bridge
Arriving, toward me with a look as sweet,
He turn'd him back, as that I first beheld
At the steep mountain's foot. Regarding well
The ruin, and some counsel first maintain'd
With his own thought, he open'd wide his arm
And took me up. As one, who, while he works,
Computes his labor's issue, that he seems
Still to foresee the effect; so lifting me
Up to the summit of one peak, he fix'd
His eye upon another. "Grapple that,"
Said he, "but first make proof, if it be such
As will sustain thee." For one capt with lead
This were no journey. Scarcely he, though light,
And I, though onward push'd from crag to crag,
Could mount. And if the precinct of this coast
Were not less ample than the last, for him
I know not, but my strength had surely fail'd.
But Malebolge all toward the mouth
Inclining of the nethermost abyss,
The site of every valley hence requires,
That one side upward slope, the other fall.

At length the point from whence the utmost stone
Juts down, we reach'd; soon as to that arrived,
So was the breath exhausted from my lungs
I could no further, but did seat me there.

"Now needs thy best of man"; so spake my guide:
"For not on downy plumes, nor under shade
Of canopy reposing, fame is won;
Without which whosoe'er consumes his days,
Leaveth such vestige of himself on earth,
As smoke in air or foam upon the wave.
Thou therefore rise: vanquish thy weariness
By the mind's effort, in each struggle form'd

[100]

To vanquish, if she suffer not the weight
Of her corporeal frame to crush her down.
A longer ladder yet remains to scale.
From these to have escaped sufficeth not,
If well thou note me, profit by my words."

I straightway rose, and show'd myself less spent
Than I in truth did feel me. "On," I cried,
"For I am stout and fearless." Up the rock
Our way we held, more rugged than before,
Narrower, and steeper far to climb. From talk
I ceased not, as we journey'd, so to seem
Least faint; whereat a voice from the other foss
Did issue forth, for utterance suited ill.
Though on the arch that crosses there I stood,
What were the words I knew not, but who spake
Seem'd moved in anger. Down I stoop'd to look;
But my quick eye might reach not to the depth
For shrouding darkness; wherefore thus I spake:
"To the next circle, teacher, bend thy steps,
And from the wall dismount we; for as hence
I hear and understand not, so I see
Beneath, and naught discern." "I answer not,"
Said he, "but by the deed. To fair request
Silent performance maketh best return."

We from the bridge's head descended, where
To the eighth mound it joins; and then, the chasm
Opening to view, I saw a crowd within
Of serpents terrible, so strange of shape
And hideous, that remembrance in my veins
Yet shrinks the vital current. Of her sands
Let Libya vaunt no more: if Jaculus,
Pareas and Chelyder be her brood,
Cenchris and Amphisbæna, plagues so dire
Or in such numbers swarming ne'er she show'd,
Not with all Ethiopia, and whate'er
Above the Erythræan sea is spawn'd.

Amid this dread exuberance of woe

Ran naked spirits wing'd with horrid fear,
Nor hope had they of crevice where to hide,
Or heliotrope to charm them out of view.
With serpents were their hands behind them bound,
Which through their reins infix'd the tail and head,
Twisted in folds before. And lo! on one
Near to our side, darted an adder up,
And, where the neck is on the shoulders tied,
Transpierced him. Far more quickly than e'er pen
Wrote O or I, he kindled, burn'd, and changed
To ashes all, pour'd out upon the earth.
When there dissolved he lay, the dust again
Uproll'd spontaneous, and the self-same form
Instant resumed. So mighty sages tell,
The Arabian Phœnix, when five hundred years
Have well-nigh circled, dies, and springs forthwith
Renascent: blade nor herb throughout his life
He tastes, but tears of frankincense alone
And odorous amomum: swaths of nard
And myrrh his funeral shroud. As one that falls,
He knows not how, by force demoniac dragg'd
To earth, or through obstruction fettering up
In chains invisible the powers of man,
Who, risen from his trance, gazeth around,
Bewilder'd with the monstrous agony
He hath endured, and wildly staring sighs;
So stood aghast the sinner when he rose.

Oh! how severe God's judgment, that deals out
Such blows in stormy vengeance. Who he was,
My teacher next inquired; and thus in few
He answer'd: "Vanni Fucci am I call'd,
Not long since rained down from Tuscany
To this dire gullet. Me the bestial life
And not the human pleased, mule that I was,
Who in Pistoia found my worthy den."

I then to Virgil: "Bid him stir not hence;
And ask what crime did thrust him thither: once
A man I knew him, choleric and bloody."

HELL

The sinner heard and feign'd not, but toward me
His mind directing and his face, wherein
Was dismal shame depictured, thus he spake:
"It grieves me more to have been caught by thee
In this sad plight, which thou beholdest, than
When I was taken from the other life.
I have no power permitted to deny
What thou inquirest. I am doom'd thus low
To dwell, for that the sacristy by me
Was rifled of its goodly ornaments,
And with the guilt another falsely charged.
But that thou mayst not joy to see me thus,
So as thou e'er shalt 'scape this darksome realm,
Open thine ears and hear what I forebode.
Reft of the Neri first Pistoia pines;
Then Florence changeth citizens and laws;
From Valdimagra, drawn by wrathful Mars,
A vapor rises, wrapt in turbid mists,
And sharp and eager driveth on the storm
With arrowy hurtling o'er Piceno's field,
Whence suddenly the cloud shall burst, and strike
Each helpless Bianco prostrate to the ground.
This have I told, that grief may rend thy heart."

CANTO XXV

*The sacrilegious Fucci vents his fury in blasphemy
and the poet finds the spirits of three countrymen.*

WHEN he had spoke, the sinner raised his hands
Pointed in mockery and cried: "Take them, God!
I level them at thee." From that day forth
The serpents were my friends; for round his neck
One of them rolling twisted, as it said,
"Be silent, tongue!" Another, to his arms
Upgliding, tied them, riveting itself
So close, it took from them the power to move.

Pistoia! ah, Pistoia! why dost doubt
To turn thee into ashes, cumbering earth
No longer, since in evil act so far
Thou hast outdone thy seed? I did not mark,
Through all the gloomy circles of the abyss,
Spirit, that swell'd so proudly 'gainst his God;
Not him, who headlong fell from Thebes. He fled,
Nor utter'd more; and after him there came
A centaur full of fury, shouting, "Where,
Where is the caitiff?" On Maremma's marsh
Swarm not the serpent tribe, as on his haunch
They swarm'd, to where the human face begins.
Behind his head, upon the shoulders, lay
With open wings a dragon, breathing fire
On whomsoe'er he met. To me my guide:
"Cacus is this, who underneath the rock
Of Aventine spread oft a lake of blood.
He, from his brethren parted, here must tread
A different journey, for his fraudful theft
Of the great herd that near him stall'd; whence found
His felon deeds their end, beneath the mace
Of stout Alcides, that perchance laid on
A hundred blows, and not the tenth was felt."

While yet he spake, the centaur sped away:
And under us three spirits came, of whom
Nor I nor he was ware, till they exclaim'd,
"Say who are ye!" We then brake off discourse,
Intent on these alone. I knew them not:
But, as it chanceth oft, befell, that one
Had need to name another. "Where," said he,
"Doth Cianfa lurk?" I, for a sign my guide
Should stand attentive, placed against my lips
The finger lifted. If, O reader! now
Thou be not apt to credit what I tell,
No marvel; for myself do scarce allow
The witness of mine eyes. But as I look'd
Toward them, lo! a serpent with six feet
Springs forth on one, and fastens full upon him:
His midmost grasp'd the belly, a forefoot

HELL

Seized on each arm (while deep in either cheek
He flesh'd his fangs); the hinder on the thighs
Were spread, 'twixt which the tail inserted curl'd
Upon the reins behind. Ivy ne'er clasp'd
A dodder'd oak, as round the other's limbs
The hideous monster intertwined his own.
Then, as they both had been of burning wax,
Each melted into other, mingling hues,
That which was either now was seen no more.
Thus up the shrinking paper, ere it burns,
A brown tint glides, not turning yet to black,
And the clean white expires. The other two
Look'd on exclaiming, "Ah! how dost thou change,
Agnello! See! Thou art nor double now,
Nor only one." The two heads now became
One, and two figures blended in one form
Appear'd, where both were lost. Of the four lengths
Two arms were made: the belly and the chest,
The thighs and legs, into such members changed
As never eye hath seen. Of former shape
All trace was vanish'd. Two, yet neither, seem'd
That image miscreate, and so pass'd on
With tardy steps. As underneath the scourge
Of the fierce dog-star that lays bare the fields,
Shifting from brake to brake the lizard seems
A flash of lightning, if he thwart the road;
So toward the entrails of the other two
Approaching seem'd an adder all on fire,
As the dark pepper-grain livid and swart.
In that part, whence our life is nourish'd first,
Once he transpierced; then down before him fell
Stretch'd out. The pierced spirit look'd on him,
But spake not; yea, stood motionless and yawn'd,
As if by sleep or feverous fit assail'd.
He eyed the serpent, and the serpent him.
One from the wound, the other from the mouth
Breathed a thick smoke, whose vapory columns join'd.

Lucan in mute attention now may hear,
Nor thy disastrous fate, Sabellus, tell,

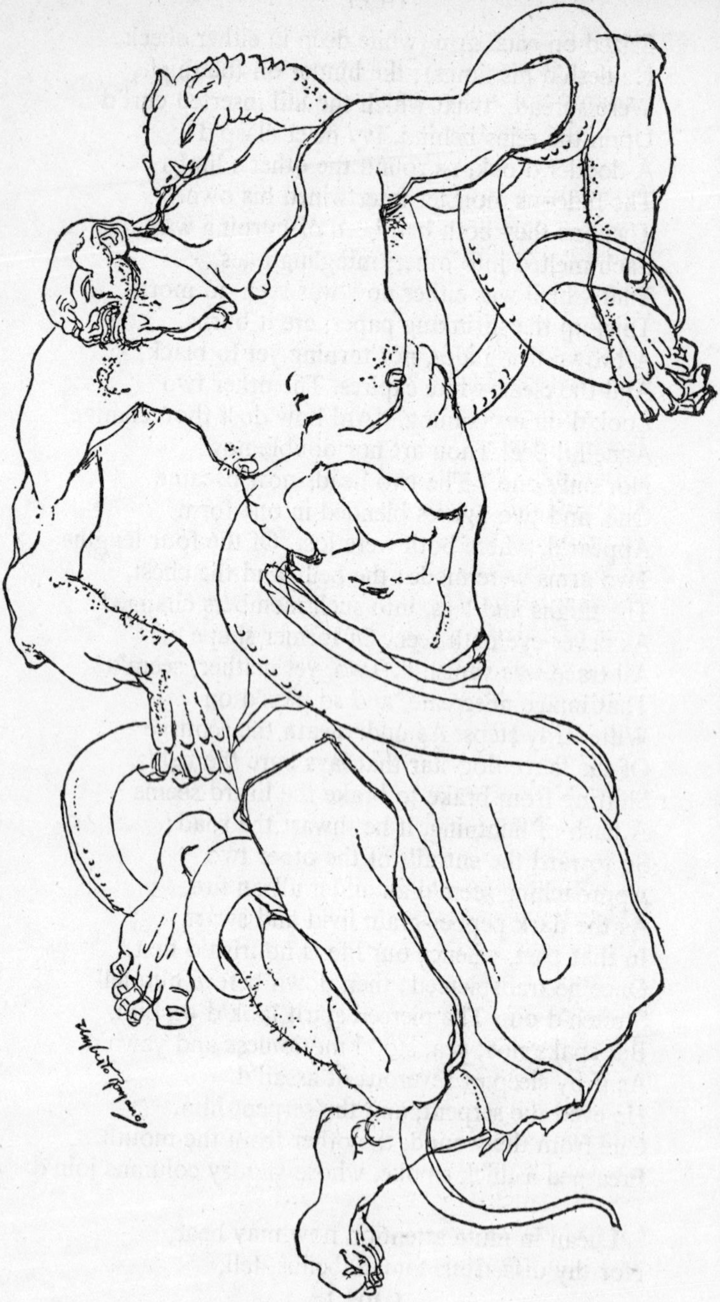

Nor thine, Nasidius. Ovid now be mute.
What if in warbling fiction he record
Cadmus and Arethusa, to a snake
Him changed, and her into a fountain clear,
I envy not; for never face to face
Two natures thus transmuted did he sing,
Wherein both shapes were ready to assume
The other's substance. They in mutual guise
So answer'd that the serpent split his train
Divided to a fork, and the pierced spirit
Drew close his steps together, legs and thighs
Compacted, that no sign of juncture soon
Was visible: the tail, disparted, took
The figure which the spirit lost; its skin
Softening, his indurated to a rind.
The shoulders next I mark'd, that entering join'd
The monster's arm-pits, whose two shorter feet
So lengthen'd, as the others dwindling shrunk.
The feet behind then twisting up became
That part that man conceals, which in the wretch
Was cleft in twain. While both the shadowy smoke
With a new color veils, and generates
The excrescent pile on one, peeling it off
From the other body, lo! upon his feet
One upright rose, and prone the other fell.
Nor yet their glaring and malignant lamps
Were shifted, though each feature changed beneath.
Of him who stood erect, the mounting face
Retreated toward the temples, and what there
Superfluous matter came, shot out in ears
From the smooth cheeks; the rest, not backward dragg'd,
Of its excess did shape the nose; and swell'd
Into due size protuberant the lips.
He, on the earth who lay, meanwhile extends
His sharpen'd visage, and draws down the ears
Into the head, as doth the slug his horns.
His tongue, continuous before and apt
For utterance, severs; and the other's fork
Closing unites. That done, the smoke was laid.
The soul, transform'd into the brute, glides off,

Hissing along the vale, and after him
The other talking sputters; but soon turn'd
His new-grown shoulders on him, and in few
Thus to another spake: "Along this path
Crawling, as I have done, speed Buoso now!"

So saw I fluctuate in successive change
The unsteady ballast of the seventh hold:
And here if aught my pen have swerved, events
So strange may be its warrant. O'er mine eyes
Confusion hung, and on my thoughts amaze.

Yet 'scaped they not so covertly, but well
I mark'd Sciancato: he alone it was
Of the three first that came, who changed not: tho'
The other's fate, Gaville! still dost rue.

CANTO XXVI

He beholds numberless flames, each containing an evil counsellor save one which holds both Ulysses and Diomedes.

FLORENCE, exult! for thou so mightily
Hast thriven, that o'er land and sea thy wings
Thou beatest, and thy name spreads over Hell.
Among the plunderers, such the three I found
Thy citizens; whence shame to me thy son,
And no proud honor to thyself redounds.

But if our minds, when dreaming near the dawn,
Are of the truth presageful, thou ere long
Shalt feel what Prato (not to say the rest)
Would fain might come upon thee; and that chance
Were in good time, if it befell thee now.
Would so it were, since it must needs befall!
For as time wears me, I shall grieve the more.

HELL

We from the depth departed; and my guide
Remounting scaled the flinty steps, which late
We downward traced, and drew me up the steep.
Pursuing thus our solitary way
Among the crags and splinters of the rock,
Sped not our feet without the help of hands.

Then sorrow seized me, which e'en now revives,
As my thought turns again to what I saw,
And, more than I am wont, I rein and curb
The powers of nature in me, lest they run
Where Virtue guides not; that, if aught of good
My gentle star or something better gave me,
I envy not myself the precious boon.

As in that season, when the sun least veils
His face that lightens all, what time the fly
Gives way to the shrill gnat, the peasant then,
Upon some cliff reclined, beneath him sees
Fire-flies innumerous spangling o'er the vale,
Vineyard or tilth, where his day-labor lies;
With flames so numberless throughout its space
Shone the eighth chasm, apparent, when the depth
Was to my view exposed. As he, whose wrongs
The bears avenged, at its departure saw
Elijah's chariot, when the steeds erect
Raised their steep flight for heaven; his eyes meanwhile,
Straining pursued them, till the flame alone,
Upsoaring like a misty speck, he kenn'd:
E'en thus along the gulf moves every flame,
A sinner so enfolded close in each,
That none exhibits token of the theft.

Upon the bridge I forward bent to look,
And grasp'd a flinty mass, or else had fallen,
Though push'd not from the height. The guide, who mark'd
How I did gaze attentive, thus began:
"Within these ardors are the spirits, each
Swathed in confining fire." "Master! thy word,"
I answer'd, "hath assured me; yet I deem'd

[109]

THE DIVINE COMEDY

Already of the truth, already wish'd
To ask thee who is in yon fire, that comes
So parted at the summit, as it seem'd
Ascending from that funeral pile where lay
The Theban brothers." He replied: "Within,
Ulysses there and Diomede endure
Their penal tortures, thus to vengeance now
Together hasting, as erewhile to wrath
These in the flame with ceaseless groans deplore
The ambush of the horse, that open'd wide
A portal for the goodly seed to pass,
Which sow'd imperial Rome; nor less the guile
Lament they, whence, of her Achilles reft,
Deïdamia yet in death complains.
And there is rued the stratagem that Troy
Of her Palladium spoil'd."—"If they have power
Of utterance from within these sparks," said I,
"O master! think my prayer a thousand-fold
In repetition urged, that thou vouchsafe
To pause till here the horned flame arrive.
See, how toward it with desires I bend."

He thus: "Thy prayer is worthy of much praise,
And I accept it therefore; but do thou
Thy tongue refrain: to question them be mine;
For I divine thy wish; and they perchance,
For they were Greeks, might shun discourse with thee."

When there the flame had come, where time and place
Seem'd fitting to my guide, he thus began:
"O ye, who dwell two spirits in one fire!
If, living, I of you did merit aught,
Whate'er the measure were of that desert,
When in the world my lofty strain I pour'd,
Move ye not on, till one of you unfold
In what clime death o'ertook him self-destroy'd."

Of the old flame forthwith the greater horn
Began to roll, murmuring, as a fire
That labors with the wind, then to and fro

HELL

Wagging the top, as a tongue uttering sounds,
Threw out its voice, and spake: "When I escaped
From Circe, who beyond a circling year
Had held me near Caieta by her charms,
Ere thus Æneas yet had named the shore;
Nor fondness for my son, nor reverence
Of my old father, nor return of love,
That should have crown'd Penelope with joy,
Could overcome in me the zeal I had
To explore the world, and search the ways of life,
Man's evil and his virtue. Forth I sail'd
Into the deep illimitable main,
With but one bark, and the small faithful band
That yet cleaved to me. As Iberia far,
Far as Marocco, either shore I saw,
And the Sardinian and each isle beside
Which round that ocean bathes. Tardy with age
Were I and my companions, when we came
To the strait pass, where Hercules ordain'd
The boundaries not to be o'erstepp'd by man.
The walls of Seville to my right I left,
On the other hand already Ceuta past.
'O brothers!' I began, 'who to the west
Through perils without number now have reach'd;
To this the short remaining watch, that yet
Our senses have to wake, refuse not proof
Of the unpeopled world, following the track
Of Phœbus. Call to mind from whence ye sprang:
Ye were not form'd to live the life of brutes,
But virtue to pursue and knowledge high.'
With these few words I sharpen'd for the voyage
The mind of my associates, that I then
Could scarcely have withheld them. To the dawn
Our poop we turn'd, and for the witless flight
Made our oars wings, still gaining on the left.
Each star of the other pole night now beheld,
And ours so low, that from the ocean floor
It rose not. Five times reillumed, as oft
Vanish'd the light from underneath the moon,
Since the deep way we enter'd, when from far

[111]

Appear'd a mountain dim, loftiest methought
Of all I e'er beheld. Joy seized us straight;
But soon to mourning changed. From the new land
A whirlwind sprung, and at her foremost side
Did strike the vessel. Thrice it whirl'd her round
With all the waves; the fourth time lifted up
The poop, and sank the prow: so fate decreed:
And over us the booming billow closed."

CANTO XXVII

The poet converses with Count Guido da Montefeltro on the state of Romagna.

Now upward rose the flame, and still'd its light
To speak no more, and now pass'd on with leave
From the mild poet gain'd; when following came
Another, from whose top a sound confused,
Forth issuing, drew our eyes that way to look.

As the Sicilian bull, that rightfully
His cries first echoed who had shaped its mould,
Did so rebellow, with the voice of him
Tormented, that the brazen monster seem'd
Pierced through with pain; thus, while no way they found,
Nor avenue immediate through the flame,
Into its language turn'd the dismal words:
But soon as they had won their passage forth,
Up from the point, which vibrating obey'd
Their motion at the tongue, these sounds were heard:
"O thou! to whom I now direct my voice,
That lately didst exclaim in Lombard phrase,
'Depart thou; I solicit thee no more';
Though somewhat tardy I perchance arrive,
Let it not irk thee here to pause awhile,
And with me parley: lo! it irks not me,
And yet I burn. If but e'en now thou fall
Into this blind world, from that pleasant land

[112]

HELL

Of Latium, whence I draw my sum of guilt,
Tell me if those who in Romagna dwell
Have peace or war. For of the mountains there
Was I, betwixt Urbino and the height
Whence Tiber first unlocks his mighty flood."

Leaning I listen'd yet with heedful ear,
When, as he touch'd my side, the leader thus:
"Speak thou: he is a Latian." My reply
Was ready, and I spake without delay:
"O spirit! who art hidden here below,
Never was thy Romagna without war
In her proud tyrants' bosoms, nor is now:
But open war there left I none. The state,
Ravenna hath maintain'd this many a year,
Is steadfast. There Polenta's eagle broods;
And in his broad circumference of plume
O'ershadows Cervia. The green talons grasp
The land, that stood erewhile the proof so long
And piled in bloody heap the host of France.

"The old mastiff of Verruchio and the young,
That tore Montagna in their wrath, still make,
Where they are wont, an auger of their fangs.

"Lamone's city, and Santerno's, range
Under the lion of the snowy lair,
Inconstant partisan, that changeth sides,
Or ever summer yields to winter's frost.
And she, whose flank is wash'd of Savio's wave,
As 'twixt the level and the steep she lies,
Lives so 'twixt tyrant power and liberty.

"Now tell us, I entreat thee, who art thou:
Be not more hard than others. In the world,
So may thy name still rear its forehead high."

Then roar'd awhile the fire, its sharpen'd point
On either side waved, and thus breathed at last:
"If I did think my answer were to one

THE DIVINE COMEDY

Who ever could return unto the world,
This flame should rest unshaken. But since ne'er,
If true be told me, any from this depth
Has found his upward way, I answer thee,
Nor fear lest infamy record the words.

"A man of arms at first, I clothed me, then
In good Saint Francis' girdle, hoping so
To have made amends. And certainly my hope
Had fail'd not, but that he, whom curses light on,
The high priest, again seduced me into sin.
And how, and wherefore, listen while I tell.
Long as this spirit moved the bones and pulp
My mother gave me, less my deeds bespake
The nature of the lion than the fox.
All ways of winding subtlety I knew,
And with such art conducted, that the sound
Reach'd the world's limit. Soon as to that part
Of life I found me come, when each behoves
To lower sails and gather in the lines;
That, which before had pleased me, then I rued,
And to repentance and confession turn'd,
Wretch that I was; and well it had bested me.
The chief of the new Pharisees meantime,
Waging his warfare near the Lateran,
Not with the Saracens or Jews (his foes
All Christians were, nor against Acre one
Had fought, nor traffick'd in the Soldan's land),
He, his great charge nor sacred ministry,
In himself reverenced, nor in me that cord
Which used to mark with leanness whom it girded.
As in Soracte, Constantine besought,
To cure his leprosy, Sylvester's aid;
So me, to cure the fever of his pride,
This man besought: my counsel to that end
He ask'd; and I was silent; for his words
Seem'd drunken: but forthwith he thus resumed:
'From thy heart banish fear: of all offence
I hitherto absolve thee. In return,
Teach me my purpose so to execute,

HELL

That Penestrino cumber earth no more.
Heaven, as thou knowest, I have power to shut
And open: and the keys are therefore twain,
The which my predecessor meanly prized.'

"Then, yielding to the forceful arguments,
Of silence as more perilous I deem'd,
And answer'd: 'Father! since thou washest me
Clear of that guilt wherein I now must fall,
Large promise with performance scant, be sure,
Shall make thee triumph in thy lofty seat.'

"When I was number'd with the dead, then came
Saint Francis for me; but a cherub dark
He met, who cried, 'Wrong me not; he is mine,
And must below to join the wretched crew,
For the deceitful counsel which he gave.
E'er since I watch'd him, hovering at his hair.
No power can the impenitent absolve;
Nor to repent, and will, at once consist,
By contradiction absolute forbid.'
Oh misery! how I shook myself, when he
Seized me, and cried, 'Thou haply thought'st me not
A disputant in logic so exact!'
To Minos down he bore me; and the judge
Twined eight times round his callous back the tail,
Which biting with excess of rage, he spake:
'This is a guilty soul, that in the fire
Must vanish.' Hence, perdition-doom'd, I rove
A prey to rankling sorrow, in this garb."

When he had thus fulfil'd his words, the flame
In dolor parted, beating to and fro,
And writhing its sharp horn. We onward went,
I and my leader, up along the rock,
Far as another arch, that overhangs
The foss, wherein the penalty is paid
Of those who load them with committed sin.

CANTO XXVIII

In the ninth gulf, the sowers of scandal, schismatics and heretics are seen with their limbs miserably maimed and divided.

WHO, e'en words unfetter'd, might at full
Tell of the wounds and blood that now I saw,
Though he repeated oft the tale? No tongue
So vast a theme could equal, speech and thought
Both impotent alike. If in one band
Collected, stood the people all, who e'er
Pour'd on Apulia's happy soil their blood,
Slain by the Trojans, and in that long war,
When of the rings the measured booty made
A pile so high, as Rome's historian writes
Who errs not; with the multitude, that felt
The grinding force of Guiscard's Norman steel,
And those the rest, whose bones are gather'd yet
At Ceperano, there where treachery
Branded the Apulian name, or where beyond
Thy walls, O Tagliacozzo, without arms
The old Alardo conquer'd; and his limbs
One were to show transpierced, another his
Clean lopt away; a spectacle like this
Were but a thing of naught, to the hideous sight
Of the ninth chasm. A rundlet, that hath lost
Its middle or side stave, gapes not so wide
As one I mark'd, torn from the chin throughout
Down to the hinder passage: 'twixt the legs
Dangling his entrails hung, the midriff lay
Open to view, and wretched ventricle,
That turns the englutted aliment to dross.

Whilst eagerly I fix on him my gaze,
He eyed me, with his hands laid his breast bare,
And cried, "Now mark how I do rip me: lo!
How is Mohammed mangled: before me

HELL

Walks Ali weeping, from the chin his face
Cleft to the forelock; and the others all,
Whom here thou seest, while they lived, did sow
Scandal and schism, and therefore thus are rent.
A fiend is here behind, who with his sword
Hacks us thus cruelly, slivering again
Each of this ream, when we have compast round
The dismal way; for first our gashes close
Ere we repass before him. But, say who
Art thou, that standest musing on the rock,
Haply so lingering to delay the pain
Sentenced upon thy crimes." "Him death not yet,"
My guide rejoin'd, "hath overta'en, nor sin
Conducts to torment; but, that he may make
Full trial of your state, I who am dead
Must through the depths of Hell, from orb to orb,
Conduct him. Trust my words; for they are true."

More than a hundred spirits, when that they heard,
Stood in the foss to mark me through amaze
Forgetful of their pangs. "Thou, who perchance
Shalt shortly view the sun, this warning thou
Bear to Dolcino: bid him, if he wish not
Here soon to follow me, that with good store
Of food he arm him, lest imprisoning snows
Yield him a victim to Novara's power;
No easy conquest else": with foot upraised
For stepping, spake Mohammed, on the ground
Then fix'd it to depart. Another shade,
Pierced in the throat, his nostrils mutilate
E'en from beneath the eyebrows, and one ear
Lopt off, who, with the rest, through wonder stood
Gazing, before the rest advanced, and bared
His wind-pipe, that without was all o'ersmear'd
With crimson stain. "O thou!" said he, "whom sin
Condemns not, and whom erst (unless too near
Resemblance to deceive me) I aloft
Have seen on Latian ground, call thou to mind
Piero of Medicina, if again
Returning, thou behold'st the pleasant land

That from Vercelli slopes to Mercabo;
And there instruct the twain, whom Fano boasts
Her worthiest sons, Guido and Angelo,
That if 'tis given us here to scan aright
The future, they out of life's tenement
Shall be cast forth, and whelm'd under the waves
Near to Cattolica, through perfidy
Of a fell tyrant. 'Twixt the Cyprian isle
And Balearic, ne'er hath Neptune seen
An injury so foul, by pirates done,
Or Argive crew of old. That one-eyed traitor
(Whose realm there is a spirit here were fain
His eye had still lack'd sight of) them shall bring
To conference with him, then so shape his end,
That they shall need not 'gainst Focara's wind
Offer up vow nor prayer." I answering thus:
"Declare, as thou dost wish that I above
May carry tidings of thee, who is he,
In whom that sight doth wake such sad remembrance."

Forthwith he laid his hand on the cheek-bone
Of one, his fellow-spirit, and his jaws
Expanding, cried: "Lo! this is he I wot of:
He speaks not for himself: the outcast this,
Who overwhelm'd the doubt in Cæsar's mind,
Affirming that delay to men prepared
Was ever harmful." Oh! how terrified
Methought was Curio, from whose throat was cut
The tongue, which spake that hardy word. Then one,
Maim'd of each hand, uplifted in the gloom
The bleeding stumps, that they with gory spots
Sullied his face, and cried: "Remember thee
Of Mosca too; I who, alas! exclaim'd,
'The deed once done, there is an end' that proved
A seed of sorrow to the Tuscan race."

I added: "Ay, and death to thine own tribe."

Whence, heaping woe on woe, he hurried off,
As one grief-stung to madness. But I there

HELL

Still linger'd to behold the troop, and saw
Things, such as I may fear without more proof
To tell of, but that conscience makes me firm,
The boon companion, who her strong breastplate
Buckles on him, that feels no guilt within,
And bids him on and fear not. Without doubt
I saw, and yet it seems to pass before me,
A headless trunk, that even as the rest
Of the sad flock paced onward. By the hair
It bore the sever'd member, lantern-wise
Pendent in hand, which look'd at us, and said,
"Woe's me!" The spirit lighted thus himself;
And two there were in one, and one in two.
How that may be, he knows who ordereth so.

When at the bridge's foot direct he stood,
His arm aloft he rear'd, thrusting the head

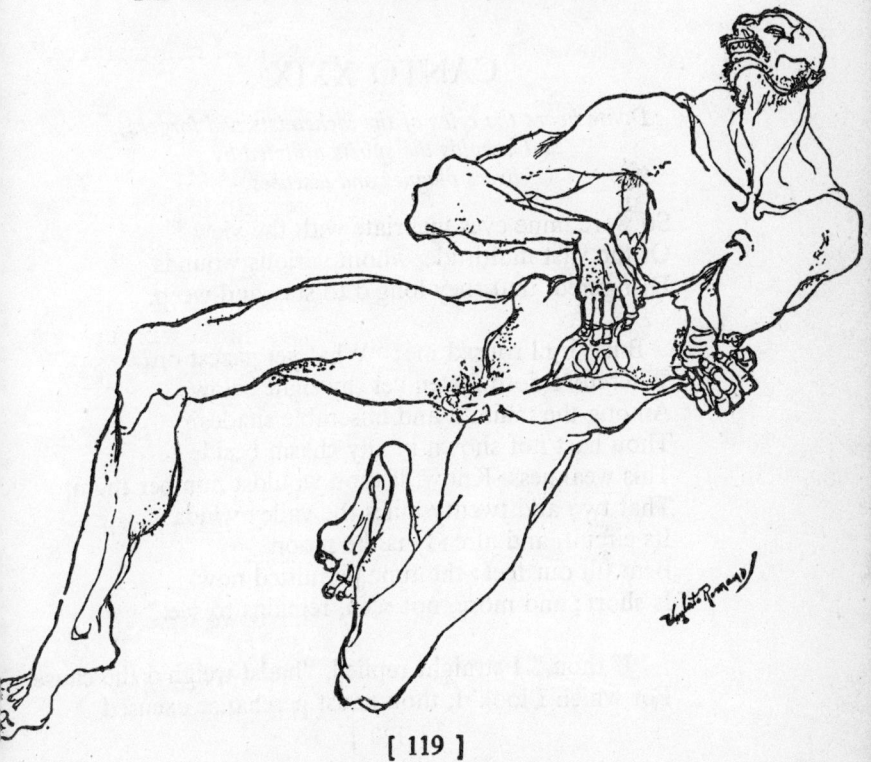

THE DIVINE COMEDY

Full in our view, that nearer we might hear
The words, which thus it utter'd: "Now behold
This grievous torment, thou, who breathing go'st
To spy the dead: behold, if any else
Be terrible as this. And, that on earth
Thou mayst bear tidings of me, know that I
Am Bertrand, he of Born, who gave King John
The counsel mischievous. Father and son
I set at mutual war. For Absalom
And David more did not Ahitophel,
Spurring them on maliciously to strife.
For parting those so closely knit, my brain
Parted, alas! I carry from its source,
That in this trunk inhabits. Thus the law
Of retribution fiercely works in me."

CANTO XXIX

*Dante hears the cries of the alchemists and forgers,
and beholds the spirits afflicted by
divers plagues and diseases.*

So were mine eyes inebriate with the view
Of the vast multitude, whom various wounds
Disfigured, that they long'd to stay and weep.

But Virgil roused me: "What yet gazest on?
Wherefore doth fasten yet thy sight below
Among the maim'd and miserable shades?
Thou hast not shown in any chasm beside
This weakness. Know, if thou wouldst number them,
That two and twenty miles the valley winds
Its circuit, and already is the moon
Beneath our feet: the time permitted now
Is short; and more, not seen, remains to see."

"If thou," I straight replied, "hadst weigh'd the cause,
For which I look'd, thou hadst perchance excused

HELL

The tarrying still." My leader part pursued
His way, the while I follow'd, answering him,
And adding thus: "Within that cave I deem,
Whereon so fixedly I held my ken,
There is a spirit dwells, one of my blood,
Wailing the crime that costs him now so dear."

Then spake my master: "Let thy soul no more
Afflict itself for him. Direct elsewhere
Its thought, and leave him. At the bridge's foot
I mark'd how he did point with menacing look
At thee, and heard him by the others named
Geri of Bello. Thou so wholly then
Wert busied with his spirit, who once ruled
The towers of Hautefort, that thou lookedst not
That way, ere he was gone." "O guide beloved!
His violent death yet unavenged," said I,
"By any, who are partners in his shame,
Made him contemptuous; therefore, as I think,
He pass'd me speechless by; and, doing so,
Hath made me more compassionate his fate."

So we discoursed to where the rock first show'd
The other valley, had more light been there,
E'en to the lowest depth. Soon as we came
O'er the last cloister in the dismal rounds
Of Malebolge, and the brotherhood
Were to our view exposed, then many a dart
Of sore lament assail'd me, headed all
With points of thrilling pity, that I closed
Both ears against the volley with mine hands.

As were the torment, if each lazar-house
Of Valdichiana, in the sultry time
'Twixt July and September, with the isle
Sardinia and Maremma's pestilent fen,
Had heap'd their maladies all in one foss
Together; such was here the torment: dire
The stench, as issuing streams from fester'd limbs.

[121]

THE DIVINE COMEDY

We on the utmost shore of the long rock
Descended still to leftward. Then my sight
Was livelier to explore the depth, wherein
The minister of the most mighty Lord,
All-searching Justice, dooms to punishment
The forgers noted on her dread record.

More rueful was it not methinks to see
The nation in Ægina droop, what time
Each living thing, e'en to the little worm,
All fell, so full of malice was the air,
(And afterward, as bards of yore have told,
The ancient people were restored anew
From seed of emmets), than was here to see
The spirits, that languish'd through the murky vale,
Up-piled on many a stack. Confused they lay,
One o'er the belly, o'er the shoulders one
Roll'd of another; sideling crawl'd a third
Along the dismal pathway. Step by step
We journey'd on, in silence looking round,
And listening those diseased, who strove in vain
To lift their forms. Then two I mark'd, that sat
Propt 'gainst each other, as two brazen pans
Set to retain the heat. From head to foot,
A tetter bark'd them round. Nor saw I e'er
Groom currying so fast, for whom his lord
Impatient waited, or himself perchance
Tired with long watching, as of these each one
Plied quickly his keen nails, through furiousness
Of ne'er abated pruriency. The crust
Came drawn from underneath, in flakes, like scales
Scraped from the bream, or fish of broader mail.

"O thou! who with thy fingers rendest off
Thy coat of proof," thus spake my guide to one,
"And sometimes makest tearing pincers of them,
Tell me if any born of Latian land
Be among these within: so may thy nails
Serve thee for everlasting to this toil."

HELL

   "Both are of Latium," weeping he replied,
"Whom tortured thus thou seest: but who art thou
That hast inquired of us?" To whom my guide:
"One that descend with this man, who yet lives,
From rock to rock, and show him Hell's abyss."

   Then started they asunder, and each turn'd
Trembling toward us, with the rest, whose ear
Those words redounding struck. To me my liege
Address'd him: "Speak to them whate'er thou list."

   And I therewith began: "So may no time
Filch your remembrance from the thoughts of men
In the upper world, but after many suns
Survive it, as ye tell me, who ye are,
And of what race ye come. Your punishment,
Unseemly and disgustful in its kind,
Deter you not from opening thus much to me."

   "Arezzo was my dwelling," answer'd one,
"And me Albero of Sienna brought
To die by fire: but that, for which I died,
Leads me not here. True is, in sport I told him,
That I had learn'd to wing my flight in air;
And he, admiring much, as he was void
Of wisdom, will'd me to declare to him
The secret of mine art: and only hence,
Because I made him not a Dædalus,
Prevail'd on one supposed his sire to burn me.
But Minos to this chasm, last of the ten,
For that I practised alchemy on earth,
Has doom'd me. Him no subterfuge eludes."

   Then to the bard I spake: "Was ever race
Light as Sienna's? Sure not France herself
Can show a tribe so frivolous and vain."

   The other leprous spirit heard my words,
And thus return'd: "Be Stricca from this charge
Exempted, he who knew so temperately

To lay out fortune's gifts; and Niccolo,
Who first the spice's costly luxury
Discover'd in that garden, where such seed
Roots deepest in the soil: and be that troop
Exempted, with whom Caccia of Asciano
Lavish'd his vineyards and wide-spreading woods,
And his rare wisdom Abbagliato show'd
A spectacle for all. That thou mayst know
Who seconds thee against the Siennese
Thus gladly, bend this way thy sharpen'd sight,
That well my face may answer to thy ken;
So shalt thou see I am Capocchio's ghost,
Who forged transmuted metals by the power
Of alchemy; and if I scan thee right,
Thou needs must well remember how I aped
Creative nature by my subtle art."

CANTO XXX

Other kinds of impostors like counterfeiters of persons, coinage, or speech are described as suffering diseases.

What time resentment burn'd in Juno's breast
For Semele against the Theban blood,
As more than once in dire mischance was rued;
Such fatal frenzy seized on Athamas,
That he his spouse beholding with a babe
Laden on either arm, "Spread out," he cried,
"The meshes, that I take the lioness
And the young lions at the pass": then forth
Stretch'd he his merciless talons, grasping one,
One helpless innocent, Learchus named,
Whom swinging down he dash'd upon a rock;
And with her other burden, self-destroy'd,
The hapless mother plunged. And when the pride
Of all presuming Troy fell from its height,
By fortune overwhelm'd, and the old king
With his realm perish'd; then did Hecuba,

HELL

A wretch forlorn and captive, when she saw
Polyxena first slaughter'd, and her son,
Her Polydorus, on the wild sea-beach
Next met the mourner's view, then reft of sense
Did she run barking even as a dog;
Such mighty power had grief to wrench her soul.
But ne'er the Furies, or of Thebes, or Troy,
With such fell cruelty were seen, their goads
Infixing in the limbs of man or beast,
As now two pale and naked ghosts I saw,
That gnarling wildly scamper'd, like the swine
Excluded from his stye. One reach'd Capocchio,
And in the neck-joint sticking deep his fangs,
Dragg'd him, that, o'er the solid pavement rubb'd
His belly stretch'd out prone. The other shape,
He of Arezzo, there left trembling, spake:
"That sprite of air is Schicchi, in like mood
Of random mischief vents he still his spite."

To whom I answering: "Oh! as thou dost hope
The other may not flesh its jaws on thee,
Be patient to inform us, who it is,
Ere it speed hence."—"That is the ancient soul
Of wretched Myrrha," he replied, "who burn'd
With most unholy flame for her own sire,
And a false shape assuming, so perform'd
The deed of sin; e'en as the other there,
That onward passes, dared to counterfeit
Donati's features, to feign'd testament
The seal affixing, that himself might gain,
For his own share, the lady of the herd."

When vanish'd the two furious shades, on whom
Mine eye was held, I turn'd it back to view
The other cursed spirits. One I saw
In fashion like a lute, had but the groin
Been sever'd where it meets the forked part.
Swol'n dropsy, disproportioning the limbs
With ill-converted moisture, that the paunch
Suits not the visage, open'd wide his lips,

THE DIVINE COMEDY

Gasping as in the hectic man for drought,
One toward the chin, the other upward curl'd.

"O ye! who in this world of misery,
Wherefore I know not, are exempt from pain,"
Thus he began, "attentively regard
Adamo's woe. When living, full supply
Ne'er lack'd me of what most I coveted;
One drop of water now, alas! I crave.
The rills, that glitter down the grassy slopes
Of Casentino, making fresh and soft
The banks whereby they glide to Arno's stream,
Stand ever in my view; and not in vain;
For more the pictured semblance dries me up,
Much more than the disease, which makes the flesh
Desert these shrivel'd cheeks. So from the place,
Where I transgress'd, stern justice urging me,
Takes means to quicken more my laboring sighs.
There is Romena, where I falsified
The metal with the Baptist's form imprest,
For which on earth I left my body burnt.
But if I here might see the sorrowing soul
Of Guido, Alessandro, or their brother,
For Branda's limpid spring I would not change
The welcome sight. One is e'en now within,
If truly the mad spirits tell, that round
Are wandering. But wherein besteads me that?
My limbs are fetter'd. Were I but so light,
That I each hundred years might move one inch,
I had set forth already on this path,
Seeking him out amidst the shapeless crew,
Although eleven miles it wind, not less
Than half of one across. They brought me down
Among this tribe; induced by them, I stamp'd
The florens with three carats of alloy."

"Who are that abject pair," I next inquired,
"That closely bounding thee upon thy right
Lie smoking, like a hand in winter steep'd

HELL

In the chill stream?" "When to this gulf I dropp'd,"
He answer'd, "here I found them; since that hour
They have not turn'd, nor ever shall, I ween,
Till time hath run his course. One is that dame,
The false accuser of the Hebrew youth;
Sinon the other, that false Greek from Troy.
Sharp fever drains the reeky moistness out,
In such a cloud upsteam'd." When that he heard,
One, gall'd perchance to be so darkly named,
With clench'd hand smote him on the braced paunch,
That like a drum resounded: but forthwith
Adamo smote him on the face, the blow
Returning with his arm, that seem'd as hard.

"Though my o'erweighty limbs have ta'en from me
The power to move," said he, "I have an arm
At liberty for such employ." To whom
Was answer'd: "When thou wentest to the fire,
Thou hadst it not so ready at command,
Then readier when it coin'd the impostor gold."

And thus the dropsied: "Ay, now speak'st thou true:
But there thou gavest not such true testimony,
When thou wast question'd of the truth, at Troy."

"If I spake false, thou falsely stamp'dst the coin,"
Said Sinon; "I am here for but one fault,
And thou for more than any imp beside."

"Remember," he replied, "O perjured one!
The horse remember, that did teem with death;
And all the world be witness to thy guilt."

"To thine," return'd the Greek, "witness the thirst
Whence thy tongue cracks, witness the fluid mound
Rear'd by the belly up before thine eyes,
A mass corrupt." To whom the coiner thus:
"Thy mouth gapes wide as ever to let pass
Its evil saying. Me if thirst assails,

Yet I am stuft with moisture. Thou art parch'd:
Pains rack thy head: no urging wouldst thou need
To make thee lap Narcissus' mirror up."

I was all fix'd to listen, when my guide
Admonish'd: "Now beware. A little more,
And I do quarrel with thee." I perceived
How angrily he spake, and toward him turn'd
With shame so poignant, as remember'd yet
Confounds me. As a man that dreams of harm
Befallen him, dreaming wishes it a dream,
And that which is, desires as if it were not;
Such then was I, who, wanting power to speak,
Wish'd to excuse myself, and all the while
Excused me, though unweeting that I did.

"More grievous fault than thine has been, less shame,"
My master cried, "might expiate. Therefore cast
All sorrow from thy soul; and if again
Chance bring thee where like conference is held,
Think I am ever at thy side. To hear
Such wrangling is a joy for vulgar minds."

CANTO XXXI

*The poets are led to the ninth circle encompassed by Giants;
Antæus places them at the bottom of the circle.*

THE very tongue, whose keen reproof before
Had wounded me, that either cheek was stain'd,
Now minister'd my cure. So have I heard,
Achilles' and his father's javelin caused
Pain first, and then the boon of health restored.

Turning our back upon the vale of woe,
We cross'd the encircled mound in silence. There
Was less than day and less than night, that far
Mine eye advanced not: but I heard a horn

[128]

HELL

Sounded so loud, the peal it rang had made
The thunder feeble. Following its course
The adverse way, my strained eyes were bent
On that one spot. So terrible a blast
Orlando blew not, when that dismal rout
O'erthrew the host of Charlemain, and quench'd
His saintly warfare. Thitherward not long
My head was raised, when many a lofty tower
Methought I spied. "Master," said I, "what land
Is this?" He answer'd straight: "Too long a space
Of intervening darkness has thine eye
To traverse: thou hast therefore widely err'd
In thy imagining. Thither arrived
Thou well shalt see, how distance can delude
The sense. A little therefore urge thee on."

Then tenderly he caught me by the hand;
"Yet know," said he, "ere further we advance,
That it less strange may seem, these are not towers,
But giants. In the pit they stand immersed,
Each from his navel downward, round the bank."

As when a fog disperseth gradually,
Our vision traces what the mist involves
Condensed in air; so piercing through the gross
And gloomy atmosphere, as more and more
We near'd toward the brink, mine error fled
And fear came o'er me. As with circling round
Of turrets, Montereggion crowns his walls;
E'en thus the shore, encompassing the abyss,
Was turreted with giants, half their length
Uprearing, horrible, whom Jove from heaven
Yet threatens, when his muttering thunder rolls.

Of one already I descried the face,
Shoulders, and breast, and of the belly huge
Great part, and both arms down along his ribs.

All-teeming Nature, when her plastic hand
Left framing of these monsters, did display

[129]

Past doubt her wisdom, taking from mad War
Such slaves to do his bidding; and if she
Repent her not of the elephant and whale,
Who ponders well confesses her therein
Wiser and more discreet; for when brute force
And evil will are back'd with subtlety,
Resistance none avails. His visage seem'd
In length and bulk, as doth the pine that tops
Saint Peter's Roman fane; and the other bones
Of like proportion, so that from above
The bank, which girdled him below, such height
Arose his stature, that three Friezelanders
Had striven in vain to reach but to his hair.
Full thirty ample palms was he exposed
Downward from whence a man his garment loops.
"Raphel baï ameth, sabì almi":
So shouted his fierce lips, which sweeter hymns
Became not; and my guide address'd him thus:
"O senseless spirit! let thy horn for thee
Interpret: therewith vent thy rage, if rage
Or other passion wring thee. Search thy neck.
There shalt thou find the belt that binds it on.
Spirit confused! lo, on thy mighty breast
Where hangs the baldrick!" Then to me he spake:
"He doth accuse himself. Nimrod is this,
Through whose ill counsel in the world no more
One tongue prevails. But pass we on, nor waste
Our words; for so each language is to him,
As his to others, understood by none."

Then to the leftward turning sped we forth,
And at a sling's throw found another shade
Far fiercer and more huge. I cannot say
What master hand had girt him; but he held
Behind the right arm fetter'd, and before,
The other, with a chain, that fasten'd him
From the neck down; and five times round his form
Apparent met the wreathed links. "This proud one
Would of his strength against almighty Jove
Make trial," said my guide: "whence he is thus

HELL

Requited: Ephialtes him they call.
Great was his prowess, when the giants brought
Fear on the gods: those arms, which then he plied,
Now moves he never." Forthwith I return'd:
"Fain would I, if 'twere possible, mine eyes,
Of Briareus immeasurable, gain'd
Experience next." He answered: "Thou shalt see
Not far from hence Antæus, who both speaks
And is unfetter'd, who shall place us there
Where guilt is at its depth. Far onward stands
Whom thou wouldst fain behold, in chains, and made
Like to this spirit, save that in his looks
More fell he seems." By violent earthquake rock'd
Ne'er shook a tower, so reeling to its base,
As Ephialtes. More than ever then
I dreaded death; nor than the terror more
Had needed, if I had not seen the cords
That held him fast. We, straightway journeying on,
Came to Antæus, who, five ells complete
Without the head, forth issued from the cave.

"O thou, who in the fortunate vale, that made
Great Scipio heir of glory, when his sword
Drove back the troop of Hannibal in flight,
Who thence of old didst carry for thy spoil
An hundred lions; and if thou hadst fought
In the high conflict on thy brethren's side,
Seems as men yet believed, that through thine arm
The sons of earth had conquer'd; now vouchsafe
To place us down beneath, where numbing cold
Locks up Cocytus. Force not that we crave
Or Tityus' help or Typhon's. Here is one
Can give what in this realm ye covet. Stoop
Therefore, nor scornfully distort thy lip.
He in the upper world can yet bestow
Renown on thee; for he doth live, and looks
For life yet longer, if before the time
Grace call him not unto herself." Thus spake
The teacher. He in haste forth stretch'd his hands
And caught my guide. Alcides whilom felt

That grapple, straiten'd sore. Soon as my guide
Had felt it, he bespake me thus: "This way,
That I may clasp thee;" then so caught me up,
That we were both one burden. As appears
The tower of Carisenda, from beneath
Where it doth lean, if chance a passing cloud
So sail across, that opposite it hangs;
Such then Antæus seem'd, as at mine ease
I mark'd him stooping. I were fain at times
To have passed another way. Yet in the abyss,
That Lucifer with Judas low ingulfs,
Lightly he placed us; nor, there leaning, stay'd;
But rose, as in a bark the stately mast.

CANTO XXXII

This canto treats of the first two rounds of the last or frozen circle of Hell.

COULD I command rough rhymes and hoarse, to suit
That hole of sorrow o'er which every rock
His firm abutment rears, then might the vein
Of fancy rise full springing: but not mine
Such measures, and with faltering awe I touch
The mighty theme; for to describe the depth
Of all the universe, is no emprise
To jest with, and demands a tongue not used
To infant babbling. But let them assist
My song, the tuneful maidens, by whose aid
Amphion wall'd in Thebes; so with the truth
My speech shall best accord. Oh ill-starr'd folk,
Beyond all others wretched! who abide
In such a mansion, as scarce thought finds words
To speak of, better had ye here on earth
Been flocks, or mountain goats. As down we stood
In the dark pit beneath the giants' feet,
But lower far than they, and I did gaze
Still on the lofty battlement, a voice

HELL

Bespake me thus: "Look how thou walkest. Take
Good heed, thy soles do tread not on the heads
Of thy poor brethren." Thereupon I turn'd,
And saw before and underneath my feet
A lake, whose frozen surface liker seem'd
To glass than water. Not so thick a veil
In winter e'er hath Austrian Danube spread
O'er his still course, nor Tanaïs far remote
Under the chilling sky. Roll'd o'er that mass
Had Tabernich or Pietrapana fallen,
Not e'en its rim had creak'd. As peeps the frog
Croaking above the wave, what time in dreams
The village gleaner oft pursues her toil,
So, to where modest shame appears, thus low
Blue pinch'd and shrined in ice the spirits stood,
Moving their teeth in shrill note like the stork.
His face each downward held; their mouth the cold,
Their eyes express'd the dolor of their heart.

A space I look'd around, then at my feet
Saw two so strictly join'd, that of their head
The very hairs were mingled. "Tell me ye,
Whose bosoms thus together press," said I,
"Who are ye?" At that sound their necks they bent;
And when their looks were lifted up to me,
Straightway their eyes, before all moist within,
Distill'd upon their lips, and the frost bound
The tears betwixt those orbs, and held them there.
Plank unto plank hath never cramp closed up
So stoutly. Whence, like two enraged goats,
They clash'd together: them such fury seized.

And one, from whom the cold both ears had reft,
Exclaim'd, still looking downward: "Why on us
Dost speculate so long? If thou wouldst know
Who are these two, the valley, whence his wave
Bisenzio slopes, did for its master own
Their sire Alberto, and next him themselves.
They from one body issued: and throughout
Caïna thou mayst search, nor find a shade

[133]

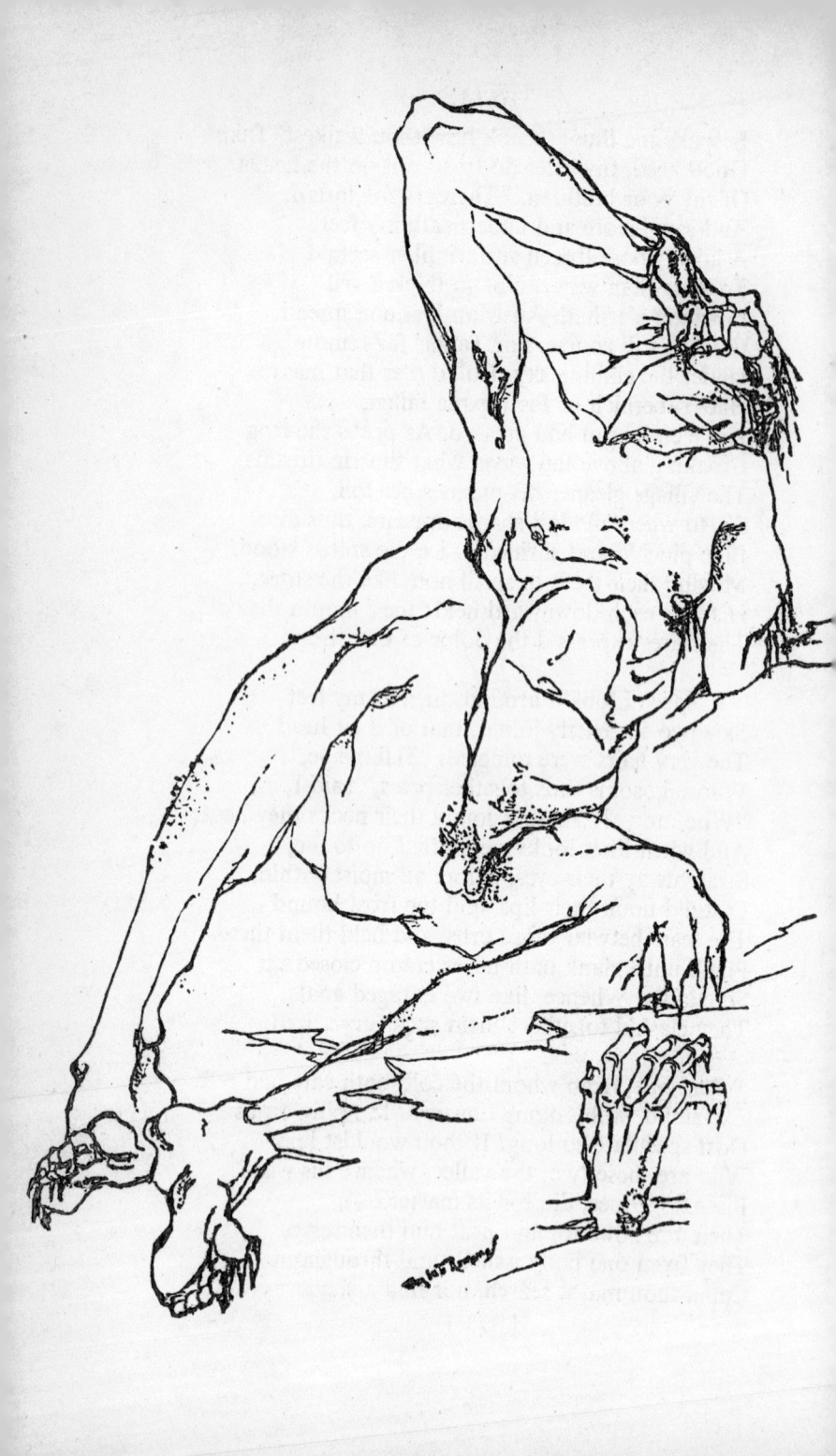

More worthy in congealment to be fix'd;
Not him, whose breast and shadow Arthur's hand
At that one blow dissever'd; not Focaccia;
No, not this spirit, whose o'erjutting head
Obstructs my onward view: he bore the name
Of Mascheroni: Tuscan if thou be,
Well knowest who he was. And to cut short
All further question, in my form behold
What once was Camiccione. I await
Carlino here my kinsman, whose deep guilt
Shall wash out mine." A thousand visages
Then mark'd I, which the keen and eager cold
Had shaped into a doggish grin; whence creeps
A shivering horror o'er me, at the thought
Of those frore shallows. While we journey'd on
Toward the middle, at whose point unites
All heavy substance, and I trembling went
Through that eternal chillness, I know not
If will it were, or destiny, or chance,
But, passing 'midst the heads, my foot did strike
With violent blow against the face of one.

"Wherefore dost bruise me?" weeping he exclaim'd
"Unless thy errand be some fresh revenge
For Montaperto, wherefore troublest me?"

I thus: "Instructor, now await me here,
That I through him may rid me of my doubt:
Thenceforth what haste thou wilt." The teacher paused
And to that shade I spake, who bitterly
Still cursed me in his wrath. "What art thou, speak,
That railest thus on others?" He replied:
"Now who art thou, that smiting others' cheeks,
Through Antenora roamest, with such force
As were past sufferance, wert thou living still?"

"And I am living, to thy joy perchance,"
Was my reply, "if fame be dear to thee,
That with the rest I may thy name enroll."

[135]

THE DIVINE COMEDY

"The contrary of what I covet most,"
Said he, "thou tender'st: hence! nor vex me more.
Ill knowest thou to flatter in this vale."

Then seizing on his hinder scalp I cried:
"Name thee, or not a hair shall tarry here."

"Rend all away," he answer'd, "yet for that
I will not tell, nor show thee, who I am,
Though at my head thou pluck a thousand times."

Now I had grasp'd his tresses, and stript off
More than one tuft, he barking, with his eyes
Drawn in and downward, when another cried,
"What ails thee, Bocca? Sound not loud enough
Thy chattering teeth, but thou must bark outright?
What devil wrings thee?"—"Now," said I, "be dumb,
Accursed traitor! To thy shame, of thee
True tidings will I bear."—"Off!" he replied;
"Tell what thou list: but, as thou 'scape from hence,
To speak of him whose tongue hath been so glib,
Forget not: here he wails the Frenchman's gold.
'Him of Duera,' thou canst say, 'I mark'd,
Where the starved sinners pine.' If thou be ask'd
What other shade was with them, at thy side
Is Beccaria, whose red gorge distain'd
The biting axe of Florence. Further on,
If I misdeem not, Soldanieri bides,
With Ganellon, and Tribaldello, him
Who oped Faenza when the people slept."

We now had left him, passing on our way,
When I beheld two spirits by the ice
Pent in one hollow, that the head of one
Was cowl unto the other; and as bread
Is raven'd up through hunger, the uppermost
Did so apply his fangs to the other's brain,
Where the spine joins it. Not more furiously
On Menalippus' temples Tydeus gnawed,
Than on that skull and on its garbage he.

HELL

"O thou! who show'st so beastly sign of hate
'Gainst him thou prey'st on, let me hear," said I,
"The cause, on such condition, that if right
Warrant thy grievance, knowing who ye are,
And what the color of his sinning was,
I may repay thee in the world above,
If that, wherewith I speak, be moist so long."

CANTO XXXIII

Count Ugolino de' Gherardeschi tells of the cruel manner in which he and his children famished to death and discourses of the third round called Ptolomea.

His jaws uplifting from their fell repast,
That sinner wiped them on the hairs o' the head,
Which he behind had mangled, then began:
"Thy will obeying, I call up afresh
Sorrow past cure; which, but to think of, wrings
My heart, or ere I tell on't. But if words,
That I may utter, shall prove seed to bear
Fruit of eternal infamy to him,
The traitor whom I gnaw at, thou at once
Shalt see me speak and weep. Who thou mayst be
I know not, nor how here below art come:
But Florentine thou seemest of a truth,
When I do hear thee. Know, I was on earth
Count Ugolino, and the Archbishop he
Ruggieri. Why I neighbor him so close,
Now list. That through effect of his ill-thoughts
In him my trust reposing, I was ta'en
And after murder'd, need is not I tell.
What therefore thou canst not have heard, that is,
How cruel was the murder, shalt thou hear,
And know if he have wrong'd me. A small grate
Within that mew, which for my sake the name
Of Famine bears, where others yet must pine,
Already through its opening several moons

[137]

THE DIVINE COMEDY

Had shown me, when I slept the evil sleep
That from the future tore the curtain off.
This one, methought, as master of the sport,
Rode forth to chase the gaunt wolf, and his whelps,
Unto the mountain which forbids the sight
Of Lucca to the Pisan. With lean brachs
Inquisitive and keen, before him ranged
Lanfranchi with Sismondi and Gualandi.
After short course the father and the sons
Seem'd tired and lagging, and methought I saw
The sharp tusks gore their sides. When I awoke,
Before the dawn, amid their sleep I heard
My sons (for they were with me) weep and ask
For bread. Right cruel art thou, if no pang
Thou feel at thinking what my heart foretold;
And if not now, why use thy tears to flow?
Now had they waken'd; and the hour drew near
When they were wont to bring us food; the mind
Of each misgave him through his dream, and I
Heard, at its outlet underneath lock'd up
The horrible tower: whence, uttering not a word,
I look'd upon the visage of my sons.
I wept not: so all stone I felt within.
They wept: and one, my little Anselm, cried,
'Thou lookest so! Father, what ails thee?' Yet
I shed no tear, nor answer'd all that day
Nor the next night, until another sun
Came out upon the world. When a faint beam
Had to our doleful prison made its way,
And in four countenances I descried
The image of my own, on either hand
Through agony I bit; and they, who thought
I did it through desire of feeding, rose
O' the sudden, and cried, 'Father, we should grieve
Far less, if thou wouldst eat of us: thou gavest
These weeds of miserable flesh we wear;
And do thou strip them off from us again.'
Then, not to make them sadder, I kept down
My spirit in stillness. That day and the next
We all were silent. Ah, obdurate earth!

HELL

Why open'dst not upon us? When we came
To the fourth day, then Gaddo at my feet
Outstretch'd did fling him, crying, 'Hast no help
For me, my father!' There he died; and e'en
Plainly as thou seest me, saw I the three
Fall one by one 'twixt the fifth day and sixth:
Whence I betook me, now grown blind, to grope
Over them all, and for three days aloud
Call'd on them who were dead. Then, fasting got
The mastery of grief." Thus having spoke,
Once more upon the wretched skull his teeth
He fasten'd like a mastiff's 'gainst the bone,
Firm and unyielding. O thou Pisa! shame
Of all the people, who their dwelling make
In that fair region, where the Italian voice
Is heard; since that thy neighbors are so slack
To punish, from their deep foundations rise
Capraia and Gorgona, and dam up
The mouth of Arno; that each soul in thee
May perish in the waters. What if fame
Reported that thy castles were betray'd
By Ugolino, yet no right hadst thou
To stretch his children on the rack. For them,
Brigata, Uguccione, and the pair
Of gentle ones, of whom my song hath told,
Their tender years, thou modern Thebes, did make
Uncapable of guilt. Onward we pass'd,
Where others, skarf'd in rugged folds of ice,
Not on their feet were turn'd, but each reversed.

There, very weeping suffers not to weep;
For, at their eyes, grief, seeking passage, finds
Impediment, and rolling inward turns
For increase of sharp anguish: the first tears
Hang cluster'd, and like crystal vizors show,
Under the socket brimming all the cup.

Now though the cold had from my face dislodged
Each feeling, as 'twere callous, yet me seem'd
Some breath of wind I felt. "Whence cometh this,"

THE DIVINE COMEDY

Said I, "my Master? Is not here below
All vapor quench'd?" "Thou shalt be speedily,"
He answer'd, "where thine eyes shall tell thee whence,
The cause descrying of this airy shower."

Then cried out one, in the chill crust who mourn'd:
"O souls! so cruel, that the farthest post
Hath been assign'd you, from this face remove
The harden'd veil; that I may vent the grief
Impregnate at my heart, some little space,
Ere it congeal again." I thus replied:
"Say who thou wast, if thou wouldst have mine aid;
And if I extricate thee not, far down
As to the lowest ice may I descend."

"The friar Alberigo," answer'd he,
"Am I, who from the evil garden pluck'd
Its fruitage, and am here repaid, the date
More luscious for my fig." "Hah!" I exclaim'd,
"Art thou, too, dead?" "How in the world aloft
It fareth with my body," answer'd he,
"I am right ignorant. Such privilege
Hath Ptolomea, that ofttimes the soul
Drops hither, ere by Atropos divorced.
And that thou mayst wipe out more willingly
The glazed tear-drops that o'erlay mine eyes,
Know that the soul, that moment she betrays,
As I did, yields her body to a fiend
Who after moves and governs it at will,
Till all its time be rounded: headlong she
Falls to this cistern. And perchance above
Doth yet appear the body of a ghost,
Who here behind me winters. Him thou know'st,
If thou but newly art arrived below.
The years are many that have passed away,
Since to this fastness Branca Doria came."

"Now," answer'd I, "methinks thou mockest me;
For Branca Doria never yet hath died,

HELL

But doth all natural functions of a man,
Eats, drinks, and sleeps, and putteth raiment on."

He thus: "Not yet unto that upper foss
By th' evil talons guarded, where the pitch
Tenacious boils, had Michel Zanche reach'd,
When this one left a demon in his stead
In his own body, and of one his kin,
Who with him treachery wrought. But now put forth
Thy hand, and ope mine eyes." I oped them not.
Ill manners were best courtesy to him.

Ah Genoese! men perverse in every way,
With every foulness stain'd, why from the earth
Are ye not cancel'd? Such an one of yours
I with Romagna's darkest spirit found,
As, for his doings, even now in soul
Is in Cocytus plunged, and yet doth seem
In body still alive upon the earth.

CANTO XXXIV

In the last round is Lucifer on whose back Dante and Virgil ascend to the other hemisphere of the earth.

"THE banners of Hell's Monarch do come forth
Toward us; therefore look," so spake my guide,
"If thou discern him." As, when breathes a cloud
Heavy and dense, or when the shades of night
Fall on our hemisphere, seems view'd from far
A windmill, which the blast stirs briskly round;
Such was the fabric then methought I saw.

To shield me from the wind, forthwith I drew
Behind my guide: no covert else was there.

THE DIVINE COMEDY

Now came I (and with fear I bid my strain
Record the marvel) where the souls were all
Whelm'd underneath, transparent, as through glass
Pellucid the frail stem. Some prone were laid;
Others stood upright, this upon the soles,
That on his head, a third with face to feet
Arch'd like a bow. When to the point we came,
Whereat my guide was pleased that I should see
The creature eminent in beauty once,
He from before me stepp'd and made me pause.

"Lo!" he exclaim'd, "lo! Dis; and lo! the place,
Where thou hast need to arm thy heart with strength."

How frozen and how faint I then became,
Ask me not, reader! for I write it not;
Since words would fail to tell thee of my state.
I was not dead nor living. Think thyself,
If quick conception work in thee at all,
How I did feel. That emperor, who sways
The realm of sorrow, at mid breast from the ice
Stood forth; and I in stature am more like
A giant, than the giants are his arms.
Mark now how great that whole must be, which suits
With such a part. If he were beautiful
As he is hideous now, and yet did dare
To scowl upon his Maker, well from him
May all our misery flow. Oh what a sight!
How passing strange it seem'd, when I did spy
Upon his head three faces: one in front
Of hue vermilion, the other two with this
Midway each shoulder join'd and at the crest;
The right 'twixt wan and yellow seem'd; the left
To look on, such as come from whence old Nile
Stoops to the lowlands. Under each shot forth
Two mighty wings, enormous as became
A bird so vast. Sails never such I saw
Outstretch'd on the wide sea. No plumes had they,
But were in texture like a bat; and these
He flapp'd i' th' air, that from him issued still

HELL

Three winds, wherewith Cocytus to its depth
Was frozen. At six eyes he wept: the tears
Adown three chins distill'd with bloody foam.
At every mouth his teeth a sinner champ'd,
Bruised as with ponderous engine; so that three
Were in this guise tormented. But far more
Than from that gnawing, was the foremost pang'd
By the fierce rending, whence ofttimes the back
Was stript of all its skin. "That upper spirit,
Who hath worst punishment," so spake my guide,
"Is Judas, he that hath his head within
And plies the feet without. Of th' other two,
Whose heads are under, from the murky jaw
Who hangs, is Brutus: lo! how he doth writhe
And speaks not. The other, Cassius, that appears
So large of limb. But night now reascends;
And it is time for parting. All is seen."

I clipp'd him round the neck; for so he bade:
And noting time and place, he, when the wings
Enough were oped, caught fast the shaggy sides,
And down from pile to pile descending stepp'd
Between the thick fell and the jagged ice.

Soon as he reach'd the point, whereat the thigh
Upon the swelling of the haunches turns,
My leader there, with pain and struggling hard,
Turn'd round his head where his feet stood before,
And grappled at the fell as one who mounts;
That into hell methought we turn'd again.

"Expect that by such stairs as these," thus spake
The teacher, panting like a man forespent,
"We must depart from evil so extreme":
Then at a rocky opening issued forth,
And placed me on the brink to sit, next join'd
With wary step my side. I raised mine eyes,
Believing that I Lucifer should see
Where he was lately left, but saw him now
With legs held upward. Let the grosser sort,

THE DIVINE COMEDY

Who see not what the point was I had past,
Bethink them if sore toil oppress'd me then.

"Arise," my master cried, "upon thy feet.
The way is long, and much uncouth the road;
And now within one hour and half of noon
The sun returns." It was no palace-hall
Lofty and luminous wherein we stood,
But natural dungeon where ill-footing was
And scant supply of light. "Ere from the abyss
I separate," thus when risen I began:
"My guide! vouchsafe few words to set me free
From error's thraldom. Where is now the ice?
How standeth he in posture thus reversed?
And how from eve to morn in space so brief
Hath the sun made his transit?" He in few
Thus answering spake: "Thou deemest thou art still
On the other side the centre, where I grasp'd
The abhorred worm that boreth through the world.
Thou wast on the other side, so long as I
Descended; when I turn'd, thou didst o'erpass
That point, to which from every part is dragg'd
All heavy substance. Thou art now arrived
Under the hemisphere opposed to that,
Which the great continent doth overspread,
And underneath whose canopy expired
The Man, that was born sinless and so lived.
Thy feet are planted on the smallest sphere,
Whose other aspect is Judecca. Morn
Here rises, when there evening sets: and he,
Whose shaggy pile we scaled, yet standeth fix'd,
As at the first. On this part he fell down
From heaven; and th' earth, here prominent before,
Through fear of him did veil her with the sea,
And to our hemisphere retired. Perchance,
To shun him, was the vacant space left here,
By what of firm land on this side appears,
That sprang aloof." There is a place beneath,
From Belzebub as distant, as extends
The vaulted tomb; discover'd not by sight,

HELL

But by the sound of brooklet, that descends
This way along the hollow of a rock,
Which, as it winds with no precipitous course,
The wave hath eaten. By that hidden way
My guide and I did enter, to return
To the fair world: and heedless of repose
We climb'd, he first, I following his steps,
Till on our view the beautiful lights of heaven
Dawn'd through a circular opening in the cave:
Thence issuing we again beheld the stars.

HILLS.

But by the sound of brookles that dissonous
Thus way, along the hollow of a rock,
Which, as it winds, with no precipitous bound,
The wave hath cut its, by that hidden way
My guide and I adventure to return
To the fair world; and heedless of repose
We climb'd, he first, I following his steps,
Till on our view the beautiful lights of heaven
Dawn'd, through a circular opening in the cave:
Thence issuing we again beheld the stars.

Purgatory

CANTO I

The poet comes to Purgatory, beholds four stars seen only by our first parents, and meets Cato of Utica.

O'ER better waves to speed her rapid course
The light bark of my genius lifts the sail,
Well pleased to leave so cruel sea behind;
And of that second region will I sing,
In which the human spirit from sinful blot
Is purged, and for ascent to Heaven prepares.

    Here, O ye hallow'd Nine! for in your train
I follow, here the deaden'd strain revive;
Nor let Calliope refuse to sound
A somewhat higher song, of that loud tone
Which when the wretched birds of chattering note
Had heard, they of forgiveness lost all hope.

    Sweet hue of eastern sapphire, that was spread
O'er the serene aspect of the pure air,
High up as the first circle, to mine eyes
Unwonted joy renew'd, soon as I 'scaped
Forth from the atmosphere of deadly gloom,
That had mine eyes and bosom fill'd with grief.
The radiant planet, that to love invites,
Made all the orient laugh, and veil'd beneath
The Pisces' light, that in his escort came.

[149]

THE DIVINE COMEDY

To the right hand I turn'd, and fix'd my mind
On the other pole attentive, where I saw
Four stars ne'er seen before save by the ken
Of our first parents. Heaven of their rays
Seem'd joyous. O thou northern site! bereft
Indeed, and widow'd, since of these deprived.

As from this view I had desisted, straight
Turning a little toward the other pole,
There from whence now the wain had disappear'd,
I saw an old man standing by my side
Alone, so worthy of reverence in his look,
That ne'er from son to father more was owed.
Low down his beard, and mix'd with hoary white,
Descended, like his locks, which, parting, fell
Upon his breast in double fold. The beams
Of those four luminaries on his face
So brightly shone, and with such radiance clear
Deck'd it, that I beheld him as the sun.

"Say who are ye, that stemming the blind stream,
Forth from the eternal prison-house have fled?"
He spoke and moved those venerable plumes.
"Who hath conducted, or with lantern sure
Lights you emerging from the depth of night,
That makes the infernal valley ever black?
Are the firm statutes of the dread abyss
Broken, or in high heaven new laws ordain'd,
That thus, condemn'd, ye to my caves approach?"

My guide, then laying hold on me, by words
And intimations given with hand and head,
Made my bent knees and eye submissive pay
Due reverence; then thus to him replied:

"Not of myself I come; a Dame from heaven
Descending, him besought me in my charge
To bring. But since thy will implies, that more
Our true condition I unfold at large,
Mine is not to deny thee thy request.

[150]

PURGATORY

This mortal ne'er hath seen the furthest gloom;
But erring by his folly had approach'd
So near, that little space was left to turn.
Then, as before I told, I was despatch'd
To work his rescue; and no way remain'd
Save this which I have ta'en. I have display'd
Before him all the regions of the bad;
And purpose now those spirits to display,
That under thy command are purged from sin.
How I have brought him would be long to say.
From high descends the virtue, by whose aid
I to thy sight and hearing him have led.
Now may our coming please thee. In the search
Of liberty he journeys: that how dear,
They know who for her sake have life refused.
Thou knowest, to whom death for her was sweet
In Utica, where thou didst leave those weeds,
That in the last great day will shine so bright.
He breathes, and I of Minos am not bound,
For us the eternal edicts are unmoved
Abiding in that circle, where the eyes
Of thy chaste Marcia beam, who still in look
Prays thee, O hallow'd spirit! to own her thine.
Then by her love we implore thee, let us pass
Through thy seven regions; for which, best thanks
I for thy favor will to her return,
If mention there below thou not disdain."

"Marcia so pleasing in my sight was found,"
He then to him rejoin'd, "while I was there,
That all she ask'd me I was fain to grant.
Now that beyond the accursed stream she dwells,
She may no longer move me, by that law,
Which was ordain'd me, when I issued thence.
Not so, if Dame from heaven, as thou sayst,
Moves and directs thee; then no flattery needs.
Enough for me that in her name thou ask.
Go therefore now: and with a slender reed
See that thou duly gird him, and his face
Lave, till all sordid stain thou wipe from thence.

For not with eye, by any cloud obscured,
Would it be seemly before him to come,
Who stands the foremost minister in Heaven.
This islet all around, there far beneath,
Where the wave beats it, on the oozy bed
Produces store of reeds. No other plant,
Cover'd with leaves, or harden'd in its stalk,
There lives, not bending to the water's sway.
After, this way return not; but the sun
Will show you, that now rises, where to take
The mountain in its easiest ascent."

He disappear'd; and I myself upraised
Speechless, and to my guide retiring close,
Toward him turn'd mine eyes. He thus began:
"My son! observant thou my steps pursue.
We must retreat to rereward; for that way
The champain to its low extreme declines."

The dawn had chased the matin hour of prime,
Which fled before it, so that from afar
I spied the trembling of the ocean stream.

We traversed the deserted plain, as one
Who, wander'd from his track, thinks every step
Trodden in vain till he regain the path.

When we had come, where yet the tender dew
Strove with the sun, and in a place where fresh
The wind breathed o'er it, while it slowly dried;
Both hands extended on the watery grass
My master placed, in graceful act and kind.
Whence I of his intent before apprised,
Stretch'd out to him my cheeks suffused with tears.
There to my visage he anew restored
That hue which the dun shades of hell conceal'd.

Then on the solitary shore arrived,
That never sailing on its waters saw
Man that could after measure back his course,

PURGATORY

He girt me in such manner as had pleased
Him who instructed; and, oh strange to tell!
As he selected every humble plant,
Wherever one was pluck'd another there
Resembling, straightway in its place arose.

CANTO II

*Dante and Virgil see a vessel bringing spirits to Purgatory,
and Dante recognizes his friend, Casella.*

Now had the sun to that horizon reach'd,
That covers, with the most exalted point
Of its meridian circle, Salem's walls;
And night, that opposite to him her orb
Rounds, from the stream of Ganges issued forth,
Holding the scales, that from her hands are dropt
When she reigns highest: so that where I was,
Aurora's white and vermeil-tinctured cheek
To orange turn'd as she in age increased.

   Meanwhile we linger'd by the water's brink,
Like men, who, musing on their road, in thought
Journey, while motionless the body rests.
When lo! as near upon the hour of dawn,
Through the thick vapors Mars with fiery beam
Glares down in the West, over the ocean floor;
So seem'd, what once again I hope to view,
A light, so swiftly coming through the sea,
No winged course might equal its career.
From which when for a space I had withdrawn
Mine eyes, to make inquiry of my guide,
Again I look'd, and saw it grown in size
And brightness: then on either side appear'd
Something, but that I knew not, of bright hue,
And by degrees from underneath it came
Another. My preceptor silent yet
Stood, while the brightness, that we first discern'd,
Open'd the form of wings: then when he knew

[153]

THE DIVINE COMEDY

The pilot, cried aloud, "Down! Down! Bend low
Thy knees! Behold God's angel! Fold thy hands!
Now shalt thou see true ministers indeed!
Lo! how all human means he sets at naught;
So that nor oar he needs, nor other sail
Except his wings, between such distant shores.
Lo! how straight up to heaven he holds them rear'd,
Winnowing the air with those eternal plumes,
That not like mortal hairs fall off or change."

As more and more toward us came, more bright
Appear'd the bird of God, nor could the eye
Endure his splendor near: I mine bent down.
He drove ashore in a small bark so swift
And light, that in its course no wave it drank.
The heavenly steersman at the prow was seen,
Visibly written "Blessed" in his looks.
Within, a hundred spirits and more there sat.

"In Exitu Israel de Egypto,"
All with one voice together sang, with what
In the remainder of that hymn is writ.
Then soon as with the sign of Holy Cross
He bless'd them, they at once leap'd out on land:
He, swiftly as he came, return'd. The crew,
There left, appear'd astounded with the place,
Gazing around, as one who sees new sights.

From every side the sun darted his beams,
And with his arrowy radiance from mid heaven
Had chased the Capricorn, when that strange tribe,
Lifting their eyes toward us: "If ye know,
Declare what path will lead us to the mount."

Them Virgil answer'd: "Ye suppose, perchance,
Us well acquainted with this place: but here,
We, as yourselves, are strangers. Not long erst
We came, before you but a little space,
By other road so rough and hard, that now
The ascent will seem to us as play." The spirits,

PURGATORY

Who from my breathing had perceived I lived,
Grew pale with wonder. As the multitude
Flock round a herald sent with olive branch,
To hear what news he brings, and in their haste
Tread one another down; e'en so at sight
Of me those happy spirits were fix'd, each one
Forgetful of its errand to depart
Where, cleansed from sin, it might be made all fair.

Then one I saw darting before the rest
With such fond ardor to embrace me, I
To do the like was moved. O shadows vain!
Except in outward semblance: thrice my hands
I clasp'd behind it, they as oft return'd
Empty into my breast again. Surprise
I need must think was painted in my looks,
For that the shadow smiled and backward drew.
To follow it I hasten'd, but with voice
Of sweetness it enjoin'd me to desist.
Then who it was I knew, and pray'd of it,
To talk with me it would a little pause.
It answer'd: "Thee as in my mortal frame
I loved, so loosed from it I love thee still,
And therefore pause: but why walkest thou here?"

"Not without purpose once more to return,
Thou find'st me, my Casella, where I am,
Journeying this way"; I said: "but how of thee
Hath so much time been lost?" He answer'd straight:

"No outrage hath been done to me, if he,
Who when and whom he chooses takes, hath oft
Denied me passage here; since of just will
His will he makes. These three months past indeed,
He, who so chose to enter, with free leave
Hath taken; whence I wandering by the shore
Where Tiber's wave grows salt, of him gain'd kind
Admittance, at that river's mouth, toward which
His wings are pointed; for there always throng
All such as not to Acheron descend."

[155]

Then I: "If new law taketh not from thee
Memory or custom of love-tuned song,
That whilom all my cares had power to 'swage;
Please thee therewith a little to console
My spirit, that encumber'd with its frame,
Travelling so far, of pain is overcome."

"Love, that discourses in my thoughts," he then
Began in such soft accents, that within
The sweetness thrills me yet. My gentle guide,
And all who came with him, so well were pleased,
That seem'd naught else might in their thoughts have room.

Fast fix'd in mute attention to his notes
We stood, when lo! that old man venerable
Exclaiming, "How is this, ye tardy spirits?
What negligence detains you loitering here?
Run to the mountain to cast off those scales,
That from your eyes the sight of God conceal."

As a wild flock of pigeons, to their food
Collected, blade or tares, without their pride
Accustom'd, and in still and quiet sort,
If aught alarm them, suddenly desert
Their meal, assail'd by more important care;
So I that new-come troop beheld, the song
Deserting, hasten to the mountain's side,
As one who goes, yet, where he tends, knows **not**.

Nor with less hurried step did we depart.

CANTO III

Arriving at the foot of the mountain of Purgatory, they are shown the ascent by a troop of spirits.

THEM sudden flight had scatter'd o'er the plain,
Turn'd toward the mountain, whither reason's voice

[156]

PURGATORY

Drives us: I, to my faithful company
Adhering, left it not. For how, of him
Deprived, might I have sped? or who, beside,
Would o'er the mountainous tract have led my steps?
He, with the bitter pang of self-remorse,
Seem'd smitten. O clear conscience, and upright!
How doth a little failing wound thee sore.

Soon as his feet desisted (slackening pace)
From haste, that mars all decency of act,
My mind, that in itself before was wrapt,
Its thought expanded, as with joy restored;
And full against the steep ascent I set
My face, where highest to heaven its top o'erflows.

The sun, that flared behind, with ruddy beam
Before my form was broken; for in me
His rays resistance met. I turn'd aside
With fear of being left, when I beheld
Only before myself the ground obscured.
When thus my solace, turning him around,
Bespake me kindly: "Why distrustest thou?
Believest not I am with thee, thy sure guide?
It now is evening there, where buried lies
The body in which I cast a shade, removed
To Naples from Brundusium's wall. Nor thou
Marvel, if before me no shadow fall,
More than that in the skyey element
One ray obstructs not other. To endure
Torments of heat and cold extreme, like frames
That virtue hath disposed, which, how it works,
Wills not to us should be reveal'd. Insane,
Who hopes our reason may that space explore,
Which holds three persons in one substance knit.
Seek not the wherefore, race of human kind;
Could ye have seen the whole, no need had been
For Mary to bring forth. Moreover, ye
Have seen such men desiring fruitlessly;
To whose desires, repose would have been given,
That now but serve them for eternal grief.

THE DIVINE COMEDY

I speak of Plato, and the Stagirite,
And others many more." And then he bent
Downward his forehead, and in troubled mood
Broke off his speech. Meanwhile we had arrived
Far as the mountain's foot, and there the rock
Found of so steep ascent, that nimblest steps
To climb it had been vain. The most remote,
Most wild, untrodden path, in all the tract
'Twixt Lerice and Turbia, were to this
A ladder easy and open of access.

"Who knows on which hand now the steep declines,"
My master said, and paused; "so that he may
Ascend, who journeys without aid of wing?"
And while, with looks directed to the ground,
The meaning of the pathway he explored,
And I gazed upward round the stony height;
On the left hand appear'd to us a troop
Of spirits, that toward us moved their steps;
Yet moving seem'd not, they so slow approach'd.

I thus my guide address'd: "Upraise thine eyes:
Lo! that way some, of whom thou mayst obtain
Counsel, if of thyself thou find'st it not."

Straightway he look'd, and with free speech replied:
"Let us tend thither: they but softly come.
And thou be firm in hope, my son beloved."

Now was that crowd from us distant as far,
(When we some thousand steps, I say, had past)
As at a throw the nervous arm could fling;
When all drew backward on the massy crags
Of the steep bank, and firmly stood unmoved,
As one, who walks in doubt, might stand to look.

"O spirits perfect! O already chosen!"
Virgil to them began: "by that blest peace,
Which, as I deem, is for you all prepared,
Instruct us where the mountain low declines,

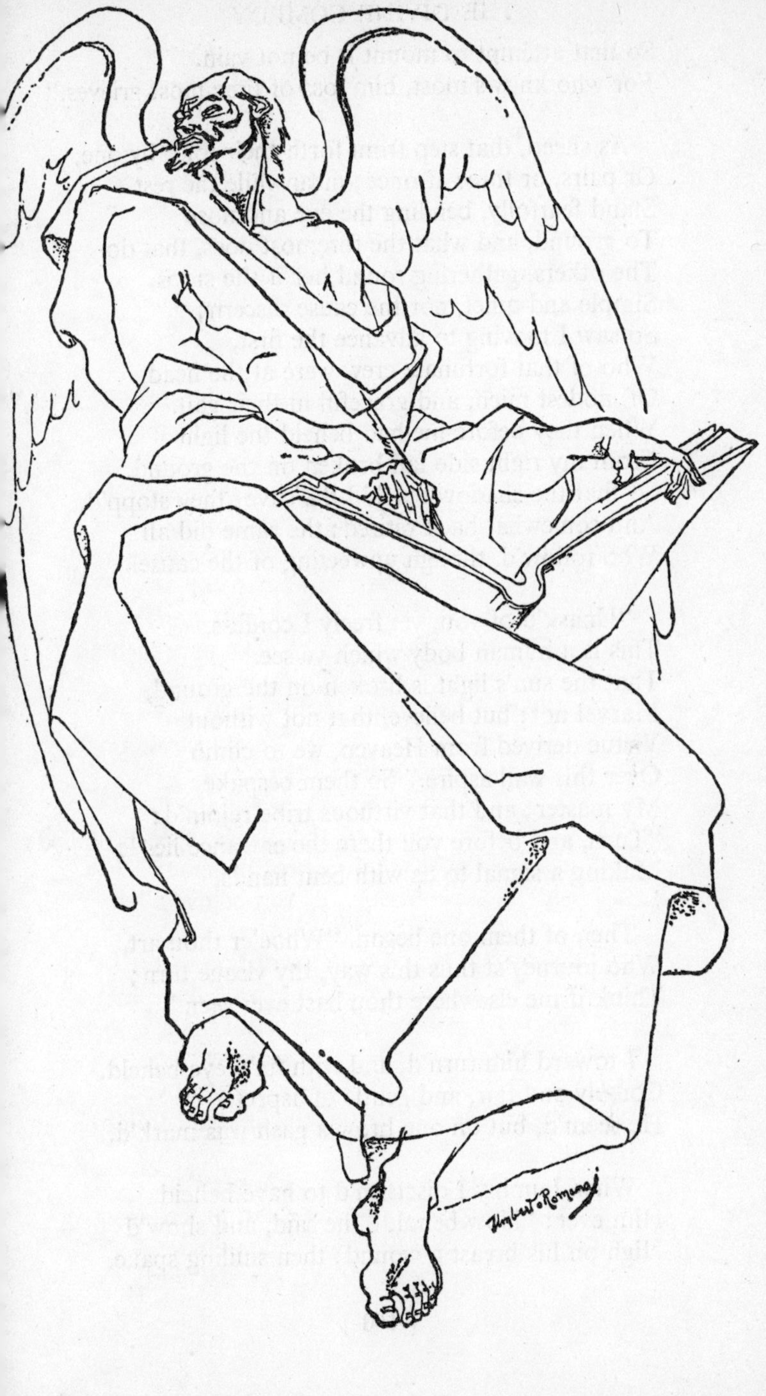
Umberto Romano

THE DIVINE COMEDY

So that attempt to mount it be not vain.
For who knows most, him loss of time most grieves."

    As sheep, that step from forth their fold, by one,
Or pairs, or three at once; meanwhile the rest
Stand fearfully, bending the eye and nose
To ground, and what the foremost does, that do
The others, gathering round her if she stops,
Simple and quiet, nor the cause discern;
So saw I moving to advance the first,
Who of that fortunate crew were at the head,
Of modest mien, and graceful in their gait.
When they before me had beheld the light
From my right side fall broken on the ground,
So that the shadow reach'd the cave; they stopp'd,
And somewhat back retired: the same did all
Who follow'd, though unweeting of the cause.

    "Unask'd of you, yet freely I confess,
This is a human body which ye see.
That the sun's light is broken on the ground,
Marvel not: but believe, that not without
Virtue derived from Heaven, we to climb
Over this wall aspire." So them bespake
My master; and that virtuous tribe rejoin'd:
"Turn, and before you there the entrance lies";
Making a signal to us with bent hands.

    Then of them one began. "Whoe'er thou art,
Who journey'st thus this way, thy visage turn;
Think if me elsewhere thou hast ever seen."

    I toward him turn'd, and with fix'd eye beheld.
Comely and fair, and gentle of aspect
He seem'd, but on one brow a gash was mark'd.

    When humbly I disclaim'd to have beheld
Him ever: "Now behold!" he said, and show'd
High on his breast a wound: then smiling spake.

PURGATORY

"I am Manfredi, grandson to the Queen
Costanza: whence I pray thee, when return'd,
To my fair daughter go, the parent glad
Of Aragonia and Sicilia's pride;
And of the truth inform her, if of me
Aught else be told. When by two mortal blows
My frame was shatter'd, I betook myself
Weeping to him, who of free will forgives.
My sins were horrible: but so wide arms
Hath goodness infinite, that it receives
All who turn to it. Had this text divine
Been of Cosenza's shepherd better scann'd,
Who then by Clement on my hunt was set,
Yet at the bridge's head my bones had lain,
Near Benevento, by the heavy mole
Protected; but the rain now drenches them,
And the wind drives, out of the kingdom's bounds,
Far as the stream of Verde, where, with lights
Extinguish'd, he removed them from their bed.
Yet by their curse we are not so destroy'd,
But that the eternal love may turn, while hope
Retains her verdant blossom. True it is,
That such one as in contumacy dies
Against the holy Church, though he repent,
Must wander thirty-fold for all the time
In his presumption past: if such decree
Be not by prayers of good men shorter made.
Look therefore if thou canst advance my bliss;
Revealing to my good Costanza, how
Thou hast beheld me, and beside the terms
Laid on me of that interdict; for here
By means of those below much profit comes."

CANTO IV

*Dante and Virgil ascend the mountain by a steep and
narrow path until they reach a ledge where
they find several spirits.*

When by sensations of delight or pain,
That any of our faculties hath seized,
Entire the soul collects herself, it seems
She is intent upon that power alone;
And thus the error is disproved, which holds
The soul not singly lighted in the breast.
And therefore when as aught is heard or seen,
That firmly keeps the soul toward it turn'd,
Time passes, and a man perceives it not.
For that, whereby we hearken, is one power;
Another that, which the whole spirit hath:
This is as it were bound, while that is free.

This found I true by proof, hearing that spirit,
And wondering; for full fifty steps aloft
The sun had measured, unobserved of me,
When we arrived where all with one accord
The spirits shouted, "Here is what ye ask."

A larger aperture ofttimes is stopt,
With forked stake of thorn by villager,
When the ripe grape imbrowns, than was the path,
By which my guide, and I behind him close,
Ascended solitary, when that troop
Departing left us. On Sanleo's road
Who journeys, or to Noli low descends,
Or mounts Bismantua's height, must use his feet;
But here a man had need to fly, I mean
With the swift wing and plumes of high desire,
Conducted by his aid, who gave me hope,
And with light furnish'd to direct my way.

PURGATORY

We through the broken rock ascended, close
Pent on each side, while underneath the ground
Ask'd help of hands and feet. When we arrived
Near on the highest ridge of the steep bank,
Where the plain level open'd, I exclaim'd,
"O Master! say, which way can we proceed."

He answer'd, "Let no step of thine recede.
Behind me gain the mountain, till to us
Some practised guide appear." That eminence
Was lofty, that no eye might reach its point;
And the side proudly rising, more than line
From the mid quadrant to the centre drawn.
I, wearied, thus began: "Parent beloved!
Turn and behold how I remain alone,
If thou stay not." "My son!" he straight replied,
"Thus far put forth thy strength"; and to a track
Pointed, that, on this side projecting, round
Circles the hill. His words so spurr'd me on,
That I, behind him, clambering, forced myself,
Till my feet press'd the circuit plain beneath.
There both together seated, turn'd we round
To eastward, whence was our ascent: and oft
Many beside have with delight look'd back.

First on the nether shores I turn'd mine eyes,
Then raised them to the sun, and wondering mark'd
That from the left it smote us. Soon perceived
That poet sage, how at the car of light
Amazed I stood, where 'twixt us and the north
Its course it enter'd. Whence he thus to me:
"Were Leda's offspring now in company
Of that broad mirror, that high up and low
Imparts his light beneath, thou mightst behold
The ruddy Zodiac nearer to the Bears
Wheel, if its ancient course it not forsook.
How that may be, if thou wouldst think; within
Pondering, imagine Sion with this mount
Placed on the earth, so that to both be one
Horizon, and two hemispheres apart,

[163]

Where lies the path that Phaëton ill knew
To guide his erring chariot: thou wilt see
How of necessity by this, on one,
He passes, while by that on the other side;
If with that clear view thine intellect attend."

"Of truth, kind teacher!" I exclaim'd, "so clear
Aught saw I never, as I now discern,
Where seem'd my ken to fail, that the mid orb
Of the supernal motion (which in terms
Of art is call'd the Equator), and remains
Still 'twixt the sun and winter, for the cause
Thou hast assign'd, from hence toward the north
Departs, when those, who in the Hebrew land
Were dwellers, saw it toward the warmer part.
But if it please thee, I would gladly know,
How far we have to journey: for the hill
Mounts higher, than this sight of mine can mount."

He thus to me: "Such is this steep ascent,
That it is ever difficult at first,
But more a man proceeds, less evil grows.
When pleasant it shall seem to thee, so much
That upward going shall be easy to thee
As in a vessel to go down the tide,
Then of this path thou wilt have reach'd the end.
There hope to rest thee from thy toil. No more
I answer, and thus far for certain know."
As he his words had spoken, near to us
A voice there sounded: "Yet ye first perchance
May to repose you by constraint be led."
At sound thereof each turn'd; and on the left
A huge stone we beheld, of which nor I
Nor he before was ware. Thither we drew;
And there were some, who in the shady place
Behind the rock were standing, as a man
Through idleness might stand. Among them one,
Who seem'd to be much wearied, sat him down,
And with his arms did fold his knees about,
Holding his face between them downward bent.

PURGATORY

"Sweet Sir!" I cried, "behold that man who shows
Himself more idle than if laziness
Were sister to him." Straight he turn'd to us,
And, o'er the thigh lifting his face, observed,
Then in these accents spake: "Up then, proceed,
Thou valiant one." Straight who it was I knew;
Nor could the pain I felt (for want of breath
Still somewhat urged me) hinder my approach.
And when I came to him, he scarce his head
Uplifted, saying, "Well hast thou discern'd,
How from the left the sun his chariot leads."

His lazy acts and broken words my lips
To laughter somewhat moved; when I began:
"Belacqua, now for thee I grieve no more.
But tell, why thou art seated upright there.
Waitest thou escort to conduct thee hence?
Or blame I only thine accustom'd ways?"
Then he: "My brother! of what use to mount,
When, to my suffering, would not let me pass
The bird of God, who at the portal sits?
Behoves so long that heaven first bear me round
Without its limits, as in life it bore;
Because I, to the end, repentant sighs
Delay'd; if prayer do not aid me first,
That riseth up from heart which lives in grace,
What other kind avails, not heard in heaven?"

Before me now the poet, up the mount
Ascending, cried: "Haste thee: for see the sun
Has touch'd the point meridian; and the night
Now covers with her foot Marocco's shore."

CANTO V

*They meet others who had deferred their repentance
until overtaken by a violent death.*

Now had I left those spirits, and pursued
The steps of my conductor; when behind,
Pointing the finger at me, one exclaim'd:
"See, how it seems as if the light not shone
From the left hand of him beneath, and he,
As living, seems to be led on." Mine eyes,
I at that sound reverting, saw them gaze,
Through wonder, first at me; and then at me
And the light broken underneath, by turns.
"Why are thy thoughts thus riveted," my guide
Exclaim'd, "that thou hast slack'd thy pace? or how
Imports it thee, what thing is whisper'd here?
Come after me, and to their babblings leave
The crowd. Be as a tower, that, firmly set,
Shakes not its top for any blast that blows.
He, in whose bosom thought on thought shoots out,
Still of his aim is wide, in that the one
Sicklies and wastes to naught the other's strength."

What other could I answer, save "I come"?
I said it, somewhat with that color tinged,
Which ofttimes pardon meriteth for man.

Meanwhile traverse along the hill there came,
A little way before us, some who sang
The "Miserere" in responsive strains.
When they perceived that through my body I
Gave way not for the rays to pass, their song
Straight to a long and hoarse exclaim they changed;
And two of them, in guise of messengers,
Ran on to meet us, and inquiring ask'd:
"Of your condition we would gladly learn."

PURGATORY

 To them my guide: "Ye may return, and bear
Tidings to them who sent you, that his frame
Is real flesh. If, as I deem, to view
His shade they paused, enough is answer'd them:
Him let them honor: they may prize him well."

 Ne'er saw I fiery vapors with such speed
Cut through the serene air at fall of night,
Nor August's clouds athwart the setting sun
That upward these did not in shorter space
Return; and, there arriving, with the rest
Wheel back on us, as with loose rein a troop.

 "Many," exclaim'd the bard, "are these, who throng
Around us: to petition thee, they come.
Go therefore on, and listen as thou go'st."

 "O spirit! who go'st on to blessedness,
With the same limbs that clad thee at thy birth,"
Shouting they came: "a little rest thy step.
Look if thou any one amongst our tribe
Hast e'er beheld, that tidings of him there
Thou mayst report. Ah! wherefore go'st thou on?
Ah! wherefore tarriest thou not? We all
By violence died, and to our latest hour
Were sinners, but then warn'd by light from heaven;
So that, repenting and forgiving, we
Did issue out of life at peace with God,
Who, with desire to see him, fills our heart."

 Then I: "The visages of all I scan,
Yet none of ye remember. But if aught
That I can do may please you, gentle spirits!
Speak, and I will perform it; by that peace,
Which, on the steps of guide so excellent
Following, from world to world, intent I seek."

 In answer he began: "None here distrusts
Thy kindness, though not promised with an oath;
So as the will fail not for want of power.

THE DIVINE COMEDY

Whence I, who sole before the other speak,
Entreat thee, if thou ever see that land
Which lies between Romagna and the realm
Of Charles, that of thy courtesy thou pray
Those who inhabit Fano, that for me
Their adorations duly be put up,
By which I may purge off my grievous sins.
From thence I came. But the deep passages,
Whence issued out the blood wherein I dwelt,
Upon my bosom in Antenor's land
Were made, where to be more secure I thought.
The author of the deed was Este's prince,
Who, more than right could warrant, with his wrath
Pursued me. Had I toward Mira fled,
When overta'en at Oriaco, still
Might I have breathed. But to the marsh I sped;
And in the mire and rushes tangled there
Fell, and beheld my life-blood float the plain."

Then said another: "Ah! so may the wish,
That takes thee o'er the mountain, be fulfill'd,
As thou shalt graciously give aid to mine.
Of Montefeltro I; Buonconte I:
Giovanna nor none else have care for me;
Sorrowing with these I therefore go." I thus:
"From Campaldino's field what force or chance
Drew thee, that ne'er thy sepulture was known?"

"Oh!" answer'd he, "at Casentino's foot
A stream there courseth, named Archiano, sprung
In Apennine above the hermit's seat,
E'en where its name is cancel'd, there came I,
Pierced in the throat, fleeing away on foot,
And bloodying the plain. Here sight and speech
Fail'd me; and, finishing with Mary's name,
I fell, and tenantless my flesh remain'd.
I will report the truth; which thou again
Tell to the living. Me God's angel took,
Whilst he of hell exclaim'd: 'O thou from heaven:
Say wherefore hast thou robb'd me? Thou of him

PURGATORY

The eternal portion bear'st with thee away,
For one poor tear that he deprives me of.
But of the other, other rule I make.'

"Thou know'st how in the atmosphere collects
That vapor dank, returning into water
Soon as it mounts where cold condenses it.
That evil will, which in his intellect
Still follows evil, came; and raised the wind
And smoky mist, by virtue of the power
Given by his nature. Thence the valley, soon
As day was spent, he cover'd o'er with cloud,
From Pratomagno to the mountain range;
And stretch'd the sky above; so that the air
Impregnate changed to water. Fell the rain;
And to the fosses came all that the land
Contain'd not; and, as mightiest streams are wont,
To the great river, with such headlong sweep,
Rush'd, that naught stay'd its course. My stiffen'd frame
Laid at his mouth, the fell Archiano found,
And dashed it into Arno; from my breast
Loosening the cross, that of myself I made
When overcome with pain. He hurl'd me on,
Along the banks and bottom of his course;
Then in his muddy spoils encircling wrapt."

"Ah! when thou to the world shalt be return'd,
And rested after thy long road," so spake
Next the third spirit; "then remember me.
I once was Pia. Sienna gave me life;
Maremma took it from me. That he knows,
Who me with jewel'd ring had first espoused."

[169]

CANTO VI

The spirits beseech Dante to obtain for them the prayers of their friends; the poet is led into an invective against the unnatural dissensions in Italy.

WHEN from their game of dice men separate,
He who hath lost remains in sadness fix'd,
Revolving in his mind what luckless throws
He cast: but, meanwhile, all the company
Go with the other; one before him runs,
And one behind his mantle twitches, one
Fast by his side bids him remember him.
He stops not; and each one, to whom his hand
Is stretch'd, well knows he bids him stand aside;
And thus he from the press defends himself.
E'en such was I in that close-crowding throng;
And turning so my face around to all,
And promising, I 'scaped from it with pains.

Here of Arezzo him I saw, who fell
By Ghino's cruel arm; and him beside,
Who in his chase was swallow'd by the stream.
Here Frederic Novello with his hand
Stretch'd forth, entreated; and of Pisa he,
Who put the good Marzuco to such proof
Of constancy. Count Orso I beheld;
And from its frame a soul dismiss'd for spite
And envy, as it said, but for no crime;
I speak of Peter de la Brosse: and here,
While she yet lives, that Lady of Brabant,
Let her beware; lest for so false a deed
She herd with worse than these. When I was freed
From all those spirits, who pray'd for other's prayers
To hasten on their state of blessedness;
Straight I began: "O thou, my luminary!
It seems expressly in thy text denied,
That heaven's supreme decree can ever bend

PURGATORY

To supplication; yet with this design
Do these entreat. Can then their hope be vain?
Or is thy saying not to me reveal'd?"

  He thus to me: "Both what I write is plain,
And these deceived not in their hope; if well
Thy mind consider, that the sacred height
Of judgment doth not stoop, because love's flame
In a short moment all fulfils, which he,
Who sojourns here, in right should satisfy.
Besides, when I this point concluded thus,
By praying no defect could be supplied;
Because the prayer had none access to God.
Yet in this deep suspicion rest thou not
Contented, unless she assure thee so,
Who betwixt truth and mind infuses light:
I know not if thou take me right; I mean
Beatrice. Her thou shalt behold above,
Upon this mountain's crown, fair seat of joy."

  Then I: "Sir! let us mend our speed; for now
I tire not as before: and lo! the hill
Stretches its shadow far." He answer'd thus:
"Our progress with this day shall be as much
As we may now despatch; but otherwise
Than thou supposest is the truth. For there
Thou canst not be, ere thou once more behold
Him back returning, who behind the steep
Is now so hidden, that, as erst, his beam
Thou dost not break. But lo! a spirit there
Stands solitary, and toward us looks:
It will instruct us in the speediest way."

  We soon approach'd it. O thou Lombard spirit!
How didst thou stand, in high abstracted mood,
Scarce moving with slow dignity thine eyes.
It spoke not aught, but let us onward pass,
Eying us as a lion on his watch.
But Virgil, with entreaty mild, advanced,
Requesting it to show the best ascent.

It answer to his question none return'd;
But of our country and our kind of life
Demanded. When my courteous guide began,
"Mantua," the shadow, in itself absorb'd,
Rose toward us from the place in which it stood,
And cried, "Mantuan! I am thy countryman,
Sordello." Each the other then embraced.

Ah, slavish Italy! thou inn of grief!
Vessel without a pilot in loud storm!
Lady no longer of fair provinces,
But brothel-house impure! this gentle spirit,
Even from the pleasant sound of his dear land
Was prompt to greet a fellow-citizen
With such glad cheer: while now thy living ones
In thee abide not without war; and one
Malicious gnaws another; ay, of those
Whom the same wall and the same moat contains.
Seek, wretched one! around the sea-coasts wide;
Then homeward to thy bosom turn; and mark,
If any part of thee sweet peace enjoy.
What boots it, that thy reins Justinian's hand
Refitted, if thy saddle be unprest?
Naught doth he now but aggravate thy shame.
Ah, people! thou obedient still should'st live,
And in the saddle let thy Cæsar sit,
If well thou marked'st that which God commands.

Look how that beast to fellness hath relapsed,
From having lost correction of the spur,
Since to the bridle thou hast set thine hand,
O German Albert! who abandon'st her
That is grown savage and unmanageable,
When thou shouldst clasp her flanks with forked heels,
Just judgment from the stars fall on thy blood;
And be it strange and manifest to all;
Such as may strike thy successor with dread;
For that thy sire and thou have suffer'd thus,
Through greediness of yonder realms detain'd,
The garden of the empire to run waste.

PURGATORY

Come, see the Capulets and Montagues.
The Filippeschi and Monaldi, man
Who carest for naught! those sunk in grief, and these
With dire suspicion rack'd. Come, cruel one!
Come, and behold the oppression of the nobles,
And mark their injuries; and thou mayst see
What safety Santafiore can supply.
Come and behold thy Rome, who calls on thee,
Desolate widow, day and night with moans,
"My Cæsar, why dost thou desert my side?"
Come, and behold what love among thy people:
And if no pity touches thee for us,
Come, and blush for thine own report. For me,
If it be lawful, O Almighty Power!
Who wast in earth for our sakes crucified,
Are thy just eyes turn'd elsewhere? or is this
A preparation, in the wondrous depth
Of thy sage counsel made, for some good end,
Entirely from our reach of thought cut off?
So are the Italian cities all o'erthrong'd
With tyrants, and a great Marcellus made
Of every petty factious villager.

   My Florence! thou mayst well remain unmoved
At this digression, which affects not thee:
Thanks to thy people, who so wisely speed.
Many have justice in their heart, that long
Waiteth for counsel to direct the bow,
Or ere it dart unto its aim: but thine
Have it on their lips' edge. Many refuse
To bear the common burdens: readier thine
Answer uncall'd, and cry, "Behold I stoop!"

   Make thyself glad, for thou hast reason now,
Thou wealthy! thou at peace! thou wisdom-fraught!
Facts best will witness if I speak the truth.
Athens and Lacedæmon, who of old
Enacted laws, for civil arts renown'd,
Made little progress in improving life
Toward thee, who usest such nice subtlety,

That to the middle of November scarce
Reaches the thread thou in October weavest.
How many times within thy memory,
Customs, and laws, and coins, and offices
Have been by thee renew'd, and people changed.

If thou remember'st well and canst see clear,
Thou wilt perceive thyself like a sick wretch,
Who finds no rest upon her down, but oft
Shifting her side, short respite seeks from pain.

CANTO VII

Sordello conducts the poets to an eminence where they see a pleasant recess and many famous spirits.

AFTER their courteous greetings joyfully
Seven times exchanged, Sordello backward drew
Exclaiming, "Who are ye?" "Before this mount
By spirits worthy of ascent to God
Was sought, my bones had by Octavius' care
Been buried. I am Virgil; for no sin
Deprived of heaven, except for lack of faith."
So answer'd him in few my gentle guide.

As one, who aught before him suddenly
Beholding, whence his wonder riseth, cries,
"It is, yet is not," wavering in belief;
Such he appear'd; then downward bent his eyes,
And, drawing near with reverential step,
Caught him, where one of mean estate might clasp
His lord. "Glory of Latium!" he exclaim'd,
"In whom our tongue its utmost power display'd;
Boast of my honor'd birth-place! what desert
Of mine, what favor, rather, undeserved,
Shows thee to me? If I to hear that voice
Am worthy, say if from below thou comest,
And from what cloister's pale." "Through every orb

PURGATORY

Of that sad region," he replied, "thus far
Am I arrived, by heavenly influence led:
And with such aid I come. Not for my doing,
But for not doing, have I lost the sight
Of that high Sun, whom thou desirest, and who
By me too late was known. There is a place
There underneath, not made by torments sad,
But by dun shades alone; where mourning's voice
Sounds not of anguish sharp, but breathes in sighs.
There I with little innocents abide,
Who by death's fangs were bitten, ere exempt
From human taint. There I with those abide,
Who the three holy virtues put not on,
But understood the rest, and without blame
Follow'd them all. But, if thou know'st, and canst,
Direct us how we soonest may arrive,
Where Purgatory its true beginning takes."

He answer'd thus: "We have no certain place
Assign'd us: upward I may go, or round.
Far as I can, I join thee for thy guide.
But thou beholdest now how day declines;
And upward to proceed by night, our power
Excels: therefore it may be well to choose
A place of pleasant sojourn. To the right
Some spirits sit apart retired. If thou
Consentest, I to these will lead thy steps:
And thou wilt know them, not without delight."

"How chances this?" was answer'd: "whoso wish'd
To ascend by night, would he be thence debarr'd
By other, or through his own weakness fail?"

The good Sordello then, along the ground
Trailing his finger, spoke: "Only this line
Thou shalt not overpass, soon as the sun
Hath disappear'd; not that aught else impedes
Thy going upward, save the shades of night.
These, with the want of power, perplex the will.
With them thou haply mightst return beneath,

THE DIVINE COMEDY

Or to and fro around the mountain's side
Wander, while day is in the horizon shut."

My master straight, as wondering at his speech,
Exclaim'd: "Then lead us quickly, where thou sayst
That, while we stay, we may enjoy delight."

A little space we were removed from thence,
When I perceived the mountain hollow'd out,
Even as large valleys hollow'd out on earth.

"That way," the escorting spirit cried, "we go,
Where in a bosom the high bank recedes:
And thou await renewal of the day."

Betwixt the steep and plain, a crooked path
Led us traverse into the ridge's side,
Where more than half the sloping edge expires.
Refulgent gold, and silver thrice refined,
And scarlet grain and ceruse, Indian wood
Of lucid dye serene, fresh emeralds
But newly broken, by the herbs and flowers
Placed in that fair recess, in color all
Had been surpass'd, as great surpasses less.
Nor nature only there lavish'd her hues,
But of the sweetness of a thousand smells
A rare and undistinguish'd fragrance made.

"Salve Regina," on the grass and flowers,
Here chanting, I beheld those spirits sit,
Who not beyond the valley could be seen.

"Before the westering sun sink to his bed,"
Began the Mantuan, who our steps had turn'd,
" 'Mid those, desire not that I lead ye on.
For from this eminence ye shall discern
Better the acts and visages of all,
Than, in the nether vale, among them mix'd.
He, who sits high above the rest, and seems
To have neglected that he should have done,

[176]

PURGATORY

And to the others' song moves not his lip,
The Emperor Rodolph call, who might have heal'd
The wounds whereof fair Italy hath died,
So that by others she revives but slowly.
He, who with kindly visage comforts him,
Sway'd in that country, where the water springs,
That Moldaw's river to the Elbe, and Elbe
Rolls to the ocean: Ottocar his name:
Who in his swaddling-clothes was of more worth
Than Wenceslaus his son, a bearded man,
Pamper'd with rank luxuriousness and ease,
And that one with the nose deprest, who close
In counsel seems with him of gentle look,
Flying, expired, withering the lily's flower.
Look there, how he doth knock against his breast.
The other ye behold, who for his cheek
Makes of one hand a couch, with frequent signs.
They are the father and the father-in-law
Of Gallia's bane: his vicious life they know
And foul; thence comes the grief that rends them thus.

"He, so robust of limb, who measure keeps
In song with him of feature prominent,
With every virtue bore his girdle braced.
And if that stripling, who behind him sits,
King after him had lived, his virtue then
From vessel to like vessel had been pour'd;
Which may not of the other heirs be said.
By James and Frederick his realms are held;
Neither the better heritage obtains.
Rarely into the branches of the tree
Doth human worth mount up: and so ordains
He who bestows it, that as his free gift
It may be call'd. To Charles my words apply
No less than to his brother in the song;
Which Pouille and Provençe now with grief confess.
So much that plant degenerates from its seed,
As, more than Beatrix and Margaret,
Costanza still boasts of her valorous spouse.

THE DIVINE COMEDY

"Behold the King of simple life and plain,
Harry of England, sitting there alone:
He through his branches better issue spreads.

"That one, who, on the ground, beneath the rest,
Sits lowest, yet his gaze directs aloft,
Is William, that brave Marquis, for whose cause,
The deed of Alexandria and his war
Makes Montferrat and Canavese weep."

CANTO VIII

*Two angels keep watch over the valley where Dante meets
a former friend. Three bright stars appear and
a serpent flees before the angelic guards.*

Now was the hour that wakens fond desire
In men at sea, and melts their thoughtful heart
Who in the morn have bid sweet friends farewell,
And pilgrim newly on his road with love
Thrills, if he hear the vesper bell from far,
That seems to mourn for the expiring day:
When I, no longer taking heed to hear,
Began, with wonder, from those spirits to mark
One risen from its seat, which with its hand
Audience implored. Both palms it join'd and raised,
Fixing its steadfast gaze toward the east,
As telling God, "I care for naught beside."

"Te Lucis Ante," so devoutly then
Came from its lip, and in so soft a strain,
That all my sense in ravishment was lost.
And the rest after, softly and devout,
Follow'd through all the hymn, with upward gaze
Directed to the bright supernal wheels.

PURGATORY

Here, reader! for the truth make thine eyes keen:
For of so subtle texture is this veil,
That thou with ease mayst pass it through unmark'd.

I saw that gentle band silently next
Look up, as if in expectation held,
Pale and in lowly guise; and, from on high,
I saw, forth issuing descend beneath,
Two angels, with two flame-illumined swords,
Broken and mutilated of their points.
Green as the tender leaves but newly born,
Their vesture was, the which, by wings as green
Beaten, they drew behind them, fann'd in air.
A little over us one took his stand;
The other lighted on the opposing hill;
So that the troop were in the midst contain'd.

Well I descried the whiteness on their heads;
But in their visages the dazzled eye
Was lost, as faculty that by too much
Is overpower'd. "From Mary's bosom both
Are come," exclaim'd Sordello, "as a guard
Over the vale, 'gainst him, who hither tends,
The serpent." Whence, not knowing by which path
He came, I turn'd me round; and closely press'd,
All frozen, to my leader's trusted side.

Sordello paused not: "To the valley now
(For it is time) let us descend; and hold
Converse with those great shadows: haply much
Their sight may please ye." Only three steps down
Methinks I measured, ere I was beneath,
And noted one who look'd as with desire
To know me. Time was now that air grew dim;
Yet not so dim, that, 'twixt his eyes and mine,
It clear'd not up what was conceal'd before.
Mutually toward each other we advanced.
Nino, thou courteous judge! what joy I felt,
When I perceived thou wert not with the bad.

[179]

THE DIVINE COMEDY

No salutation kind on either part
Was left unsaid. He then inquired: "How long,
Since thou arrived'st at the mountain's foot,
Over the distant waves?" "Oh!" answer'd I,
"Through the sad seats of woe this morn I came;
And still in my first life, thus journeying on,
The other strive to gain." Soon as they heard
My words, he and Sordello backward drew,
As suddenly amazed. To Virgil one,
The other to a spirit turn'd, who near
Was seated, crying: "Conrad! up with speed:
Come, see what of his grace high God hath will'd."
Then turning round to me: "By that rare mark
Of honor, which thou owest to him, who hides
So deeply his first cause it hath no ford;
When thou shalt be beyond the vast of waves,
Tell my Giovanna, that for me she call
There, where reply to innocence is made.
Her mother, I believe, loves me no more;
Since she has changed the white and wimpled folds,
Which she is doom'd once more with grief to wish.
By her it easily may be perceived,
How long in woman lasts the flame of love,
If sight and touch do not relume it oft.
For her so fair a burial will not make
The viper, which calls Milan to the field,
As had been made by shrill Gallura's bird."

He spoke, and in his visage took the stamp
Of that right zeal, which with due temperature
Glows in the bosom. My insatiate eyes
Meanwhile to heaven had travel'd, even there
Where the bright stars are slowest, as a wheel
Nearest the axle; when my guide inquired:
"What there aloft, my son, has caught thy gaze?"

I answer'd: "The three torches, with which here
The pole is all on fire." He then to me:
"The four resplendent stars, thou saw'st this morn,
Are there beneath; and these, risen in their stead."

PURGATORY

While yet he spoke, Sordello to himself
Drew him, and cried: "Lo there our enemy!"
And with his hand pointed that way to look.

Along the side, where barrier none arose
Around the little vale, a serpent lay,
Such haply as gave Eve the bitter food.
Between the grass and flowers, the evil snake
Came on, reverting oft his lifted head;
And, as a beast that smooths its polish'd coat,
Licking his back. I saw not, nor can tell,
How those celestial falcons from their seat
Moved, but in motion each one well descried.
Hearing the air cut by their verdant plumes,
The serpent fled; and, to their stations, back
The angels up return'd with equal flight.

The spirit (who to Nino, when he call'd,
Had come), from viewing me with fixed ken,
Through all that conflict, loosen'd not his sight.

"So may the lamp, which leads thee up on high,
Find, in thy free resolve, of wax so much,
As may suffice thee to the enamel'd height,"
It thus began: "If any certain news
Of Valdimagra and the neighbor part
Thou know'st, tell me, who once was mighty there.
They call'd me Conrad Malaspina; not
That old one; but from him I sprang. The love
I bore my people is now here refined."

"In your domains," I answer'd, "ne'er was I.
But, through all Europe, where do those men dwell,
To whom their glory is not manifest?
The fame, that honors your illustrious house,
Proclaims the nobles, and proclaims the land;
So that he knows it, who was never there.
I swear to you, so may my upward route
Prosper, your honored nation not impairs
The value of her coffer and her sword.

[181]

THE DIVINE COMEDY

Nature and use give her such privilege,
That while the world is twisted from his course
By a bad head, she only walks aright,
And has the evil way in scorn." He then:
"Now pass thee on: seven times the tired sun
Revisits not the couch, which with four feet
The forked Aries covers, ere that kind
Opinion shall be nail'd into thy brain
With stronger nails than other's speech can drive;
If the sure course of judgment be not stay'd."

CANTO IX

Asleep and dreaming, Dante is carried up the mountain by Lucia, and on wakening, finds himself with Virgil at the gate of Purgatory.

Now the fair consort of Tithonus old,
Arisen from her mate's beloved arms,
Look'd palely o'er the eastern cliff; her brow,
Lucent with jewels, glitter'd, set in sign
Of that chill animal, who with his train
Smites fearful nations: and where then we were,
Two steps of her ascent the night had past;
And now the third was closing up its wing,
When I, who had so much of Adam with me,
Sank down upon the grass, o'ercome with sleep,
There where all five were seated. In that hour,
When near the dawn the swallow her sad lay,
Remembering haply ancient grief, renews;
And when our minds, more wanderers from the flesh,
And less by thought restrain'd, are, as 'twere, full
Of holy divination in their dreams;
Then, in a vision, did I seem to view
A golden-feather'd eagle in the sky,
With open wings, and hovering for descent;
And I was in that place, methought, from whence

PURGATORY

Young Ganymede, from his associates reft,
Was snatch'd aloft to the high consistory.

"Perhaps," thought I within me, "here alone
He strikes his quarry, and elsewhere disdains
To pounce upon the prey." Therewith, it seem'd,
A little wheeling in his aery tour,
Terrible as the lightning, rush'd he down,
And snatch'd me upward, even to the fire.
There both, I thought, the eagle and myself
Did burn; and so intense the imagined flames,
That needs my sleep was broken off. As erst
Achilles shook himself, and round him roll'd
His waken'd eyeballs, wondering where he was,
Whenas his mother had from Chiron fled
To Scyros, with him sleeping in her arms;
(There whence the Greeks did after sunder him);
E'en thus I shook me, soon as from my face
The slumber parted, turning deadly pale,
Like one ice-struck with dread. Sole at my side
My comfort stood: and the bright sun was now
More than two hours aloft: and to the sea
My looks were turn'd. "Fear not," my master cried,
"Assured we are at happy point. Thy strength
Shrink not, but rise dilated. Thou art come
To Purgatory now. Lo! there the cliff
That circling bounds it. Lo! the entrance there,
Where it doth seem disparted. Ere the dawn
Usher'd the day-light, when thy wearied soul
Slept in thee, o'er the flowery vale beneath
A lady came, and thus bespake me: 'I
Am Lucia. Suffer me to take this man,
Who slumbers. Easier so his way shall speed.'
Sordello and the other gentle shapes
Tarrying, she bare thee up: and, as day shone,
This summit reach'd: and I pursued her steps.
Here did she place thee. First, her lovely eyes
That open entrance show'd me; then at once
She vanish'd with thy sleep." Like one, whose doubts

THE DIVINE COMEDY

Are chased by certainty, and terror turn'd
To comfort on discovery of the truth,
Such was the change in me: and as my guide
Beheld me fearless, up along the cliff
He moved, and I behind him, toward the height.

Reader! thou markest how my theme doth rise;
Nor wonder therefore, if more artfully
I prop the structure. Nearer now we drew,
Arrived whence, in that part, where first a breach
As of a wall appear'd, I could descry
A portal, and three steps beneath, that led
For inlet there, of different color each;
And one who watch'd, but spake not yet a word.
As more and more mine eye did stretch its view,
I mark'd him seated on the highest step,
In visage such, as past my power to bear.
Grasp'd in his hand, a naked sword glanced back
The rays so toward me, that I oft in vain
My sight directed. "Speak, from whence ye stand;"
He cried: "What would ye? Where is your escort?
Take heed your coming upward harm ye not."

"A heavenly dame, not skilless of these things,"
Replied the instructor, "told us, even now,
'Pass that way: here the gate is.' " "And may she,
Befriending, prosper your ascent," resumed
The courteous keeper of the gate: "Come then
Before our steps." We straightway thither came.

The lowest stair was marble white, so smooth
And polish'd, that therein my mirror'd form
Distinct I saw. The next of hue more dark
Than sablest grain, a rough and singed block,
Crack'd lengthwise and across. The third, that lay
Massy above, seem'd porphyry, that flamed
Red as the life-blood spouting from a vein.
On this God's angel either foot sustain'd,
Upon the threshold seated, which appear'd
A rock of diamond. Up the trinal steps

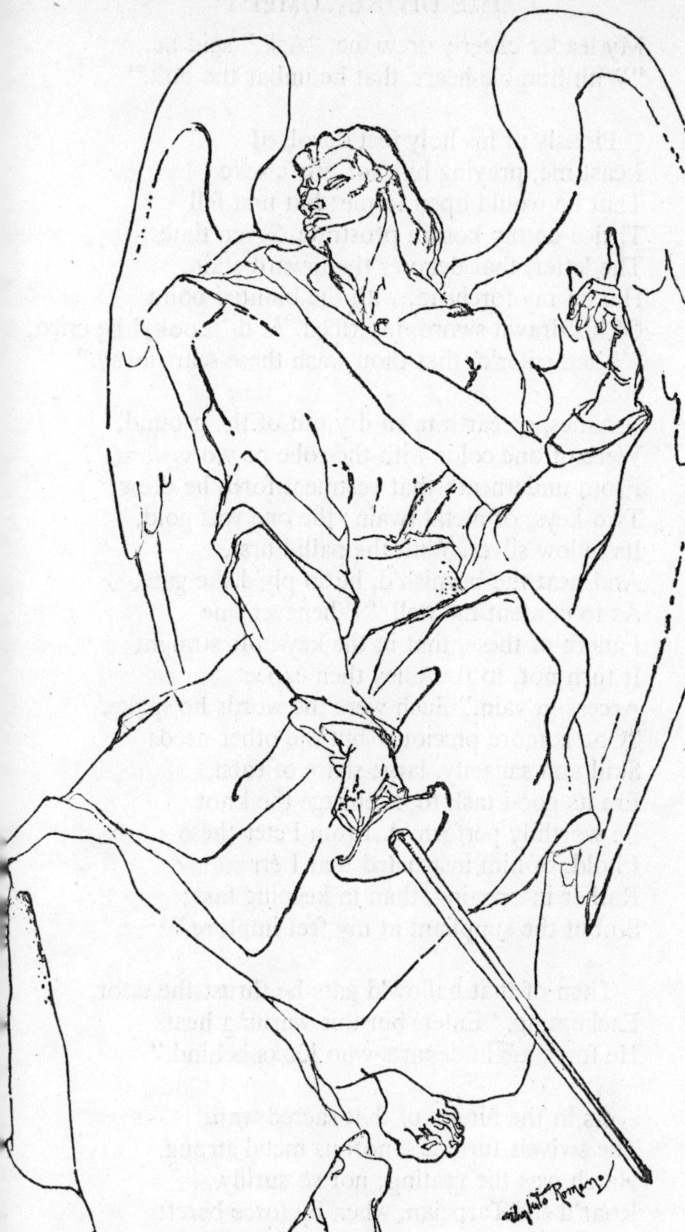

My leader cheerly drew me. "Ask," said he,
"With humble heart, that he unbar the bolt."

 Piously at his holy feet devolved
I cast me, praying him for pity's sake
That he would open to me; but first fell
Thrice on my bosom prostrate. Seven times
The letter, that denotes the inward stain,
He, on my forehead, with the blunted point
Of his drawn sword, inscribed. And "Look," he cried,
"When enter'd, that thou wash these scars away."

 Ashes, or earth ta'en dry out of the ground,
Were of one color with the robe he wore.
From underneath that vestment forth he drew
Two keys, of metal twain: the one was gold,
Its fellow silver. With the pallid first,
And next the burnish'd, he so ply'd the gate,
As to content me well. "Whenever one
Faileth of these, that in the key-hole straight
It turn not, to this alley then expect
Access in vain." Such were the words he spake.
"One is more precious: but the other needs
Skill and sagacity, large share of each,
Ere its good task to disengage the knot
Be worthily perform'd. From Peter these
I hold, of him instructed that I err
Rather in opening, than in keeping fast;
So but the suppliant at my feet implore."

 Then of that hallow'd gate he thrust the door,
Exclaiming, "Enter, but this warning hear:
He forth again departs who looks behind."

 As in the hinges of that sacred ward
The swivels turn'd, sonorous metal strong,
Harsh was the grating; nor so surlily
Roar'd the Tarpeian, when by force bereft
Of good Metellus, thenceforth from his loss
To leanness doom'd. Attentively I turn'd,

PURGATORY

Listening the thunder that first issued forth;
And "We praise thee, O God," methought I heard,
In accents blended with sweet melody.
The strains came o'er mine ear, e'en as the sound
Of choral voices, that in solemn chant
With organ mingle, and, now high and clear
Come swelling, now float indistinct away.

CANTO X

*On a level space within Purgatory, the poets see
artfully engraved stories of humility and
spirits expiating the sin of pride.*

WHEN we had passed the threshold of the gate
(Which the soul's ill affection doth disuse,
Making the crooked seem the straighter path),
I heard its closing sound. Had mine eyes turn'd,
For that offence what plea might have avail'd?

We mounted up the riven rock, that wound
On either side alternate, as the wave
Flies and advances. "Here some little art
Behoves us," said my leader, "that our steps
Observe the varying flexure of the path."

Thus we so slowly sped, that with cleft orb
The moon once more o'erhangs her watery couch,
Ere we that strait have threaded. But when free,
We came, and open, where the mount above
One solid mass retires; I spent with toil,
And both uncertain of the way, we stood,
Upon a plain more lonesome than the roads
That traverse desert wilds. From whence the brink
Borders upon vacuity, to foot
Of the steep bank that rises still, the space
Had measured thrice the stature of a man:
And, distant as mine eye could wing its flight,

[187]

THE DIVINE COMEDY

To leftward now and now to right despatch'd,
That cornice equal in extent appear'd.

  Not yet our feet had on that summit moved,
When I discover'd that the bank, around
Whose proud uprising all ascent denied,
Was marble white; and so exactly wrought
With quaintest sculpture, that not there alone
Had Polycletus, but e'en nature's self
Been shamed. The angel (who came down to earth
With tidings of the peace so many years
Wept for in vain, that oped the heavenly gates
From their long interdict) before us seem'd,
In a sweet act, so sculptured to the life,
He look'd no silent image. One had sworn
He had said "Hail!" for she was imaged there,
By whom the key did open to God's love;
And in her act as sensibly imprest
That word, "Behold the handmaid of the Lord,"
As figure seal'd on wax. "Fix not thy mind
On one place only," said the guide beloved,
Who had me near him on that part where lies
The heart of man. My sight forthwith I turn'd,
And mark'd, behind the virgin mother's form,
Upon that side where he that moved me stood,
Another story graven on the rock.

  I pass'd athwart the bard, and drew me near,
That it might stand more aptly for my view.
There, in the self-same marble, were engraved
The cart and kine, drawing the sacred ark,
That from unbidden office awes mankind.
Before it came much people; and the whole
Parted in seven quires. One sense cried "Nay,"
Another, "Yes, they sing." Like doubt arose
Betwixt the eye and smell, from the curl'd fume
Of incense breathing up the well-wrought toil.
Preceding the blest vessel, onward came,
With light dance leaping, girt in humble guise,
Israel's sweet harper: in that hap he seem'd

PURGATORY

Less, and yet more, than kingly. Opposite,
At a great palace, from the lattice forth
Look'd Michol, like a lady full of scorn
And sorrow. To behold the tablet next,
Which, at the back of Michol, whitely shone,
I moved me. There, was storied on the rock
The exalted glory of the Roman prince,
Whose mighty worth moved Gregory to earn
His mighty conquest, Trajan the Emperor.
A widow at his bridle stood, attired
In tears and mourning. Round about them troop'd
Full throng of knights; and overhead in gold
The eagles floated, struggling with the wind.
The wretch appear'd amid all these to say:
"Grant vengeance, Sire! for, woe beshrew this heart,
My son is murder'd." He replying seem'd:
"Wait now till I return." And she, as one
Made hasty by her grief: "O Sire! if thou
Dost not return?" "Where I am, who then is,
May right thee." "What to thee is other's good,
If thou neglect thy own?" "Now comfort thee";
At length he answers. "It beseemeth well
My duty be perform'd, ere I move hence:
So justice wills; and pity bids me stay."

He, whose ken nothing new surveys, produced
That visible speaking, new to us and strange,
The like not found on earth. Fondly I gazed
Upon those patterns of meek humbleness,
Shapes yet more precious for their artist's sake;
When "Lo!" the poet whisper'd, "where this way
(But slack their pace) a multitude advance.
These to the lofty steps shall guide us on."

Mine eyes, though bent on view of novel sights,
Their loved allurement, were not slow to turn.

Reader! I would not that amazed thou miss
Of thy good purpose, hearing how just God
Decrees our debts be cancel'd. Ponder not

[189]

The form of suffering. Think on what succeeds:
Think that, at worst, beyond the mighty doom
It cannot pass. "Instructor!" I began,
"What I see hither tending, bears no trace
Of human semblance, nor of aught beside
That my foil'd sight can guess." He answering thus:
"So curb'd to earth, beneath their heavy terms
Of torment stoop they, that mine eye at first
Struggled as thine. But look intently thither;
And disentangle with thy laboring view,
What, underneath those stones, approacheth: now,
E'en now, mayst thou discern the pangs of each."

Christians and proud! O poor and wretched ones!
That, feeble in the mind's eye, lean your trust
Upon unstaid perverseness: know ye not
That we are worms, yet made at last to form
The winged insect, imp'd with angel plumes,
That to heaven's justice unobstructed soars?
Why buoy ye up aloft your unfledged souls?
Abortive then and shapeless ye remain,
Like the untimely embryon of a worm.

As, to support incumbent floor or roof,
For corbel, is a figure sometimes seen,
That crumples up its knees unto its breast;
With the feign'd posture, stirring ruth unfeign'd
In the beholder's fancy; so I saw
These fashion'd, when I noted well their guise.

Each, as his back was laden, came indeed
Or more or less contracted; and it seem'd
As he, who show'd most patience in his look,
Wailing exclaim'd: "I can endure no more."

PURGATORY

CANTO XI

*After a prayer uttered by the spirits, Virgil inquires
the way upward. He and Dante discourse
with several spirits.*

"O THOU Almighty Father! who dost make
The heavens thy dwelling, not in bounds confined,
But that, with love intenser, there thou view'st
Thy primal effluence; hallow'd be thy name:
Join, each created being, to extol
Thy might; for worthy humblest thanks and praise
Is thy blest Spirit. May thy kingdom's peace
Come unto us; for we, unless it come,
With all our striving, thither tend in vain.
As, of their will, the angels unto thee
Tender meet sacrifice, circling thy throne
With loud hosannas; so of theirs be done
By saintly men on earth. Grant us, this day,
Our daily manna, without which he roams
Through this rough desert retrograde, who most
Toils to advance his steps. As we to each
Pardon the evil done us, pardon thou
Benign, and of our merit take no count.
'Gainst the old adversary, prove thou not
Our virtue, easily subdued; but free
From his incitements, and defeat his wiles.
This last petition, dearest Lord! is made
Not for ourselves; since that were needless now;
But for their sakes who after us remain."

Thus for themselves and us good speed imploring,
Those spirits went beneath a weight like that
We sometimes feel in dreams; all, sore beset,
But with unequal anguish; wearied all;
Round the first circuit; purging as they go
The world's gross darkness off. In our behoof
If their vows still be offer'd, what can here

For them be vow'd and done by such, whose wills
Have root of goodness in them? Well beseems
That we should help them wash away the stains
They carried hence; that so, made pure and light,
They may spring upward to the starry spheres.

"Ah! so may mercy-temper'd justice rid
Your burdens speedily; that ye have power
To stretch your wing, which e'en to your desire
Shall lift you; as ye show us on which hand
Toward the ladder leads the shortest way.
And if there be more passages than one,
Instruct us of that easiest to ascend:
For this man, who comes with me, and bears yet
The charge of fleshly raiment Adam left him,
Despite his better will, but slowly mounts."
From whom the answer came unto these words,
Which my guide spake, appear'd not; but 'twas said:
"Along the bank to rightward come with us;
And ye shall find a pass that mocks not toil
Of living man to climb: and were it not
That I am hinder'd by the rock, wherewith
This arrogant neck is tamed, whence needs I stoop
My visage to the ground; him, who yet lives,
Whose name thou speak'st not, him I fain would view;
To mark if e'er I knew him, and to crave
His pity for the fardel that I bear.
I was of Latium; of a Tuscan born,
A mighty one: Aldobrandesco's name
My sire's, I know not if ye e'er have heard.
My old blood and forefathers' gallant deeds
Made me so haughty, that I clean forgot
The common mother; and to such excess
Wax'd in my scorn of all men, that I fell,
Fell therefore; by what fate, Sienna's sons,
Each child in Campagnatico, can tell.
I am Omberto: not me, only, pride
Hath injured, but my kindred all involved
In mischief with her. Here my lot ordains
Under this weight to groan, till I appease

PURGATORY

God's angry justice, since I did it not
Amongst the living, here amongst the dead."

   Listening I bent my visage down: and one
(Not he who spake) twisted beneath the weight
That urged him, saw me, knew me straight, and call'd;
Holding his eyes with difficulty fix'd
Intent upon me, stooping as I went
Companion of their way. "O!" I exclaim'd,
"Art thou not Oderigi? art not thou
Agobbio's glory, glory of that art
Which they of Paris call the limner's skill?"

   "Brother!" said he, "with tints, that gayer smile,
Bolognian Franco's pencil lines the leaves.
His all the honor now; my light obscured.
In truth, I had not been thus courteous to him
The whilst I lived, through eagerness of zeal
For that pre-eminence my heart was bent on.
Here, of such pride, the forfeiture is paid.
Nor were I even here, if, able still
To sin, I had not turn'd me unto God.
O powers of man! how vain your glory, nipt
E'en in its height of verdure, if an age
Less bright succeed not. Cimabue thought
To lord it over painting's field; and now
The cry is Giotto's, and his name eclipsed.
Thus hath one Guido from the other snatch'd
The letter'd prize: and he, perhaps, is born,
Who shall drive either from their nest. The noise
Of worldly fame is but a blast of wind,
That blows from diverse points, and shifts its name,
Shifting the point it blows from. Shalt thou more
Live in the mouths of mankind, if thy flesh
Part shrivel'd from thee, than if thou hadst died
Before the coral and the pap were left;
Or e'er some thousand years have pass'd? and that
Is, to eternity compared, a space
Briefer than is the twinkling of an eye
To the heaven's slowest orb. He there, who treads

THE DIVINE COMEDY

So leisurely before me, far and wide
Through Tuscany resounded once; and now
Is in Sienna scarce with whispers named:
There was he sovereign, when destruction caught
The maddening rage of Florence, in that day
Proud as she now is loathsome. Your renown
Is as the herb, whose hue doth come and go;
And his might withers it, by whom it sprang
Crude from the lap of earth." I thus to him:
"True are thy sayings: to my heart they breathe
The kindly spirit of meekness, and allay
What tumors rankle there. But who is he,
Of whom thou speakest but now?" "This," he replied,
"Is Provenzano. He is here, because
He reach'd, with a grasp presumptuous, at the sway
Of all Sienna. Thus he still hath gone,
Thus goeth never-resting, since he died.
Such is the acquittance render'd back of him,
Who, in the mortal life, too much hath dared."
I then: "If soul, that to life's verge delays
Repentance, linger in that lower space,
Nor hither mount (unless good prayers befriend),
Or ever time, long as it lived, be past;
How chanced admittance was vouchsafed to him?"

"When at his glory's topmost height," said he,
"Respect of dignity all cast aside,
Freely he fix'd him on Sienna's plain,
A suitor to redeem his suffering friend,
Who languish'd in the prison-house of Charles;
Nor, for his sake, refused through every vein
To tremble. More I will not say: and dark,
I know, my words are; but thy neighbors soon
Shall help thee to a comment on the text.
This is the work, that from these limits freed him."

CANTO XII

*Dante observes the ground is covered with imagery
exhibiting instances of pride in history and fable.*

WITH equal pace, as oxen in the yoke,
I, with that laden spirit, journey'd on,
Long as the mild instructor suffer'd me;
But, when he bade me quit him, and proceed,
(For "Here," said he, "behoves with sail and oars
Each man, as best he may, push on his bark,")
Upright, as one disposed for speed, I raised
My body, still in thought submissive bow'd.

I now my leader's track not loth pursued;
And each had shown how light we fared along,
When thus he warned me: "Bend thine eyesight down:
For thou, to ease the way, shalt find it good
To ruminate the bed beneath thy feet."

As, in memorial of the buried, drawn
Upon earth-level tombs, the sculptured form
Of what was once, appears (at sight whereof
Tears often stream forth, by remembrance waked,
Whose sacred stings the piteous often feel),
So saw I there, but with more curious skill
Of portraiture o'erwrought, whate'er of space
From forth the mountain stretches. On one part
Him I beheld, above all creatures erst
Created noblest, lightening fall from heaven:
On the other side, with bolt celestial pierced,
Briareus; cumbering earth he lay, through dint
Of mortal ice-stroke. The Thymbræan god,
With Mars, I saw, and Pallas, round their sire,
Arm'd still, and gazing on the giants' limbs
Strewn o'er the ethereal field. Nimrod I saw:
At foot of the stupendous work he stood,

As if bewilder'd, looking on the crowd
Leagued in his proud attempt on Sennaar's plain.

    O Niobe! in what a trance of woe
Thee I beheld, upon that highway drawn,
Seven sons on either side thee slain. O Saul!
How ghastly didst thou look, on thine own sword
Expiring, in Gilboa, from that hour
Ne'er visited with rain from heaven, or dew.

    O fond Arachne! thee I also saw,
Half spider now, in anguish, crawling up
The unfinish'd web thou weaved'st to thy bane.

    O Rehoboam! here thy shape doth seem
Louring no more defiance; but fear-smote,
With none to chase him, in his chariot whirl'd.

    Was shown beside upon the solid floor,
How dear Alcmæon forced his mother rate
That ornament, in evil hour received:
How, in the temple, on Sennacherib fell
His sons, and how a corpse they left him there.
Was shown the scath, and cruel mangling made
By Tomyris on Cyrus, when she cried,
"Blood thou didst thirst for: take thy fill of blood."
Was shown how routed in the battle fled
The Assyrians, Holofernes slain, and e'en
The relics of the carnage. Troy I mark'd,
In ashes and in caverns. Oh! how fallen,
How abject, Ilion, was thy semblance there.

    What master of the pencil or the style
Had traced the shades and lines, that might have made
The subtlest workman wonder? Dead, the dead;
The living seem'd alive: with clearer view,
His eye beheld not, who beheld the truth,
Than mine what I did tread on, while I went
Low bending. Now swell out, and with stiff necks

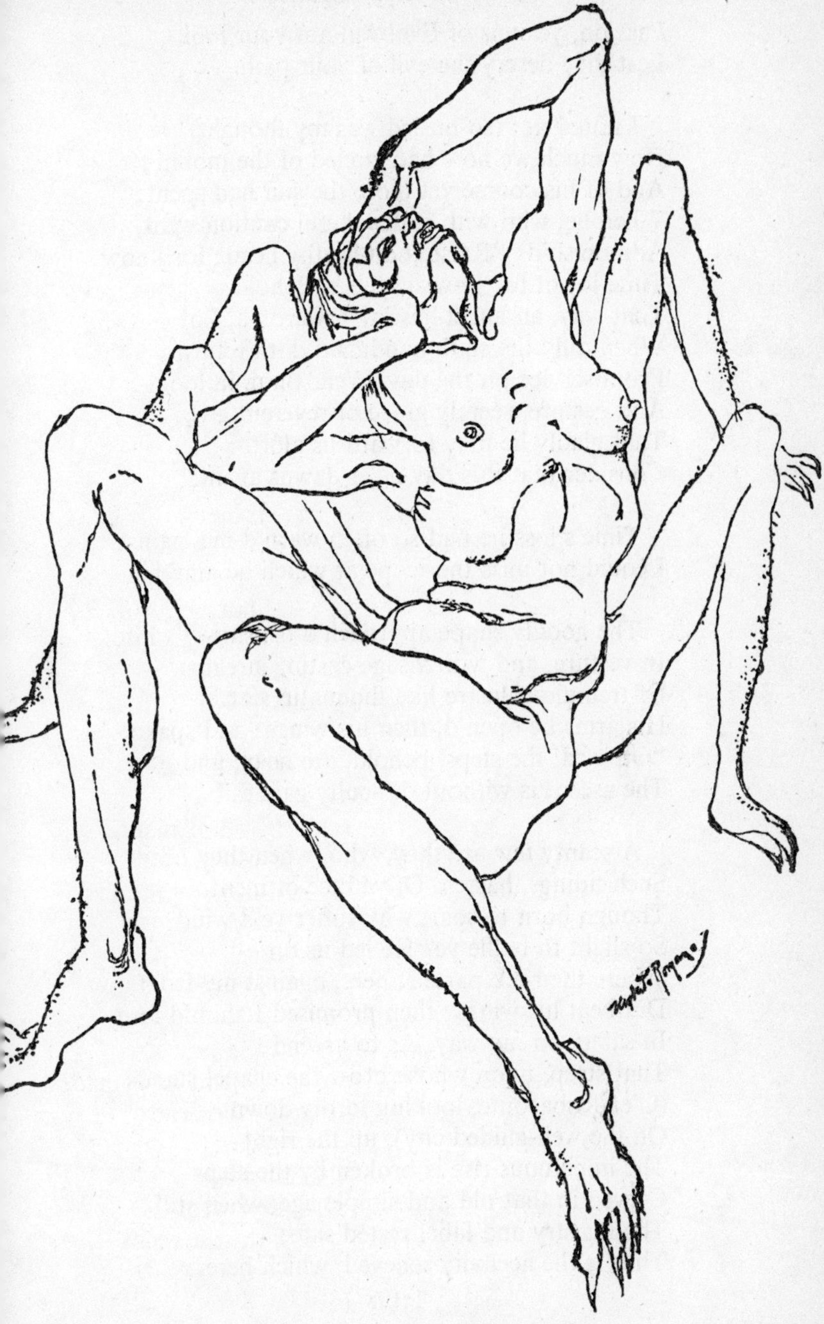

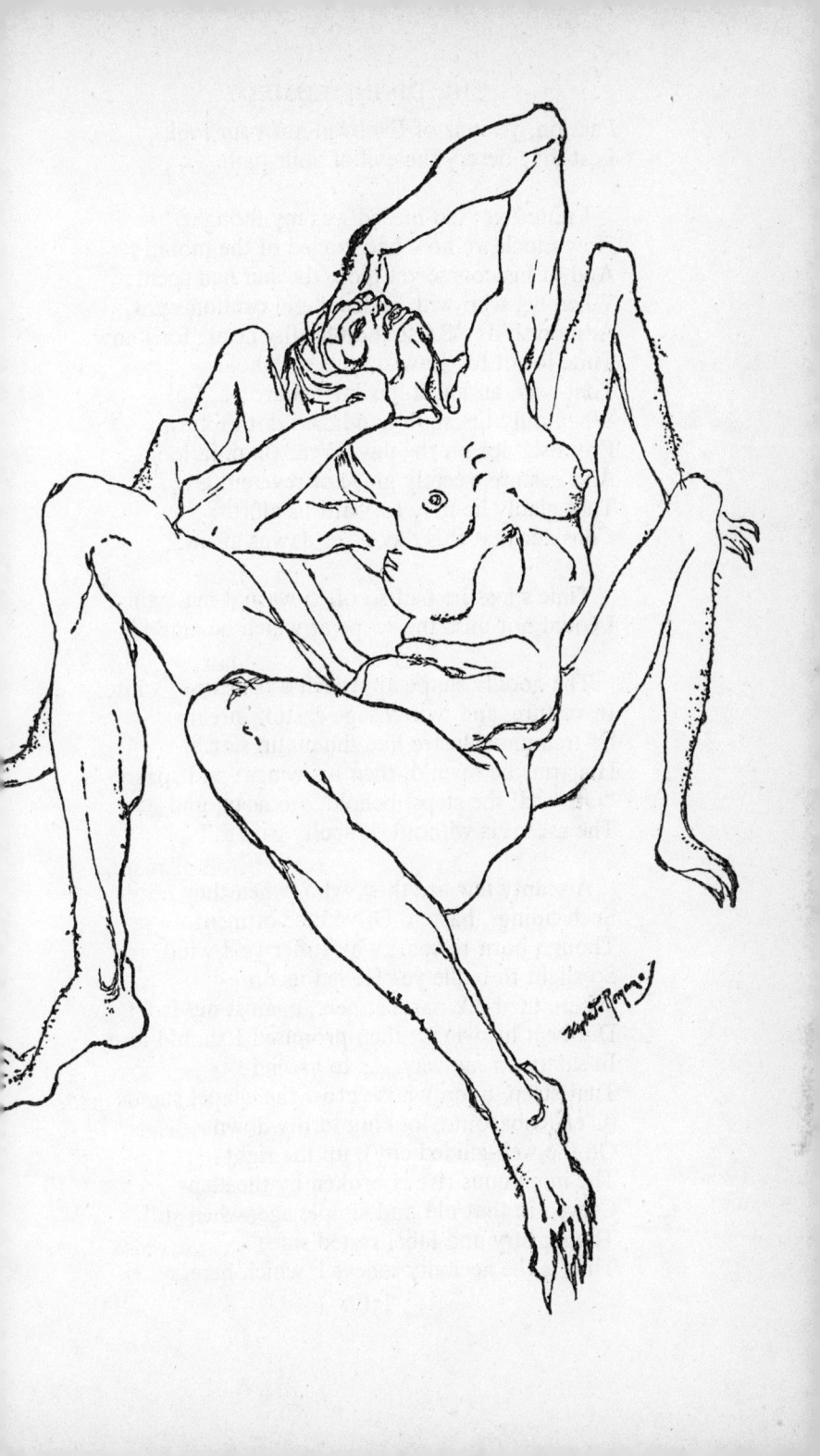

Pass on, ye sons of Eve! veil not your looks,
Lest they descry the evil of your path.

I noted not (so busied was my thought)
How much we now had circled of the mount;
And of his course yet more the sun had spent;
When he, who with still wakeful caution went,
Admonish'd: "Raise thou up thy head: for know
Time is not for slow suspense. Behold,
That way, an angel hasting toward us. Lo!
When duly the sixth handmaid doth return
From service on the day. Wear thou, in look
And gesture, seemly grace of reverent awe;
That gladly he may forward us aloft.
Consider that this day ne'er dawns again."

Time's loss he had so often warn'd me 'gainst,
I could not miss the scope at which he aim'd.

The goodly shape approach'd us, snowy white
In vesture, and with visage casting streams
Of tremulous lustre like the matin star.
His arms he open'd, then his wings; and spake:
"Onward! the steps, behold, are near; and now
The ascent is without difficulty gain'd."

A scanty few are they, who, when they hear
Such tidings, hasten. O, ye race of men!
Though born to soar, why suffer ye a wind
So slight to baffle ye? He led us on
Where the rock parted; here, against my front,
Did beat his wings; then promised I should fare
In safety on my way. As to ascend
That steep, upon whose brow the chapel stands
(O'er Rubaconte, looking lordly down
On the well-guided city), up the right
The impetuous rise is broken by the steps
Carved in that old and simple age, when still
The registry and label rested safe;
Thus is the acclivity relieved, which here,

PURGATORY

Precipitous, from the other circuit falls:
But, on each hand, the tall cliff presses close.

   As, entering, there we turn'd, voices, in strain
Ineffable, sang: "Blessed are the poor
In spirit." Ah! how far unlike to these
The straits of hell: here songs to usher us,
There shrieks of woe. We climb the holy stairs:
And lighter to myself by far I seem'd
Than on the plain before; whence thus I spake:
"Say, master, of what heavy thing have I
Been lighten'd; that scarce aught the sense of toil
Affects me journeying?" He in few replied:
"When sin's broad characters, that yet remain
Upon thy temples, though well nigh effaced,
Shall be, as one is, all clean razed out:
Then shall thy feet by heartiness of will
Be so o'ercome, they not alone shall feel
No sense of labor, but delight much more
Shall wait them, urged along their upward way."

   Then like to one, upon whose head is placed
Somewhat he deems not of, but from the becks
Of others, as they pass him by; his hand
Lends therefore help to assure him, searches, finds,
And well performs such office as the eye
Wants power to execute; so stretching forth
The fingers of my right hand, did I find
Six only of the letters, which his sword,
Who bare the keys, had traced upon my brow.
The leader, as he mark'd mine action, smiled.

CANTO XIII

*They gain the second cornice where sin of envy is purged,
hear voices recounting famous examples of charity,
and behold the shades of the envious.*

We reach'd the summit of the scale, and stood
Upon the second buttress of that mount
Which healeth him who climbs. A cornice there,
Like to the former, girdles round the hill;
Save that its arch, with sweep less ample, bends.

Shadow, nor image there, is seen: all smooth
The rampart and the path, reflecting naught
But the rock's sullen hue. "If here we wait
For some to question," said the bard, "I fear
Our choice may haply meet too long delay."

Then fixedly upon the sun his eyes
He fasten'd; made his right the central point
From whence to move; and turn'd the left aside.
"O pleasant light, my confidence and hope!
Conduct us thou," he cried, "on this new way,
Where now I venture; leading to the bourn
We seek. The universal world to thee
Owes warmth and lustre. If no other cause
Forbid, thy beams should ever be our guide."

Far, as is measured for a mile on earth,
In brief space had we journey'd; such prompt will
Impell'd; and toward us flying, now were heard
Spirits invisible, who courteously
Unto love's table bade the welcome guest.
The voice, that first flew by, call'd forth aloud,
"They have no wine," so on behind us past,
Those sounds reiterating, nor yet lost
In the faint distance, when another came

[200]

PURGATORY

Crying, "I am Orestes," and alike
Wing'd fleet away. "O father!" I exclaim'd,
"What tongues are these?" and as I question'd, lo!
A third exclaiming, "Love ye those have wrong'd you."

"This circuit," said my teacher, "knots the scourge
For envy; and the cords are therefore drawn
By charity's correcting hand. The curb
Is of a harsher sound; as thou shalt hear
(If I deem rightly) ere thou reach the pass,
Where pardon sets them free. But fix thine eyes
Intently through the air; and thou shalt see
A multitude before thee seated, each
Along the shelving grot." Then more than erst
I oped mine eyes; before me view'd; and saw
Shadows with garments dark as was the rock;
And when we pass'd a little forth, I heard
A crying, "Blessed Mary! pray for us,
Michael and Peter! all ye saintly host!"

I do not think there walks on earth this day
Man so remorseless, that he had not yearn'd
With pity at the sight that next I saw.
Mine eyes a load of sorrow teem'd, when now
I stood so near them, that their semblances
Came clearly to my view. Of sackcloth vile
Their covering seem'd; and, on his shoulder, one
Did stay another, leaning; and all lean'd
Against the cliff. E'en thus the blind and poor,
Near the confessionals, to crave an alms,
Stand, each his head upon his fellow's sunk;
So most to stir compassion, not by sound
Of words alone, but that which moves not less,
The sight of misery. And as never beam
Of noon-day visiteth the eyeless man,
E'en so was heaven a niggard unto these
Of this fair light: for, through the orbs of all,
A thread of wire, impiercing, knits them up,
As for the taming of a haggard hawk.

THE DIVINE COMEDY

It were a wrong, methought, to pass and look
On others, yet myself the while unseen.
To my sage counsel therefore did I turn.
He knew the meaning of the mute appeal,
Nor waited for my questioning, but said:
"Speak; and be brief, be subtile in thy words."

On that part of the cornice, whence no rim
Engarlands its steep fall, did Virgil come;
On the other side me were the spirits, their cheeks
Bathing devout with penitential tears,
That through the dread impalement forced a way.

I turn'd me to them, and "O shades!" said I,
"Assured that to your eyes unveil'd shall shine
The lofty light, sole object of your wish,
So may heaven's grace clear whatsoe'er of foam
Floats turbid on the conscience, that thenceforth
The stream of mind roll limpid from its source;
As ye declare (for so shall ye impart
A boon I dearly prize) if any soul
Of Latium dwell among ye: and perchance
That soul may profit, if I learn so much."

"My brother! we are, each one, citizens
Of one true city. Any, thou wouldst say,
Who lived a stranger in Italia's land."

So heard I answering, as appear'd, a voice
That onward came some space from whence I stood.

A spirit I noted, in whose look was mark'd
Expectance. Ask ye how? The chin was raised
As in one reft of sight. "Spirit," said I,
"Who for thy rise art tutoring (if thou be
That which didst answer to me), or by place,
Or name, disclose thyself, that I may know thee."

"I was," it answer'd, "of Sienna: here
I cleanse away with these the evil life,

PURGATORY

Soliciting with tears that He, who is,
Vouchsafe him to us. Though Sapia named,
In sapience I excell'd not; gladder far
Of other's hurt, than of the good befell me.
That thou mayst own I now deceive thee not,
Hear, if my folly were not as I speak it.
When now my tears sloped waning down the arch,
It so bechanced, my fellow-citizens
Near Colle met their enemies in the field;
And I pray'd God to grant what He had will'd.
There were they vanquish'd, and betook themselves
Unto the bitter passages of flight.
I mark'd the hunt; and waxing out of bounds
In gladness, lifted up my shameless brow,
And, like the merlin cheated by a gleam,
Cried, 'It is over. Heaven! I fear thee not.'
Upon my verge of life I wish'd for peace
With God; nor yet repentance had supplied
What I did lack of duty, were it not
The hermit Piero, touch'd with charity,
In his devout orisons thought on me.
But who art thou that question'st of our state,
Who go'st, as I believe, with lids unclosed,
And breathest in thy talk?" "Mine eyes," said I,
"May yet be here ta'en from me; but not long;
For they have not offended grievously
With envious glances. But the woe beneath
Urges my soul with more exceeding dread.
That nether load already weighs me down."

She thus: "Who then, among us here aloft,
Hath brought thee, if thou weenest to return?"

"He," answered I, "who standeth mute beside me.
I live: of me ask therefore, chosen spirit!
If thou desire I yonder yet should move
For thee my mortal feet." "Oh!" she replied,
"This is so strange a thing, it is a great sign
That God doth love thee. Therefore with thy prayer
Sometime assist me: and, by that I crave,

Which most thou covetest, that if thy feet
E'er tread on Tuscan soil, thou save my fame
Among my kindred. Them shalt thou behold
With that vain multitude, who set their hope
On Telamone's haven; there to fail
Confounded, more than when the fancied stream
They sought, of Dian call'd: but they, who lead
Their navies, more than ruin'd hopes shall mourn."

CANTO XIV

The poet listens to certain souls inveigh against dwellers on the banks of the Arno and in Romagna, and hears more instances of envy.

"SAY, who is he around our mountain winds,
Or ever death has pruned his wing for flight;
That opes his eyes, and covers them at will?"

"I know not who he is, but know thus much;
He comes not singly. Do thou ask of him,
For thou art nearer to him; and take heed,
Accost him gently, so that he may speak."

Thus on the right two spirits, bending each
Toward the other, talk'd of me; then both
Addressing me, their faces backward lean'd,
And thus the one began: "O soul, who yet
Pent in the body, tendest toward the sky!
For charity, we pray thee, comfort us;
Recounting whence thou comest, and who thou art:
For thou dost make us, at the favor shown thee,
Marvel, as at a thing that ne'er hath been."

"There stretches through the midst of Tuscany,"
I straight began, "a brooklet, whose well-head
Springs up in Falterona; with his race
Not satisfied, when he some hundred miles
Hath measured. From his banks bring I this frame.

PURGATORY

To tell you who I am were words mis-spent:
For yet my name scarce sounds on rumor's lip."

"If well I do incorporate with my thought
The meaning of thy speech," said he, who first
Address'd me, "thou dost speak of Arno's wave."

To whom the other: "Why hath he conceal'd
The title of that river, as a man
Doth of some horrible thing?" The spirit, who
Thereof was question'd, did acquit him thus:
"I know not: but 'tis fitting well the name
Should perish of that vale; for from the source,
Where teems so plenteously the Alpine steep
Maim'd of Pelorus (that doth scarcely pass
Beyond that limit), even to the point
Where unto ocean is restored what heaven
Drains from the exhaustless store for all earth's streams,
Throughout the space is virtue worried down,
As 'twere a snake by all, for mortal foe;
Or through disastrous influence on the place,
Or else distortion of misguided wills
That custom goads to evil: whence in those,
The dwellers in that miserable vale,
Nature is so transform'd, it seems as they
Had shared of Circe's feeding. 'Midst brute swine,
Worthier of acorns than of other food
Created for man's use, he shapeth first
His obscure way; then, sloping onward, finds
Curs, snarlers more in spite than power, from whom
He turns with scorn aside: still journeying down,
By how much more the curst and luckless foss
Swells out to largeness, e'en so much it finds
Dogs turning into wolves. Descending still
Through yet more hollow eddies, next he meets
A race of foxes, so replete with craft,
They do not fear that skill can master it.
Nor will I cease because my words are heard
By other ears than thine. It shall be well
For this man, if he keep in memory

[205]

What from no erring spirit I reveal.
Lo! I behold thy grandson, that becomes
A hunter of those wolves, upon the shore
Of the fierce stream; and cows them all with dread.
Their flesh, yet living, sets he up to sale,
Then, like an aged beast, to slaughter dooms.
Many of life he 'reaves, himself of worth
And goodly estimation. Smear'd with gore,
Mark how he issues from the rueful wood;
Leaving such havoc, that in thousand years
It spreads not to prime lustihood again."

As one, who tidings hears of woe to come,
Changes his looks perturb'd, from whate'er part
The peril grasp him; so beheld I change
That spirit, who had turn'd to listen; struck
With sadness, soon as he had caught the word.

His visage, and the other's speech, did raise
Desire in me to know the names of both;
Whereof, with meek entreaty, I inquired.

The shade, who late address'd me, thus resumed:
"Thy wish imports, that I vouchsafe to do
For thy sake what thou wilt not do for mine.
But, since God's will is that so largely shine
His grace in thee, I will be liberal too.
Guido of Duca know then that I am.
Envy so parch'd my blood, that had I seen
A fellow man made joyous, thou hadst mark'd
A livid paleness overspread my cheek.
Such harvest reap I of the seed I sow'd.
O man! why place thy heart where there doth need
Exclusion of participants in good?
This is Rinieri's spirit; this, the boast
And honor of the house of Calboli;
Where of his worth no heritage remains.
Nor his the only blood, that hath been stript
('Twixt Po, the mount, the Reno, and the shore)
Of all that truth or fancy asks for bliss:

PURGATORY

But, in those limits, such a growth has sprung
Of rank and venom'd roots, as long would mock
Slow culture's toil. Where is good Lizio? where
Manardi, Traversaro, and Carpigna?
O bastard slips of old Romagna's line!
When in Bologna the low artisan,
And in Faenza yon Bernardin sprouts,
A gentle cyon from ignoble stem.
Wonder not, Tuscan, if thou see me weep,
When I recall to mind those once loved names,
Guido of Prata, and of Azzo him
That dwelt with us; Tignoso and his troop,
With Traversaro's house and Anastagio's
(Each race disherited); and beside these,
The ladies and the knights, the toils and ease,
That witch'd us into love and courtesy;
Where now such malice reigns in recreant hearts.
O Brettinoro! wherefore tarriest still,
Since forth of thee thy family hath gone,
And many, hating evil, join'd their steps?
Well doeth he, that bids his lineage cease,
Bagnacavallo; Castracaro ill,
And Conio worse, who care to propagate
A race of Counties from such blood as theirs.
Well shall ye also do, Pagani, then
When from among you hies your demon child;
Not so, howe'er, that thenceforth there remain
True proof of what ye were. O Hugolin,
Thou sprung of Fantolini's line! thy name
Is safe; since none is look'd for after thee
To cloud its lustre, warping from thy stock.
But, Tuscan! go thy ways; for now I take
Far more delight in weeping, than in words.
Such pity for your sakes hath wrung my heart."

We knew those gentle spirits, at parting, heard
Our steps. Their silence therefore, of our way,
Assured us. Soon as we had quitted them,
Advancing onward, lo! a voice, that seem'd
Like volley'd lightning, when it rives the air,

Met us, and shouted, "Whosoever finds
Will slay me"; and then fled from us, as the bolt
Lanced sudden from a downward-rushing cloud.
When it had given short truce unto our hearing,
Behold the other with a crash as loud
As the quick-following thunder: "Mark in me
Aglauros, turn'd to rock." I, at the sound
Retreating, drew more closely to my guide.

Now in mute stillness rested all the air;
And thus he spake: "There was the galling bit
Which should keep man within his boundary.
But your old enemy so baits the hook,
He drags you eager to him. Hence nor curb
Avails you, nor reclaiming all. Heaven calls,
And, round about you wheeling, courts your gaze
With everlasting beauties. Yet your eye
Turns with fond doting still upon the earth.
Therefore He smites you who discerneth all."

CANTO XV

When they reach the third cornice where the sin of anger is purged, the poet beholds remarkable instances of patience.

As much as 'twixt the third hour's close and dawn,
Appeareth of heaven's sphere, that ever whirls
As restless as an infant in his play;
So much appear'd remaining to the sun
Of his slope journey toward the western goal.

Evening was there, and here the noon of night;
And full upon our forehead smote the beams.
For round the mountain, circling, so our path
Has led us, that toward the sunset now
Direct we journey'd; when I felt a weight
Of more exceeding splendor, than before,
Press on my front. The cause unknown, amaze

PURGATORY

Possess'd me! and both hands against my brows
Lifting, I interposed them, as a screen,
That of its gorgeous superflux of light
Clips the diminish'd orb. As when the ray,
Striking on water or the surface clear
Of mirror, leaps unto the opposite part,
Ascending at a glance, e'en as it fell,
And as much differs from the stone, that falls
Through equal space (so practic skill hath shown);
Thus with refracted light, before me seem'd
The ground there smitten; whence, in sudden haste,
My sight recoil'd. "What is this, sire beloved!
'Gainst which I strive to shield the sight in vain?"
Cried I, "and which toward us moving seems?"

"Marvel not, if the family of heaven,"
He answer'd, "yet with dazzling radiance dim
Thy sense. It is a messenger who comes,
Inviting man's ascent. Such sights ere long,
Not grievous, shall impart to thee delight,
As thy perception is by nature wrought
Up to their pitch." The blessed angel, soon
As we had reach'd him, hailed us with glad voice:
"Here enter on a ladder far less steep
Than ye have yet encounter'd." We forthwith
Ascending, heard behind us chanted sweet,
"Blessed the merciful," and "Happy thou,
That conquer'st." Lonely each, my guide and I,
Pursued our upward way; and as we went,
Some profit from his words I hoped to win,
And thus of him inquiring, framed my speech:
"What meant Romagna's spirit, when he spake
Of bliss exclusive, with no partner shared?"

He straight replied: "No wonder, since he knows
What sorrow waits on his own worst defect,
If he chide others, that they less may mourn.
Because ye point your wishes at a mark,
Where, by communion of possessors, part
Is lessen'd, envy bloweth up men's sighs.

THE DIVINE COMEDY

No fear of that might touch ye, if the love
Of higher sphere exalted your desire.
For there, by how much more they call it *ours*,
So much propriety of each in good
Increases more, and heighten'd charity
Wraps that fair cloister in a brighter flame."

"Now lack I satisfaction more," said I,
"Than if thou hadst been silent at the first;
And doubt more gathers on my laboring thought.
How can it chance, that good distributed,
The many, that possess it, makes more rich,
Than if 'twere shared by few?" He answering thus:
"Thy mind reverting still to things of earth,
Strikes darkness from true light. The highest good
Unlimited, ineffable, doth so speed
To love, as beam to lucid body darts,
Giving as much of ardor as it finds.
The sempiternal effluence streams abroad,
Spreading, wherever charity extends.
So that the more aspirants to that bliss
Are multiplied, more good is there to love,
And more is loved; as mirrors, that reflect,
Each unto other, propagated light.
If these my words avail not to allay
Thy thirsting, Beatrice thou shalt see,
Who of this want, and of all else thou hast,
Shall rid thee to the full. Provide but thou,
That from thy temples may be soon erased,
E'en as the two already, those five scars,
That, when they pain thee worst, then kindliest heal."

"Thou," I had said, "content'st me"; when I saw
The other round was gain'd, and wondering eyes
Did keep me mute. There suddenly I seem'd
By an ecstatic vision wrapt away;
And in a temple saw, methought, a crowd
Of many persons; and at the entrance stood
A dame, whose sweet demeanor did express

PURGATORY

A mother's love, who said, "Child! why hast thou
Dealt with us thus? Behold thy sire and I
Sorrowing have sought thee"; and so held her peace;
And straight the vision fled. A female next
Appear'd before me, down whose visage coursed
Those waters, that grief forces out from one
By deep resentment stung who seem'd to say:
"If thou, Pisistratus, be lord indeed
Over this city, named with such debate
Of adverse gods, and whence each science sparkles,
Avenge thee of those arms, whose bold embrace
Hath clasp'd our daughter"; and to her, meseem'd,
Benign and meek, with visage undisturb'd,
Her sovereign spake: "How shall we those requite
Who wish us evil, if we thus condemn
The man that loves us?" After that I saw
A multitude, in fury burning, slay
With stones a stripling youth, and shout amain

THE DIVINE COMEDY

"Destroy, destroy"; and him I saw, who bow'd
Heavy with death unto the ground, yet made
His eyes, unfolded upward, gates to heaven,
Praying forgiveness of the Almighty Sire,
Amidst that cruel conflict, on his foes,
With looks that win compassion to their aim.

Soon as my spirit, from her airy flight
Returning, sought again the things whose truth
Depends not on her shaping, I observed
She had not roved to falsehood in her dreams.

Meanwhile the leader, who might see I moved
As one who struggles to shake off his sleep,
Exclaim'd: "What ails thee, that thou canst not hold
Thy footing firm; but more than half a league
Hast travell'd with closed eyes and tottering gait,
Like to a man by wine or sleep o'ercharged?"

"Beloved father! so thou deign," said I,
"To listen, I will tell thee what appear'd
Before me, when so fail'd my sinking steps."

He thus: "Not if thy countenance were mask'd
With hundred visors could a thought of thine,
How small soe'er, elude me. What thou saw'st
Was shown, that freely thou mightst ope thy heart
To the waters of peace, that flow diffused
From their eternal fountain. I not ask'd,
What ails thee? for such cause as he doth, who
Looks only with that eye, which sees no more,
When spiritless the body lies; but ask'd,
To give fresh vigor to thy foot. Such goads,
The slow and loitering need; that they be found
Not wanting when their hour of watch returns."

So on we journey'd, through the evening sky
Gazing intent, far onward as our eyes,
With level view, could stretch against the bright
Vespertine ray: and lo! by slow degrees

Gathering, a fog made toward us, dark as night.
There was no room for 'scaping; and that mist
Bereft us, both of sight and the pure air.

CANTO XVI

*Marco Lombardo shows that much human depravity
results from the mixture of spiritual and
temporal authority in rulers.*

HELL'S dunnest gloom, or night unlustrous, dark,
Of every planet reft, and pall'd in clouds,
Did never spread before the sight a veil
In thickness like that fog, nor to the sense
So palpable and gross. Entering its shade,
Mine eye endured not with unclosed lids;
Which marking, near me drew the faithful guide,
Offering me his shoulder for a stay.

As the blind man behind his leader walks,
Lest he should err, or stumble unawares
On what might harm him or perhaps destroy;
I journey'd through that bitter air and foul,
Still listening to my escort's warning voice,
"Look that from me thou part not." Straight I heard
Voices, and each one seem'd to pray for peace,
And for compassion, to the Lamb of God
That taketh sins away. Their prelude still
Was "Agnus Dei"; and through all the quire,
One voice, one measure ran, that perfect seem'd
The concord of their song. "Are these I hear
Spirits, O master?" I exclaim'd; and he,
"Thou aim'st aright: these loose the bonds of wrath."

"Now who art thou, that through our smoke dost cleave,
And speak'st of us, as thou thyself e'en yet
Dividest time by calends?" So one voice

Bespake me; whence my master said, "Reply;
And ask, if upward hence the passage lead."

"O being! who dost make thee pure, to stand
Beautiful once more in thy Maker's sight;
Along with me: and thou shalt hear and wonder."
Thus I, whereto the spirit answering spake:
"Long as 'tis lawful for me, shall my steps
Follow on thine; and since the cloudy smoke
Forbids the seeing, hearing in its stead
Shall keep us join'd." I then forthwith began:
"Yet in my mortal swathing, I ascend
To higher regions; and am hither come
Through the fearful agony of Hell.
And, if so largely God hath doled his grace,
That, clean beside all modern precedent,
He wills me to behold his kingly state;
From me conceal not who thou wast, ere death
Had loosed thee; but instruct me: and instruct
If rightly to the pass I tend; thy words
The way directing, as a safe escort."

"I was of Lombardy, and Marco call'd:
Not inexperienced of the world, that worth
I still affected, from which all have turn'd
The nerveless bow aside. Thy course tends right
Unto the summit": and, replying thus,
He added, "I beseech thee pray for me,
When thou shalt come aloft." And I to him:
"Accept my faith for pledge I will perform
What thou requirest. Yet one doubt remains,
That wrings me sorely, if I solve it not.
Singly before it urged me, doubled now
By thine opinion, when I couple that
With one elsewhere declared; each strengthening other.
The world indeed is even so forlorn
Of all good, as thou speak'st it, and so swarms
With every evil. Yet, beseech thee, point
The cause out to me, that myself may see,

[214]

PURGATORY

And unto others show it: for in heaven
One places it, and one on earth below."

   Then heaving forth a deep and audible sigh,
"Brother!" he thus began, "the world is blind;
And thou in truth comest from it. Ye, who live,
Do so each cause refer to Heaven above,
E'en as its motion, of necessity,
Drew with it all that moves. If this were so,
Free choice in you were none; nor justice would
There should be joy for virtue, woe for ill.
Your movements have their primal bent from heaven;
Not all: yet said I all: what then ensues?
Light have ye still to follow evil or good,
And of the will free power, which, if it stand
Firm and unwearied in Heaven's first assay,
Conquers at last, so it be cherish'd well,
Triumphant over all. To mightier force,
To better nature subject, ye abide
Free, not constrain'd by that which forms in you
The reasoning mind uninfluenced of the stars.
If then the present race of mankind err,
Seek in yourselves the cause, and find it there.
Herein thou shalt confess me no false spy.

   "Forth from his plastic hand, who charm'd beholds
Her image ere she yet exist, the soul
Comes like a babe, that wantons sportively,
Weeping and laughing in its wayward moods;
As artless, and as ignorant of aught,
Save that her Maker being one who dwells
With gladness ever, willingly she turns
To whate'er yields her joy. Of some slight good
The flavor soon she tastes; and, snared by that,
With fondness she pursues it; if no guide
Recall, no rein direct her wandering course.
Hence it behoved, the law should be a curb;
A sovereign hence behoved, whose piercing view
Might mark at least the fortress and main tower

THE DIVINE COMEDY

Of the true city. Laws indeed there are:
But who is he who observes them? None; not he,
Who goes before, the shepherd of the flock,
Who chews the cud but doth not cleave the hoof.
Therefore the multitude, who see their guide
Strike at the very good they covet most,
Feed there and look no further. Thus the cause
Is not corrupted nature in yourselves,
But ill-conducting, that hath turn'd the world
To evil. Rome, that turn'd it unto good,
Was wont to boast two suns, whose several beams
Cast light on either way, the world's and God's.
One since hath quench'd the other; and the sword
Is grafted on the crook; and, so conjoin'd,
Each must perforce decline to worse, unawed
By fear of other. If thou doubt me, mark
The blade: each herb is judged of by its seed.
That land, through which Adice and the Po
Their waters roll, was once the residence
Of courtesy and valor, ere the day
That frown'd on Frederick; now secure may pass
Those limits, whosoe'er hath left, for same,
To talk with good men, or come near their haunts.
Three aged ones are still found there, in whom
The old time chides the new: these deem it long
Ere God restore them to a better world:
The good Gherardo; of Plazzo he,
Conrad; and Guido of Castello, named
In Gallic phrase more fitly the plain Lombard.
On this at last conclude. The church of Rome,
Mixing two governments that ill assort,
Hath miss'd her footing, fallen into the mire,
And there herself and burden much defiled."

"O Marco!" I replied, "thine arguments
Convince me: and the cause I now discern,
Why of the heritage no portion came
To Levi's offspring. But resolve me this:
Who that Gherardo is, that as thou say'st

PURGATORY

Is left a sample of the perish'd race,
And for rebuke to this untoward age?"

"Either thy words," said he, "deceive, or else
Are meant to try me; that thou, speaking Tuscan,
Appear'st not to have heard of good Gherardo;
The sole addition that, by which I know him;
Unless I borrow'd from his daughter Gaïa
Another name to grace him. God be with you.
I bear you company no more. Behold
The dawn with white ray glimmering through the mist.
I must away—the angel comes—ere he
Appear." He said, and would not hear me more.

CANTO XVII

The poet imagines some noted instances of anger, and an angel takes them to the fourth cornice where the sin of gloominess or indifference is purged.

CALL to remembrance, reader, if thou e'er
Hast on an Alpine height been ta'en by cloud,
Through which thou saw'st no better than the mole
Doth through opacous membrane; then, whene'er
The watery vapors dense began to melt
Into thin air, how faintly the sun's sphere
Seem'd wading through them: so thy nimble thought
May image, how at first I rebeheld
The sun, that bedward now his couch o'erhung.

Thus, with my leader's feet still equalling pace,
From forth that cloud I came, when now expired
The parting beams from off the nether shores.

O quick and forgetive power! that sometimes dost
So rob us of ourselves, we take no mark
Though round about us thousand trumpets clang;

What moves thee, if the senses stir not? Light
Moves thee from heaven, spontaneous, self-inform'd;
Or, likelier, gliding down with swift illapse
By will divine. Portray'd before me came
The traces of her dire impiety,
Whose form was changed into the bird, that most
Delights itself in song: and here my mind
Was inwardly so wrapt, it gave no place
To aught that ask'd admittance from without.
Next shower'd into my fantasy a shape
As of one crucified, whose visage spake
Fell rancor, malice deep, wherein he died;
And round in Ahasuerus the great king;
Esther his bride; and Mordecai the just,
Blameless in word and deed. As of itself
That unsubstantial coinage of the brain
Burst, like a bubble, when the water fails
That fed it; in my vision straight uprose
A damsel weeping loud, and cried, "O queen!
O mother! wherefore has intemperate ire
Driven thee to loathe thy being? Not to lose
Lavinia, desperate thou hast slain thyself.
Now hast thou lost me. I am she, whose tears
Mourn, ere I fall, a mother's timeless end."

E'en as a sleep breaks off, if suddenly
New radiance strike upon the closed lids,
The broken slumber quivering ere it dies;
Thus, from before me, sunk the imagery,
Vanishing, soon as on my face there struck
The light, outshining far our earthly beam.
As round I turn'd me to survey what place
I had arrived at, "Here ye mount": exclaim'd
A voice, that other purpose left me none
Save will so eager to behold who spake,
I could not choose but gaze. As 'fore the sun,
That weighs our vision down, and veils his form
In light transcendent, thus my virtue fail'd
Unequal. "This is Spirit from above,
Who marshals us our upward way, unsought;

[218]

PURGATORY

And in his own light shrouds him. As a man
Doth for himself, so now is done for us.
For whoso waits imploring, yet sees need
Of his prompt aidance, sets himself prepared
For blunt denial, ere the suit be made.
Refuse we not to lend a ready foot
At such inviting: haste we to ascend,
Before it darken: for we may not then,
Till morn again return." So spake my guide;
And to one ladder both address'd our steps;
And the first stair approaching, I perceived
Near me as 'twere the waving of a wing,
That fann'd my face, and whisper'd: "Blessed they,
The peace-makers: they know not evil wrath."

Now to such height above our heads were raised
The last beams, follow'd close by hooded night,
That many a star on all sides through the gloom
Shone out. "Why partest from me, O my strength?"
So with myself I communed; for I felt
My o'ertoil'd sinews slacken. We had reach'd
The summit, and were fix'd like to a bark
Arrived at land. And waiting a short space,
If aught should meet mine ear in that new round,
Then to my guide I turn'd, and said: "Loved sire!
Declare what guilt is on this circle purged.
If our feet rest, no need thy speech should pause."

He thus to me: "The love of good, whate'er
Wanted of just proportion, here fulfils.
Here plies afresh the oar, that loiter'd ill.
But that thou mayst yet clearlier understand,
Give ear unto my words; and thou shalt cull
Some fruit may please thee well, from this delay.

"Creator, nor created being, e'er,
My son," he thus began, "was without love,
Or natural, or the free spirit's growth,
Thou hast not that to learn. The natural still
Is without error: but the other swerves,

If on ill object bent, or thought excess
Of vigor, or defect. While e'er it seeks
The primal blessings, or with measure due
The inferior, no delight, that flows from it,
Partakes of ill. But let it warp to evil,
Or with more ardor than behoves, or less,
Pursue the good; the thing created then
Works 'gainst its Maker. Hence thou must infer
That love is germin of each virtue in ye,
And of each act no less, that merits pain.
Now since it may not be, but love intend
The welfare mainly of the thing it loves,
All from self-hatred are secure: and since
No being can be thought to exist apart,
And independent of the first, a bar
Of equal force restrains from hating that.

"Grant the distinction just; and it remains
The evil must be another's, which is loved.
Three ways such love is gender'd in your clay.
There is who hopes (his neighbor's worth deprest)
Pre-eminence himself; and covets hence,
For his own greatness, that another fall.
There is who so much fears the loss of power,
Fame, favor, glory (should his fellow mount
Above him), and so sickens at the thought,
He loves their opposite: and there is he,
Whom wrong or insult seems to gall and shame,
That he doth thirst for vengeance; and such needs
Must dote on other's evil. Here beneath,
This threefold love is mourn'd. Of the other sort
Be now instructed; that which follows good,
But with disorder'd and irregular course.

"All indistinctly apprehend a bliss,
On which the soul may rest; the hearts of all
Yearn after it; and to that wished bourn
All therefore strive to tend. If ye behold,
Or seek it, with a love remiss and lax;
This cornice, after just repenting, lays

[220]

PURGATORY

Its penal torment on ye. Other good
There is, where man finds not his happiness:
It is not true fruition; not that blest
Essence, of every good the branch and root.
The love too lavishly bestow'd on this,
Along three circles over us, is mourn'd.
Account of that division tripartite
Expect not, fitter for thine own research."

CANTO XVIII

Virgil discourses on the nature of love. Two spirits record instances of zeal and fervent affection, and others shout memorable examples of sin for which they suffer.

THE teacher ended, and his high discourse
Concluding, earnest in my looks inquired
If I appear'd content; and I, whom still
Unsated thirst to hear him urged, was mute,
Mute outwardly, yet inwardly I said:
"Perchance my too much questioning offends."
But he, true father, mark'd the secret wish
By diffidence restrain'd; and, speaking, gave
Me boldness thus to speak: "Master! my sight
Gathers so lively virtue from thy beams,
That all, thy words convey, distinct is seen.
Wherefore I pray thee, father, whom this heart
Holds dearest, thou wouldst deign by proof t' unfold
That love, from which, as from their source, thou bring'st
All good deeds and their opposite." He then:
"To what I now disclose be thy clear ken
Directed; and thou plainly shalt behold
How much those blind have err'd, who make themselves
The guides of men. The soul, created apt
To love, moves versatile which way soe'er
Aught pleasing prompts her, soon as she is waked
By pleasure into act. Of substance true
Your apprehension forms its counterfeit;

And, in you the ideal shape presenting,
Attracts the soul's regard. If she, thus drawn,
Incline toward it; love is that inclining,
And a new nature knit by pleasure in ye.
Then, as the fire points up, and mounting seeks
His birth-place and his lasting seat, e'en thus
Enters the captive soul into desire,
Which is a spiritual motion, that ne'er rests
Before enjoyment of the thing it loves.
Enough to show thee, how the truth from those
Is hidden, who aver all love a thing
Praiseworthy in itself; although perhaps
Its matter seem still good. Yet if the wax
Be good, it follows not the impression must."

"What love is," I return'd, "thy words, O guide!
And my own docile mind, reveal. Yet thence
New doubts have sprung. For, from without, if love
Be offer'd to us, and the spirit knows
No other footing; tend she right or wrong,
Is no desert of hers." He answering thus:
"What reason here discovers, I have power
To show thee: that which lies beyond, expect
From Beatrice, faith not reason's task.
Spirit, substantial form, with matter join'd,
Not in confusion mix'd, hath in itself
Specific virtue of that union born,
Which is not felt except it work, nor proved
But through effect, as vegetable life
By the green leaf. From whence his intellect
Deduced its primal notices of things,
Man therefore knows not, or his appetites
Their first affections; such in you, as zeal
In bees to gather honey; at the first,
Volition, meriting nor blame nor praise.
But o'er each lower faculty supreme,
That, as she list, are summon'd to her bar,
Ye have that virtue in you, whose just voice
Uttereth counsel, and whose word should keep
The threshold of assent. Here is the source,

PURGATORY

Whence cause of merit in you is derived;
E'en as the affections, good or ill, she takes,
Or severs, winnow'd as the chaff. Those men,
Who, reasoning, went to depth profoundest, mark'd
That innate freedom; and were thence induced
To leave their moral teaching to the world.
Grant then, that from necessity arise
All love that glows within you; to dismiss
Or harbor it, the power is in yourselves.
Remember, Beatrice, in her style,
Denominates free choice by eminence
The noble virtue; if in talk with thee
She touch upon that theme." The moon, well nigh
To midnight hour belated, made the stars
Appear to wink and fade; and her broad disk
Seem'd like a crag on fire, as up the vault
That course she journey'd, which the sun then warms;
When they of Rome behold him at his set
Betwixt Sardinia and the Corsic isle.
And now the weight, that hung upon my thought,
Was lighten'd by the aid of that clear spirit,
Who raiseth Andes above Mantua's name.
I therefore, when my questions had obtain'd
Solution plain and ample, stood as one
Musing in dreamy slumber; but not long
Slumber'd; for suddenly a multitude,
The steep already turning from behind,
Rush'd on. With fury and like random rout,
As echoing on their shores at midnight heard
Ismenus and Asopus, for his Thebes
If Bacchus' help were needed; so came these
Tumultuous, curving each his rapid step,
By eagerness impell'd of holy love.

Soon they o'ertook us; with such swiftness moved
The mighty crowd. Two spirits at their head
Cried, weeping, "Blessed Mary sought with haste
The hilly region. Cæsar, to subdue
Ilerda, darted in Marseilles his sting,
And flew to Spain." "Oh, tarry not: away!"

THE DIVINE COMEDY

The others shouted; "let not time be lost
Through slackness of affection. Hearty zeal
To serve reanimates celestial grace."

"O ye! in whom intenser fervency
Haply supplies, where lukewarm erst ye fail'd,
Slow or neglectful, to absolve your part
Of good and virtuous; this man, who yet lives
(Credit my tale, though strange), desires to ascend,
So morning rise to light us. Therefore say
Which hand leads nearest to the rifted rock."

So spake my guide; to whom a shade return'd:
"Come after us, and thou shalt find the cleft.
We may not linger: such resistless will
Speeds our unwearied course. Vouchsafe us then
Thy pardon, if our duty seem to thee
Discourteous rudeness. In Verona I
Was Abbot of San Zeno, when the hand
Of Barbarossa grasp'd imperial sway,
That name e'er utter'd without tears in Milan
And there is he, hath one foot in his grave,
Who for that monastery ere long shall weep,
Ruing his power misused: for that his son,
Of body ill compact, and worse in mind,
And born in evil, he hath set in place
Of its true pastor." Whether more he spake,
Or here was mute, I know not: he had sped
E'en now so far beyond us. Yet thus much
I heard, and in remembrance treasured it.

He then, who never fail'd me at my need,
Cried, "Hither turn. Lo! two with sharp remorse
Chiding their sin." In rear of all the troop
These shouted: "First they died, to whom the sea
Open'd, or ever Jordan saw his heirs:
And they, who with Æneas to the end
Endured not suffering, for their portion chose
Life without glory." Soon as they had fled
Past reach of sight, new thought within me rose

[224]

PURGATORY

By others follow'd fast, and each unlike
Its fellow: till led on from thought to thought,
And pleasured with the fleeting train, mine eye
Was closed, and meditation changed to dream.

CANTO XIX

*After describing his dream, the poet ascends to the fifth
cornice where the sin of avarice is cleansed.*

It was the hour, when of diurnal heat
No reliques chafe the cold beams of the moon,
O'erpower'd by earth, or planetary sway
Of Saturn; and the geomancer sees
His Greater Fortune up the east ascend,
Where gray dawn checkers first the shadowy cone;
When, 'fore me in my dream, a woman's shape
There came, with lips that stammer'd, eyes aslant,
Distorted feet, hands maim'd, and color pale.

I look'd upon her: and, as sunshine cheers
Limbs numb'd by nightly cold, e'en thus my look
Unloosed her tongue; next, in brief space, her form
Decrepit raised erect, and faded face
With love's own hue illumed. Recovering speech,
She forthwith, warbling, such a strain began,
That I, how loath soe'er, could scarce have held
Attention from the song. "I," thus she sang,
"I am the Siren, she, whom mariners
On the wide sea are wilder'd when they hear:
Such fulness of delight the listener feels.
I, from his course, Ulysses by my lay
Enchanted drew. Whoe'er frequents me once,
Parts seldom: so I charm him, and his heart
Contented knows no void." Or ere her mouth
Was closed, to shame her, at my side appear'd
A dame of semblance holy. With stern voice
She utter'd: "Say, O Virgil! who is this?"

Which hearing, he approach'd, with eyes still bent
Toward that goodly presence: the other seized her,
And, her robes tearing, open'd her before,
And show'd the belly to me, whence a smell,
Exhaling loathsome, waked me. Round I turn'd
Mine eyes: and thus the teacher: "At the least
Three times my voice hath call'd thee. Rise, begone.
Let us the opening find where thou mayst pass."

I straightway rose. Now day, pour'd down from high,
Fill'd all the circuits of the sacred mount;
And, as we journey'd, on our shoulder smote
The early ray. I follow'd, stooping low
My forehead, as a man, o'ercharged with thought,
Who bends him to the likeness of an arch
That midway spans the flood; when thus I heard,
"Come, enter here," in tone so soft and mild,
As never met the ear on mortal strand.

With swan-like wings dispread and pointing up,
Who thus had spoken marshal'd us along,
Where, each side of the solid masonry,
The sloping walls retired; then moved his plumes,
And fanning us, affirm'd that those, who mourn,
Are blessed, for that comfort shall be theirs.

"What aileth thee, that still thou look'st to earth?"
Began my leader; while the angelic shape
A little over us his station took.

"New vision," I replied, "hath raised in me
Surmisings strange and anxious doubts, whereon
My soul intent allows no other thought
Or room, or entrance." "Hast thou seen," said he,
"That old enchantress, her, whose wiles alone
The spirits o'er us weep for? Hast thou seen
How man may free him of her bonds? Enough.
Let thy heels spurn the earth; and thy raised ken
Fix on the lure, which heaven's eternal King
Whirls in the rolling spheres." As on his feet

PURGATORY

The falcon first looks down, then to the sky
Turns, and forth stretches eager for the food,
That woos him thither; so the call I heard:
So onward, far as the dividing rock
Gave way, I journey'd, till the plain was reach'd.

On the fifth circle when I stood at large,
A race appear'd before me, on the ground
All downward lying prone and weeping sore.
"My soul hath cleaved to the dust," I heard
With sighs so deep, they well nigh choked the words.

"O ye elect of God! whose penal woes
Both hope and justice mitigate, direct
Toward the steep rising our uncertain way."

"If ye approach secure from this our doom,
Prostration, and would urge your course with speed,
See that ye still to rightward keep the brink."

So them the bard besought; and such the words,
Beyond us some short space, in answer came.

I noted what remain'd yet hidden from them:
Thence to my liege's eyes mine eyes I bent,
And he, forthwith interpreting their suit,
Beckon'd his glad assent. Free then to act
As pleased me, I drew near, and took my stand
Over that shade whose words I late had mark'd.
And, "Spirit!" I said, "in whom repentant tears
Mature that blessed hour when thou with God
Shalt find acceptance, for a while suspend
For me that mightier care. Say who thou wast;
Why thus ye grovel on your bellies prone;
And if, in naught, ye wish my service there,
Whence living I am come." He answering spake:
"The cause why Heaven our back toward his cope
Reverses, shalt thou know: but me know first,
The successor of Peter, and the name
And title of my lineage, from that stream

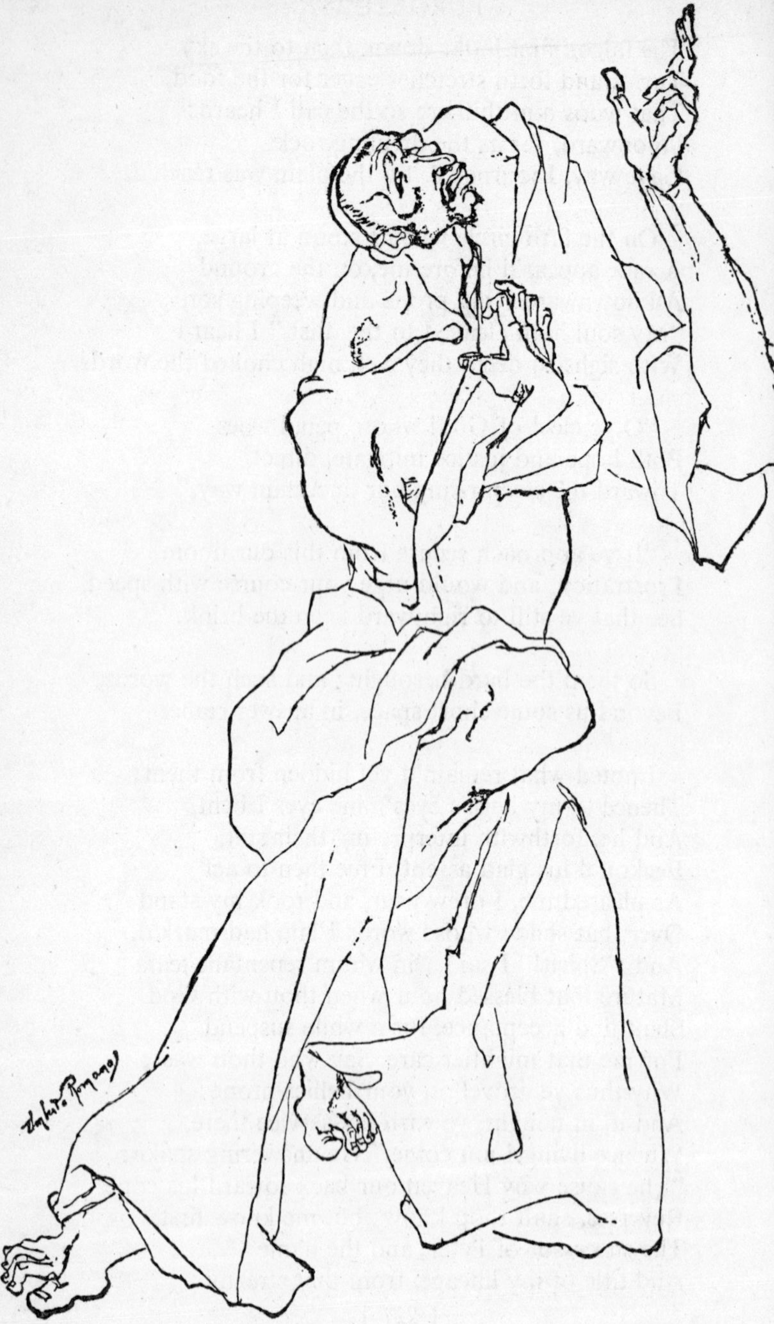
Umberto Romano

PURGATORY

That 'twixt Chiaveri and Siestri draws
His limpid waters through the lowly glen.
A month and little more by proof I learnt,
With what a weight that robe of sovereignty
Upon his shoulder rests, who from the mire
Would guard it; that each other fardel seems
But feathers in the balance. Late, alas!
Was my conversion: but, when I became
Rome's pastor, I discern'd at once the dream
And cozenage of life; saw that the heart
Rested not there, and yet no prouder height
Lured on the climber: wherefore, of that life
No more enamor'd, in my bosom love
Of purer being kindled. For till then
I was a soul in misery, alienate
From God, and covetous of all earthly things;
Now, as thou seest, here punish'd for my doting.
Such cleansing from the taint of avarice,
Do spirits, converted, need. This mount inflicts
No direr penalty. E'en as our eyes
Fasten'd below, nor e'er to loftier clime
Were lifted; thus hath justice level'd us,
Here on the earth. As avarice quench'd our love
Of good, without which is no working; thus
Here justice holds us prison'd, hand and foot
Chain'd down and bound, while heaven's just Lord shall please,
So long to tarry, motionless, outstretch'd."

My knees I stoop'd and would have spoke; but he,
Ere my beginning, by his ear perceived
I did him reverence; and "What cause," said he,
"Hath bow'd thee thus?" "Compunction," I rejoin'd,
"And inward awe of your high dignity."

"Up," he exclaim'd, "brother! upon thy feet
Arise; err not: thy fellow-servant I,
(Thine and all others') of one Sovereign Power.
If thou hast ever mark'd those holy sounds
Of gospel truth, 'nor shall be given in marriage,'
Thou mayst discern the reasons of my speech.

[229]

Go thy ways now; and linger here no more.
Thy tarrying is a let unto the tears,
With which I hasten that whereof thou speakest.
I have on earth a kinswoman; her name
Alagia, worthy in herself, so ill
Example of our house corrupt her not:
And she is all remaineth of me there."

CANTO XX

*Hugh Capet tells of illustrious examples of voluntary poverty
and bounty, and some noted instances of avarice.*

ILL strives the will, 'gainst will more wise that strives:
His pleasure therefore to mine own preferr'd,
I drew the sponge yet thirsty from the wave.

Onward I moved: he also onward moved,
Who led me, coasting still, wherever place
Along the rock was vacant; as a man
Walks near the battlements on narrow wall.
For those on the other part, who drop by drop
Wring out their all-infecting malady,
Too closely press the verge. Accurst be thou,
Inveterate wolf! whose gorge ingluts more prey,
Than every beast beside, yet is not fill'd;
So bottomless thy maw.—Ye spheres of heaven!
To whom there are, as seems, who attribute
All change in mortal state, when is the day
Of his appearing, for whom fate reserves
To chase her hence?—With wary steps and slow
We pass'd; and I attentive to the shades,
Whom piteously I heard lament and wail;
And, 'midst the wailing, one before us heard
Cry out "O blessed Virgin!" as a dame
In the sharp pangs of childbed; and "How poor
Thou wast," it added, "witness that low roof
Where thou didst lay thy sacred burden down.

PURGATORY

O good Fabricius! thou didst virtue choose
With poverty, before great wealth with vice."

The words so pleased me, that desire to know
The spirit, from whose lip they seem'd to come,
Did draw me onward. Yet it spake the gift
Of Nicholas, which on the maidens he
Bounteous bestow'd, to save their youthful prime
Unblemish'd. "Spirit! who dost speak of deeds
So worthy, tell me who thou wast," I said,
"And why thou dost with single voice renew
Memorial of such praise. That boon vouchsafed
Haply shall meet reward; if I return
To finish the short pilgrimage of life,
Still speeding to its close on restless wing."

"I," answer'd he, "will tell thee; not for help,
Which thence I look for; but that in thyself
Grace so exceeding shines, before thy time
Of mortal dissolution. I was root
Of that ill plant whose shade such poison sheds
O'er all the Christian land, that seldom thence
Good fruit is gather'd. Vengeance soon should come,
Had Ghent and Douay, Lille and Bruges power;
And vengeance I of heaven's great Judge implore.
Hugh Capet was I hight: from me descend
The Philips and the Louis, of whom France
Newly is govern'd: born of one, who plied
The slaughterer's trade at Paris. When the race
Of ancient kings had vanish'd (all save one
Wrapt up in sable weeds) within my gripe
I found the reins of empire, and such powers
Of new acquirement, with full store of friends,
That soon the widow'd circlet of the crown
Was girt upon the temples of my son,
He, from whose bones the anointed race begins.
Till the great dower of Provence had removed
The stains, that yet obscured our lowly blood,
Its sway indeed was narrow; but howe'er
It wrought no evil: there, with force and lies,

[231]

Began its rapine: after, for amends,
Poitou it seized, Navarre and Gascony.
To Italy came Charles; and for amends,
Young Conradine, an innocent victim, slew;
And sent the angelic teacher back to heaven,
Still for amends. I see the time at hand,
That forth from France invites another Charles
To make himself and kindred better known.
Unarm'd he issues, saving with that lance,
Which the arch-traitor tilted with, and that
He carries with so home a thrust, as rives
The bowels of poor Florence. No increase
Of territory hence, but sin and shame
Shall be his guerdon; and so much the more
As he more lightly deems of such foul wrong.
I see the other (who a prisoner late
Had stepped on shore) exposing to the mart
His daughter, whom he bargains for, as do
The Corsairs for their slaves. O avarice!
What canst thou more, who hast subdued our blood
So wholly to thyself, they feel no care
Of their own flesh? To hide with direr guilt
Past ill and future, lo! the flower-de-luce
Enters Alagna; in his Vicar Christ
Himself a captive, and his mockery
Acted again. Lo! to his holy lip
The vinegar and gall once more applied;
And he 'twixt living robbers doom'd to bleed.
Lo! the new Pilate, of whose cruelty
Such violence cannot fill the measure up,
With no decree to sanction, pushes on
Into the temple his yet eager sails.

"O sovereign Master! when shall I rejoice
To see the vengeance, which thy wrath, well-pleased,
In secret silence broods?—While daylight lasts,
So long what thou didst hear of her, sole spouse
Of the Great Spirit, and on which thou turn'dst
To me for comment, is the general theme
Of all our prayers: but, when it darkens, then

PURGATORY

A different strain we utter; then record
Pygmalion, whom his gluttonous thirst of gold
Made traitor, robber, parricide: the woes
Of Midas, which his greedy wish ensued,
Mark'd for derision to all future times:
And the fond Achan, how he stole the prey,
That yet he seems by Joshua's ire pursued.
Sapphira with her husband next to blame;
And praise the fore feet, that with furious ramp
Spurn'd Heliodorus. All the mountain round
Rings with the infamy of Thracia's king,
Who slew his Phrygian charge: and last a shout
Ascends: 'Declare, O Crassus! for thou know'st,
The flavor of thy gold.' The voice of each
Now high, now low, as each his impulse prompts,
Is led through many a pitch, acute or grave.
Therefore, not singly, I erewhile rehearsed
That blessedness we tell of in the day:
But near me, none, beside, his accent raised."

From him we now had parted, and essay'd
With utmost efforts to surmount the way;
When I did feel, as nodding to its fall,
The mountain tremble; whence an icy chill
Seized on me, as on one to death convey'd.
So shook not Delos, when Latona there
Couch'd to bring forth the twin-born eyes of heaven.

Forthwith from every side a shout arose
So vehement, that suddenly my guide
Drew near, and cried: "Doubt not, while I conduct thee."
"Glory!" all shouted (such the sounds mine ear
Gather'd from those, who near me swell'd the sounds)
"Glory in the highest be to God." We stood
Immovably suspended, like to those,
The shepherds, who first heard in Bethlehem's field
That song: till ceased the trembling, and the song
Was ended: then our hallow'd path resumed,
Eying the prostrate shadows, who renew'd
Their custom'd mourning. Never in my breast

[233]

Did ignorance so struggle with desire
Of knowledge, if my memory do not err,
As in that moment; nor through haste dared I
To question, nor myself could aught discern.
So on I fared, in thoughtfulness and dread.

CANTO XXI

*The two poets are overtaken by the spirit of Statius
who is on his way to Paradise.*

THE natural thirst, ne'er quench'd but from the well
Whereof the woman of Samaria craved,
Excited; haste, along the cumber'd path,
After my guide, impell'd; and pity moved
My bosom for the 'vengeful doom though just.
When lo! even as Luke relates, that Christ
Appear'd unto the two upon their way,
New-risen from his vaulted grave; to us
A shade appear'd, and after us approach'd,
Contemplating the crowd beneath its feet.
We were not ware of it; so first it spake,
Saying, "God give you peace, my brethren!" then
Sudden we turn'd: and Virgil such salute,
As fitted that kind greeting, gave; and cried:
"Peace in the blessed council be thy lot,
Awarded by that righteous court which me
To everlasting banishment exiles."

"How!" he exclaim'd, nor from his speed meanwhile
Desisting; "If that ye be spirits whom God
Vouchsafes not room above; who up the height
Has been thus far your guide?" To whom the bard:
"If thou observe the tokens, which this man,
Traced by the finger of the angel, bears;
'Tis plain that in the kingdom of the just
He needs must share. But sithence she, whose wheel
Spins day and night, for him not yet had drawn

[234]

PURGATORY

That yarn, which on the fatal distaff piled,
Clotho apportions to each wight that breathes;
His soul, that sister is to mine and thine,
Not of herself could mount; for not like ours
Her ken: whence I, from forth the ample gulf
Of Hell, was ta'en, to lead him, and will lead
Far as my lore avails. But, if thou know,
Instruct us for what cause, the mount erewhile
Thus shook, and trembled: wherefore all at once
Seem'd shouting, even from his wave-wash'd foot."

That questioning so tallied with my wish,
The thirst did feel abatement of its edge
E'en from expectance. He forthwith replied:
"In its devotion, naught irregular
This mount can witness, or by punctual rule
Unsanction'd; here from every change exempt,
Other than that, which heaven in itself
Doth of itself receive, no influence
Can reach us. Tempest none, shower, hail, or snow,
Hoar frost, or dewy moistness, higher falls
Than that brief scale of threefold steps: thick clouds,
Nor scudding rack, are ever seen: swift glance
Ne'er lightens; nor Thaumantian Iris gleams,
That yonder often shifts on each side Heaven.
Vapor adust doth never mount above
The highest of the trinal stairs, whereon
Peter's vicegerent stands. Lower perchance,
With various motion rock'd, trembles the soil:
But here, through wind in earth's deep hollow pent,
I know not how, yet never trembled: then
Trembles, when any spirit feels itself
So purified, that it may rise, or move
For rising; and such loud acclaim ensues.
Purification, by the will alone,
Is proved, that free to change society
Seizes the soul rejoicing in her will.
Desire of bliss is present from the first;
But strong propension hinders, to that wish
By the just ordinance of heaven opposed;

[235]

THE DIVINE COMEDY

Propension now as eager to fulfil
The allotted torment, as erewhile to sin.
And I, who in this punishment had lain
Five hundred years and more, but now have felt
Free wish for happier clime. Therefore thou felt'st
The mountain tremble; and the spirits devout
Heard'st, over all his limits, utter praise
To that liege Lord, whom I entreat their joy
To hasten." Thus he spake: and, since the draught
Is grateful ever as the thirst is keen,
No words may speak my fulness of content.

"Now," said the instructor sage, "I see the net
That takes ye here; and how the toils are loosed;
Why rocks the mountain, and why ye rejoice.
Vouchsafe, that from thy lips I next may learn
Who on the earth thou wast; and wherefore here,
So many an age, were prostrate." "In that time,
When the good Titus, with heaven's King to help,
Avenged those piteous gashes, whence the blood
By Judas sold did issue; with the name
Most lasting and most honor'd, there, was I
Abundantly renown'd," the shade replied,
"Not yet with faith endued. So passing sweet
My vocal spirit; from Tolosa, Rome
To herself drew me, where I merited
A myrtle garland to inwreathe my brow.
Statius they name me still. Of Thebes I sang,
And next of great Achilles; but i' the way
Fell with the second burden. Of my flame
Those sparkles were the seeds, which I derived
From the bright fountain of celestial fire
That feeds unnumber'd lamps; the song I mean
Which sounds Æneas' wanderings: that the breast
I hung at; that the nurse, from whom my veins
Drank inspiration: whose authority
Was ever sacred with me. To have lived
Coeval with the Mantuan, I would bide
The revolution of another sun
Beyond my stated years in banishment."

PURGATORY

The Mantuan, when he heard him, turn'd to me;
And holding silence, by his countenance
Enjoin'd me silence: but the power, which wills,
Bears not supreme control: laughter and tears
Follow so closely on the passion prompts them,
They wait not for the motions of the will
In nature most sincere. I did but smile,
As one who winks; and thereupon the shade
Broke off, and peer'd into mine eyes, where best
Our looks interpret. "So to good event
Mayst thou conduct such great emprise," he cried,
"Say, why across thy visage beam'd, but now,
The lightning of a smile." On either part
Now am I straiten'd; one conjures me speak,
The other to silence binds me: whence a sigh
I utter, and the sigh is heard. "Speak on,"
The teacher cried: "and do not fear to speak;
But tell him what so earnestly he asks."
Whereon I thus: "Perchance, O ancient spirit!
Thou marvel'st at my smiling. There is room
For yet more wonder. He, who guides my ken
On high, he is that Mantuan, led by whom
Thou didst presume of men and gods to sing.
If other cause thou deem'dst for which I smiled,
Leave it as not the true one: and believe
Those words, thou spakest of him, indeed the cause."

Now down he bent to embrace my teacher's feet;
But he forbade him: "Brother! do it not:
Thou art a shadow, and behold'st a shade."
He, rising, answer'd thus: "Now hast thou proved
The force and ardor of the love I bear thee,
When I forget we are but things of air,
And, as a substance, treat an empty shade."

CANTO XXII

Dante, Virgil, and Statius mount to the sixth cornice where the sin of gluttony is purged. Voices record examples of temperance.

Now we had left the angel, who had turn'd
To the sixth circle our ascending step;
One gash from off my forehead razed; while they,
Whose wishes tend to justice, shouted forth,
"Blessed!" and ended with "I thirst": and I,
More nimble than along the other straits,
So journey'd, that, without the sense of toil,
I follow'd upward the swift-footed shades;
When Virgil thus began: "Let its pure flame
From virtue flow, and love can never fail
To warm another's bosom, so the light
Shine manifestly forth. Hence, from that hour,
When, 'mongst us in the purlieus of the deep,
Came down the spirit of Aquinum's bard,
Who told of thine affection, my good will
Hath been for thee of quality as strong
As ever link'd itself to one not seen.
Therefore these stairs will now seem short to me.
But tell me: and, if too secure, I loose
The rein with a friend's license, as a friend
Forgive me, and speak now as with a friend:
How chanced it covetous desire could find
Place in that bosom, 'midst such ample store
Of wisdom, as thy zeal had treasured there?"

First somewhat moved to laughter by his words,
Statius replied: "Each syllable of thine
Is a dear pledge of love. Things oft appear,
That minister false matter to our doubts,
When their true causes are removed from sight.
Thy question doth assure me, thou believest
I was on earth a covetous man; perhaps

PURGATORY

Because thou found'st me in that circle placed.
Know then I was too wide of avarice:
And e'en for that excess, thousands of moons
Have wax'd and waned upon my sufferings.
And were it not that I with heedful care
Noted, where thou exclaim'st as if in ire
With human nature, 'Why, thou cursed thirst
Of gold! dost not with juster measure guide
The appetite of mortals?' I had met
The fierce encounter of the voluble rock.
Then was I ware that, with too ample wing,
The hands may haste to lavishment; and turn'd,
As from my other evil, so from this,
In penitence. How many from their grave
Shall with shorn locks arise, who living, ay,
And at life's last extreme, of this offence,
Through ignorance, did not repent! And know,
The fault, which lies direct from any sin
In level opposition, here, with that,
Wastes its green rankness on one common heap.
Therefore, if I have been with those, who wail
Their avarice, to cleanse me; through reverse
Of their transgression, such hath been my lot."

To whom the sov'reign of the pastoral song:
"While thou didst sing that cruel warfare waged
By the twin sorrow of Jocasta's womb,
From thy discourse with Clio there, it seems
As faith had not been thine; without the which,
Good deeds suffice not. And if so, what sun
Rose on thee, or what candle pierced the dark,
That thou didst after see to hoist the sail,
And follow where the fisherman had led?"

He answering thus: "By thee conducted first,
I enter'd the Parnassian grots, and quaff'd
Of the clear spring: illumined first by thee,
Open'd mine eyes to God. Thou didst, as one,
Who, journeying through the darkness, bears a light
Behind, that profits not himself, but makes

His followers wise, when thou exclaimed'st, 'Lo!
A renovated world, Justice return'd,
Times of primeval innocence restored,
And a new race descended from above.'
Poet and Christian both to thee I owed.
That thou mayst mark more clearly what I trace,
My hand shall stretch forth to inform the lines
With livelier coloring. Soon o'er all the world,
By messengers from Heaven, the true belief
Teem'd now prolific; and that word of thine,
Accordant, to the new instructors chimed.
Induced by which agreement, I was wont
Resort to them; and soon their sanctity
So won upon me, that, Domitian's rage
Pursuing them, I mix'd my tears with theirs;
And, while on earth I stay'd, still succor'd them;
And their most righteous customs made me scorn
All sects besides. Before I led the Greeks,
In tuneful fiction, to the streams of Thebes,
I was baptized: but secretly, through fear,
Remain'd a Christian, and conform'd long time
To Pagan rites. Four centuries and more
I, for that lukewarmness, was fain to pace
Round the fourth circle. Thou then, who hast raised
The covering which did hide such blessing from me,
Whilst much of this ascent is yet to climb,
Say, if thou know, where our old Terence bides,
Cæcilius, Plautus, Varro: if condemn'd
They dwell, and in what province of the deep."
"These," said my guide, "with Persius and myself,
And others many more, are with that Greek,
Of mortals, the most cherish'd by the nine,
In the first ward of darkness. There, ofttimes,
We of that mount hold converse, on whose top
For aye our nurses live. We have the bard
Of Pella and the Teian, Agatho,
Simonides, and many a Grecian else
Ingarlanded with laurel. Of thy train,
Antigone is there, Deïphile,
Argia, and as sorrowful as erst

PURGATORY

Ismene, and who show'd Langia's wave:
Deïdamia with her sisters there,
And blind Tiresias' daughter, and the bride
Sea-born of Peleus." Either poet now
Was silent; and no longer by the ascent
Or the steep walls obstructed, round them cast
Inquiring eyes. Four handmaids of the day
Had finish'd now their office, and the fifth
Was at the chariot-beam, directing still
Its flamy point aloof; when thus my guide:
"Methinks, it well behoves us to the brink
Bend the right shoulder, circuiting the mount,
As we have ever used." So custom there
Was usher to the road; the which we chose
Less doubtful, as that worthy shade complied.

They on before me went: I sole pursued,
Listening their speech, that to my thoughts convey'd
Mysterious lessons of sweet poesy.
But soon they ceased; for midway of the road
A tree we found, with goodly fruitage hung,
And pleasant to the smell: and as a fir,
Upward from bough to bough, less ample spreads;
So downward this less ample spread; that none,
Methinks, aloft may climb. Upon the side,
That closed our path, a liquid crystal fell
From the steep rock, and through the sprays above
Stream'd showering. With associate step the bards
Drew near the plant; and, from amidst the leaves,
A voice was heard: "Ye shall be chary of me";
And after added: "Mary took more thought
For joy and honor of the nuptial feast,
Than for herself, who answers now for you.
The women of old Rome were satisfied
With water for their beverage. Daniel fed
On pulse, and wisdom gain'd. The primal age
Was beautiful as gold: and hunger then
Made acorns tasteful; thirst, each rivulet
Run nectar. Honey and locusts were the food,
Whereon the Baptist in the wilderness

Fed, and that eminence of glory reach'd
And greatness, which the Evangelist records."

CANTO XXIII

*They are overtaken by the spirit of Forese who inveighs
bitterly against the immodest dress of their
countrywomen of Florence.*

On the green leaf mine eyes were fix'd, like his
Who throws away his days in idle chase
Of the diminutive birds, when thus I heard
The more than father warn me: "Son! our time
Asks thriftier using. Linger not: away!"

Thereat my face and steps at once I turn'd
Toward the sages, by whose converse cheer'd
I journey'd on, and felt no toil: and lo!
A sound of weeping, and a song: "My lips,
O Lord!" and these so mingled, it gave birth
To pleasure and to pain. "O Sire beloved!
Say what is this I hear." Thus I inquired.

"Spirits," said he, "who, as they go, perchance,
Their debt of duty pay." As on their road
The thoughtful pilgrims, overtaking some
Not known unto them, turn to them, and look,
But stay not; thus, approaching from behind
With speedier motion, eyed us, as they pass'd,
A crowd of spirits, silent and devout.
The eyes of each were dark and hollow; pale
Their visage, and so lean withal, the bones
Stood staring through the skin. I do not think
Thus dry and meagre Erisichthon show'd,
When pinch'd by sharp-set famine to the quick.

"Lo!" to myself I mused, "the race, who lost
Jerusalem, when Mary with dire beak

PURGATORY

Prey'd on her child." The sockets seem'd as rings,
From which the gems were dropt. Who reads the name
Of man upon his forehead, there the M
Had traced most plainly. Who would deem, that scent
Of water and an apple could have proved
Powerful to generate such pining want,
Not knowing how it wrought? While now I stood,
Wondering what thus could waste them (for the cause
Of their gaunt hollowness and scaly rind
Appear'd not), lo! a spirit turn'd his eyes
In their deep-sunken cells, and fasten'd them
On me, then cried with vehemence aloud:
"What grace is this vouchsafed me?" By his looks
I ne'er had recognized him: but the voice
Brought to my knowledge what his cheer conceal'd.
Remembrance of his altered lineaments
Was kindled from that spark; and I agnized
The visage of Forese. "Ah! respect
This wan and leprous-wither'd skin," thus he
Suppliant implored, "this macerated flesh.
Speak to me truly of thyself. And who
Are those twain spirits, that escort thee there?
Be it not said thou scorn'st to talk with me."

"That face of thine," I answer'd him, "which dead
I once bewail'd, disposes me not less
For weeping, when I see it thus transform'd.
Say then, by Heaven, what blasts ye thus? The whilst
I wonder, ask not speech from me: unapt
Is he to speak, whom other will employs."

He thus: "The water and the plant, we pass'd,
With power are gifted, by the eternal will
Infused; the which so pines me. Every spirit,
Whose song bewails his gluttony indulged
Too grossly, here in hunger and in thirst
Is purified. The odor, which the fruit
And spray that showers upon the verdure, breathe,
Inflames us with desire to feed and drink.
Nor once alone, encompassing our route,

We come to add fresh fuel to the pain:
Pain, said I? solace rather: for that will
To the tree leads us, by which Christ was led
To call on Eli, joyful, when he paid
Our ransom from his vein." I answering thus:
"Forese! from that day, in which the world
For better life thou changedst, not five years
Have circled. If the power of sinning more
Were first concluded in thee, ere thou knew'st
That kindly grief which re-espouses us
To God, how hither art thou come so soon?
I thought to find thee lower, there, where time
Is recompense for time." He straight replied:
"To drink up the sweet wormwood of affliction
I have been brought thus early, by the tears
Stream'd down my Nella's cheeks. Her prayers devout,
Her sighs have drawn me from the coast, where oft
Expectance lingers; and have set me free
From the other circles. In the sight of God
So much the dearer is my widow prized.
She whom I loved so fondly, as she ranks
More singly eminent for virtuous deeds.
The tract, most barbarous of Sardinia's isle,
Hath dames more chaste, and modester by far,
Than that wherein I left her. O sweet brother!
What wouldst thou have me say? A time to come
Stands full within my view, to which this hour
Shall not be counted of an ancient date,
When from the pulpit shall be loudly warn'd
The unblushing dames of Florence, lest they bare
Unkerchief'd bosoms to the common gaze.
What savage women hath the world e'er seen,
What Saracens, for whom there needed scourge
Of spiritual or other discipline,
To force them walk with covering on their limbs?
But did they see, the shameless ones, what Heaven
Wafts on swift wing toward them while I speak,
Their mouths were oped for howling: they shall taste
Of sorrow (unless foresight cheat me here)
Or e'er the cheek of him be clothed with down,

PURGATORY

Who is now rock'd with lullaby asleep.
Ah! now, my brother, hide thyself no more;
Thou seest how not I alone, but all,
Gaze, where thou veil'st the intercepted sun."

Whence I replied: "If thou recall to mind
What we were once together, even yet
Remembrance of those days may grieve thee sore.
That I forsook that life, was due to him
Who there precedes me, some few evenings past,
When she was round, who shines with sister lamp
To his great glisters yonder," and I show'd
The sun. " 'Tis he, who through profoundest night
Of the true dead has brought me, with this flesh
As true, that follows. From that gloom the aid
Of his sure comfort drew me on to climb,
And, climbing, wind along this mountain-steep,
Which rectifies in you whate'er the world
Made crooked and depraved. I have his word,
That he will bear me company as far
As till I come where Beatrice dwells:
But there must leave me. Virgil is that spirit,
Who thus hath promised," and I pointed to him:
"The other is that shade, for whom so late
Your realm, as he arose, exulting, shook
Through every pendent cliff and rocky bound."

CANTO XXIV

*Forese points out several purifying themselves of gluttony,
and predicts the violent end of Dante's political enemy,
Corso Donati; the three poets
proceed to the next cornice.*

OUR journey was not slacken'd by our talk,
Nor yet our talk by journeying. Still we spake,
And urged our travel stoutly, like a ship
When the wind sits astern. The shadowy forms,

THE DIVINE COMEDY

That seem'd things dead and dead again, drew in
At their deep-delved orbs rare wonder of me,
Perceiving I had life; and I my words
Continued, and thus spake: "He journeys up
Perhaps more tardily than else he would,
For others' sake. But tell me, if thou know'st,
Where is Piccarda? Tell me, if I see
Any of mark, among this multitude
Who eye me thus." "My sister (she for whom,
'Twixt beautiful and good, I cannot say
Which name was fitter) wears e'en now her crown,
And triumphs in Olympus." Saying this,
He added: "Since spare diet hath so worn
Our semblance out, 'tis lawful here to name
Each one. This," and his finger then he raised,
"Is Buonaggiunta—Buonaggiunta, he
Of Lucca: and that face beyond him, pierced
Unto a leaner fineness than the rest,
Had keeping of the church; he was of Tours,
And purges by wan abstinence away
Bolsena's eels and cups of muscadel."

He show'd me many others, one by one:
And all, as they were named, seem'd well content;
For no dark gesture I discern'd in any.
I saw, through hunger, Ubaldino, grind
His teeth on emptiness; and Boniface,
That waved the crozier o'er a numerous flock:
I saw the Marquis, who had time erewhile
To swill at Forli with less drought; yet so,
Was one ne'er sated. I howe'er, like him
That, gazing 'midst a crowd, singles out one,
So singled him of Lucca; for methought
Was none among them took such note of me.
Somewhat I heard him whisper of Gentucca:
The sound was indistinct, and murmur'd there,
Where justice, that so strips them, fix'd her sting.

PURGATORY

"Spirit!" said I, "it seems as thou wouldst fain
Speak with me. Let me hear thee. Mutual wish
To converse prompts, which let us both indulge."

He, answering, straight began: "Woman is born,
Whose brow no wimple shades yet, that shall make
My city please thee, blame it as they may.
Go then with this forewarning. If aught false
My whisper too implied, the event shall tell.
But say, if of a truth I see the man
Of that new lay the inventor, which begins
With 'Ladies, ye that con the lore of love.' "

To whom I thus: "Count of me but as one,
Who am the scribe of love; that, when he breathes,
Take up my pen, and, as he dictates, write."

"Brother!" said he, "the hindrance, which once held
The notary, with Guittone and myself,
Short of that new and sweeter style I hear,
Is now disclosed: I see how ye your plumes
Stretch, as the inditer guides them; which, no question,
Ours did not. He that seeks a grace beyond,
Sees not the distance parts one style from other."
And, as contented, here he held his peace.

Like as the birds, that winter near the Nile,
In squared regiment direct their course,
Then stretch themselves in file for speedier flight;
Thus all the tribe of spirits, as they turn'd
Their visage, faster fled, nimble alike
Through leanness and desire. And as a man,
Tired with the motion of a trotting steed,
Slacks pace, and stays behind his company,
Till his o'erbreathed lungs keep temperate time;
E'en so Forese let that holy crew
Proceed, behind them lingering at my side,
And saying: "When shall I again behold thee?"

[247]

THE DIVINE COMEDY

"How long my life may last," said I, "I know not.
This know, how soon soever I return,
My wishes will before me have arrived:
Sithence the place, where I am set to live,
Is, day by day, more scoop'd of all its good;
And dismal ruin seems to threaten it."

"Go now," he cried: "lo! he, whose guilt is most
Passes before my vision, dragg'd at heels
Of an infuriate beast. Toward the vale,
Where guilt hath no redemption, on it speeds,
Each step increasing swiftness on the last;
Until a blow it strikes, that leaveth him
A corse most vilely shatter'd. No long space
Those wheels have yet to roll" (therewith his eyes
Look'd up to heaven), "ere thou shalt plainly see
That which my words may not more plainly tell.
I quit thee: time is precious here: I lose
Too much, thus measuring my pace with thine."

As from a troop of well-rank'd chivalry,
One knight, more enterprising than the rest,
Pricks forth at gallop, eager to display
His prowess in the first encounter proved;
So parted he from us, with lengthen'd strides;
And left me on the way with those twain spirits,
Who were such mighty marshals of the world.

When he beyond us had so fled, mine eyes
No nearer reach'd him, than my thought his words;
The branches of another fruit, thick hung,
And blooming fresh, appear'd. E'en as our steps
Turn'd thither; not far off, it rose to view.
Beneath it were a multitude, that raised
Their hands, and shouted forth I know not what
Unto the boughs; like greedy and fond brats,
That beg, and answer none obtain from him,
Of whom they beg; but more to draw them on,
He, at arm's length, the object of their wish
Above them holds aloft, and hides it not.

PURGATORY

At length, as undeceived, they went their way:
And we approach the tree, whom vows and tears
Sue to in vain; the mighty tree. "Pass on,
And come not near. Stands higher up the wood,
Whereof Eve tasted: and from it was ta'en
This plant." Such sounds from midst the thickets came
Whence I, with either bard, close to the side
That rose, pass'd forth beyond. "Remember," next
We heard, "those unblest creatures of the clouds,
How they their twifold bosoms, overgorged,
Opposed in fight to Theseus: call to mind
The Hebrews, how, effeminate, they stoop'd
To ease their thirst; whence Gideon's ranks were thinn'd,
As he to Madian march'd adown the hills."

Thus near one border coasting, still we heard
The sins of gluttony, with woe erewhile
Reguerdon'd. Then along the lonely path,
Once more at large, full thousand paces on
We travel'd, each contemplative and mute.

"Why pensive journey so ye three alone?"
Thus suddenly a voice exclaim'd: whereat
I shook, as doth a scared and paltry beast;
Then raised my head, to look from whence it came.

Was ne'er, in furnace, glass, or metal, seen
So bright and glowing red, as was the shape
I now beheld. "If ye desire to mount,"
He cried; "here must ye turn. This way he goes,
Who goes in quest of peace." His countenance
Had dazzled me; and to my guides I faced
Backward, like one who walks as sound directs.

As when, to harbinger the dawn, springs up
On freshen'd wing the air of May, and breathes
Of fragrance, all impregn'd with herb and flowers;
E'en such a wind I felt upon my front
Blow gently, and the moving of a wing
Perceived, that, moving, shed ambrosial smell;

[249]

And then a voice: "Blessed are they, whom grace
Doth so illume, that appetite in them
Exhaleth no inordinate desire,
Still hungering as the rule of temperance wills."

CANTO XXV

*At the last cornice where the sin of incontinence
is purged, the spirits record illustrious
instances of chastity.*

It was an hour, when he who climbs had need
To walk uncrippled; for the sun had now
To Taurus the meridian circle left,
And to the Scorpion left the night. As one,
That makes no pause, but presses on his road,
Whate'er betide him, if some urgent need
Impel; so enter'd we upon our way,
One before other; for, but singly, none
That steep and narrow scale admits to climb.

E'en as the young stork lifteth up his wing
Through wish to fly, yet ventures not to quit
The nest, and drops it; so in me desire
Of questioning my guide arose, and fell,
Arriving even to the act that marks
A man prepared for speech. Him all our haste
Restrain'd not; but thus spake the sire beloved:
"Fear not to speed the shaft, that on thy lip
Stands trembling for its flight." Encouraged thus,
I straight began: "How there can leanness come,
Where is no want of nourishment to feed?"

"If thou," he answer'd, "hadst remember'd thee,
How Meleager with the wasting brand
Wasted alike, by equal fires consumed;
This would not trouble thee: and hadst thou thought,
How in the mirror your reflected form

PURGATORY

With mimic motion vibrates; what now seems
Hard, and appear'd no harder than the pulp
Of summer-fruit mature. But that thy will
In certainty may find its full repose,
Lo Statius here! on him I call, and pray
That he would now be healer of thy wound."

"If, in thy presence, I unfold to him
The secrets of heaven's vengeance, let me plead
Thine own injunction to exculpate me."
So Statius answer'd, and forthwith began:
"Attend my words, O son, and in thy mind
Receive them; so shall they be light to clear
The doubt thou offer'st. Blood, concocted well,
Which by the thirsty veins is ne'er imbibed,
And rests as food superfluous, to be ta'en
From the replenish'd table, in the heart
Derives effectual virtue, that informs
The several human limbs, as being that
Which passes through the veins itself to make them.
Yet more concocted it descends, where shame
Forbids to mention: and from thence distils
In natural vessels on another's blood.
There each unite together; one disposed
To endure, to act the other, through that power
Derived from whence it came; and being met,
It 'gins to work, coagulating first;
Then vivifies what its own substance made
Consist. With animation now endued,
The active virtue (differing from a plant
No further, than that this is on the way,
And at its limit that) continues yet
To operate, that now it moves, and feels,
As sea-sponge clinging to the rock: and there
Assumes the organic powers its seed convey'd.
This is the moment, son! at which the virtue,
That from the generating heart proceeds,
Is pliant and expansive; for each limb
Is in the heart by forgeful nature plann'd.
How babe of animal becomes, remains

[251]

For thy considering. At this point, more wise,
Than thou, has err'd, making the soul disjoin'd
From passive intellect, because he saw
No organ for the latter's use assign'd.

"Open thy bosom to the truth that comes.
Know, soon as in the embryo, to the brain
Articulation is complete, then turns
The primal Mover with a smile of joy
On such great work of nature; and imbreathes
New spirit replete with virtue, that what here
Active it finds, to its own substance draws;
And forms an individual soul, that lives,
And feels, and bends reflective on itself.
And that thou less may'st marvel at the word,
Mark the sun's heat; how that to wine doth change,
Mix'd with the moisture filter'd through the vine.

"When Lachesis hath spun the thread, the soul
Takes with her both the human and divine,
Memory, intelligence, and will, in act
Far keener than before; the other powers
Inactive all and mute. No pause allow'd,
In wondrous sort self-moving, to one strand
Of those, where the departed roam, she falls:
Here learns her destined path. Soon as the place
Receives her, round the plastic virtue beams,
Distinct as in the living limbs before:
And as the air, when saturate with showers,
The casual beam refracting, decks itself
With many a hue; so here the ambient air
Weareth that form, which influence of the soul
Imprints on it: and like the flame, that where
The fire moves, thither follows; so, henceforth,
The new form on the spirit follows still:
Hence hath it semblance, and is shadow call'd,
With each sense, even to the sight, endued:
Hence speech is ours, hence laughter, tears and sighs,
Which thou mayst oft have witness'd on the mount.
The obedient shadow fails not to present

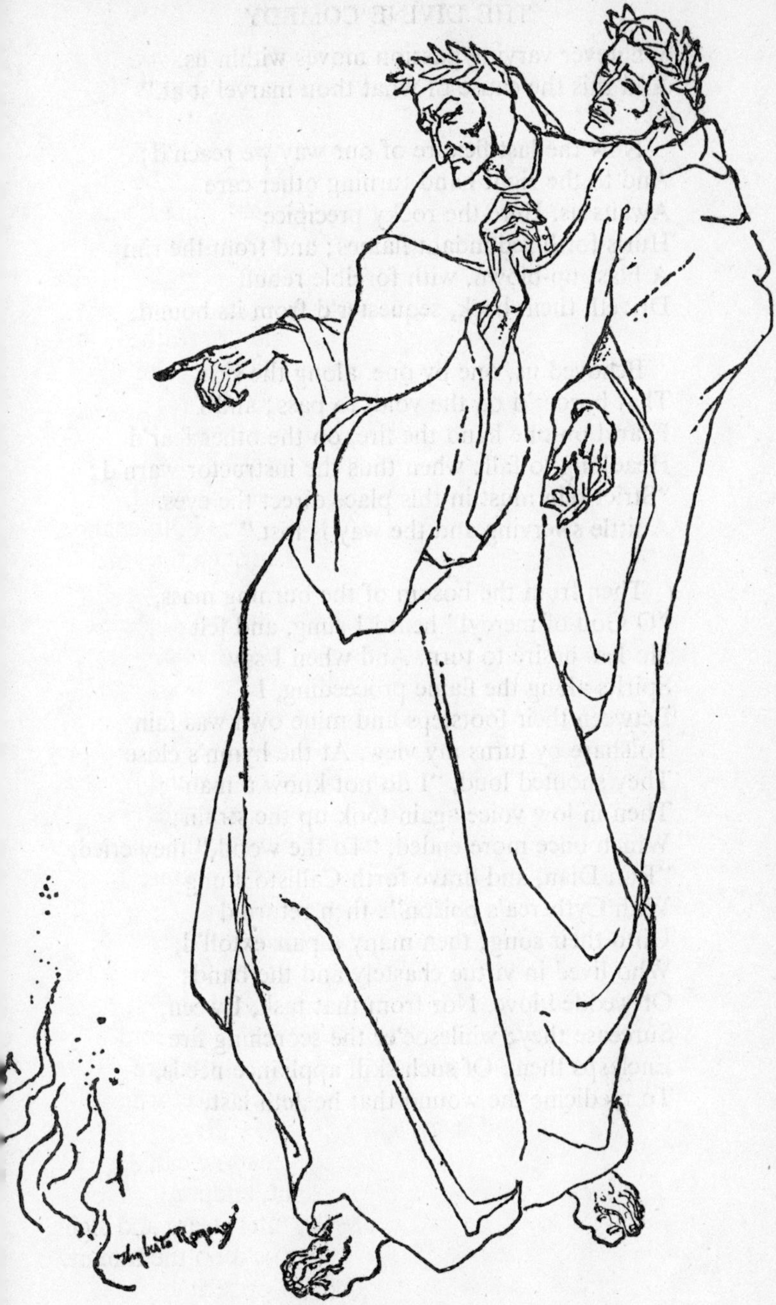

THE DIVINE COMEDY

Whatever varying passion moves within us.
And this the cause of what thou marvel'st at."

Now the last flexure of our way we reach'd;
And to the right hand turning other care
Awaits us. Here the rocky precipice
Hurls forth redundant flames; and from the rim
A blast up-blown, with forcible rebuff
Driveth them back, sequester'd from its bound.

Behoved us, one by one, along the side,
That border'd on the void, to pass; and I
Fear'd on one hand the fire, on the other fear'd
Headlong to fall: when thus the instructor warn'd;
"Strict rein must in this place direct the eyes.
A little swerving and the way is lost."

Then from the bosom of the burning mass,
"O God of mercy!" heard I sung, and felt
No less desire to turn. And when I saw
Spirits along the flame proceeding, I
Between their footsteps and mine own was fain
To share by turns my view. At the hymn's close
They shouted loud, "I do not know a man";
Then in low voice again took up the strain;
Which once more ended, "To the wood," they cried,
"Ran Dian, and drave forth Callisto stung
With Cytherea's poison": then return'd
Unto their song; then many a pair extoll'd,
Who lived in virtue chastely and the bands
Of wedded love. Nor from that task, I ween,
Surcease they; whilesoe'er the scorching fire
Enclasps them. Of such skill appliance needs,
To medicine the wound that healeth last.

PURGATORY

CANTO XXVI

A spirit wondering at the shadow cast by Dante's body addresses him and proves to be Guido Guinicelli, the Italian poet.

WHILE singly thus along the rim we walk'd,
Oft the good master warn'd me, "Look thou well.
Avail it that I caution thee." The sun
Now all the western clime irradiate changed
From azure tinct to white; and, as I pass'd,
My passing shadow made the umber'd flame
Burn ruddier. At so strange a sight I mark'd
That many a spirit marvel'd on his way.

   This bred occasion first to speak of me.
"He seems," said they, "no insubstantial frame";
Then, to obtain what certainty they might,
Stretch'd toward me, careful not to overpass
The burning pale. "O thou! who followest
The others, haply not more slow than they,
But moved by reverence; answer me, who burn
In thirst and fire: nor I alone, but these
All for thine answer do more thirst, than doth
Indian or Æthiop for the cooling stream.
Tell us, how is it that thou makest thyself
A wall against the sun, as thou not yet
Into the inextricable toils of death
Hadst enter'd?" Thus spake one: and I had straight
Declared me, if attention had not turn'd
To new appearance. Meeting these, there came,
Midway the burning path, a crowd, on whom
Earnestly gazing, from each part I view
The shadows all press forward, severally
Each snatch a hasty kiss, and then away.
E'en so the emmets, 'mid their dusky troops,
Peer closely one at other, to spy out
Their mutual road perchance, and how they thrive.

[255]

THE DIVINE COMEDY

That friendly greeting parted, ere despatch
Of the first onward step, from either tribe
Loud clamor rises: those, who newly come,
Shout "Sodom and Gomorrah!" these, "The cow
Pasiphaë enter'd, that the beast she woo'd
Might rush unto her luxury." Then as cranes,
That part toward the Riphæn mountains fly,
Part toward the Lybic sands, these to avoid
The ice, and those the sun; so hasteth off
One crowd, advances the other; and resume
Their first song, weeping, and their several shout.

Again drew near my side the very same,
Who had erewhile besought me; and their looks
Mark'd eagerness to listen. I, who twice
Their will had noted, spake: "O spirits! secure,
Whene'er the time may be, of peaceful end;

"My limbs, nor crude, nor in mature old age,
Have I left yonder: here they bear me, fed
With blood, and sinew-strung. That I no more
May live in blindness, hence I tend aloft.
There is a dame on high, who wins for us
This grace, by which my mortal through your realm
I bear. But may your utmost wish soon meet
Such full fruition, that the orb of heaven,
Fullest of love, and of most ample space,
Receive you; as ye tell (upon my page
Henceforth to stand recorded) who ye are;
And what this multitude, that at your backs
Have pass'd behind us." As one, mountain-bred,
Rugged and clownish, if some city's walls
He chance to enter, round him stares agape,
Confounded and struck dumb; e'en such appear'd
Each spirit. But when rid of that amaze
(Not long the inmate of a noble heart),
He, who before had question'd, thus resumed:
"O blessed! who, for death preparing takest
Experience of our limits, in thy bark;
Their crime, who not with us proceed, was that

PURGATORY

For which, as he did triumph, Cæsar heard
The shout of 'Queen!' to taunt him. Hence their cry
Of 'Sodom!' as they parted; to rebuke
Themselves, and aid the burning by their shame.
Our sinning was Hermaphrodite: but we,
Because the law of human kind we broke,
Following like beasts our vile concupiscence,
Hence parting from them, to our own disgrace
Record the name of her, by whom the beast
In bestial tire was acted. Now our deeds
Thou know'st, and how we sinn'd. If thou by name
Wouldst haply know us, time permits not now
To tell so much, nor can I. Of myself
Learn what thou wishest. Guinicelli I;
Who having truly sorrow'd ere my last,
Already cleanse me." With such pious joy,
As the two sons upon their mother gazed
From sad Lycurgus rescued; such my joy
(Save that I more repress'd it) when I heard
From his own lips the name of him pronounced,
Who was a father to me, and to those
My betters, who have ever used the sweet
And pleasant rhymes of love. So naught I heard,
Nor spake; but long time thoughtfully I went
Gazing on him; and, only for the fire,
Approach'd not nearer. When my eyes were fed
By looking on him; with such solemn pledge,
As forces credence, I devoted me
Unto his service wholly. In reply
He thus bespake me: "What from thee I hear
Is graved so deeply on my mind, the waves
Of Lethe shall not wash it off, nor make
A whit less lively. But as now thy oath
Has seal'd the truth, declare what cause impels
That love, which both thy looks and speech bewray."

"Those dulcet lays," I answer'd; "which, as long
As of our tongue the beauty does not fade,
Shall make us love the very ink that traced them."

[257]

THE DIVINE COMEDY

"Brother!" he cried, and pointed at the shade
Before him, "there is one, whose mother speech
Doth owe to him a fairer ornament.
He in love ditties, and the tales of prose,
Without a rival stands; and let the fools
Talk on, who think the songster of Limoges
O'ertops him. Rumor and the popular voice
They look to, more than truth; and so confirm
Opinion, ere by art or reason taught.
Thus many of the elder time cried up
Guittone, giving him the prize, till truth
By strength of numbers vanquish'd. If thou own
So ample privilege, as to have gain'd
Free entrance to the cloister, whereof Christ
Is Abbot of the college; say to him
One paternoster for me, far as needs
For dwellers in this world, where power to sin
No longer tempts us." Haply to make way
For one that follow'd next, when that was said,
He vanish'd through the fire, as through the wave
A fish, that glances diving to the deep.

I, to the spirit he had shown me, drew
A little onward, and besought his name,
For which my heart, I said, kept gracious room.
He frankly thus began: "Thy courtesy
So wins on me, I have nor power nor will
To hide me. I am Arnault; and with songs,
Sorely lamenting for my folly past,
Through this ford of fire I wade, and see
The day, I hope for, smiling in my view.
I pray ye by the worth that guides ye up
Unto the summit of the scale, in time
Remember ye my sufferings." With such words
He disappear'd in the refining flame.

PURGATORY

CANTO XXVII

The fall of night hinders their further ascent, and the poet dreams of two females representing the active and contemplative life.

Now was the sun so station'd, as when first
His early radiance quivers on the heights,
Where stream'd his Maker's blood; while Libra hangs
Above Hesperian Ebro; and new fires,
Meridian, flash on Ganges' yellow tide.

So day was sinking, when the angel of God
Appear'd before us. Joy was in his mien.
Forth of the flame he stood upon the brink;
And with a voice, whose lively clearness far
Surpass'd our human, "Blessed are the pure
In heart," he sang: then near him as we came,
"Go ye not further, holy spirits!" he cried,
"Ere the fire pierce you: enter in; and list
Attentive to the song ye hear from thence."

I, when I heard his saying, was as one
Laid in the grave. My hands together clasp'd,
And upward stretching, on the fire I look'd;
And busy fancy conjured up the forms
Erewhile beheld alive consumed in flames.
The escorting spirits turn'd with gentle looks
Toward me; and the Mantuan spake: "My son,
Here torment thou mayst feel, but canst not death.
Remember thee, remember thee, if I
Safe e'en on Geryon brought thee; now I come
More near to God, wilt thou not trust me now?
Of this be sure; though in its womb that flame
A thousand years contain'd thee, from thy head
No hair should perish. If thou doubt my truth,
Approach; and with thy hands thy vesture's hem
Stretch forth, and for thyself confirm belief.

[259]

THE DIVINE COMEDY

Lay now all fear, oh! lay all fear aside.
Turn hither, and come onward undismay'd."

I still, though conscience urged, no step advanced.

When still he saw me fix'd and obstinate,
Somewhat disturb'd he cried: "Mark now, my son,
From Beatrice thou art by this wall
Divided." As at Thisbe's name the eye
Of Pyramus was open'd (when life ebb'd
Fast from his veins), and took one parting glance,
While vermeil dyed the mulberry; thus I turn'd
To my sage guide, relenting, when I heard
The name that springs for ever in my breast.

He shook his forehead; and, "How long," he said,
"Linger we now?" then smiled, as one would smile
Upon a child that eyes the fruit and yields.
Into the fire before me then he walk'd;
And Statius, who erewhile no little space
Had parted us, he pray'd to come behind.

I would have cast me into molten glass
To cool me, when I enter'd; so intense
Raged the conflagrant mass. The sire beloved,
To comfort me, as he proceeded, still
Of Beatrice talk'd. "Her eyes," saith he,
"E'en now I seem to view." From the other side
A voice, that sang, did guide us; and the voice
Following, with heedful ear, we issued forth,
There where the path led upward. "Come," we heard,
"Come, blessed of my Father." Such the sounds,
That hail'd us from within a light, which shone
So radiant, I could not endure the view.
"The sun," it added, "hastes: and evening comes.
Delay not: ere the western sky is hung
With blackness, strive ye for the pass." Our way
Upright within the rock arose, and faced
Such part of heaven, that from before my steps
The beams were shrouded of the sinking sun.

PURGATORY

Nor many stairs were overpast, when now
By fading of the shadow we perceived
The sun behind us couch'd; and ere one face
Of darkness o'er its measureless expanse
Involved the horizon, and the night her lot
Held individual, each of us had made
A stair his pallet; not that will, but power,
Had fail'd us, by the nature of that mount
Forbidden further travel. As the goats,
That late have skipt and wanton'd rapidly
Upon the craggy cliffs, ere they had ta'en
Their supper on the herb, now silent lie
And ruminate beneath the umbrage brown,
While noon-day rages; and the goatherd leans
Upon his staff, and leaning watches them:
And as the swain, that lodges out all night
In quiet by his flock, lest beast of prey
Disperse them: even so all three abode,
I as a goat, and as the shepherds they,
Close pent on either side by shelving rock.

A little glimpse of sky was seen above;
Yet by that little I beheld the stars,
In magnitude and lustre shining forth
With more than wonted glory. As I lay,
Gazing on them, and in that fit of musing
Sleep overcame me, sleep, that bringeth oft
Tidings of future hap. About the hour,
As I believe, when Venus from the east
First lighten'd on the mountain, she whose orb
Seems always glowing with the fire of love,
A lady young and beautiful, I dream'd,
Was passing o'er a lea; and, as she came,
Methought I saw her ever and anon
Bending to cull the flowers; and thus she sang:
"Know ye, whoever of my name would ask,
That I am Leah: for my brow to weave
A garland, these fair hands unwearied ply.
To please me at the crystal mirror, here
I deck me. But my sister Rachel, she

Before her glass abides the livelong day,
Her radiant eyes beholding, charm'd no less,
Than I with this delightful task. Her joy
In contemplation, as in labor mine."

And now as glimmering dawn appear'd, that breaks
More welcome to the pilgrim still, as he
Sojourns less distant on his homeward way,
Darkness from all sides fled, and with it fled
My slumber; whence I rose, and saw my guide
Already risen. "That delicious fruit,
Which through so many a branch the zealous care
Of mortals roams in quest of, shall this day
Appease thy hunger." Such the words I heard
From Virgil's lip; and never greeting heard,
So pleasant as the sounds. Within me straight
Desire so grew upon desire to mount,
Thenceforward at each step I felt the wings
Increasing for my flight. When we had run
O'er all the ladder to its topmost round,
As there we stood, on me the Mantuan fix'd
His eyes, and thus he spake: "Both fires, my son,
The temporal and eternal, thou hast seen;
And art arrived, where of itself my ken
No further reaches. I, with skill and art,
Thus far have drawn thee. Now thy pleasure take
For guide. Thou hast o'ercome the steeper way,
O'ercome the straiter. Lo! the sun, that darts
His beam upon my forehead: lo! the herb,
The arborets and flowers, which of itself
This land pours forth profuse. Till those bright eyes
With gladness come, which, weeping, made me haste
To succor thee, thou mayst or seat thee down,
Or wander where thou wilt. Expect no more
Sanction of warning voice or sign from me,
Free of thy own arbitrament to choose,
Discreet, judicious. To distrust thy sense
Were henceforth error. I invest thee then
With crown and mitre, sovereign o'er thyself."

CANTO XXVIII

*Wandering through terrestrial Paradise, Dante is stopped
by a stream on the other side of which he sees
a fair lady culling flowers.*

THROUGH that celestial forest, whose thick shade
With lively greenness the new-springing day
Attemper'd, eager now to roam, and search
Its limits round, forthwith I left the bank;
Along the champain leisurely my way
Pursuing, o'er the ground, that on all sides
Delicious odor breathed. A pleasant air,
That intermitted never, never veer'd,
Smote on my temples, gently, as a wind
Of softest influence: at which the sprays,
Obedient all, lean'd trembling to that part
Where first the holy mountain casts his shade;
Yet were not so disorder'd, but that still
Upon their top the feather'd choristers
Applied their wonted art, and with full joy
Welcomed those hours of prime, and warbled shrill
Amid the leaves, that to their jocund lays
Kept tenor; even as from branch to branch,
Along the piny forests on the shore
Of Chiassi, rolls the gathering melody,
When Eolus hath from his cavern loosed
The dripping south. Already had my steps,
Though slow, so far into that ancient wood
Transported me, I could not ken the place
Where I had enter'd; when, behold! my path
Was bounded by a rill, which, to the left,
With little rippling waters bent the grass
That issued from its brink. On earth no wave,
How clean soe'er, that would not seem to have
Some mixture in itself, compared with this,
Transpicuous clear; yet darkly on it roll'd,

Darkly beneath perpetual gloom, which ne'er
Admits or sun or moonlight there to shine.

   My feet advanced not; but my wondering eyes
Pass'd onward, o'er the streamlet, to survey
The tender may-bloom, flush'd through many a hue,
In prodigal variety: and there,
As object, rising suddenly to view,
That from our bosom every thought beside
With the rare marvel chases, I beheld
A lady all alone, who, singing, went,
And culling flower from flower, wherewith her way
Was all o'er painted. "Lady beautiful!
Thou, who (if looks, that use to speak the heart,
Are worthy of our trust), with love's own beam
Dost warm thee," thus to her my speech I framed;
"Ah! please thee hither toward the streamlet bend
Thy steps so near, that I may list thy song.
Beholding thee and this fair place, methinks,
I call to mind where wander'd and how look'd
Proserpine, in that season, when her child
The mother lost, and she the bloomy spring."

   As when a lady, turning in the dance,
Doth foot it featly, and advances scarce
One step before the other to the ground;
Over the yellow and vermilion flowers,
Thus turn'd she at my suit, most maiden-like
Veiling her sober eyes; and came so near,
That I distinctly caught the dulcet sound.
Arriving where the limpid waters now
Laved the greensward, her eyes she deign'd to raise,
That shot such splendor on me, as I ween
Ne'er glanced from Cytherea's, when her son
Had sped his keenest weapon to her heart.
Upon the opposite bank she stood and smiled;
As through her graceful fingers shifted still
The intermingling dyes, which without seed
That lofty land unbosoms. By the stream
Three paces only were we sunder'd: yet,

PURGATORY

The Hellespont, where Xerxes pass'd it o'er
(A curb for ever to the pride of man),
Was by Leander not more hateful held
For floating, with inhospitable wave,
'Twixt Sestus and Abydos, than by me
That flood, because it gave no passage thence.

"Strangers ye come; and haply in this place,
That cradled human nature in her birth,
Wondering, ye not without suspicion view
My smiles: but that sweet strain of psalmody,
'Thou, Lord! hast made me glad,' will give ye light,
Which may uncloud your minds. And thou, who stand'st
The foremost, and didst make thy suit to me,
Say if aught else thou wish to hear: for I
Came prompt to answer every doubt of thine."

She spake; and I replied: "I know not how
To reconcile this wave, and rustling sound
Of forest leaves, with what I late have heard
Of opposite report." She answering thus:
"I will unfold the cause, whence that proceeds,
Which makes thee wonder; and so purge the cloud
That hath enwrapt thee. The First Good, whose joy
Is only in himself, created man,
For happiness; and gave this goodly place,
His pledge and earnest of eternal peace.
Favor'd thus highly, through his own defect
He fell; and here made short sojourn; he fell,
And, for the bitterness of sorrow changed
Laughter unblamed and ever-new delight.
That vapors none, exhaled from earth beneath,
Or from the waters (which, wherever heat
Attracts them, follow), might ascend thus far
To vex man's peaceful state, this mountain rose
So high toward the heaven, nor fears the rage
Of elements contending; from that part
Exempted, where the gate his limit bars.
Because the circumambient air, throughout,
With its first impulse circles still, unless

[265]

Aught interpose to check or thwart its course;
Upon the summit, which on every side
To visitation of the impassive air
Is open, doth that motion strike, and makes
Beneath its sway the umbrageous wood resound:
And in the shaken plant such power resides,
That it impregnates with its efficacy
The voyaging breeze, upon whose subtle plume
That, wafted, flies abroad; and the other land,
Receiving (as 'tis worthy in itself,
Or in the clime, that warms it), doth conceive;
And from its womb produces many a tree
Of various virtue. This when thou hast heard,
The marvel ceases, if in yonder earth
Some plant, without apparent seed, be found
To fix its fibrous stem. And further learn,
That with prolific foison of all seeds
This holy plain is fill'd, and in itself
Bears fruit that ne'er was pluck'd on other soil.

"The water, thou behold'st, springs not from vein,
Restored by vapor, that the cold converts;
As stream that intermittently repairs
And spends his pulse of life; but issues forth
From fountain, solid, undecaying, sure:
And, by the will omnific, full supply
Feeds whatsoe'er on either side it pours;
On this, devolved with power to take away
Remembrance of offence; on that, to bring
Remembrance back of every good deed done.
From whence its name of Lethe on this part;
On the other, Eunoë: both of which must first
Be tasted, ere it work; the last exceeding
All flavors else. Albeit thy thirst may now
Be well contented, if I here break off,
No more revealing; yet a corollary
I freely give beside: nor deem my words
Less grateful to thee, if they somewhat pass
The stretch of promise. They, whose verse of yore
The golden age recorded and its bliss,

On the Parnassian mountain, of this place
Perhaps had dream'd. Here was man guiltless; here
Perpetual spring, and every fruit; and this
The far-famed nectar." Turning to the bards,
When she had ceased, I noted in their looks
A smile at her conclusion; then my face
Again directed to the lovely dame.

CANTO XXIX

*The lady moves along the side of the stream and Dante
keeps pace with her on the opposite bank.*

Singing, as if enamor'd, she resumed
And closed the song, with "Blessed they whose sins
Are cover'd." Like the wood-nymphs then, that tripp'd
Singly across the sylvan shadows; one
Eager to view, and one to escape the sun;
So moved she on, against the current, up
The verdant rivage. I, her mincing step
Observing, with as tardy step pursued.

Between us not an hundred paces trod,
The bank, on each side bending equally,
Gave me to face the orient. Nor our way
Far onward brought us, when to me at once
She turn'd, and cried: "My brother! look, and hearken."
And lo! a sudden lustre ran across
Through the great forest on all parts, so bright,
I doubted whether lightning were abroad;
But that, expiring ever in the spleen
That doth unfold it, and this during still,
And waxing still in splendor, made me question
What it might be: and a sweet melody
Ran through the luminous air. Then did I chide,
With warrantable zeal, the hardihood
Of our first parent; for that there, where earth
Stood in obedience to the heavens, she only,

THE DIVINE COMEDY

Woman, the creature of an hour, endured not
Restraint of any veil, which had she borne
Devoutly, joys, ineffable as these,
Had from the first, and long time since, been mine.

    While, through that wilderness of primy sweets
That never fade, suspense I walk'd, and yet
Expectant of beatitude more high;
Before us, like a blazing fire, the air
Under the green boughs glow'd; and, for a song,
Distinct the sound of melody was heard.

    O ye thrice holy virgins! for your sakes
If e'er I suffer'd hunger, cold, and watching,
Occasion calls on me to crave your bounty.
Now through my breast let Helicon his stream
Pour copious, and Urania with her choir
Arise to aid me; while the verse unfolds
Things, that do almost mock the grasp of thought.

    Onward a space, what seem'd seven trees of gold
The intervening distance to mine eye
Falsely presented; but, when I was come
So near them, that no lineament was lost
Of those, with which a doubtful object, seen
Remotely, plays on the misdeeming sense;
Then did the faculty, that ministers
Discourse to reason, these for tapers of gold
Distinguish; and i' the singing trace the sound
"Hosanna!" Above, their beauteous garniture
Flamed with more ample lustre, than the moon
Through cloudless sky at midnight, in her noon.

    I turn'd me, full of wonder, to my guide;
And he did answer with a countenance
Charged with no less amazement: whence my view
Reverted to those lofty things, which came
So slowly moving toward us, that the bride
Would have outstript them on her bridal day.

PURGATORY

The lady call'd aloud: "Why thus yet burns
Affection in thee for these living lights,
And dost not look on that which follows them?"

I straightway mark'd a tribe behind them walk,
As if attendant on their leaders, clothed
With raiment of such whiteness, as on earth
Was never. On my left, the watery gleam
Borrow'd, and gave me back, when there I look'd,
As in a mirror, my left side portray'd.

When I had chosen on the river's edge
Such station, that the distance of the stream
Alone did separate me; there I stay'd
My steps for clearer prospect, and beheld
The flames go onward, leaving, as they went,
The air behind them painted as with trail
Of liveliest pencils; so distinct were mark'd
All those seven listed colors, whence the sun
Maketh his bow, and Cynthia her zone.
These streaming gonfalons did flow beyond
My vision; and ten paces, as I guess,
Parted the outermost. Beneath a sky
So beautiful, came four and twenty elders,
By two and two, with flower-de-luces crown'd.
All sang one song: "Blessed be thou among
The daughters of Adam! and thy loveliness
Blessed forever!" After that the flowers,
And the fresh herblets, on the opposite brink,
Were free from that elected race; as light
In heaven doth second light, came after them
Four animals, each crown'd with verdurous leaf.
With six wings each was plumed; the plumage full
Of eyes; and the eyes of Argus would be such,
Were they endued with life. Reader! more rhymes
I will not waste in shadowing forth their form:
For other need so straitens, that in this
I may not give my bounty room. But read
Ezekiel; for he paints them, from the north
How he beheld them come by Chebar's flood,

THE DIVINE COMEDY

In whirlwind, cloud, and fire; and even such
As thou shalt find them character'd by him,
Here were they; save as to the pennons: there,
From him departing, John accords with me.

The space, surrounded by the four, enclosed
A car triumphal: on two wheels it came,
Drawn at a Gryphon's neck; and he above
Stretch'd either wing uplifted, 'tween the midst
And the three listed hues, on each side, three;
So that the wings did cleave or injure none;
And out of sight they rose. The members, far
As he was bird, were golden; white the rest,
With vermeil intervein'd. So beautiful
A car, in Rome, ne'er graced Augustus' pomp,
Or Africanus': e'en the sun's itself
Were poor to this; that chariot of the sun,
Erroneous, which in blazing ruin fell
At Tellus' prayer devout, by the just doom

PURGATORY

Mysterious of all-seeing Jove. Three nymphs,
At the right wheel, came circling in smooth dance:
The one so ruddy, that her form had scarce
Been known within a furnace of clear flame;
The next did look, as if the flesh and bones
Were emerald; snow new-fallen seem'd the third.
Now seem'd the white to lead, the ruddy now;
And from her song who led, the others took
Their measure, swift or slow. At the other wheel,
A band quaternion, each in purple clad,
Advanced with festal step, as, of them, one
The rest conducted; one, upon whose front
Three eyes were seen. In rear of all this group,
Two old men I beheld, dissimilar
In raiment, but in port and gesture like,
Solid and mainly grave; of whom, the one
Did show himself some favor'd counsellor
Of the great Coan, him, whom nature made
To serve the costliest creature of her tribe:
His fellow mark'd an opposite intent;
Bearing a sword, whose glitterance and keen edge,
E'en as I viewed it with the flood between,
Appall'd me. Next, four others I beheld
Of humble seeming; and, behind them all,
One single old man, sleeping as he came,
With a shrewd visage. And these seven, each
Like the first troop were habited; but wore
No braid of lilies on their temples wreathed.
Rather, with roses and each vermeil flower,
A sight, but little distant, might have sworn,
That they were all on fire above their brow.

When as the car was o'er against me, straight
Was heard a thundering, at whose voice it seem'd
The chosen multitude were stay'd; for there,
With the first ensigns, made they solemn halt.

THE DIVINE COMEDY

CANTO XXX

Beatrice descends from heaven and rebukes the poet.

SOON as that polar light, fair ornament
Of the first heaven, which hath never known
Setting nor rising, nor the shadowy veil
Of other cloud than sin, to duty there
Each one convoying, as that lower doth
The steersman to his port, stood firmly fix'd;
Forthwith the saintly tribe, who in the van
Between the Gryphon and its radiance came,
Did turn them to the car, as to their rest:
And one, as if commission'd from above,
In holy chant thrice shouted forth aloud;
"Come, spouse! from Libanus": and all the rest
Took up the song.—At the last audit, so
The blest shall rise, from forth his cavern each
Uplifting lightly his new-vested flesh;
As, on the sacred litter, at the voice
Authoritative of that elder, sprang
A hundred ministers and messengers
Of life eternal. "Blessed thou, who comest!"
And, "Oh!" they cried, "from full hands scatter ye
Unwithering lilies": and, so saying, cast
Flowers over head and round them on all sides.

I have beheld, ere now, at break of day,
The eastern clime all roseate; and the sky
Opposed, one deep and beautiful serene;
And the sun's face so shaded, and with mists
Attemper'd, at his rising, that the eye
Long while endured the sight: thus, in a cloud
Of flowers, that from those hands angelic rose,
And down within and outside of the car
Fell showering, in white veil with olive wreathed,
A virgin in my view appear'd, beneath
Green mantle, robed in hue of living flame:

[272]

PURGATORY

And o'er my spirit, that so long a time
Had from her presence felt no shuddering dread,
Albeit mine eyes discern'd her not, there moved
A hidden virtue from her, at whose touch
The power of ancient love was strong within me.

No sooner on my vision streaming, smote
The heavenly influence, which, years past, and e'en
In childhood, thrill'd me, than toward Virgil I
Turn'd me to leftward; panting, like a babe,
That flees for refuge to his mother's breast,
If aught have terrified or work'd him woe:
And would have cried, "There is no dram of blood,
That doth not quiver in me. The old flame
Throws out clear tokens of reviving fire."
But Virgil had bereaved us of himself;
Virgil, my best-beloved father; Virgil, he
To whom I gave me up for safety: nor
All, our prime mother lost, avail'd to save
My undew'd cheeks from blur of soiling tears.

"Dante! weep not that Virgil leaves thee; nay,
Weep thou not yet: behoves thee feel the edge
Of other sword; and thou shalt weep for that."

As to the prow or stern, some admiral
Paces the deck, inspiriting his crew,
When 'mid the sail-yards all hands ply aloof;
Thus, on the left side of the car, I saw
(Turning me at the sound of mine own name,
Which here I am compell'd to register)
The virgin station'd, who before appear'd
Veil'd in that festive shower angelical.

Toward me, across the stream, she bent her eyes;
Though from her brow the veil descending, bound
With foliage of Minerva, suffer'd not
That I beheld her clearly: then with act
Full royal, still insulting o'er her thrall,
Added, as one who, speaking, keepeth back

THE DIVINE COMEDY

The bitterest saying, to conclude the speech:
"Observe me well. I am, in sooth, I am
Beatrice. What! and hast thou deign'd at last
Approach the mountain? Knewest not, O man!
Thy happiness is here?" Down fell mine eyes
On the clear fount; but there, myself espying,
Recoil'd, and sought the greensward; such a weight
Of shame was on my forehead. With a mien
Of that stern majesty, which doth surround
A mother's presence to her awe-struck child,
She look'd; a flavor of such bitterness
Was mingled in her pity. There her words
Brake off; and suddenly the angels sang,
"In thee, O gracious Lord! my hope hath been":
But went no further than, "Thou, Lord! hast set
My feet in ample room." As snow, that lies,
Amidst the living rafters on the back
Of Italy, congeal'd, when drifted high
And closely piled by rough Sclavonian blasts;
Breathe but the land whereon no shadow falls,
And straightway melting it distils away,
Like a fire-wasted taper: thus was I,
Without a sigh or tear, or ever these
Did sing, that, with the chiming of heaven's sphere,
Still in their warbling chime: but when the strain
Of dulcet symphony express'd for me
Their soft compassion, more than could the words,
"Virgin! why so consumest him?" then, the ice
Congeal'd about my bosom, turn'd itself
To spirit and water; and with anguish forth
Gush'd, through the lips and eyelids, from the heart.

Upon the chariot's same edge still she stood,
Immovable; and thus address'd her words
To those bright semblances with pity touch'd:
"Ye in the eternal day your vigils keep;
So that nor night nor slumber, with close stealth,
Conveys from you a single step, in all
The goings on of time: thence, with more heed
I shape mine answer, for his ear intended,

PURGATORY

Who there stands weeping; that the sorrow now
May equal the transgression. Not alone
Through operation of the mighty orbs,
That mark each seed to some predestined aim,
As with aspect or fortunate or ill
The constellations meet; but through benign
Largess of heavenly graces, which rain down
From such a height as mocks our vision, this man
Was, in the freshness of his being, such,
So gifted virtually, that in him
All better habits wonderously had thrived.
The more of kindly strength is in the soil,
So much doth evil seed and lack of culture
Mar it the more, and make it run to wildness.
These looks sometime upheld him; for I show'd
My youthful eyes, and led him by their light
In upright walking. Soon as I had reach'd
The threshold of my second age, and changed
My mortal for immortal; then he left me,
And gave himself to others. When from flesh
To spirit I had risen, and increase
Of beauty and of virtue circled me,
I was less dear to him, and valued less.
His steps were turn'd into deceitful ways,
Following false images of good, that make
No promise perfect. Nor avail'd me aught
To sue for inspirations, with the which,
I, both in dreams of night, and otherwise,
Did call him back; of them, so little reck'd him.
Such depth he fell, that all device was short
Of his preserving, save that he should view
The children of perdition. To this end
I visited the purlieus of the dead:
And one, who hath conducted him thus high,
Received my supplications urged with weeping.
It were a breaking of God's high decree,
If Lethe should be pass'd, and such food tasted,
Without the cost of some repentant tear."

CANTO XXXI

Dante confesses his error, is drawn through the waters of Lethe, and then presented to the four virgins personifying the cardinal virtues and to the Gryffon, a symbol of our Saviour.

"O THOU!" her words she thus without delay
Resuming, turn'd their point on me, to whom
They, with but lateral edge, seem'd harsh before:
"Say thou, who stand'st beyond the holy stream,
If this be true. A charge, so grievous, needs
Thine own avowal." On my faculty
Such strange amazement hung, the voice expired
Imperfect, ere its organs gave it birth.

A little space refraining, then she spake:
"What dost thou muse on? Answer me. The wave
On thy remembrances of evil yet
Hath done no injury." A mingled sense
Of fear and of confusion, from my lips
Did such a "Yea" produce, as needed help
Of vision to interpret. As when breaks,
In act to be discharged, a cross-bow bent
Beyond its pitch, both nerve and bow o'erstretch'd;
The flagging weapon feebly hits the mark:
Thus, tears and sighs forth gushing, did I burst,
Beneath the heavy load: and thus my voice
Was slacken'd on its way. She straight began:
"When my desire invited thee to love
The good, which sets a bound to our aspirings;
What bar of thwarting foss or linked chain
Did meet thee, that thou so shouldst quit the hope
Of further progress? or what a bait of ease,
Or promise of allurement, led thee on
Elsewhere, that thou elsewhere shouldst rather wait?"

PURGATORY

A bitter sigh I drew, then scarce found voice
To answer; hardly to these sounds my lips
Gave utterance, wailing: "Thy fair looks withdrawn,
Things present, with deceitful pleasures, turn'd
My steps aside." She answering spake: "Hadst thou
Been silent, or denied what thou avow'st,
Thou hadst not hid thy sin the more; such eye
Observes it. But whene'er the sinner's cheek
Breaks forth into the precious-streaming tears
Of self-accusing, in our court the wheel
Of justice doth run counter to the edge.
Howe'er, that thou mayst profit by the shame
For errors past, and that henceforth more strength
May arm thee, when thou hear'st the Siren-voice;
Lay thou aside the motive to this grief,
And lend attentive ear, while I unfold
How opposite a way my buried flesh
Should have impell'd thee. Never didst thou spy,
In art or nature, aught so passing sweet,
As were the limbs that in their beauteous frame
Enclosed me, and are scatter'd now in dust.
If sweetest thing thus fail'd thee with my death,
What, afterward, of mortal, should thy wish
Have tempted? When thou first hadst felt the dart
Of perishable things, in my departing
For better realms, thy wing thou shouldst have pruned
To follow me; and never stoop'd again,
To 'bide a second blow, for a slight girl,
Or other gaud as transient and as vain.
The new and inexperienced bird awaits,
Twice it may be, or thrice, the fowler's aim;
But in the sight of one whose plumes are full,
In vain the net is spread, the arrow wing'd."

I stood, as children silent and ashamed
Stand, listening, with their eyes upon the earth,
Acknowledging their fault, and self-condemn'd.
And she resumed: "If, but to hear, thus pains thee;
Raise thou thy beard, and lo! what sight shall do."

With less reluctance yields a sturdy holm,
Rent from its fibres by a blast, that blows
From off the pole, or from Iarbas' land,
Than I at her behest my visage raised:
And thus the face denoting by the beard,
I mark'd the secret sting her words convey'd.

No sooner lifted I mine aspect up,
Than I perceived those primal creatures cease
Their flowery sprinkling; and mine eyes beheld
(Yet unassured and wavering in their view)
Beatrice; she, who toward the mystic shape,
That joins two natures in one form, had turn'd:
And, even under shadow of her veil,
And parted by the verdant rill that flow'd
Between, in loveliness she seem'd as much
Her former self surpassing, as on earth
All others she surpass'd. Remorseful goads
Shot sudden through me. Each thing else, the more
Its love had late beguiled me, now the more
Was loathsome. On my heart so keenly smote
The bitter consciousness, that on the ground
O'erpower'd I fell: and what my state was then,
She knows, who was the cause. When now my strength
Flow'd back, returning outward from the heart,
The lady, whom alone I first had seen,
I found above me. "Loose me not," she cried:
"Loose not thy hold": and lo! had dragg'd me high
As to my neck into the stream; while she,
Still as she drew me after, swept along,
Swift as a shuttle, bounding o'er the wave.

The blessed shore approaching, then was heard
So sweetly, "*Tu asperges me*," that I
May not remember, much less tell the sound.

The beauteous dame, her arms expanding, clasp'd
My temples, and immerged me where 'twas fit
The wave should drench me: and, thence raising up,
Within the fourhold dance of lovely nymphs

PURGATORY

Presented me so laved; and with their arm
They each did cover me. "Here are we nymphs,
And in the heaven are stars. Or ever earth
Was visited of Beatrice, we,
Appointed for her handmaids, tended on her.
We to her eyes will lead thee: but the light
Of gladness, that is in them, well to scan,
Those yonder three, of deeper ken than ours,
Thy sight shall quicken." Thus began their song:
And then they led me to the Gryphon's breast,
Where, turn'd toward us, Beatrice stood.
"Spare not thy vision. We have station'd thee
Before the emeralds, whence love, erewhile,
Hath drawn his weapons on thee." As they spake,
A thousand fervent wishes riveted
Mine eyes upon her beaming eyes, that stood,
Still fix'd toward the Gryphon, motionless.
As the sun strikes a mirror, even thus
Within those orbs the twifold being shone;
Forever varying, in one figure now
Reflected, now in other. Reader! muse
How wondrous in my sight it seem'd, to mark
A thing, albeit steadfast in itself,
Yet in its imaged semblance mutable.

Full of amaze, and joyous, while my soul
Fed on the viand, whereof still desire
Grows with satiety; the other three,
With gesture that declared a loftier line,
Advanced: to their own carol, on they came
Dancing, in festive ring angelical.

"Turn, Beatrice!" was their song: "Oh! turn
Thy saintly sight on this thy faithful one,
Who, to behold thee, many a wearisome pace
Hath measured. Gracious at our prayer, vouchsafe
Unveiled to him thy cheeks; that he may mark
Thy second beauty, now conceal'd." O splendor!
O sacred light eternal! who is he,
So pale with musing in Pierian shades,

[279]

THE DIVINE COMEDY

Or with that fount so lavishly imbued,
Whose spirit should not fail him in the essay
To represent thee such as thou didst seem,
When under cope of the still-chiming heaven
Thou gavest to open air thy charms reveal'd?

CANTO XXXII

The procession moves on, accompanied by Matilda, Statius and Dante, until it reaches an exceedingly lofty tree.

MINE eyes with such an eager coveting
Were bent to rid them of their ten years' thirst,
No other sense was waking: and e'en they
Were fenced on either side from heed of aught;
So tangled, in its custom'd toils, that smile
Of saintly brightness drew me to itself:
When forcibly, toward the left, my sight
The sacred virgins turn'd; for from their lips
I heard the warning sounds: "Too fix'd a gaze!"

Awhile my vision labor'd; as when late
Upon the o'erstrained eyes the sun hath smote:
But soon, to lesser object, as the view
Was now recover'd (lesser in respect
To that excess of sensible, whence late
I had perforce been sunder'd), on their right
I mark'd that glorious army wheel, and turn,
Against the sun and sevenfold lights, their front.
As when, their bucklers for protection raised,
A well-ranged troop, with portly banners curl'd,
Wheel circling, ere the whole can change their ground,
E'en thus the goodly regiment of heaven,
Proceeding, all did pass us ere the car
Had sloped his beam. Attendant at the wheels
The damsels turn'd; and on the Gryphon moved
The sacred burden, with a pace so smooth,
No feather on him trembled. The fair dame,
Who through the wave had drawn me, companied

[280]

PURGATORY

By Statius and myself, pursued the wheel,
Whose orbit, rolling, mark'd a lesser arch.

   Through the high wood, now void (the more her blame,
Who by the serpent was beguiled) I pass'd,
With step in cadence to the harmony
Angelic. Onward had we moved, as far,
Perchance, as arrow at three several flights
Full wing'd had sped, when from her station down
Descended Beatrice. With one voice
All murmur'd "Adam"; circling next a plant
Despoil'd of flowers and leaf, on every bough.
Its tresses, spreading more as more they rose,
Were such, as 'midst their forest wilds, for height,
The Indians might have gazed at. "Blessed thou,
Gryphon! whose beak hath never pluck'd that tree
Pleasant to taste: for hence the appetite
Was warp'd to evil." Round the stately trunk
Thus shouted forth the rest, to whom return'd
The animal twice-gender'd: "Yea! for so
The generation of the just are saved."
And turning to the chariot-pole, to foot
He drew it of the widow'd branch, and bound
There, left unto the stock whereon it grew.

   As when large floods of radiance from above
Stream, with that radiance mingled, which ascends
Next after setting of the scaly sign,
Our plants then bourgeon, and each wears anew
His wonted colors, ere the sun have yoked
Beneath another star his flamy steeds;
Thus putting forth a hue more faint than rose,
And deeper than the violet, was renew'd
The plant, erewhile in all its branches bare.
Unearthly was the hymn, which then arose.
I understood it not, nor to the end
Endured the harmony. Had I the skill
To pencil forth how closed the unpitying eyes
Slumbering, when Syrinx warbled (eyes that paid
So dearly for their watching), then, like painter,

[281]

That with a model paints, I might design
The manner of my falling into sleep.
But feign who will the slumber cunningly,
I pass it by to when I waked; and tell,
How suddenly a flash of splendor rent
The curtain of my sleep, and one cries out,
"Arise: what dost thou?" As the chosen three,
On Tabor's mount, admitted to behold
The blossoming of that fair tree, whose fruit
Is coveted of angels, and doth make
Perpetual feast in Heaven; to themselves
Returning, at the word whence deeper sleeps
Were broken, they their tribe diminish'd saw;
Both Moses and Elias gone, and changed
The stole their master wore; thus to myself
Returning, over me beheld I stand
The piteous one, who cross the stream had brought
My steps. "And where," all doubting, I exclaim'd,
"Is Beatrice?" "See her," she replied,
"Beneath the fresh leaf, seated on its root.
Behold the associate quire that circles her.
The others, with a melody more sweet
And more profound, journeying to higher realms,
Upon the Gryphon tend." If there her words
Were closed, I know not; but mine eyes had now
Ta'en view of her, by whom all other thoughts
Were barr'd admittance. On the very ground
Alone she sat, as she had there been left
A guard upon the wain, which I beheld
Bound the twiform beast. The seven nymphs
Did make themselves a cloister round about her;
And, in their hands, upheld those lights secure
From blast septentrion and the gusty south.

"A little while thou shalt be forester here;
And citizen shalt be, forever with me,
Of that true Rome, wherein Christ dwells a Roman.
To profit the misguided world, keep now
Thine eyes upon the car; and what thou seest,
Take heed thou write, returning to that place."

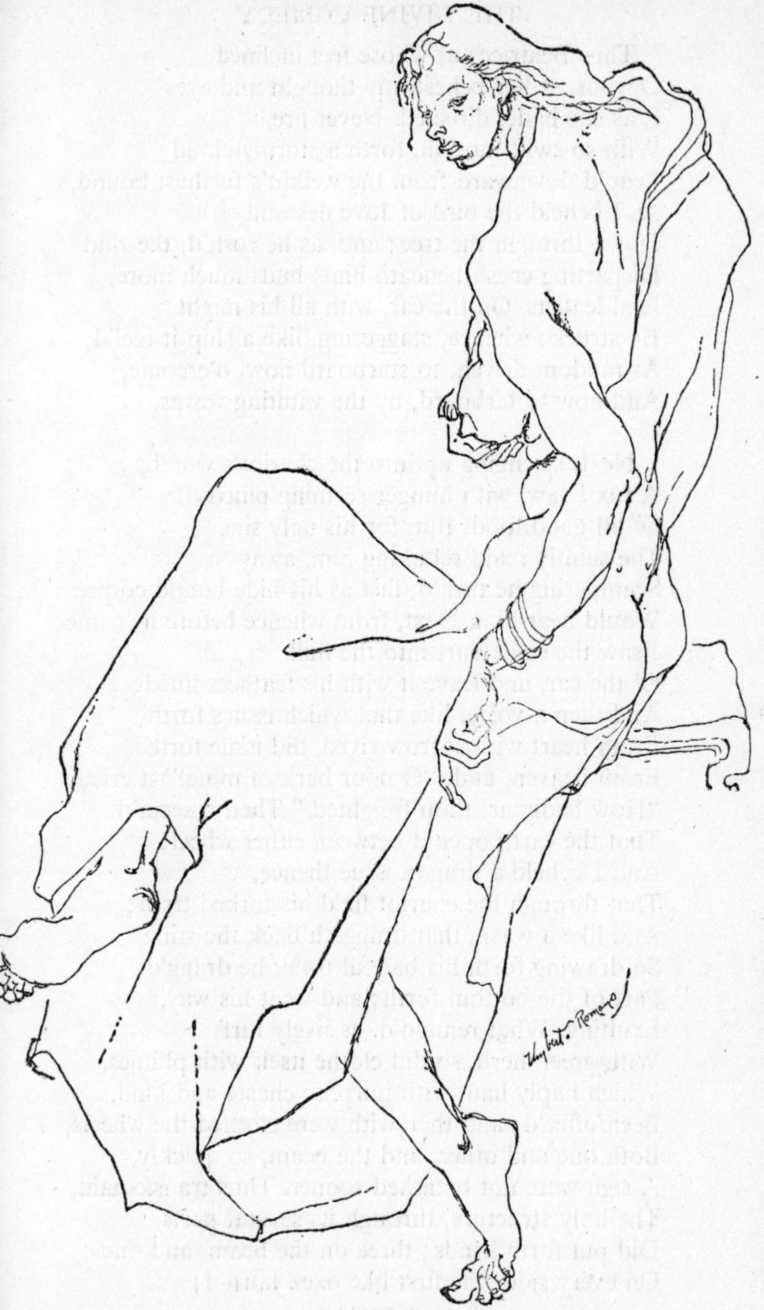

THE DIVINE COMEDY

Thus Beatrice: at whose feet inclined
Devout, at her behest, my thought and eyes
I, as she bade, directed. Never fire,
With so swift motion, forth a stormy cloud
Leap'd downward from the welkin's furthest bound,
As I beheld the bird of Jove descend
Down through the tree; and, as he rush'd, the rind
Disparting crush beneath him; buds much more,
And leaflets. On the car, with all his might
He struck; whence, staggering, like a ship it reel'd,
At random driven, to starboard now, o'ercome,
And now to larboard, by the vaulting waves.

Next, springing up into the chariot's womb,
A fox I saw, with hunger seeming pined
Of all good food. But, for his ugly sins
The saintly maid rebuking him, away
Scampering he turn'd, fast as his hide-bound corpse
Would bear him. Next, from whence before he came,
I saw the eagle dart into the hull
O' the car, and leave it with his feathers lined:
And then a voice, like that which issues forth
From heart with sorrow rived, did issue forth
From heaven, and, "O poor bark of mine!" it cried,
"How badly art thou freighted." Then it seem'd
That the earth open'd between either wheel;
And I beheld a dragon issue thence,
That through the chariot fix'd his forked train;
And like a wasp, that draggeth back the sting,
So drawing forth his baleful train, he dragg'd
Part of the bottom forth; and went his way,
Exulting. What remain'd, as lively turf
With green herb, so did clothe itself with plumes,
Which haply had, with purpose chaste and kind,
Been offer'd; and therewith were clothed the wheels,
Both one and other, and the beam, so quickly,
A sigh were not breathed sooner. Thus transform'd,
The holy structure, through its several parts,
Did put forth heads; three on the beam, and one
On every side: the first like oxen horn'd;

PURGATORY

But with a single horn upon their front,
The four. Like monster, sight hath never seen.
O'er it methought there sat, secure as rock
On mountain's lofty top, a shameless whore,
Whose ken roved loosely round her. At her side,
As 'twere that none might bear her off, I saw
A giant stand; and ever and anon
They mingled kisses. But, her lustful eyes
Chancing on me to wander, that fell minion
Scourged her from head to foot all o'er; then full
Of jealousy, and fierce with rage, unloosed
The monster, and dragg'd on, so far across
The forest, that from me its shades alone
Shielded the harlot and the new-form'd brute.

CANTO XXXIII

After the singing of a hymn, Beatrice and the whole band proceed to the fountain which is the source of Lethe and Eunoë.

"THE heathen, Lord! are come": responsive thus,
The trinal now, and now the virgin band
Quaternion, their sweet psalmody began,
Weeping; and Beatrice listen'd, sad
And sighing, to the song, in such a mood,
That Mary, as she stood beside the cross,
Was scarce more changed. But when they gave her place
To speak, then, risen upright on her feet,
She, with a color glowing bright as fire,
Did answer: "Yet a little while, and ye
Shall see me not; and, my beloved sisters!
Again a little while, and ye shall see me."

Before her then she marshal'd all the seven;
And, beckoning only, motion'd me, the dame,
And that remaining sage, to follow her.

[285]

THE DIVINE COMEDY

So on she pass'd; and had not set, I ween,
Her tenth step to the ground, when, with mine eyes,
Her eyes encountered; and, with visage mild,
"So mend thy pace," she cried, "that if my words
Address thee, thou mayst still be aptly placed
To hear them." Soon as duly to her side
I now had hasten'd: "Brother!" she began,
"Why makest thou no attempt at questioning,
As thus we walk together?" Like to those
Who, speaking with too reverent an awe
Before their betters, draw not forth the voice
Alive unto their lips, befell me then
That I in sounds imperfect thus began:
"Lady! what I have need of, that thou know'st;
And what will suit my need." She answering thus:
"Of fearfulness and shame, I will that thou
Henceforth do rid thee; that thou speak no more,
As one who dreams. Thus far be taught of me:
The vessel which thou saw'st the serpent break,
Was, and is not: let him, who hath the blame,
Hope not to scare God's vengeance with a sop.
Without an heir forever shall not be
That eagle, he, who left the chariot plumed,
Which monster made it first and next a prey.
Plainly I view, and therefore speak, the stars
E'en now approaching, whose conjunction, free
From all impediment and bar, brings on
A season, in the which, one sent from God
(Five hundred, five, and ten, do mark him out),
That foul one, and the accomplice of her guilt,
The giant, both, shall slay. And if perchance
My saying, dark as Themis or as Sphinx,
Fail to persuade thee (since like them it foils
The intellect with blindness), yet erelong
Events shall be the Naïads, that will solve
This knotty riddle; and no damage light
On flock or field. Take heed; and as these words
By me are utter'd, teach them even so
To those who live that life, which is a race
To death: and when thou writest them, keep in mind

PURGATORY

Not to conceal how thou hast seen the plant,
That twice hath now been spoil'd. This whoso robs,
This whoso plucks, with blasphemy of deed
Sins against God, who for his use alone
Creating hallow'd it. For taste of this,
In pain and in desire, five thousand years
And upward, the first soul did yearn for him
Who punish'd in himself the fatal gust.

"Thy reason slumbers, if it deem this height,
And summit thus inverted, of the plant,
Without due cause: and were not vainer thoughts,
As Elsa's numbing waters, to thy soul,
And their fond pleasures had not dyed it dark
As Pyramus the mulberry; thou hadst seen,
In such momentous circumstance alone,
God's equal justice morally implied
In the forbidden tree. But since I mark thee,
In understanding, harden'd into stone,
And, to that hardness, spotted too and stain'd,
So that thine eye is dazzled at my word;
I will, that, if not written, yet at least
Painted thou take it in thee, for the cause,
That one brings home his staff inwreathed with palm."

I thus: "As wax by seal, that changeth not
Its impress, now is stamp'd my brain by thee.
But wherefore soars thy wish'd-for speech so high
Beyond my sight, that loses it the more,
The more it strains to reach it?" "To the end
That thou mayst know," she answer'd straight, "the school,
That thou hast follow'd; and how far behind,
When following my discourse, its learning halts:
And mayst behold your art, from the divine
As distant, as the disagreement is
'Twixt earth and heaven's most high and rapturous orb."

"I not remember," I replied, "that e'er
I was estranged from thee; nor for such fault
Doth conscience chide me." Smiling she return'd:

[287]

THE DIVINE COMEDY

"If thou canst not remember, call to mind
How lately thou hast drunk of Lethe's wave;
And, sure as smoke doth indicate a flame,
In that forgetfulness itself conclude
Blame from thy alienated will incurr'd.
From henceforth, verily, my words shall be
As naked, as will suit them to appear
In thy unpractised view." More sparkling now,
And with retarded course, the sun possess'd
The circle of mid-day, that varies still
As the aspect varies of each several clime;
When, as one, sent in vaward of a troop
For escort, pauses, if perchance he spy
Vestige of somewhat strange and rare; so paused
The sevenfold band, arriving at the verge
Of a dun umbrage hoar, such as is seen,
Beneath green leaves and gloomy branches, oft
To overbrow a bleak and Alpine cliff.
And, where they stood, before them, as it seem'd,
I, Tigris and Euphrates both, beheld
Forth from one fountain issue; and, like friends,
Linger at parting. "O enlightening beam!
O glory of our kind! beseech thee say
What water this, which, from one source derived,
Itself removes to distance from itself?"

To such entreaty answer thus was made:
"Entreat Matilda, that she teach thee this."

And here, as one who clears himself of blame
Imputed, the fair dame return'd: "Of me
He this and more hath learnt; and I am safe
That Lethe's water hath not hid it from him."

And Beatrice: "Some more pressing care,
That oft the memory 'reaves, perchance hath made
His mind's eye dark. But lo, where Eunoë flows!
Lead thither; and, as thou art wont, revive
His fainting virtue." As a courteous spirit,
That proffers no excuses, but as soon

PURGATORY

As he hath token of another's will,
Makes it his own; when she had ta'en me, thus
The lovely maiden moved her on, and call'd
To Statius, with an air most lady-like:
"Come thou with him." Were further space allow'd,
Then, Reader! might I sing, though but in part,
That beverage, with whose sweetness I had ne'er
Been sated. But, since all the leaves are full,
Appointed for this second strain, mine art
With warning bridle checks me. I return'd
From the most holy wave, regenerate,
E'en as new plants renew'd with foliage new,
Pure and made apt for mounting to the stars.

Paradise

CANTO I

The poet ascends with Beatrice towards the first heaven, and is resolved of certain doubts he entertains.

His glory, by whose might all things are moved,
Pierces the universe, and in one part
Sheds more resplendence, elsewhere less. In Heaven,
That largeliest of his light partakes, was I,
Witness of things, which, to relate again,
Surpasseth power of him who comes from thence;
For that, so near approaching its desire,
Our intellect is to such depth absorb'd,
That memory cannot follow. Nathless all,
That in my thoughts I of that sacred realm
Could store, shall now be matter of my song.
Benign Apollo! this last labor aid;
And make me such a vessel of thy worth,
As thy own laurel claims, of me beloved.
Thus far hath one of steep Parnassus' brows
Sufficed me; henceforth, there is need of both
For my remaining enterprise. Do thou
Enter into my bosom, and there breathe
So, as when Marsyas by thy hand was dragg'd
Forth from his limbs, unsheathed. O power divine!
If thou to me of thine impart so much,
That of that happy realm the shadow'd form
Traced in my thoughts I may set forth to view;
Thou shalt behold me of thy favor'd tree,
Come to the foot, and crown myself with leaves:

THE DIVINE COMEDY

For to that honor thou, and my high theme
Will fit me. If but seldom, mighty Sire!
To grace his triumph, gathers thence a wreath
Cæsar, or bard (more shame for human wills
Depraved), joy to the Delphic god must spring
From the Peneian foliage, when one breast
Is with such thirst inspired. From a small spark
Great flame hath risen: after me, perchance,
Others with better voice may pray, and gain,
From the Cyrrhæan city, answer kind.

Through divers passages, the world's bright lamp
Rises to mortals; but through that which joins
Four circles with the threefold cross, in best
Course, and in happiest constellation set,
He comes; and, to the worldly wax, best gives
Its temper and impression. Morning there,
Here eve was well-nigh by such passage made;
And whiteness had o'erspread that hemisphere,
Blackness the other part; when to the left
I saw Beatrice turn'd, and on the sun
Gazing, as never eagle fix'd his ken.
As from the first a second beam is wont
To issue, and reflected upward rise,
Even as a pilgrim bent on his return;
So of her act, that through the eyesight pass'd
Into my fancy, mine was form'd: and straight,
Beyond our mortal wont, I fix'd mine eyes
Upon the sun. Much is allow'd us there,
That here exceeds our power; thanks to the place
Made for the dwelling of the human kind.

I suffer'd it not long; and yet so long,
That I beheld it bickering sparks around,
As iron that comes boiling from the fire.
And suddenly upon the day appear'd
A day new-risen; as he, who hath the power,
Had with another sun bedeck'd the sky.

Her eyes fast fix'd on the eternal wheels,

[294]

PARADISE

Beatrice stood unmoved; and I with ken
Fix'd upon her, from upward gaze removed,
At her aspect, such inwardly became
As Glaucus, when he tasted of the herb
That made him peer among the ocean gods:
Words may not tell of that trans-human change;
And therefore let the example serve, though weak,
For those whom grace hath better proof in store.

If I were only what thou didst create,
Then newly, Love! by whom the heaven is ruled;
Thou know'st, who by thy light didst bear me up.
Whenas the wheel which thou dost ever guide,
Desired Spirit! with its harmony,
Temper'd of thee and measured, charm'd mine ear
Then seem'd to me so much of heaven to blaze
With the sun's flame, that rain or flood ne'er made
A lake so broad. The newness of the sound,
And that great light, inflamed me with desire,
Keener than e'er was felt, to know their cause.

Whence she, who saw me, clearly as myself,
To calm my troubled mind, before I ask'd,
Open'd her lips, and gracious thus began:
"With false imagination thou thyself
Makest dull; so that thou seest not the thing,
Which thou hadst seen, had that been shaken off.
Thou art not on the earth as thou believest;
For lightning, scaped from its own proper place,
Ne'er ran, as thou hast hither now return'd."

Although divested of my first-raised doubt
By those brief words accompanied with smiles,
Yet in new doubt was I entangled more,
And said: "Already satisfied, I rest
From admiration deep; but now admire
How I above those lighter bodies rise."

Whence, after utterance of a piteous sigh,
She toward me bent her eyes, with such a look,

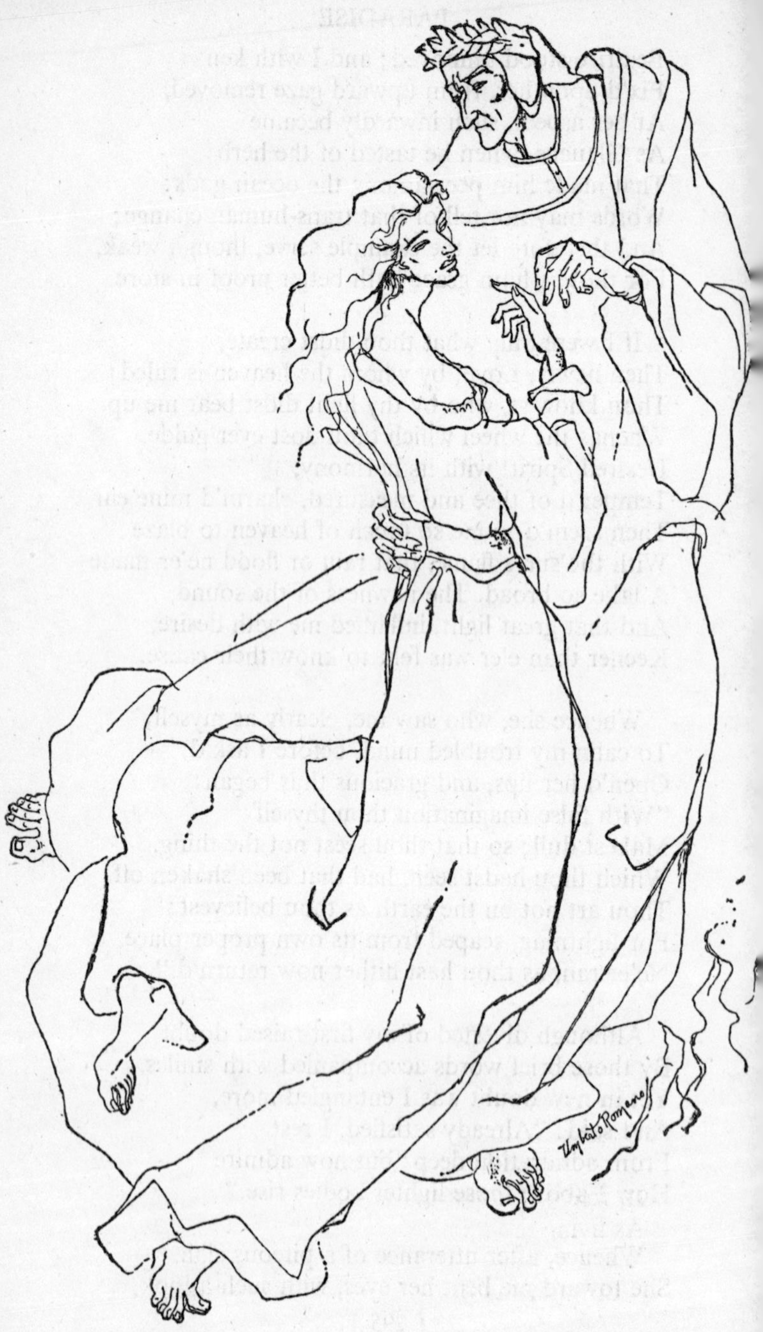
Umberto Romano

PARADISE

As on her frenzied child a mother casts;
Then thus began: "Among themselves all things
Have order; and from hence the form, which makes
The universe resemble God. In this
The higher creatures see the printed steps
Of that eternal worth, which is the end
Whither the line is drawn. All natures lean,
In this their order, diversly; some more,
Some less approaching to their primal source.
Thus they to different havens are moved on
Through the vast sea of being, and each one
With instinct given, that bears it in its course:
This to the lunar sphere directs the fire;
This moves the hearts of mortal animals;
This the brute earth together knits, and binds.
Nor only creatures, void of intellect,
Are aim'd at by this vow; but even those,
That have intelligence and love, are pierced.
That Providence, who so well orders all,
With her own light makes ever calm the heaven,
In which the substance, that hath greatest speed,
Is turn'd: and thither now, as to our seat
Predestined, we are carried by the force
Of that strong cord, that never looses dart
But at fair aim and glad. Yet it is true,
That as, ofttimes, but ill accords the form
To the design of art, through sluggishness
Or unreplying matter; so this course
Is sometimes quitted by the creature, who
Hath power, directed thus, to bend elsewhere;
As from a cloud the fire is seen to fall,
From its original impulse warp'd to earth,
By vicious fondness. Thou no more admire
Thy soaring (if I rightly deem), than lapse
Of torrent downward from a mountain's height.
There would in thee for wonder be more cause,
If, free of hindrance, thou hadst stay'd below,
As living fire unmoved upon the earth."

So said, she turn'd toward the heaven her face.

CANTO II

*Dante and his celestial guide enter the moon. The cause
of the spots or shadows is explained to him.*

ALL ye, who in small bark have following sail'd,
Eager to listen, on the adventurous track
Of my proud keel, that singing cuts her way,
Backward return with speed, and your own shores
Revisit; nor put out to open sea,
Where losing me, perchance ye may remain
Bewilder'd in deep maze. The way I pass,
Ne'er yet was run: Minerva breathes the gale;
Apollo guides me; and another Nine,
To my rapt sight, the arctic beams reveal.
Ye other few who have outstretch'd the neck
Timely for food of angels, on which here
They live, yet never know satiety;
Through the deep brine ye fearless may put out
Your vessel; marking well the furrow broad
Before you in the wave, that on both sides
Equal returns. Those, glorious, who pass'd o'er
To Colchos, wonder'd not as ye will do,
When they saw Jason following the plough.

The increate perpetual thirst, that draws
Toward the realm of God's own form, bore us
Swift almost as the heaven ye behold.

Beatrice upward gazed, and I on her;
And in such space as on the notch a dart
Is placed, then loosen'd flies, I saw myself
Arrived, where wonderous thing engaged my sight.
Whence she, to whom no care of mine was hid,
Turning to me, with aspect glad as fair,
Bespake me: "Gratefully direct thy mind
To God, through whom to this first star we come."

PARADISE

Meseem'd as if a cloud had cover'd us,
Translucent, solid, firm, and polish'd bright,
Like adamant, which the sun's beam had smit.
Within itself the ever-during pearl
Received us; as the wave a ray of light
Receives, and rests unbroken. If I then
Was of corporeal frame, and it transcend
Our weaker thought, how one dimension thus
Another could endure, which needs must be
If body enter body; how much more
Must the desire inflame us to behold
That essence, which discovers by what means
God and our nature join'd! There will be seen
That, which we hold through faith; not shown by proof,
But in itself intelligibly plain,
E'en as the truth that man at first believes.

I answer'd: "Lady! I with thoughts devout,
Such as I best can frame, give thanks to him,
Who hath removed me from the mortal world.
But tell, I pray thee, whence the gloomy spots
Upon this body, which below on earth
Give rise to talk of Cain in fabling quaint?"

She somewhat smiled, then spake: "If mortals err
In their opinion, when the key of sense
Unlocks not, surely wonder's weapon keen
Ought not to pierce thee: since thou find'st, the wings
Of reason to pursue the senses' flight
Are short. But what thy own thought is, declare."

Then I: "What various here above appears,
Is caused, I deem, by bodies dense or rare."

She then resumed: "Thou certainly wilt see
In falsehood thy belief o'erwhelm'd, if well
Thou listen to the arguments which I
Shall bring to face it. The eighth sphere displays
Numberless lights, the which, in kind and size,
May be remark'd of different aspects:

[299]

THE DIVINE COMEDY

If rare or dense of that were cause alone,
One single virtue then would be in all;
Alike distributed, or more, or less.
Different virtues needs must be the fruits
Of formal principles; and these, save one,
Will by thy reasoning be destroy'd. Beside,
If rarity were of that dusk the cause,
Which thou inquirest, either in some part
That planet must throughout be void, nor fed
With its own matter; or, as bodies share
Their fat and leanness, in like manner this
Must in its volume change the leaves. The first,
If it were true, had through the sun's eclipse
Been manifested, by transparency
Of light, as through aught rare beside effused.
But this is not. Therefore remains to see
The other cause: and, if the other fall,
Erroneous so must prove what seem'd to thee.
If not from side to side this rarity
Pass through, there needs must be a limit, whence
Its contrary no further lets it pass.
And hence the beam, that from without proceeds,
Must be pour'd back; as color comes, through glass
Reflected, which behind it lead conceals.
Now wilt thou say, that there of murkier hue,
Than, in the other part, the ray is shown,
By being thence refracted further back.
From this perplexity will free thee soon
Experience, if thereof thou trial make,
The fountain whence your arts derive their streams.
Three mirrors shalt thou take, and two remove
From thee alike; and more remote the third,
Betwixt the former pair, shall meet thine eyes:
Then turn'd toward them, cause behind thy back
A light to stand, that on the three shall shine,
And thus reflected come to thee from all.
Though that, beheld most distant, do not stretch
A space so ample, yet in brightness thou
Wilt own it equalling the rest. But now,
As under snow the ground, if the warm ray

PARADISE

Smites it, remains dismantled of the hue
And cold, that cover'd it before; so thee,
Dismantled in thy mind, I will inform
With light so lively, that the tremulous beam
Shall quiver where it falls. Within the heaven,
Where peace divine inhabits, circles round
A body, in whose virtue lies the being
Of all that it contains. The following heaven,
That hath so many lights, this being divides,
Through different essences, from it distinct,
And yet contain'd within it. The other orbs
Their separate distinctions variously
Dispose, for their own seed and produce apt.
Thus do these organs of the world proceed,
As thou beholdest now, from step to step;
Their influences from above deriving,
And thence transmitting downward. Mark me well;
How through this passage to the truth I ford,
The truth thou lovest; that thou henceforth, alone,
Mayst know to keep the shallows, safe, untold.

"The virtue and motion of the sacred orbs,
As mallet by the workman's hand, must needs
By blessed movers be inspired. This heaven,
Made beauteous by so many luminaries,
From the deep spirit, that moves its circling sphere,
Its image takes and impress as a seal:
And as the soul, that dwells within your dust,
Through members different, yet together form'd,
In different powers resolves itself; e'en so
The intellectual efficacy unfolds
Its goodness multiplied throughout the stars;
On its own unity revolving still.
Different virtue compact different
Makes with the precious body it enlivens,
With which it knits, as life in you is knit.
From its original nature full of joy,
The virtue mingled through the body shines,
As joy through pupil of the living eye.
From hence proceeds that which from light to light

THE DIVINE COMEDY
Seems different, and not from dense or rare.
This is the formal cause, that generates,
Proportion'd to its power, the dusk or clear."

CANTO III

Dante meets Piccarda, the sister of Forese, who tells him the moon is allotted to those who had been compelled to break their vows of chastity and the religious life.

THAT sun, which erst with love my bosom warm'd,
Had of fair truth unveil'd the sweet aspect,
By proof of right, and of the false reproof;
And I, to own myself convinced and free
Of doubt, as much as needed, raised my head
Erect for speech. But soon a sight appear'd,
Which, so intent to mark it, held me fix'd,
That of confession I no longer thought.

As through translucent and smooth glass, or wave
Clear and unmoved, and flowing not so deep
As that its bed is dark, the shape returns
So faint of our impictured lineaments,
That, on white forehead set, a pearl as strong
Comes to the eye; such saw I many a face,
All stretch'd to speak; from whence I straight conceived,
Delusion opposite to that, which raised,
Between the man and fountain, amorous flame.

Sudden, as I perceived them, deeming these
Reflected semblances, to see of whom
They were, I turn'd mine eyes, and nothing saw;
Then turn'd them back, directed on the light
Of my sweet guide, who, smiling, shot forth beams
From her celestial eyes. "Wonder not thou,"
She cried, "at this my smiling, when I see
Thy childish judgment; since not yet on truth
It rests the foot, but, as it still is wont,

[302]

PARADISE

Makes thee fall back in unsound vacancy.
True substances are these, which thou behold'st,
Hither through failure of their vow exiled.
But speak thou with them; listen, and believe,
That the true light, which fills them with desire,
Permits not from its beams their feet to stray."

Straight to the shadow, which for converse seem'd
Most earnest, I address'd me: and began
As one by over-eagerness perplex'd:
"O spirit, born for joy! who in the rays
Of life eternal, of that sweetness know'st
The flavor, which, not tasted, passes far
All apprehension; me it well would please,
If thou wouldst tell me of thy name, and this
Your station here." Whence she with kindness prompt,
And eyes glistering with smiles: "Our charity,
To any wish by justice introduced,
Bars not the door; no more than she above,
Who would have all her court be like herself.
I was a virgin sister in the earth:
And if thy mind observe me well, this form,
With such addition graced of loveliness,
Will not conceal me long; but thou wilt know
Piccarda, in the tardiest sphere thus placed,
Here 'mid these other blessed also blest.
Our hearts, whose high affections burn alone
With pleasure from the Holy Spirit conceived,
Admitted to his order, dwell in joy.
And this condition, which appears so low,
Is for this cause assign'd us, that our vows
Were, in some part, neglected and made void."

Whence I to her replied: "Something divine
Beams in your countenances wonderous fair;
From former knowledge quite transmuting you.
Therefore to recollect was I so slow.
But what thou say'st hath to my memory
Given now such aid, that to retrace your forms
Is easier. Yet inform me, ye, who here

Are happy; long ye for a higher place,
More to behold, and more in love to dwell?"

She with those other spirits gently smiled;
Then answer'd with such gladness, that she seem'd
With love's first flame to glow: "Brother! our will
Is, in composure, settled by the power
Of charity, who makes us will alone
What we possess, and naught beyond desire:
If we should wish to be exalted more,
Then must our wishes jar with the high will
Of him, who sets us here; which in these orbs
Thou wilt confess not possible, if here
To be in charity must needs befall,
And if her nature well thou contemplate.
Rather it is inherent in this state
Of blessedness, to keep ourselves within
The divine will, by which our wills with his
Are one. So that as we, from step to step,
Are placed throughout this kingdom, pleases all,
Even as our King, who in us plants his will;
And in his will is our tranquillity:
It is the mighty ocean, whither tends
Whate'er creates and Nature makes."

Then saw I clearly how each spot in heaven
Is Paradise, though with like gracious dew
The supreme virtue shower not over all.

But as it chances, if one sort of food
Hath satiated, and of another still
The appetite remains, that this is ask'd,
And thanks for that return'd; e'en so did I,
In word and motion, bent from her to learn
What web it was, through which she had not drawn
The shuttle to its point. She thus began:
"Exalted worth and perfectness of life
The Lady higher up inshrine in heaven,
By whose pure laws upon your nether earth
The robe and veil they wear; to that intent,

PARADISE

That e'en till death they may keep watch, or sleep,
With their great bridegroom, who accepts each vow,
Which to his gracious pleasure love conforms.
I from the world, to follow her, when young
Escaped; and, in her vesture mantling me,
Made promise of the way her sect enjoins.
Thereafter men, for ill than good more apt,
Forth snatch'd me from the pleasant cloister's pale.
God knows how, after that, my life was framed.
This other splendid shape, which thou behold'st
At my right side, burning with all the light
Of this our orb, what of myself I tell
May to herself apply. From her, like me
A sister, with like violence were torn
The saintly folds, that shaded her fair brows.
E'en when she to the world again was brought
In spite of her own will and better wont,
Yet not for that the bosom's inward veil
Did she renounce. This is the luminary
Of mighty Constance, who from that loud blast,
Which blew the second over Suabia's realm,
That power produced, which was the third and last."

She ceased from further talk, and then began
"Ave Maria" singing; and with that song
Vanish'd, as heavy substance through deep wave.

Mine eye, that, far as it was capable,
Pursued her, when in dimness she was lost,
Turn'd to the mark where greater want impell'd,
And bent on Beatrice all its gaze.
But she, as lightning, beam'd upon my looks;
So that the sight sustain'd it not at first.
Whence I to question her became less prompt.

CANTO IV

Beatrice removes Dante's doubts about the place assigned to the blessed and the will absolute or conditional.

BETWEEN two kinds of food, both equally
Remote and tempting, first a man might die
Of hunger, ere he one could freely chuse.
E'en so would stand a lamb between the maw
Of two fierce wolves, in dread of both alike:
E'en so between two deer a dog would stand.
Wherefore, if I was silent, fault nor praise
I to myself impute; by equal doubts
Held in suspense; since of necessity
It happen'd. Silent was I, yet desire
Was painted in my looks; and thus I spake
My wish more earnestly than language could.

As Daniel, when the haughty king he freed
From ire, that spurr'd him on to deeds unjust
And violent; so did Beatrice then.

"Well I discern," she thus her words address'd,
"How thou art drawn by each of these desires;
So that thy anxious thought is in itself
Bound up and stifled, nor breathes freely forth.
Thou arguest: if the good intent remain;
What reason that another's violence
Should stint the measure of my fair desert?

"Cause too thou find'st for doubt, in that it seems,
That spirits to the stars, as Plato deem'd,
Return. These are the questions which thy will
Urge equally; and therefore I, the first,
Of that will treat which hath the more of gall.
Of seraphim he who is most enskied,

[306]

PARADISE

Moses and Samuel, and either John,
Chuse which thou wilt, nor even Mary's self,
Have not in any other heaven their seats,
Than have those spirits which so late thou saw'st;
Nor more or fewer years exist; but all
Make the first circle beauteous, diversly
Partaking of sweet life, as more or less
Afflation of eternal bliss pervades them.
Here were they shown thee, not that fate assigns
This for their sphere, but for a sign to thee
Of that celestial furthest from the height.
Thus needs, that ye may apprehend, we speak:
Since from things sensible alone ye learn
That, which, digested rightly, after turns
To intellectual. For no other cause
The Scripture, condescending graciously
To your perception, hands and feet to God
Attributes, nor so means: and holy church
Doth represent with human countenance,
Gabriel, and Michel, and him who made
Tobias whole. Unlike what here thou seest.
The judgment of Timæus, who affirms
Each soul restored to its particular star;
Believing it to have been taken thence,
When nature gave it to inform her mould:
Yet to appearance his intention is
Not what his words declare: and so to shun
Derision, haply thus he hath disguised
His true opinion. If his meaning be,
That to the influencing of these orbs revert
The honor and the blame in human acts,
Perchance he doth not wholly miss the truth.
This principle, not understood aright,
Erewhile perverted well-nigh all the world;
So that it fell to fabled names of Jove,
And Mercury, and Mars. That other doubt,
Which moves thee, is less harmful; for it brings
No peril of removing thee from me.

"That, to the eye of man, our justice seems
Unjust, is argument for faith, and not
For heretic declension. But, to the end
This truth may stand more clearly in your view,
I will content thee even to thy wish.

"If violence be, when that which suffers, naught
Consents to that which forceth, not for this
These spirits stood exculpate. For the will,
That wills not, still survives unquench'd, and doth,
As nature doth in fire, though violence
Wrest it a thousand times; for, if it yield
Or more or less, so far it follows force.
And thus did these, when they had power to seek
The hallow'd place again. In them, had will
Been perfect, such as once upon the bars
Held Laurence firm, or wrought in Scævola
To his own hand remorseless; to the path,
Whence they were drawn, their steps had hasten'd back,
When liberty return'd: but in too few,
Resolve, so steadfast, dwells. And by these words,
If duly weigh'd, that argument is void,
Which oft might have perplex'd thee still. But now
Another question thwarts thee, which, to solve,
Might try thy patience without better aid.
I have, no doubt, instill'd into thy mind,
That blessed spirit may not lie; since near
The source of primal truth it dwells for aye:
And thou mightst after of Piccarda learn
That Constance held affection to the veil;
So that she seems to contradict me here.
Not seldom, brother, it hath chanced for men
To do what they had gladly left undone;
Yet, to shun peril, they have done amiss:
E'en as Alcmæon, at his father's suit
Slew his own mother; so made pitiless,
Not to lose pity. On this point bethink thee,
That force and will are blended in such wise
As not to make the offence excusable.
Absolute will agrees not to the wrong;

PARADISE

But inasmuch as there is fear of woe
From non-compliance, it agrees. Of will
Thus absolute, Piccarda spake, and I
Of the other; so that both have truly said."

Such was the flow of that pure rill, that well'd
From forth the fountain of all truth; and such
The rest, that to my wandering thoughts I found.

"O thou, of primal love the prime delight,
Goddess!" I straight replied, "whose lively words
Still shed new heat and vigor through my soul;
Affection fails me to requite thy grace
With equal sum of gratitude: be his
To recompense, who sees and can reward thee.
Well I discern, that by that truth alone
Enlighten'd, beyond which no truth may roam,
Our mind can satisfy her thirst to know:
Therein she resteth, e'en as in his lair
The wild beast, soon as she hath reach'd that bound.
And she hath power to reach it; else desire
Were given to no end. And thence doth doubt
Spring, like a shoot, around the stock of truth;
And it is nature which, from height to height,
On to the summit prompts us. This invites,
This doth assure me, Lady! reverently
To ask thee of another truth, that yet
Is dark to me. I fain would know, if man
By other works well done may so supply
The failure of his vows, that in your scale
They lack not weight." I spake; and on me straight
Beatrice look'd, with eyes that shot forth sparks
Of love celestial, in such copious stream,
That, virtue sinking in me overpower'd,
I turn'd; and downward bent, confused, my sight.

[309]

CANTO V

Dante ascends with Beatrice to Mercury, the second heaven, where he meets a multitude of spirits.

If beyond earthly wont, the flame of love
Illume me, so that I o'ercome thy power
Of vision, marvel not: but learn the cause
In that perfection of the sight, which, soon
As apprehending, hasteneth on to reach
The good it apprehends. I well discern,
How in thine intellect already shines
The light eternal, which to view alone
Ne'er fails to kindle love; and if aught else
Your love seduces, 'tis but that it shows
Some ill-mark'd vestige of that primal beam.

"This wouldst thou know: if failure of the vow
By other service may be so supplied,
As from self-question to assure the soul."

Thus she her words, not heedless of my wish,
Began; and thus, as one who breaks not off
Discourse, continued in her saintly strain.
"Supreme of gifts, which God, creating, gave
Of his free bounty, sign most evident
Of goodness, and in his account most prized
Was liberty of will; the boon, wherewith
All intellectual creatures, and them sole,
He hath endow'd. Hence now thou mayst infer
Of what high worth the vow, which so is framed
That when man offers, God well-pleased accepts:
For in the compact between God and him,
This treasure such as I describe it to thee,
He makes the victim; and of his own act.
What compensation therefore may he find?
If that, whereof thou hast oblation made,
By using well thou think'st to consecrate,

PARADISE

Thou wouldst of theft do charitable deed.
Thus I resolve thee of the greater point.

"But forasmuch as holy church, herein
Dispensing, seems to contradict the truth
I have discover'd to thee, yet behoves
Thou rest a little longer at the board,
Ere the crude aliment which thou hast ta'en,
Digested fitly, to nutrition turn.
Open thy mind to what I now unfold;
And give it inward keeping. Knowledge comes
Of learning well retain'd, unfruitful else.

"This sacrifice, in essence, of two things
Consisteth; one is that, whereof 'tis made;
The covenant, the other. For the last,
It ne'er is cancel'd, if not kept: and hence
I spake, erewhile, so strictly of its force.
For this it was enjoin'd the Israelites,
Though leave were given them, as thou know'st, to change
The offering, still to offer. The other part,
The matter and the substance of the vow,
May well be such, as that, without offence,
It may for other substance be exchanged.
But, at his own discretion, none may shift
The burden on his shoulders; unreleased
By either key, the yellow and the white.
Nor deem of any change, as less than vain,
If the last bond be not within the new
Included, as the quatre in the six.
No satisfaction therefore can be paid
For what so precious in the balance weighs,
That all in counterpoise must kick the beam.
Take then no vow at random: ta'en, with faith
Preserve it; yet not bent, as Jephthah once,
Blindly to execute a rash resolve,
Whom better it had suited to exclaim,
'I have done ill,' than to redeem his pledge
By doing worse: or, not unlike to him
In folly, that great leader of the Greeks;

[311]

Whence, on the altar, Iphigenia mourn'd
Her virgin beauty, and hath since made mourn
Both wise and simple, even all, who hear
Of so fell sacrifice. Be ye more staid,
O Christian! not, like feather, by each wind
Removable; nor think to cleanse yourselves
In every water. Either testament,
The old and new, is yours: and for your guide,
The shepherd of the church. Let this suffice
To save you. When by evil lust enticed,
Remember ye be men, not senseless beasts;
Nor let the Jew, who dwelleth in your streets,
Hold you in mockery. Be not, as the lamb,
That, fickle wanton, leaves its mother's milk,
To dally with itself in idle play."

Such were the words that Beatrice spake:
These ended, to that region, where the world
Is liveliest, full of fond desire she turn'd.

Though mainly prompt new question to propose,
Her silence and changed look did keep me dumb.
And as the arrow, ere the cord is still,
Leapeth unto its mark; so on we sped
Into the second realm. There I beheld
The dame, so joyous, enter, that the orb
Grew brighter at her smiles; and, if the star
Were moved to gladness, what then was my cheer,
Whom nature hath made apt for every change!

As in a quiet and clear lake the fish,
If aught approach them from without, do draw
Toward it, deeming it their food; so drew
Full more than thousand splendors toward us;
And in each one was heard: "Lo! one arrived
To multiply our loves!" and as each came,
The shadow, streaming forth effulgence new,
Witness'd augmented joy. Here, Reader! think,
If thou didst miss the sequel of my tale,
To know the rest how sorely thou wouldst crave;

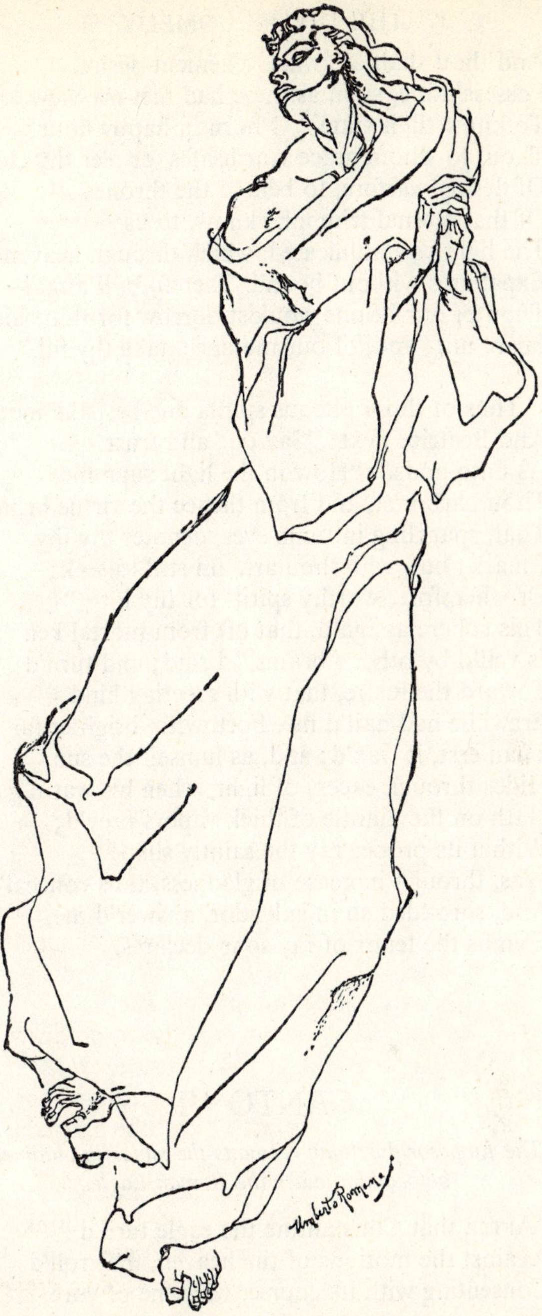
Umberto Romano

And thou shalt see what vehement desire
Possess'd me, soon as these had met my view,
To know their state. "O born in happy hour!
Thou, to whom grace vouchsafes, or e'er thy close
Of fleshly warfare, to behold the thrones
Of that eternal triumph; know, to us
The light communicated, which through heaven
Expatiates without bound. Therefore, if aught
Thou of our beams wouldst borrow for thine aid,
Spare not; and, of our radiance, take thy fill."

Thus of those piteous spirits one bespake me;
And Beatrice next: "Say on; and trust
As unto gods." "How in the light supreme
Thou harbor'st, and from thence the virtue bring'st,
That, sparkling in thine eyes, denotes thy joy,
I mark; but, who thou art, am still to seek;
Or wherefore, worthy spirit! for thy lot
This sphere assign'd, that oft from mortal ken
Is veil'd by other's beams." I said; and turn'd
Toward the lustre, that with greeting kind
Erewhile had hail'd me. Forthwith, brighter far
Than erst, it wax'd: and, as himself the sun
Hides through excess of light, when his warm gaze
Hath on the mantle of thick vapors prey'd;
Within its proper ray the saintly shape
Was, through increase of gladness, thus conceal'd;
And, shrouded so in splendor, answer'd me,
E'en as the tenor of my song declares.

CANTO VI

The Emperor Justinian recounts the victories obtained before him under the Roman Eagle.

"AFTER that Constantine the eagle turn'd
Against the motions of the heaven, that roll'd
Consenting with its course, when he of yore,

PARADISE

Lavinia's spouse, was leader of the flight;
A hundred years twice told and more, his seat
At Europe's extreme point, the bird of Jove
Held, near the mountains, whence he issued first;
There under shadow of his sacred plumes
Swaying the world, till through successive hands
To mine he came devolved. Cæsar I was;
And am Justinian; destined by the will
Of that prime love, whose influence I feel,
From vain excess to clear the incumber'd laws.
Or e'er that work engaged me, I did hold
In Christ one nature only; with such faith
Contented. But the blessed Agapete,
Who was chief shepherd, he with warning voice
To the true faith recall'd me. I believed
His words: and what he taught, now plainly see,
As thou in every contradiction seest
The true and false opposed. Soon as my feet
Were to the church reclaim'd, to my great task,
By inspiration of God's grace impell'd,
I gave me wholly; and consign'd mine arms
To Belisarius, with whom heaven's right hand
Was link'd in such conjointment, 'twas a sign
That I should rest. To thy first question thus
I shape mine answer, which were ended here,
But that its tendency doth prompt perforce
To some addition; that thou well mayst mark,
What reason on each side they had to plead,
By whom that holiest banner is withstood,
Both who pretend its power and who oppose.

"Beginning from that hour, when Pallas died
To give it rule, behold the valorous deeds
Have made it worthy reverence. Not unknown
To thee, how for three hundred years and more
It dwelt in Alba, up to those fell lists
Where, for its sake, were met the rival three;
Nor aught unknown to thee, which it achieved
Down from the Sabines' wrong to Lucrece's woe;
With its seven kings conquering the nations round;

[315]

Nor all it wrought, by Roman worthies borne
'Gainst Brennus and the Epirot prince, and hosts
Of single chiefs, or states in league combined
Of social warfare: hence, Torquatus stern,
And Quintius named of his neglected locks,
The Decii, and the Fabii hence acquired
Their fame, which I with duteous zeal embalm.
By it the pride of Arab hordes was quell'd,
When they, led on by Hannibal, o'erpass'd
The Alpine rocks, whence glide thy currents, Po!
Beneath its guidance, in their prime of days
Scipio and Pompey triumph'd; and that hill
Under whose summit thou didst see the light,
Rued its stern bearing. After, near the hour,
When Heaven was minded that o'er all the world
His own deep calm should brood, to Cæsar's hand
Did Rome consign it; and what then it wrought
From Var unto the Rhine, saw Isere's flood,
Saw Loire and Seine, and every vale, that fills
The torrent Rhone. What after that it wrought,
When from Ravenna it came forth, and leap'd
The Rubicon, was of so bold a flight,
That tongue nor pen may follow it. Toward Spain
It wheel'd its bands, then toward Dyrrachium smote,
And on Pharsalia, with so fierce a plunge,
E'en the warm Nile was conscious to the pang;
Its native shores Antandros, and the streams
Of Simois revisited, and there
Where Hector lies; then ill for Ptolemy
His pennons shook again; lightning thence fell
On Juba, and the next, upon your west,
At sound of the Pompeian trump, return'd.

"What following, and in its next bearer's gripe,
It wrought, is now by Cassius and Brutus
Bark'd of in Hell; and by Perugia's sons,
And Modena's, was mourn'd. Hence weepeth still
Sad Cleopatra, who, pursued by it,
Took from the adder black and sudden death.
With him it ran e'en to the Red Sea coast;

[316]

PARADISE

With him composed the world to such a peace,
That of his temple Janus barr'd the door.

"But all the mighty standard yet had wrought
And was appointed to perform thereafter,
Throughout the mortal kingdom which it sway'd,
Falls in appearance dwindled and obscured,
If one with steady eye and perfect thought
On the third Cæsar look; for to his hands,
The living Justice, in whose breath I move,
Committed glory, e'en into his hands,
To execute the vengeance of its wrath.

"Hear now, and wonder at, what next I tell.
After with Titus it was sent to wreak
Vengeance for vengeance of the ancient sin.
And, when the Lombard tooth, with fang impure,
Did gore the bosom of the holy church,
Under its wings, victorious Charlemain
Sped to her rescue. Judge then for thyself
Of those, whom I erewhile accused to thee,
What they are, and how grievous their offending,
Who are the cause of all your ills. The one
Against the universal ensign rears
The yellow lilies; and with partial aim,
That, to himself, the other arrogates:
So that 'tis hard to see who most offends.
Be yours, ye Ghibellines, to veil your hearts
Beneath another standard: ill is this
Follow'd of him, who severs it and justice:
And let not with his Guelfs the new-crown'd Charles
Assail it; but those talons hold in dread,
Which from a lion of more lofty port
Have rent the casing. Many a time ere now
The sons have for the sire's transgression wail'd:
Nor let him trust the fond belief, that heaven
Will truck its armor for his lilied shield.

"This little star is furnish'd with good spirits,
Whose mortal lives were busied to that end,

[317]

That honor and renown might wait on them:
And, when desires thus err in their intention,
True love must needs ascend with slacker beam.
But it is part of our delight, to measure
Our wages with the merit; and admire
The close proportion. Hence doth heavenly justice
Temper so evenly affection in us,
It ne'er can warp to any wrongfulness.
Of diverse voices is sweet music made:
So in our life the different degrees
Render sweet harmony among these wheels.

"Within the pearl, that now encloseth us,
Shines Romeo's light, whose goodly deed and fair
Met ill acceptance. But the Provençals,
That were his foes, have little cause for mirth.
Ill shapes that man his course, who makes his wrong
Of other's worth. Four daughters were there born
To Raymond Berenger; and every one
Became a queen: and this for him did Romeo,
Though of mean state and from a foreign land.
Yet envious tongues incited him to ask
A reckoning of that just one, who return'd
Twelve-fold to him for ten. Aged and poor
He parted thence: and if the world did know
The heart he had, begging his life by morsels,
'Twould deem the praise it yields him, scantly dealt."

CANTO VII

Some doubts arise in the mind of the poet respecting human redemption which are explained by Beatrice.

"HOSANNA *Sanctus Deus Sabaoth,*
Superillustrans claritate tuâ
Felices ignes horum malahoth."
Thus chanting saw I turn that substance bright,
With fourfold lustre to its orb again,

PARADISE

Revolving; and the rest, unto their dance,
With it, moved also; and, like swiftest sparks,
In sudden distance from my sight were veil'd.

   Me doubt possess'd; and "Speak," it whisper'd me,
"Speak, speak unto thy lady; that she quench
Thy thirst with drops of sweetness." Yet blank awe,
Which lords it o'er me, even at the sound
Of Beatrice's name, did bow me down
As one in slumber held. Not long that mood
Beatrice suffer'd: she, with such a smile,
As might have made one blest amid the flames,
Beaming upon me, thus her words began:
"Thou in thy thought art pondering (as I deem,
And what I deem is truth) how just revenge
Could be with justice punish'd: from which doubt
I soon will free thee; so thou mark my words;
For they of weighty matter shall possess thee.
Through suffering not a curb upon the power
That will'd in him, to his own profiting,
That man, who was unborn, condemn'd himself;
And, in himself, all, who since him have lived,
His offspring: whence, below, the human kind
Lay sick in grievous error many an age;
Until it pleased the Word of God to come
Amongst them down, to his own person joining
The nature from its Maker far estranged,
By the mere act of his eternal love.
Contemplate here the wonder I unfold.
The nature with its Maker thus conjoin'd,
Created first was blameless, pure and good;
But, through itself alone, was driven forth
From Paradise, because it had eschew'd
The way of truth and life, to evil turn'd.
Ne'er then was penalty so just as that
Inflicted by the cross, if thou regard
The nature in assumption doom'd; ne'er wrong
So great, in reference to him, who took
Such nature on him, and endured the doom.
So different effects flow'd from one act:

THE DIVINE COMEDY

For by one death God and the Jews were pleased;
And heaven was open'd, though the earth did quake.
Count it not hard henceforth, when thou dost hear
That a just vengeance was, by righteous court,
Justly revenged. But yet I see thy mind,
By thought on thought arising, sore perplex'd;
And, with how vehement desire, it asks
Solution of the maze. What I have heard,
Is plain, thou say'st: but wherefore God this way
For our redemption chose, eludes my search.

"Brother! no eye of man not perfected,
Nor fully ripen'd in the flame of love,
May fathom this decree. It is a mark,
In sooth, much aim'd at, and but little kenn'd
And I will therefore show thee why such way
Was worthiest. The celestial love, that spurns
All envying in its bounty, in itself
With such effulgence blazeth, as sends forth
All beauteous things eternal. What distils
Immediate thence, no end of being knows;
Bearing its seal immutably imprest.
Whatever thence immediate falls, is free,
Free wholly, uncontrollable by power
Of each thing new: by such conformity
More grateful to its author, whose bright beams,
Though all partake their shining, yet in those
Are liveliest, which resemble him the most.
These tokens of pre-eminence on man
Largely bestow'd, if any of them fail,
He needs must forfeit his nobility,
No longer stainless. Sin alone is that,
Which doth disfranchise him, and make unlike
To the chief good; for that its light in him
Is darken'd. And to dignity thus lost
Is no return; unless, where guilt makes void,
He for ill-pleasure pay with equal pain.
Your nature, which entirely in its seed
Transgress'd, from these distinctions fell, no less
Than from its state in Paradise; nor means

PARADISE

Found of recovery (search all methods out
As strictly as thou may) save one of these,
The only fords were left through which to wade:
Either, that God had of his courtesy
Released him merely; or else, man himself
For his own folly by himself atoned.

"Fix now thine eye, intently as thou canst,
On the everlasting counsel; and explore,
Instructed by my words, the dread abyss.

"Man in himself had ever lack'd the means
Of satisfaction, for he could not stoop
Obeying, in humility so low,
As high, he, disobeying, thought to soar:
And, for this reason, he had vainly tried,
Out of his own sufficiency, to pay
The rigid satisfaction. Then behoved
That God should by his own ways lead him back
Unto the life, from whence he fell, restored:
By both his ways, I mean, or one alone.
But since the deed is ever prized the more,
The more the doer's good intent appears;
Goodness celestial, whose broad signature
Is on the universe, of all its ways
To raise ye up, was fain to leave out none.
Nor aught so vast or so magnificent,
Either for him who gave or who received,
Between the last night and the primal day,
Was or can be. For God more bounty show'd,
Giving himself to make man capable
Of his return to life, than had the terms
Been mere and unconditional release.
And for his justice, every method else
Were all too scant, had not the Son of God
Humbled himself to put on mortal flesh.

"Now, to content thee fully, I revert;
And further in some part unfold my speech,
That thou mayst see it clearly as myself.

[321]

"I see, thou sayst, the air, the fire I see,
The earth and water, and all things of them
Compounded, to corruption turn, and soon
Dissolve. Yet these were also things create
Because, if what were told me, had been true,
They from corruption had been therefore free.

"The angels, O my brother! and this clime
Wherein thou art, impassable and pure,
I call created, even as they are
In their whole being. But the elements,
Which thou hast named, and what of them is made,
Are by created virtue inform'd: create,
Their substance; and create, the informing virtue
In these bright stars, that round them circling move.
The soul of every brute and of each plant,
The ray and motion of the sacred lights,
Draw from complexion with meet power endued.
But this our life the eternal good inspires
Immediate, and enamors of itself;
So that our wishes rest forever here.

"And hence thou mayst by inference conclude
Our resurrection certain, if thy mind
Consider how the human flesh was framed,
When both our parents at the first were made."

CANTO VIII

*The poet ascends to Venus and meets Charles Martel,
King of Hungary, who tells him why children
differ in disposition from their parents.*

THE world was, in its day of peril dark,
Wont to believe the dotage of fond love,
From the fair Cyprian deity, who rolls
In her third epicycle, shed on men

PARADISE

By stream of potent radiance: therefore they
Of elder time, in their old error blind,
Not her alone with sacrifice adored
And invocation, but like honors paid
To Cupid and Dione, deem'd of them
Her mother, and her son, him whom they feign'd
To sit in Dido's bosom: and from her,
Whom I have sung preluding, borrow'd they
The appellation of that star, which views
Now obvious, and now averse, the sun.

I was not ware that I was wafted up
Into its orb; but the new loveliness,
That graced my lady, gave me ample proof
That we had enter'd there. And as in flame
A sparkle is distinct, or voice in voice
Discern'd, when one its even tenor keeps,
The other comes and goes; so in that light
I other luminaries saw, that coursed
In circling motion, rapid more or less,
As their eternal vision each impels.

Never was blast from vapor charged with cold,
Whether invisible to eye or no,
Descended with such speed, it had not seem'd
To linger in dull tardiness, compared
To those celestial lights, that toward us came,
Leaving the circuit of their joyous ring,
Conducted by the lofty seraphim.
And after them, who in the van appear'd,
Such an Hosanna sounded as hath left
Desire, ne'er since extinct in me, to hear
Renew'd the strain. Then, parting from the rest,
One near us drew, and sole began: "We all
Are ready at thy pleasure, well disposed
To do thee gentle service. We are they
To whom thou in the world erewhile didst sing;
'O ye! whose intellectual ministry
Moves the third heaven': and in one orb we roll,

One motion, one impulse, with those who rule
Princedoms in heaven; yet are of love so full,
That to please thee 'twill be as sweet to rest."

After mine eyes had with meek reverence
Sought the celestial guide, and were by her
Assured, they turn'd again unto the light,
Who had so largely promised; and with voice
That bare the lively pressure of my zeal,
"Tell who ye are," I cried. Forthwith it grew
In size and splendor, through augmented joy;
And thus it answer'd: "A short date, below,
The world possess'd me. Had the time been more,
Much evil, that will come, had never chanced.
My gladness hides thee from me, which doth shine
Around, and shroud me, as an animal
In its own silk enswathed. Thou lovedst me well,
And hadst good cause; for had my sojourning
Been longer on the earth, the love I bare thee
Had put forth more than blossoms. The left bank,
That Rhone, when he hath mix'd with Sorga, laves,
In me its lord expected, and that horn
Of fair Ausonia, with its boroughs old,
Bari, and Croton, and Gaeta piled,
From where the Trento disembogues his waves,
With Verde mingled, to the salt-sea flood.
Already on my temples beam'd the crown,
Which gave me sovereignty over the land
By Danube wash'd, whenas he strays beyond
The limits of his German shores. The realm,
Where, on the gulf by stormy Eurus lash'd,
Betwixt Pelorus and Pachynian heights,
The beautiful Trinacria lies in gloom
(Not through Typhoëus, but the vapory cloud
Bituminous upsteam'd), *that* too did look
To have its sceptre wielded by a race
Of monarchs, sprung through me from Charles and Rodolph,
Had not ill-lording, which doth desperate make
The people ever, in Palermo raised

PARADISE

The shout of 'death,' re-echoed loud and long.
Had but my brother's foresight kenn'd as much,
He had been warier, that the greedy want
Of Catalonia might not work his bale.
And truly need there is that he forecast,
Or other for him, lest more freight be laid
On his already over-laden bark.
Nature in him, from bounty fallen to thrift,
Would ask the guard of braver arms, than such
As only care to have their coffers fill'd."

"My liege! it doth enhance the joy thy words
Infuse into me, mighty as it is,
To think my gladness manifest to thee,
As to myself, who own it, when thou look'st
Into the source and limit of all good,
There, where thou markest that which thou dost speak,
Thence prized of me the more. Glad thou hast made me:
Now make intelligent, clearing the doubt
Thy speech hath raised in me; for much I muse,
How bitter can spring up, when sweet is sown."
I thus inquiring; he forthwith replied:
"If I have power to show one truth, soon that
Shall face thee, which thy questioning declares
Behind thee now conceal'd. The Good, that guides
And blessed makes this realm which thou dost mount,
Ordains its providence to be the virtue
In these great bodies: nor the natures only
The all-perfect mind provides for, but with them
That which preserves them too; for naught, that lies
Within the range of that unerring bow,
But is as level with the destined aim,
As ever mark to arrow's point opposed.
Were it not thus, these heavens, thou dost visit,
Would their effect so work, it would not be
Art, but destruction; and this may not chance,
If the intellectual powers, that move these stars,
Fail not, and who, first faulty made them, fail.
Wilt thou this truth more clearly evidenced?"

THE DIVINE COMEDY

To whom I thus: "It is enough: no fear
I see, lest nature in her part should tire."

He straight rejoin'd: "Say, were it worse for man,
If he lived not in fellowship on earth?"

"Yea," answer'd I; "nor here a reason needs."

"And may that be, if different estates
Grow not of different duties in your life?
Consult your teacher, and he tells you 'no.' "

Thus did he come, deducing to this point,
And then concluded: "For this cause behoves,
The roots, from whence your operations come,
Must differ. Therefore one is Solon born;
Another, Xerxes; and Melchisedec
A third; and he a fourth, whose airy voyage
Cost him his son. In her circuitous course,
Nature, that is the seal to mortal wax,
Doth well her art, but no distinction owns
'Twixt one or other household. Hence befalls
That Esau is so wide of Jacob: hence
Quirinus of so base a father springs,
He dates from Mars his lineage. Were it not
That Providence celestial overruled,
Nature, in generation, must the path
Traced by the generator still pursue
Unswervingly. Thus place I in thy sight
That, which was late behind thee. But, in sign
Of more affection for thee, 'tis my will
Thou wear this corollary. Nature ever,
Finding discordant fortune, like all seed
Out of its proper climate, thrives but ill.
And were the world below content to mark
And work on the foundation nature lays,
I would not lack supply of excellence.
But ye perversely to religion strain
Him, who was born to gird on him the sword,

PARADISE

And of the fluent phraseman make your king:
Therefore your steps have wander'd from the path."

CANTO IX

*The conversation of the amorous Cunizza is followed
by a meeting with Folco of Folques who blames
the Pope for neglecting the holy land.*

AFTER solution of my doubt, thy Charles,
O fair Clemenza, of the treachery spake,
That must befall his seed; but, "Tell it not,"
Said he, "and let the destined years come round."
Nor may I tell thee more, save that the meed
Of sorrow well-deserved shall quit your wrongs.

And now the visage of that saintly light
Was to the sun, that fills it, turn'd again,
As to the good, whose plenitude of bliss
Sufficeth all. O ye misguided souls!
Infatuate, who from such a good estrange
Your hearts, and bend your gaze on vanity,
Alas for you!—And lo! toward me, next,
Another of those splendent forms approach'd
That, by its outward brightening, testified
The will it had to pleasure me. The eyes
Of Beatrice, resting, as before,
Firmly upon me, manifested forth
Approval of my wish. "And O," I cried,
"Blest spirit! quickly be my will perform'd;
And prove thou to me, that my inmost thoughts
I can reflect on thee." Thereat the light,
That yet was new to me, from the recess,
Where it before was singing, thus began,
As one who joys in kindness: "In that part
Of the depraved Italian land, which lies
Between Rialto and the fountain-springs

[327]

THE DIVINE COMEDY

Of Brenta and of Piava, there doth rise,
But to no lofty eminence, a hill,
From whence erewhile a firebrand did descend,
That sorely shent the region. From one root
I and it sprung; my name on earth Cunizza:
And here I glitter, for that by its light
This star o'ercame me. Yet I naught repine,
Nor grudge myself the cause of this my lot:
Which haply vulgar hearts can scarce conceive.

"This jewel, that is next me in our Heaven,
Lustrous and costly, great renown hath left,
And not to perish, ere these hundred years
Five times absolve their round. Consider thou,
If to excel be worthy man's endeavor,
When such life may attend the first. Yet they
Care not for this, the crowd that now are girt
By Adice and Tagliamento, still
Impenitent, though scourged. The hour is near
When for their stubbornness, at Padua's marsh
The water shall be changed, that laves Vicenza.
And where Cagnano meets with Sile, one
Lords it, and bears his head aloft, for whom
The web is now a-warping. Feltro too
Shall sorrow for its godless shepherd's fault,
Of so deep stain, that never, for the like,
Was Malta's bar unclosed. Too large should be
The skillet that would hold Ferrara's blood,
And wearied he, who ounce by ounce would weigh it,
The which this priest, in show of party-zeal,
Courteous will give; nor will the gift ill suit
The country's custom. We descry above
Mirrors, ye call them thrones, from which to us
Reflected shine the judgments of our God:
Whence these our sayings we avouch for good."

She ended; and appear'd on other thoughts
Intent, re-entering on the wheel she late
Had left. That other joyance meanwhile wax'd
A thing to marvel at, in splendor glowing,

PARADISE

Like choicest ruby stricken by the sun.
For, in that upper clime, effulgence comes
Of gladness, as here laughter: and below,
As the mind saddens, murkier grows the shade.

"God seeth all: and in him is thy sight,"
Said I, "blest spirit! Therefore will of his
Cannot to thee be dark. Why then delays
Thy voice to satisfy my wish untold;
That voice, which joins the inexpressive song,
Pastime of Heaven, the which those ardors sing,
That cowl them with six shadowing wings outspread?
I would not wait thy asking, wert thou known
To me, as thoroughly I to thee am known."

He, forthwith answering, thus his words began:
"The valley of waters, widest next to that
Which doth the earth engarland, shapes its course,
Between discordant shores, against the sun
Inward so far, it makes meridian there,
Where was before the horizon. Of that vale
Dwelt I upon the shore, 'twixt Ebro's stream
And Macra's, that divides with passage brief
Genoan bounds from Tuscan. East and west
Are nearly one to Begga and my land
Whose haven erst was with its own blood warm.
Who knew my name, were wont to call me Folco;
And I did bear impression of this heaven,
That now bears mine: for not with fiercer flame
Glow'd Belus' daughter, injuring alike
Sichæus and Creusa, than did I,
Long as it suited the unripen'd down
That fledged my cheek; nor she of Rhodope,
That was beguiled of Demophoön;
Nor Jove's son, when the charms of Iole
Were shrined within his heart. And yet there bides
No sorrowful repentance here, but mirth,
Not for the fault (that doth not come to mind)
But for the virtue, whose o'erruling sway
And providence have wrought thus quaintly. Here

The skill is look'd into, that fashioneth
With such effectual working, and the good
Discern'd accruing to the lower world
From this above. But fully to content
Thy wishes all that in this sphere have birth,
Demands my further parle. Inquire thou wouldst,
Who of this light is denizen, that here
Beside me sparkles, as the sun-beam doth
On the clear wave. Know then, the soul of Rahab
Is in that gladsome harbor; to our tribe
United, and the foremost rank assign'd.
She to this heaven, at which the shadow ends
Of your sublunar world, was taken up,
First, in Christ's triumph, of all souls redeem'd.
For well behoved, that, in some part of heaven,
She should remain a trophy, to declare
The mighty conquest won with either palm;
For that she favor'd first the high exploit
Of Joshua on the Holy Land, whereof
The Pope recks little now. Thy city, plant
Of him, that on his Maker turn'd the back,
And of whose envying so much woe hath sprung,
Engenders and expands the cursed flower,
That hath made wander both the sheep and lambs,
Turning the shepherd to a wolf. For this,
The gospel and great teachers laid aside,
The decretals, as their stuft margins show,
Are the sole study. Pope and Cardinals,
Intent on these, ne'er journey but in thought
To Nazareth, where Gabriel oped his wings.
Yet it may chance, ere long, the Vatican,
And other most selected parts of Rome,
That were the grave of Peter's soldiery,
Shall be deliver'd from the adulterous bond."

PARADISE

CANTO X

*They next ascend to the sun where they are encompassed
by twelve blessed spirits including Thomas Aquinas.*

LOOKING into his first-born with the love,
Which breathes from both eternal, the first Might
Ineffable, wherever eye or mind
Can roam, hath in such order all disposed,
As none may see and fail to enjoy. Raise, then,
O reader! to the lofty wheels, with me,
Thy ken directed to the point, whereat
One motion strikes on the other. There begin
Thy wonder of the mighty Architect,
Who loves his work so inwardly, his eye
Doth ever watch it. See, how thence oblique
Brancheth the circle, where the planets roll
To pour their wished influence on the world;
Whose path not bending thus, in heaven above
Much virtue would be lost, and here on earth
All power well-nigh extinct: or, from direct
Were its departure distant more or less,
I' the universal order, great defect
Must, both in Heaven and here beneath, ensue.

Now rest thee, reader! on thy bench, and muse
Anticipative of the feast to come;
So shall delight make thee not feel thy toil.
Lo! I have set before thee; for thyself
Feed now: the matter I indite, henceforth
Demands entire my thought. Join'd with the part,
Which late we told of, the great minister
Of nature, that upon the world imprints
The virtue of the heaven, and doles out
Time for us with his beam, went circling on
Along the spires, where each hour sooner comes;
And I was with him, weetless of ascent,
But as a man, that weets him come, ere thinking.

[331]

THE DIVINE COMEDY

For Beatrice, she who passeth on
So suddenly from good to better, time
Counts not the act, oh then how great must needs
Have been her brightness! What there was i' th' sun,
(Where I had enter'd) not through change of hue,
But light transparent—did I summon up
Genius, art, practice—I might not so speak,
It should be e'er imagined: yet believed
It may be, and the sight be justly craved.
And if our fantasy fail of such height,
What marvel, since no eye above the sun
Hath ever travel'd? Such are they dwell here,
Fourth family of the Omnipotent Sire,
Who of his spirit and of his offspring shows;
And holds them still enraptured with the view.
And thus to me Beatrice: "Thank, oh thank
The Sun of angels, him, who by his grace
To this perceptible hath lifted thee."

Never was heart in such devotion bound,
And with complacency so absolute
Disposed to render up itself to God,
As mine was at those words: and so entire
The love for Him, that held me, it eclipsed
Beatrice in oblivion. Naught displeased
Was she, but smiled thereat so joyously,
That of her laughing eyes the radiance brake
And scatter'd my collected mind abroad.

Then saw I a bright band, in liveliness
Surpassing, who themselves did make the crown,
And us their centre: yet more sweet in voice,
Than, in their visage, beaming. Cinctured thus,
Sometime Latona's daughter we behold,
When the impregnate air retains the thread
That weaves her zone. In the celestial court,
Whence I return, are many jewels found,
So dear and beautiful, they cannot brook
Transporting from that realm: and of these lights
Such was the song. Who doth not prune his wing

PARADISE

To soar up thither, let him look from thence
For tidings from the dumb. When, singing thus,
Those burning suns had circled round us thrice,
As nearest stars around the fixed pole;
Then seem'd they like to ladies, from the dance
Not ceasing, but suspense, in silent pause,
Listening, till they have caught the strain anew:
Suspended so they stood: and, from within,
Thus heard I one, who spake: "Since with its beam
The grace, whence true love lighteth first his flame,
That after doth increase by loving, shines
So multiplied in thee, it leads thee up
Along this ladder, down whose hallow'd steps
None e'er descend, and mount them not again;
Who from his phial should refuse thee wine
To slake thy thirst, no less constrained were,
Than water flowing not unto the sea.
Thou fain wouldst hear, what plants are these, that bloom
In the bright garland, which, admiring, girds
This fair dame round, who strengthens thee for heaven.
I, then, was of the lambs, that Dominic
Leads, for his saintly flock, along the way
Where well they thrive, not swol'n with vanity.
He, nearest on my right hand, brother was,
And master to me: Albert of Cologne
Is this; and, of Aquinum, Thomas I.
If thou of all the rest wouldst be assured,
Let thine eye, waiting on the words I speak,
In circuit journey round the blessed wreath.
That next resplendence issues from the smile
Of Gratian, who to either forum lent
Such help, as favor wins in Paradise.
The other, nearest, who adorns our quire,
Was Peter, he that with the widow gave
To holy Church his treasure. The fifth light,
Goodliest of all, is by such love inspired,
That all your world craves tidings of his doom:
Within, there is the lofty light, endow'd
With sapience so profound, if truth be truth,
That with a ken of such wide amplitude

[333]

THE DIVINE COMEDY

No second hath arisen. Next behold
That taper's radiance, to whose view was shown,
Clearliest, the nature and the ministry
Angelical, while yet in flesh it dwelt.
In the other little light serenely smiles
That pleader for the Christian temples, he,
Who did provide Augustin of his lore.
Now, if thy mind's eye pass from light to light,
Upon my praises following, of the eighth
Thy thirst is next. The saintly soul, that shows
The world's deceitfulness, to all who hear him,
Is, with the sight of all the good that is,
Blest there. The limbs, whence it was driven, lie
Down in Cieldauro; and from martyrdom
And exile came it here. Lo! further on,
Where flames the arduous spirit of Isidore;
Of Bede; and Richard, more than man, erewhile,
In deep discernment. Lastly this, from whom
Thy look on me reverteth, was the beam
Of one, whose spirit, on high musings bent,
Rebuked the lingering tardiness of death.
It is the eternal light of Sigebert
Who escaped not envy, when of truth he argued,
Reading in the straw-litter'd street." Forthwith,
As clock, that calleth up the spouse of God
To win her bridegroom's love at matin's hour,
Each part of other fitly drawn and urged,
Sends out a tinkling sound, of note so sweet,
Affection springs in well-disposed breast;
Thus saw I move the glorious wheel; thus heard
Voice answering voice, so musical and soft,
It can be known but where day endless shines.

PARADISE

CANTO XI

Thomas Aquinas describes life and character of St. Francis, and a difficulty that has arisen in Dante's mind.

O FOND anxiety of mortal men!
How vain and inconclusive arguments
Are those, which make thee beat thy wings below.
For statutes one, and one for aphorisms
Was hunting; this the priesthood follow'd; that,
By force or sophistry, aspired to rule;
To rob, another; and another sought,
By civil business, wealth; one, moiling, lay
Tangled in net of sensual delight;
And one to wistless indolence resign'd;
What time from all these empty things escaped,
With Beatrice, I thus gloriously
Was raised aloft, and made the guest of heaven.

They of the circle to that point, each one,
Where erst it was, had turn'd; and steady glow'd,
As candle in his socket. Then within
The lustre, that erewhile bespake me, smiling
With merer gladness, heard I thus begin:

"E'en as his beam illumes me, so I look
Into the eternal light, and clearly mark
Thy thoughts, from whence they rise. Thou art in doubt,
And wouldst that I should bolt my words afresh
In such plain open phrase, as may be smooth
To thy perception, where I told thee late
That 'well they thrive'; and that 'no second such
Hath risen,' which no small distinction needs.

"The Providence, that governeth the world,
In depth of counsel by created ken
Unfathomable, to the end that she,
Who with loud cries was 'spoused in precious blood,

Might keep her footing toward her well-beloved,
Safe in herself and constant unto him,
Hath two ordain'd, who should on either hand
In chief escort her: one, seraphic all
In fervency; for wisdom upon earth,
The other, splendor of cherubic light.
I but of one will tell: he tells of both,
Who one commendeth, which of them soe'er
Be taken: for their deeds were to one end.

"Between Tupino, and the wave that falls
From blest Ubaldo's chosen hill, there hangs
Rich slope of mountain high, whence heat and cold
Are wafted through Perugia's eastern gate:
And Nocera with Gualdo, in its rear,
Mourn for their heavy yoke. Upon that side,
Where it doth break its steepness most, arose
A sun upon the world, as duly this
From Ganges doth: therefore let none, who speak
Of that place, say Ascesi; for its name
Were lamely so deliver'd; but the East,
To call things rightly, be it henceforth styled.
He was not yet much distant from his rising,
When his good influence 'gan to bless the earth.
A dame, to whom none openeth pleasure's gate
More than to death, was, 'gainst his father's will,
His stripling choice: and he did make her his,
Before the spiritual court, by nuptial bonds,
And in his father's sight: from day to day,
Then loved her more devoutly. She, bereaved
Of her first husband, slighted and obscure,
Thousand and hundred years and more, remain'd
Without a single suitor, till he came.
Nor aught avail'd, that, with Amyclas, she
Was found unmoved at rumor of his voice,
Who shook the world: nor aught her constant boldness
Whereby with Christ she mounted on the cross,
When Mary stay'd beneath. But not to deal
Thus closely with thee longer, take at large

PARADISE

The lovers' titles—Poverty and Francis.
Their concord and glad looks, wonder and love,
And sweet regard gave birth to holy thoughts,
So much, that venerable Bernard first
Did bare his feet, and, in pursuit of peace
So heavenly, ran, yet deem'd his footing slow.
O hidden riches! O prolific good!
Egidius bares him next, and next Sylvester,
And follow, both, the bridegroom: so the bride
Can please them. Thenceforth goes he on his way
The father and the master, with his spouse,
And with that family, whom now the cord
Girt humbly: nor did abjectness of heart
Weigh down his eyelids, for that he was son
Of Pietro Bernardone, and by men
In wonderous sort despised. But royally
His hard intention he to Innocent
Set forth; and, from him, first received the seal
On his religion. Then, when numerous flock'd
The tribe of lowly ones, that traced his steps,
Whose marvellous life deservedly were sung
In heights empyreal; through Honorius' hand
A second crown, to deck their Guardian's virtues,
Was by the eternal Spirit inwreathed: and when
He had, through thirst of martyrdom, stood up
In the proud Soldan's presence, and there preach'd
Christ and his followers, but found the race
Unripen'd for conversion; back once more
He hasted (not to intermit his toil),
And reap'd Ausonian lands. On the hard rock,
'Twixt Arno and the Tiber, he from Christ
Took the last signet, which his limbs two years
Did carry. Then, the season come that he,
Who to such good had destined him, was pleased
To advance him to the meed, which he had earn'd
By his self-humbling; to his brotherhood,
As their just heritage, he gave in charge
His dearest lady: and enjoin'd their love
And faith to her; and, from her bosom, will'd

[337]

His goodly spirit should move forth, returning
To its appointed kingdom; nor would have
His body laid upon another bier.

"Think now of one, who were a fit colleague
To keep the bark of Peter, in deep sea,
Helm'd to right point; and such our Patriarch was.
Therefore who follow him as he enjoins,
Thou mayst be certain, take good lading in.
But hunger of new viands tempts his flock;
So that they needs into strange pastures wide
Must spread them: and the more remote from him
The stragglers wander, so much more they come
Home, to the sheep-fold, destitute of milk,
There are of them, in truth, who fear their harm,
And to the shepherd cleave; but these so few,
A little stuff may furnish out their cloaks.

"Now, if my words be clear; if thou have ta'en
Good heed; if that, which I have told, recall
To mind; thy wish may be in part fulfill'd:
For thou wilt see the plant from whence they split;
And he shall see, who girds him, what that means,
'That well they thrive, not swol'n with vanity.'"

CANTO XII

Bonaventura praises St. Dominic and informs the poet about the glorified souls in this second garland.

SOON as its final word the blessed flame
Had raised for utterance, straight the holy mill
Began to wheel; nor yet had once revolved,
Or e'er another, circling, compass'd it,
Motion to motion, song to song, conjoining;
Song, that as much our muses doth excel,
Our Syrens with their tuneful pipes, as ray
Of primal splendor doth its faint reflex.

[338]

PARADISE

As when, if Juno bid her handmaid forth,
Two arches parallel, and trick'd alike,
Span the thin cloud, the outer taking birth
From that within (in manner of that voice
Whom love did melt away, as sun the mist)
And they who gaze, presageful call to mind
The compact, made with Noah, of the world
No more to be o'erflow'd; about us thus,
Of sempiternal roses, bending, wreathed
Those garlands twain; and to the innermost
E'en thus the external answer'd. When the footing,
And other great festivity, of song,
And radiance, light with light accordant, each
Jocund and blythe, had at their pleasure still'd,
(E'en as the eyes, by quick volition moved,
Are shut and raised together), from the heart
Of one amongst the new lights moved a voice,
That made me seem like needle to the star,
In turning to its whereabouts; and thus
Began: "The love, that makes me beautiful,
Prompts me to tell of the other guide, for whom
Such good of mine is spoken. Where one is,
The other worthily should also be;
That as their warfare was alike, alike
Should be their glory. Slow, and full of doubt,
And with thin ranks, after its banner moved
The army of Christ (which it so dearly cost
To reappoint), when its imperial Head,
Who reigneth ever, for the drooping host
Did make provision, through grace alone,
And not through its deserving. As thou heard'st,
Two champions to the succor of his spouse
He sent, who by their deeds and words might join
Again his scatter'd people. In that clime
Where springs the pleasant west-wind to unfold
The fresh leaves, with which Europe sees herself
New-garmented; nor from those billows far,
Beyond whose chiding, after weary course,
The sun doth sometimes hide him; safe abides
The happy Callaroga, under guard

THE DIVINE COMEDY

Of the great shield, wherein the lion lies
Subjected and supreme. And there was born
The loving minion of the Christian faith,
The hallow'd wrestler, gentle to his own,
And to his enemies terrible. So replete
His soul with lively virtue, that when first
Created, even in the mother's womb,
It prophesied. When, at the sacred font,
The spousals were complete 'twixt faith and him,
Where pledge of mutual safety was exchanged,
The dame, who was his surety, in her sleep
Beheld the wondrous fruit, that was from him
And from his heirs to issue. And that such
He might be construed, as indeed he was,
She was inspired to name him of his owner,
Whose he was wholly; and so call'd him Dominic.
And I speak of him, as the laborer,
Whom Christ in his own garden chose to be
His help-mate. Messenger he seem'd, and friend
Fast-knit to Christ; and the first love he show'd,
Was after the first counsel that Christ gave.
Many a time his nurse, at entering, found
That he had risen in silence, and was prostrate,
As who should say, 'My errand was for this.'
O happy father! Felix rightly named.
O favor'd mother! rightly named Joanna;
If that do mean, as men interpret it.
Not for the world's sake, for which now they toil
Upon Ostiense and Taddeo's lore,
But for the real manna, soon he grew
Mighty in learning; and did set himself
To go about the vineyard, that soon turns
To wan and wither'd, if not tended well:
And from the see (whose bounty to the just
And needy is gone by, not through its fault,
But his who fills it basely) he besought,
No dispensation for commuted wrong,
Nor the first vacant fortune, nor the tenths
That to God's paupers rightly appertain,
But, 'gainst an erring and degenerate world,

PARADISE

License to fight, in favor of that seed
From which the twice twelve cions gird thee round.
Then, with sage doctrine and good-will to help,
Forth on his great apostleship he fared,
Like torrent bursting from a lofty vein;
And, dashing 'gainst the stocks of heresy,
Smote fiercest, where resistance was most stout.
Thence many rivulets have since been turn'd,
Over the garden catholic to lead
Their living waters, and have fed its plants.

"If such, one wheel of that two-yoked car,
Wherein the holy Church defended her,
And rode triumphant through the civil broil;
Thou canst not doubt its fellow's excellence,
Which Thomas, ere my coming, hath declared
So courteously unto thee. But the track,
Which its smooth fellies made, is now deserted:
That, mouldy mother is, where late were lees.
His family, that wont to trace his path,
Turn backward, and invert their steps; erelong
To rue the gathering in of their ill crop,
When the rejected tares in vain shall ask
Admittance to the barn. I question not
But he, who search'd our volume, leaf by leaf,
Might still find page with this inscription on't,
'I am as I was wont.' Yet such were not
From Acquasparta nor Casale, whence,
Of those who come to meddle with the text,
One stretches and another cramps its rule.
Buonaventura's life in me behold,
From Bagnoregio; one, who, in discharge
Of my great offices, still laid aside
All sinister aim. Illuminato here,
And Agostino join me: two they were,
Among the first of those barefooted meek ones,
Who sought God's friendship in the cord: with them
Hugues of Saint Victor; Pietro Mangiadore;
And he of Spain in his twelve volumes shining;
Nathan the prophet; Metropolitan

Chrysostom; and Anselmo; and, who deign'd
To put his hand to the first art, Donatus.
Raban is here; and at my side there shines
Calabria's abbot, Joachim, endow'd
With soul prophetic. The bright courtesy
Of friar Thomas and his goodly lore,
Have moved me to the blazon of a peer
So worthy; and with me have moved this throng."

CANTO XIII

*Thomas Aquinas solves another of Dante's doubts
and warns him against assenting to any proposition
without having duly examined it.*

LET him, who would conceive what now I saw,
Imagine (and retain the image firm
As mountain rock, the whilst he hears me speak),
Of stars, fifteen, from midst the ethereal host
Selected, that, with lively ray serene,
O'ercome the massiest air: thereto imagine
The wain, that, in the bosom of our sky,
Spins ever on its axle night and day,
With the bright summit of that horn, which swells
Due from the pole, round which the first wheel rolls,
To have ranged themselves in fashion of two signs
In heaven, such as Ariadne made,
When death's chill seized her; and that one of them
Did compass in the other's beam; and both
In such sort whirl around, that each should tend
With opposite motion: and, conceiving thus,
Of that true constellation, and the dance
Twofold, that circled me, he shall attain
As 'twere the shadow; for things there as much
Surpass our usage, as the swiftest heaven
Is swifter than the Chiana. There was sung
No Bacchus, and no Io Pæan, but

PARADISE

Three Persons in the Godhead, and in one
Person that nature and the human join'd.

   The song and round were measured: and to us
Those saintly lights attended, happier made
At each new ministering. Then silence brake
Amid the accordant sons of Deity,
That luminary, in which the wondrous life
Of the meek man of God was told to me;
And thus it spake: "One ear o' the harvest thresh'd,
And its grain safely stored, sweet charity
Invites me with the other to like toil.

   "Thou know'st, that in the bosom, whence the rib
Was ta'en to fashion that fair cheek, whose taste
All the world pays for; and in that, which pierced
By the keen lance, both after and before
Such satisfaction offer'd as outweighs
Each evil in the scale; whate'er of light
To human nature is allow'd, must all
Have by his virtue been infused, who form'd
Both one and other: and thou thence admirest
In that I told thee, of beatitudes,
A second there is none to him enclosed
In the fifth radiance. Open now thine eyes
To what I answer thee; and thou shalt see
Thy deeming and my saying meet in truth,
As centre in the round. That which dies not,
And that which can die, are but each the beam
Of that idea, which our Sovereign Sire
Engendereth loving; for that lively light,
Which passeth from his splendor, not disjoin'd
From him, nor from his love triune with them,
Doth, through his bounty, congregate itself,
Mirror'd, as 'twere, in new existences;
Itself unalterable, and ever one.

   "Descending hence unto the lowest powers,
Its energy so sinks, at last it makes

THE DIVINE COMEDY

But brief contingencies; for so I name
Things generated, which the heavenly orbs
Moving, with seed or without seed, produce.
Their wax, and that which moulds it, differ much:
And thence with lustre, more or less, it shows
The ideal stamp imprest: so that one tree,
According to his kind, hath better fruit,
And worse: and, at your birth, ye, mortal men,
Are in your talents various. Were the wax
Moulded with nice exactness, and the heaven
In its disposing influence supreme,
The brightness of the seal should be complete.
But nature renders it imperfect ever;
Resembling thus the artist, in his work,
Whose faltering hand is faithless to his skill.
Therefore, if fervent love dispose, and mark
The lustrous image of the primal virtue,
There all perfection is vouchsafed; and such
The clay was made, accomplish'd with each gift,
That life can teem with; such the burden fill'd
The virgin's bosom: so that I commend
Thy judgment, that the human nature ne'er
Was, or can be, such as in them it was.

"Did I advance no further than this point;
'How then had he no peer?' thou might'st reply.
But, that what now appears not, may appear
Right plainly, ponder, who he was, and what
(When he was bidden 'Ask') the motive, sway'd
To his requesting. I have spoken thus,
That thou mayst see, he was a king, who ask'd
For wisdom, to the end he might be king
Sufficient: not, the number to search out
Of the celestial movers; or to know,
If necessary with contingent e'er
Have made necessity; or whether that
Be granted, that first motion is; or if,
Of the mid-circle, can by art be made
Triangle, with its corner blunt or sharp.

PARADISE

"Whence, noting that, which I have said, and this,
Thou kingly prudence and that ken mayst learn,
At which the dart of my intention aims.
And, marking clearly, that I told thee, 'Risen,'
Thou shalt discern it only hath respect
To kings, of whom are many, and the good
Are rare. With this distinction take my words;
And they may well consist with that which thou
Of the first human father dost believe,
And of our well-beloved. And let this
Henceforth be lead unto thy feet, to make
Thee slow in motion, as a weary man,
Both to the 'yea' and to the 'nay' thou seest not.
For he among the fools is down full low,
Whose affirmation, or denial, is
Without distinction, in each case alike.
Since it befalls, that in most instances
Current opinion leans to false: and then
Affection bends the judgment to her ply.

"Much more than vainly doth he lose from shore,
Since he returns not such as he set forth,
Who fishes for the truth and wanteth skill.
And open proofs of this unto the world
Have been afforded in Parmenides,
Melissus, Bryso, and the crowd beside,
Who journey'd on, and knew not whither: so did
Sabellius, Arius, and the other fools,
Who, like to scimitars, reflected back
The scripture-image by distortion marr'd.

"Let not the people be too swift to judge;
As one who reckons on the blades in field,
Or e'er the crop be ripe. For I have seen
The thorn frown rudely all the winter long,
And after bear the rose upon its top;
And bark, that all her way across the sea
Ran straight and speedy, perish at the last
E'en in the haven's mouth. Seeing one steal,

Another bring his offering to the priest,
Let not Dame Birtha and Sir Martin thence
Into heaven's counsels deem that they can pry:
For one of these may rise, the other fall."

CANTO XIV

After listening to Solomon, Dante and Beatrice proceed to Mars and behold the spirits of those who died fighting for the true faith.

FROM centre to the circle, and so back
From circle to the centre, water moves
In the round chalice, even as the blow
Impels it, inwardly, or from without.
Such was the image glanced into my mind,
As the great spirit of Aquinum ceased;
And Beatrice, after him, her words
Resumed alternate: "Need there is (though yet
He tells it to you not in words, nor e'en
In thought) that he should fathom to its depth
Another mystery. Tell him, if the light,
Wherewith your semblance blooms, shall stay with you
Eternally, as now; and, if it doth,
How, when ye shall regain your visible forms,
The sight may without harm endure the change,
That also tell." As those, who in a ring
Tread the light measure, in their fitful mirth
Raise loud the voice, and spring with gladder bound;
Thus, at the hearing of that pious suit,
The saintly circles, in their tourneying
And wondrous note, attested new delight.

Whoso laments, that we must doff this garb
Of frail mortality, thenceforth to live
Immortally above; he hath not seen
The sweet refreshing of that heavenly shower.

PARADISE

Him, who lives ever, and forever reigns
In mystic union of the Three in One,
Unbounded, bounding all, each spirit thrice
Sang, with such melody, as, but to hear,
For highest merit were an ample meed.
And from the lesser orb the goodliest light,
With gentle voice and mild, such as perhaps
The angel's once to Mary, thus replied:
"Long as the joy of Paradise shall last,
Our love shall shine around that raiment, bright
As fervent; fervent as, in vision, blest;
And that as far, in blessedness, exceeding,
As it hath grace, beyond its virtue, great.
Our shape, regarmented with glorious weeds
Of saintly flesh, must, being thus entire,
Show yet more gracious. Therefore shall increase
Whate'er, of light, gratuitous imparts
The Supreme Good; light, ministering aid,
The better to disclose his glory: whence,
The vision needs increasing, must increase
The fervor, which it kindles; and that too
The ray, that comes from it. But as the gleed
Which gives out flame, yet in its whiteness shines
More livelily than that, and so preserves
Its proper semblance; thus this circling sphere
Of splendor shall to view less radiant seem,
Than shall our fleshly robe, which yonder earth
Now covers. Nor will such excess of light
O'erpower us, in corporeal organs made
Firm, and susceptible of all delight."

So ready and so cordial an "Amen"
Follow'd from either choir, as plainly spoke
Desire of their dead bodies; yet perchance
Not for themselves, but for their kindred dear,
Mothers and sires, and those whom best they loved,
Ere they were made imperishable flame.

And lo! forthwith there rose up round about
A lustre, over that already there;

THE DIVINE COMEDY

Of equal clearness, like the brightening up
Of the horizon. As at evening hour
Of twilight, new appearances through heaven
Peer with faint glimmer, doubtfully descried;
So, there, new substances, methought, began
To rise in view beyond the other twain,
And wheeling, sweep their ampler circuit wide.

O genuine glitter of eternal Beam!
With what a sudden whiteness did it flow,
O'erpowering vision in me. But so fair,
So passing lovely, Beatrice show'd,
Mind cannot follow it, nor words express
Her infinite sweetness. Thence mine eyes regain'd
Power to look up; and I beheld myself,
Sole with my lady, to more lofty bliss
Translated: for the star, with warmer smile
Impurpled, well denoted our ascent.

With all the heart, and with that tongue which speaks
The same in all, a holocaust I made
To God befitting the new grace vouchsafed.
And from my bosom had not yet upsteam'd
The fuming of that incense, when I knew
The rite accepted. With such mighty sheen
And mantling crimson, in two listed rays
The splendors shot before me, that I cried,
"God of Sabaoth! that dost prank them thus!"

As leads the galaxy from pole to pole,
Distinguish'd into greater lights and less,
Its pathway, which the wisest fail to spell;
So thickly studded, in the depth of Mars,
Those rays described the venerable sign,
That quadrants in the round conjoining frame.

Here memory mocks the toil of genius. Christ
Beam'd on that cross; and pattern fails me now.
But whoso takes his cross, and follows Christ,
Will pardon me for that I leave untold,

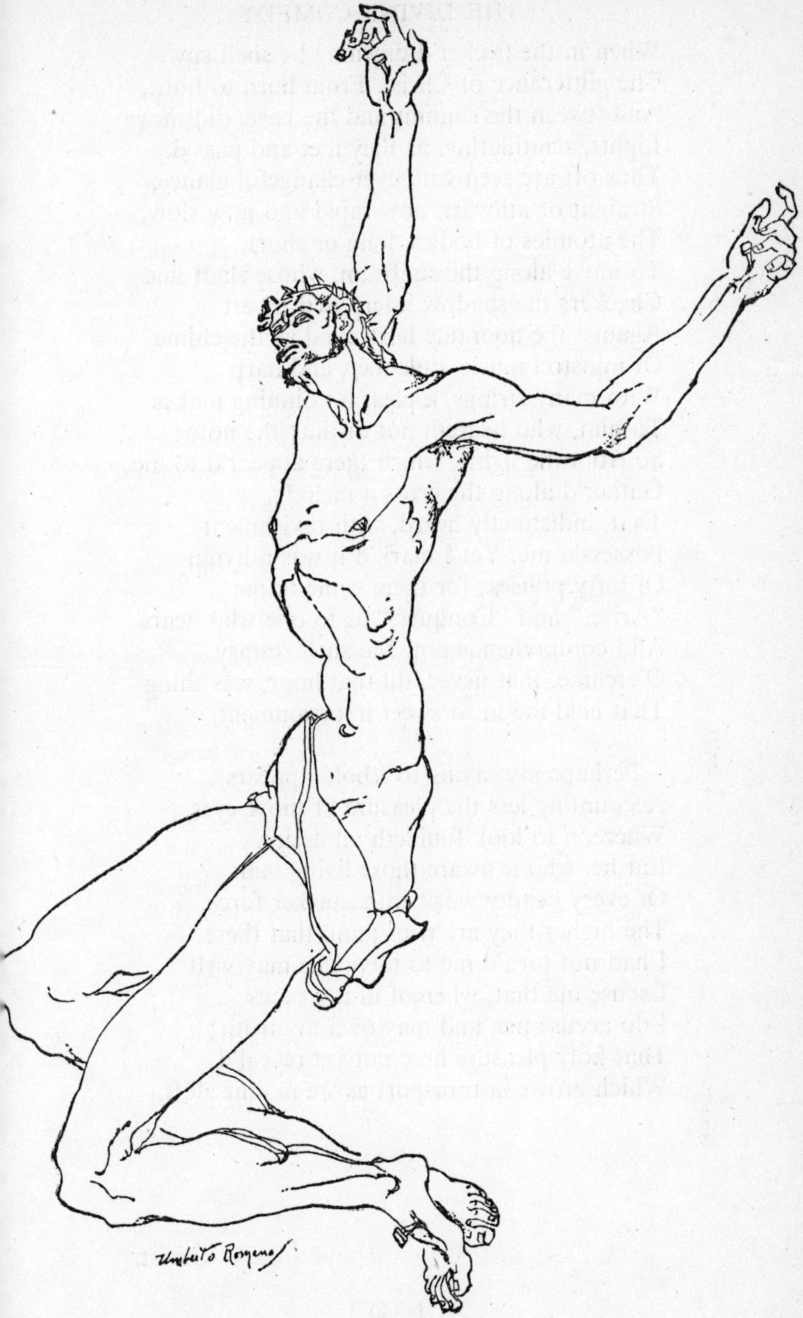
Umberto Romano

THE DIVINE COMEDY

When in the flecker'd dawning he shall spy
The glitterance of Christ. From horn to horn,
And 'tween the summit and the base, did move
Lights, scintillating, as they met and pass'd.
Thus oft are seen with ever-changeful glance,
Straight or athwart, now rapid and now slow,
The atomies of bodies, long or short,
To move along the sunbeam, whose slant line
Checkers the shadow interposed by art
Against the noontide heat. And as the chime
Of minstrel music, dulcimer, and harp
With many strings, a pleasant dinning makes
To him, who heareth not distinct the note;
So from the lights, which there appear'd to me,
Gather'd along the cross a melody,
That, indistinctly heard, with ravishment
Possess'd me. Yet I mark'd it was a hymn
Of lofty praises; for there came to me
"Arise," and "Conquer," as to one who hears
And comprehends not. Me such ecstasy
O'ercame, that never, till that hour, was thing
That held me in so sweet imprisonment.

Perhaps my saying overbold appears,
Accounting less the pleasure of those eyes,
Whereon to look fulfilleth all desire.
But he, who is aware those living seals
Of every beauty work with quicker force,
The higher they are risen; and that there
I had not turn'd me to them; he may well
Excuse me that, whereof in my excuse
I do accuse me, and may own my truth;
That holy pleasure here not yet reveal'd,
Which grows in transport as we mount aloft.

[350]

PARADISE

CANTO XV

*The spirit of Cacciaguida speaks of the simplicity
of the Florentines in his days.*

TRUE love, that ever shows itself as clear
In kindness, as loose appetite in wrong,
Silenced that lyre harmonious, and still'd
The sacred chords, that are by Heaven's right hand
Unwound and tighten'd. How to righteous prayers
Should they not hearken, who, to give me will
For praying, in accordance thus were mute?
He hath in sooth good cause for endless grief,
Who, for the love of thing that lasteth not,
Despoils himself forever of that love.

As oft along the still and pure serene,
At nightfall, glides a sudden trail of fire,
Attracting with involuntary heed
The eye to follow it, erewhile at rest;
And seems some star that shifted place in heaven,
Only that, whence it kindles, none is lost,
And it is soon extinct: thus from the horn,
That on the dexter of the cross extends,
Down to its foot, one luminary ran
From mid the cluster shone there; yet no gem
Dropp'd from its foil: and through the beamy list,
Like flame in alabaster, glow'd its course.
So forward stretch'd him (if of credence aught
Our greater muse may claim) the pious ghost
Of old Anchises, in the Elysian bower,
When he perceived his son. "O thou, my blood!
O most exceeding grace divine! to whom,
As now to thee, hath twice the heavenly gate
Been e'er unclosed?" So spake the light: whence I
Turn'd me toward him; then unto my dame
My sight directed: and on either side
Amazement waited me; for in her eyes

[351]

Was lighted such a smile, I thought that mine
Had dived unto the bottom of my grace
And of my bliss in Paradise. Forthwith,
To hearing and to sight grateful alike,
The spirit to his proem added things
I understood not, so profound he spake:
Yet not of choice, but through necessity,
Mysterious; for his high conception soar'd
Beyond the mark of mortals. When the flight
Of holy transport had so spent its rage,
That nearer to the level of our thought
The speech descended; the first sounds I heard
Were, "Blest be thou, Triunal Deity!
That hast such favor in my seed vouchsafed."
Then follow'd: "No unpleasant thirst, though long,
Which took me reading in the sacred book,
Whose leaves or white or dusky never change,
Thou hast allay'd, my son! within this light,
From whence my voice thou hear'st: more thanks to her
Who, for such lofty mounting, has with plumes
Begirt thee. Thou dost deem thy thoughts to me
From Him transmitted, who is first of all,
E'en as all numbers ray from unity;
And therefore dost not ask me who I am,
Or why to thee more joyous I appear,
Than any other in this gladsome throng.
The truth is as thou deem'st; for in this life
Both less and greater in that mirror look,
In which thy thoughts, or e'er thou think'st, are shown.
But, that the love, which keeps me wakeful ever,
Urging with sacred thirst of sweet desire,
May be contented fully; let thy voice,
Fearless, and frank, and jocund, utter forth
Thy will distinctly, utter forth the wish,
Whereto my ready answer stands decreed."

  I turn'd me to Beatrice; and she heard
Ere I had spoken, smiling an assent,
That to my will gave wings; and I began:
"To each among your tribe, what time ye kenn'd

PARADISE

The nature, in whom naught unequal dwells,
Wisdom and love were in one measure dealt;
For that they are so equal in the sun,
From whence ye drew your radiance and your heat,
As makes all likeness scant. But will and means,
In mortals, for the cause ye well discern,
With unlike wings are fledge. A mortal, I
Experience inequality like this;
And therefore give no thanks, but in the heart,
For thy paternal greeting. This howe'er
I pray thee, living topaz! that ingemm'st
This precious jewel; let me hear thy name."

"I am thy root, O leaf! whom to expect
Even, hath pleased me." Thus the prompt reply
Prefacing, next it added: "He, of whom
Thy kindred appellation comes, and who,
These hundred years and more, on its first ledge
Hath circuited the mountain, was my son,
And thy great-grandsire. Well befits, his long
Endurance should be shorten'd by thy deeds.

"Florence, within her ancient limit-mark,
Which calls her still to matin prayers and noon,
Was chaste and sober, and abode in peace.
She had no armlets and no head-tires then;
No purfled dames; no zone, that caught the eye
More than the person did. Time was not yet,
When at his daughter's birth the sire grew pale,
For fear the age and dowry should exceed,
On each side, just proportion. House was none
Void of its family: nor yet had come
Sardanapalus, to exhibit feats
Of chamber prowess. Montemalo yet
O'er our suburban turret rose; as much
To be surpassed in fall, as in its rising.
I saw Bellincion Berti walk abroad
In leathern girdle, and a clasp of bone;
And, with no artful coloring on her cheeks,
His lady leave the glass. The sons I saw

[353]

THE DIVINE COMEDY

Of Nerli, and of Vecchio, well content
With unrobed jerkin; and their good dames handling
The spindle and the flax: O happy they!
Each sure of burial in her native land,
And none left desolate a-bed for France.
One waked to tend the cradle, hushing it
With sounds that lull'd the parent's infancy;
Another, with her maidens, drawing off
The tresses from the distaff, lectured them
Old tales of Troy, and Fesole, and Rome.
A Salterello and Cianghella we
Had held as strange a marvel, as ye would
A Cincinnatus or Cornelia now.

"In such composed and seemly fellowship,
Such faithful and such fair equality,
In so sweet household, Mary at my birth
Bestow'd me, call'd on with loud cries; and there,
In your old baptistery, I was made
Christian at once and Cacciaguida; as were
My brethren Eliseo and Moronto.

"From Valdipado came to me my spouse;
And hence thy surname grew. I follow'd then
The Emperor Conrad: and his knighthood he
Did gird on me; in such good part he took
My valiant service. After him I went
To testify against that evil law,
Whose people, by the shepherd's fault, possess
Your right usurp'd. There I by that foul crew
Was disentangled from the treacherous world
Whose base affection many a spirit soils;
And from the martyrdom came to this peace."

PARADISE

CANTO XVI

Cacciaguida recounts the names of the chief Florentine families of his time and accounts for the subsequent degeneration of the city.

O SLIGHT respect of man's nobility!
I never shall account it marvellous,
That our infirm affection here below
Thou movest to boasting; when I could not chuse,
E'en in that region of unwarp'd desire,
In heaven itself, but make my vaunt in thee.
Yet cloak thou art soon shorten'd; for that Time,
Unless thou be eked out from day to day,
Goes round thee with his shears. Resuming then,
With greeting such as Rome was first to bear,
But since hath disaccustom'd, I began:
And Beatrice, that a little space
Was sevr'd, smiled; reminding me of her,
Whose cough embolden'd (as the story holds)
To first offence the doubting Guenever.

"You are my sire," said I: "you give me heart
Freely to speak my thought: above myself
You raise me. Through so many streams with joy
My soul is fill'd, that gladness wells from it;
So that it bears the mighty tide, and bursts not.
Say then, my honor'd stem! what ancestors
Were those who sprang from, and what years were mark'd
In your first childhood? Tell me of the fold,
That hath Saint John for guardian, what was then
Its state, and who in it were highest seated!"

As embers, at the breathing of the wind,
Their flame enliven; so that light I saw
Shine at my blandishments; and, as it grew
More fair to look on, so with voice more sweet,
Yet not in this our modern phrase, forthwith

[355]

It answer'd: "From the day, when it was said
'Hail Virgin!' to the throes by which my mother,
Who now is sainted, lighten'd her of me
Whom she was heavy with, this fire had come
Five hundred times and fourscore, to relume
Its radiance underneath the burning foot
Of its own lion. They, of whom I sprang,
And I, had there our birth-place, where the last
Partition of our city first is reach'd
By him that runs her annual game. Thus much
Suffice of my forefathers: who they were,
And whence they hither came, more honorable
It is to pass in silence than to tell.
All those who at that time were there, betwixt
Mars and the Baptist, fit to carry arms,
Were but the fifth, of them this day alive.
But then the citizen's blood, that now is mix'd
From Campi and Certaldo and Fighine,
Ran purely through the last mechanic's veins.
O how much better were it, that these people
Were neighbors to you; and that at Galluzzo
And at Trespiano ye should have your boundary;
Than to have them within, and bear the stench
Of Aguglione's hind, and Signa's, him,
That hath his eye already keen for bartering.
Had not the people, which of all the world
Degenerates most, been stepdame unto Cæsar,
But, as a mother to her son been kind,
Such one, as hath become a Florentine,
And trades and traffics, had been turn'd adrift
To Simifonte, where his grandsire plied
The beggar's craft: the Conti were possessed
Of Montemurlo still: the Cerchi still
Were in Acone's parish: nor had haply
From Valdigreve passed the Buondelmonti.
The city's malady hath ever source
In the confusion of its persons, as
The body's, in variety of food:
And the blind bull falls with a steeper plunge,
Than the blind lamb: and oftentimes one sword

PARADISE

Doth more and better execution,
Than five. Mark Luni; Urbisaglia mark;
How they are gone; and after them how go
Chiusi and Sinigaglia: and 'twill seem
No longer new, or strange to thee, to hear
That families fail, when cities have their end.
All things that appertain to ye, like yourselves,
Are mortal: but mortality in some
Ye mark not; they endure so long, and you
Pass by so suddenly. And as the moon
Doth, by the rolling of her heavenly sphere,
Hide and reveal the strand unceasingly;
So fortune deals with Florence. Hence admire not
At what of them I tell thee, whose renown
Time covers, the first Florentines. I saw
The Ughi, Catilini, and Filippi,
The Alberichi, Greci, and Ormanni,
Now in their wane, illustrious citizens;
And great as ancient, of Sannella him,
With him of Arca saw, and Soldanieri,
And Ardinghi, and Bostichi. At the poop
That now is laden with new felony
So cumbrous it may speedily sink the bark,
The Ravignani sat, of whom is sprung
The County Guido, and whoso hath since
His title from the famed Bellincion ta'en.
Fair governance was yet an art well prized
By him of Pressa: Galigaio show'd
The gilded hilt and pommel, in his house:
The column, clothed with verrey, still was seen
Unshaken; the Sachetti still were great,
Giouchi, Sifanti, Galli, and Barucci,
With them who blush to hear the bushel named.
Of the Calfucci still the branchy trunk
Was in its strength: and, to the curule chairs,
Sizii and Arrigucci yet were drawn.
How mighty them I saw, whom, since, their pride
Hath undone! And in all their goodly deeds
Florence was, by the bullets of bright gold,
O'erflourish'd. Such the sires of those, who now,

[357]

As surely as your church is vacant, flock
Into her consistory, and at leisure
There stall them and grow fat. The o'erweening brood,
That plays the dragon after him that flees,
But unto such as turn and show the tooth,
Ay or the purse, is gentle as a lamb,
Was on its rise, but yet so slight esteem'd,
That Ubertino of Donati grudged
His father-in-law should yoke him to its tribe.
Already Caponsacco had descended
Into the mart from Fesole: and Giuda
And Infangato were good citizens.
A thing incredible I tell, though true:
The gateway, named from those of Pera, led
Into the narrow circuit of your walls.
Each one, who bears the sightly quarterings
Of the great Baron, (he whose name and worth
The festival of Thomas still revives),
His knighthood and his privilege retain'd;
Albeit one, who borders them with gold,
This day is mingled with the common herd.
In Borgo yet the Gualterotti dwelt,
And Importuni: well for its repose,
Had it still lack'd of newer neighborhood.
The house, from whence your tears have had their spring,
Through the just anger, that hath murder'd ye
And put a period to your gladsome days,
Was honor'd; it, and those consorted with it.
O Buondelmonti! what ill counselling
Prevail'd on thee to break the plighted bond?
Many, who now are weeping, would rejoice,
Had God to Ema given thee, the first time
Thou near our city camest. But so was doom'd:
Florence! on that maim'd stone which guards the bridge,
The victim, when thy peace departed, fell.

"With these and others like to them, I saw
Florence in such assured tranquillity,
She had no cause at which to grieve: with these

PARADISE

Saw her so glorious and so just, that ne'er
The lily from the lance had hung reverse,
Or through division been with vermeil dyed."

CANTO XVII

*Cacciaguida predicts Dante's exile and exhorts
him to write the present poem.*

SUCH as the youth, who came to Clymene,
To certify himself of that reproach
Which had been fasten'd on him (he whose end
Still makes the fathers chary to their sons),
E'en such was I; nor unobserved was such
Of Beatrice, and that saintly lamp,
Who had erewhile for me his station moved;
When thus my lady: "Give thy wish free vent,
That it may issue, bearing true report
Of the mind's impress: not that aught thy words
May to our knowledge add, but to the end
That thou mayst use thyself to own thy thirst,
And men may mingle for thee when they hear."

"O plant, from whence I spring! revered and loved!
Who soar'st so high a pitch, that thou as clear,
As earthly thought determines two obtuse
In one triangle not contain'd, so clear
Dost see contingencies, ere in themselves
Existent, looking at the point whereto
All times are present; I, the whilst I scaled
With Virgil the soul-purifying mount
And visited the nether world of woe,
Touching my future destiny have heard
Words grievous, though I feel me on all sides
Well squared to fortune's blows. Therefore my will
Were satisfied to know the lot awaits me.
The arrow, seen beforehand, slacks his flight."

THE DIVINE COMEDY

So said I to the brightness, which erewhile
To me had spoken; and my will declared,
As Beatrice will'd, explicitly.
Nor with oracular response obscure,
Such as, or e'er the Lamb of God was slain,
Beguiled the credulous nations: but, in terms
Precise, and unambiguous lore, replied
The spirit of paternal love, enshrined,
Yet in his smile apparent; and thus spake:
"Contingency, whose verge extendeth not
Beyond the tablet of your mortal mould,
Is all depictured in the eternal sight;
But hence deriveth not necessity,
More than the tall ship, hurried down the flood,
Is driven by the eye that looks on it.
From thence, as to the ear sweet harmony
From organ comes, so comes before mine eye
The time prepared for thee. Such as driven out
From Athens, by his cruel stepdame's wiles,
Hippolytus departed; such must thou
Depart from Florence. This they wish, and this
Contrive, and will ere long effectuate, there,
Where gainful merchandise is made of Christ
Throughout the live-long day. The common cry,
Will, as 'tis ever wont, affix the blame
Unto the party injured: but the truth
Shall, in the vengeance it dispenseth, find
A faithful witness. Thou shalt leave each thing
Beloved most dearly: this is the first shaft
Shot from the bow of exile. Thou shalt prove
How salt the savor is of other's bread;
How hard the passage, to descend and climb
By other's stairs. But that shall gall thee most,
Will be the worthless and vile company,
With whom thou must be thrown into these straits.
For all ungrateful, impious all, and mad,
Shall turn 'gainst thee: but in a little while,
Theirs, and not thine, shall be the crimson'd brow,
Their course shall so evince their brutishness,
To have ta'en thy stand apart shall well become thee.

PARADISE

"First refuge thou must find, first place of rest,
In the great Lombard's courtesy, who bears,
Upon the ladder perch'd, the sacred bird.
He shall behold thee with such kind regard,
That 'twixt ye two, the contrary to that
Which 'falls 'twixt other men, the granting shall
Forerun the asking. With him shalt thou see
That mortal, who was at his birth impressed
So strongly from this star, that of his deeds
The nations shall take note. His unripe age
Yet holds him from observance; for these wheels
Only nine years have compassed him about.
But, ere the Gascon practise on great Harry,
Sparkles of virtue shall shoot forth in him,
In equal scorn of labors and of gold.
His bounty shall be spread abroad so widely,
As not to let the tongues, e'en of his foes,
Be idle in its praise. Look thou to him,
And his beneficence: for he shall cause
Reversal of their lot to many people;
Rich men and beggars interchanging fortunes.
And thou shalt bear this written in thy soul,
Of him, but tell it not": and things he told
Incredible to those who witness them;
Then added: "So interpret thou, my son,
What hath been told thee.—Lo! the ambushment
That a few circling seasons hide for thee.
Yet envy not thy neighbors: time extends
Thy span beyond their treason's chastisement."

Soon as the saintly spirit, by silence, mark'd
Completion of that web, which I had stretch'd
Before it, warp'd for weaving; I began,
As one, who in perplexity desires
Counsel of other, wise, benign, and friendly:
"My father! well I mark how time spurs on
Toward me, ready to inflict the blow,
Which falls most heavily on him who most
Abandoneth himself. Therefore 'tis good
I should forecast, that, driven from the place

[361]

THE DIVINE COMEDY

Most dear to me, I may not lose myself
All other by my song. Down through the world
Of infinite mourning; and along the mount,
From whose fair height my lady's eyes did lift me;
And, after, through this Heaven, from light to light:
Have I learnt that, which if I tell again,
It may with many wofully disrelish:
And, if I am a timid friend to truth,
I fear my life may perish among those,
To whom these days shall be of ancient date."

   The brightness, where enclosed the treasure smiled,
Which I had found there, first shone glisteringly,
Like to a golden mirror in the sun;
Next answer'd: "Conscience, dimm'd or by its own
Or other's shame, will feel thy saying sharp.
Thou, notwithstanding, all deceit removed,
See the whole vision be made manifest.
And let them wince, who have their withers wrung.
What though, when tasted first, thy voice shall prove
Unwelcome: on digestion, it will turn
To vital nourishment. The cry thou raisest
Shall, as the wind doth, smite the proudest summits;
Which is of honor no light argument.
For this, there only have been shown to thee,
Throughout these orbs, the mountain, and the deep,
Spirits, whom fame hath note of. For the mind
Of him who hears, is loth to acquiesce
And fix its faith, unless the instance brought
Be palpable, and proof apparent urge."

CANTO XVIII

*Dante ascends to Jupiter, the sixth heaven, where he finds
the souls of those who had administered justice
rightly in the world.*

Now in his word, sole, ruminating, joy'd
That blessed spirit: and I fed on mine,
Tempering the sweet with bitter. She meanwhile,
Who led me unto God, admonish'd: "Muse
On other thoughts: bethink thee, that near Him
I dwell, who recompenseth every wrong."

At the sweet sounds of comfort straight I turn'd;
And, in the saintly eyes what love was seen,
I leave in silence here, nor through distrust
Of my words only, but that to such bliss
The mind remounts not without aid. Thus much
Yet may I speak; that, as I gazed on her,
Affection found no room for other wish.
While the everlasting pleasure, that did full
On Beatrice shine, with second view
From her fair countenance my gladden'd soul
Contented; vanquishing me with a beam
Of her soft smile, she spake: "Turn thee, and list.
These eyes are not thy only Paradise."

As here, we sometimes in the looks may see
The affection mark'd, when that its sway hath ta'en
The spirit wholly; thus the hallow'd light,
To whom I turn'd, flashing, bewray'd its will
To talk yet further with me, and began:
"On this fifth lodgment of the tree, whose life
Is from its top, whose fruit is ever fair
And leaf unwithering, blessed spirits abide,
That were below, ere they arrived in heaven,
So mighty in renown, as every muse
Might grace her triumph with them. On the horns

THE DIVINE COMEDY

Look, therefore, of the cross: he whom I name,
Shall there enact, as doth in summer cloud
Its nimble fire." Along the cross I saw,
At the repeated name of Joshua,
A splendor gliding; nor, the word was said,
Ere it was done: then, at the naming, saw,
Of the great Maccabee, another move
With whirling speed; and gladness was the scourge
Unto that top. The next for Charlemain
And for the peer Orlando, two my gaze
Pursued, intently, as the eye pursues
A falcon flying. Last, along the cross,
William, and Renard, and Duke Godfrey drew
My ken, and Robert Guiscard. And the soul
Who spake with me, among the other lights
Did move away, and mix; and with the quire
Of heavenly songsters proved his tuneful skill.

To Beatrice on my right I bent,
Looking for intimation, or by word
Or act, what next behoved; and did descry
Such mere effulgence in her eyes, such joy,
It pass'd all former wont. And, as by sense
Of new delight, the man, who perseveres
In good deeds, doth perceive, from day to day,
His virtue growing; I e'en thus perceived,
Of my ascent, together with the heaven,
The circuit widen'd; noting the increase
Of beauty in that wonder. Like the change
In a brief moment on some maiden's cheek,
Which, from its fairness, doth discharge the weight
Of pudency, that stain'd it; such in her,
And to mine eyes so sudden was the change,
Through silvery whiteness of that temperate star
Whose sixth orb now enfolded us. I saw,
Within that jovial cresset, the clear sparks
Of love, that reign'd there, fashion to my view
Our language. And as birds, from river banks
Arisen, now in round, now lengthen'd troop,
Array them in their flight, greeting, as seems,

[364]

PARADISE

Their new-found pastures; so, within the lights,
The saintly creatures flying, sang; and made
Now D, now I, now L, figured i' the air.
First singing to their notes they moved; then, one
Becoming of these signs, a little while
Did rest them, and were mute. O nymph divine
Of Pegasean race! who souls, which thou
Inspirest, makest glorious and long-lived, as they
Cities and realms by thee; thou with thyself
Inform me; that I may set forth the shapes,
As fancy doth present them: be thy power
Display'd in this brief song. The characters,
Vocal and consonant, were five-fold seven.
In order, each, as they appear'd, I mark'd
Diligite Justitiam, the first,
Both verb and noun all blazon'd; and the extreme,
Qui judicatis terram. In the M
Of the fifth word they held their station;
Making the star seem silver streak'd with gold.
And on the summit of the M, I saw
Descending other lights, that rested there,
Singing, methinks, their bliss and primal good.
Then, as at shaking of a lighted brand,
Sparkles innumerable on all sides
Rise scatter'd, source of augury to the unwise:
Thus more than thousand twinkling lustres hence
Seem'd reascending; and a higher pitch
Some mounting, and some less, e'en as the sun,
Which kindleth them, decreed. And when each one
Had settled in his place; the head and neck
Then saw I of an eagle, livelily
Graved in that streaky fire. Who painteth there,
Hath none to guide Him: of Himself he guides:
And every line and texture of the nest
Doth own from Him the virtue fashions it.
The other bright beatitude, that seem'd
Erewhile, with lilied crowning, well content
To over-canopy the M, moved forth,
Following gently the impress of the bird.

THE DIVINE COMEDY

Sweet star! what glorious and thick-studded gems
Declared to me our justice on the earth
To be the effluence of that heaven, which thou,
Thyself a costly jewel, dost inlay.
Therefore I pray the Sovran Mind, from whom
Thy motion and thy virtue are begun,
That He would look from whence the fog doth rise,
To vitiate thy beam; so that once more
He may put forth his hand 'gainst such, as drive
Their traffic in that sanctuary, whose walls
With miracles and martyrdoms were built.
Ye host of heaven, whose glory I survey!
O beg ye grace for those, that are, on earth,
All after ill example gone astray.
War once had for his instrument the sword:
But now 'tis made, taking the bread away,
Which the good Father locks from none.—And thou,
That writest but to cancel, think, that they,
Who for the vineyard, which thou wastest, died,
Peter and Paul, live yet, and mark thy doings.
Thou hast good cause to cry, "My heart so cleaves
To him, that lived in solitude remote,
And for a dance was dragg'd to martyrdom,
I wist not of the fisherman nor Paul."

CANTO XIX

*The eagle declares the cause for which it is exalted
to the state of glory and discusses salvation
and the day of judgment.*

BEFORE my sight appear'd, with open wings,
The beauteous image; in fruition sweet,
Gladdening the thronged spirits. Each did seem
A little ruby, whereon so intense
The sun-beam glow'd, that to mine eyes it came
In clear refraction. And that, which next
Befalls me to portray, voice hath not utter'd,

PARADISE

Nor hath ink written, nor in fantasy
Was e'er conceived. For I beheld and heard
The beak discourse; and, what intention form'd
Of many, singly as of one express,
Beginning: "For that I was just and piteous,
I am exalted to this height of glory,
The which no wish exceeds: and there on earth
Have I my memory left, e'en by the bad
Commended, while they leave its course untrod."

   Thus is one heat from many embers felt;
As in that image many were the loves,
And one the voice, that issued from them all:
Whence I address'd them: "O perennial flowers
Of gladness everlasting! that exhale
In single breath your odors manifold;
Breathe now: and let the hunger be appeased,
That with great craving long hath held my soul,
Finding no food on earth. This well I know;
That if there be in heaven a realm, that shows
In faithful mirror the celestial Justice,
Yours without veil reflects it. Ye discern
The heed, wherewith I do prepare myself
To hearken; ye, the doubt, that urges me
With such inveterate craving." Straight I saw,
Like to a falcon issuing from the hood,
That rears his head, and claps him with his wings,
His beauty and his eagerness bewraying;
So saw I move that stately sign, with praise
Of grace divine inwoven, and high song
Of inexpressive joy. "He," it began,
"Who turn'd his compass on the world's extreme,
And in that space so variously hath wrought,
Both openly and in secret; in such wise
Could not, through all the universe, display
Impression of his glory, that the Word
Of his omniscience should not still remain
In infinite excess. In proof whereof,
He first through pride supplanted, who was sum
Of each created being, waited not

For light celestial; and abortive fell.
Whence needs each lesser nature is but scant
Receptacle unto that Good, which knows
No limit measured by itself alone.
Therefore your sight, of the omnipresent Mind
A single beam, its origin must own
Surpassing far its utmost potency.
The ken, your world is gifted with, descends
In the everlasting Justice as low down,
As eye doth in the sea; which, though it mark
The bottom from the shore, in the wide main
Discerns it not; and ne'ertheless it is;
But hidden through its deepness. Light is none,
Save that which cometh from the pure serene
Of ne'er disturbed ether: for the rest,
'Tis darkness all; or shadow of the flesh,
Or else its poison. Here confess reveal'd
That covert, which hath hidden from thy search
The living justice, of the which thou madest
Such frequent question; for thou said'st—'A man
Is born on Indus' banks, and none is there
Who speaks of Christ, nor who doth read nor write;
And all his inclinations and his acts,
As far as human reason sees, are good;
And he offendeth not in word or deed:
But unbaptized he dies, and void of faith.
Where is the justice that condemns him? where
His blame, if he believeth not?'—What then,
And who art thou, that on the stool wouldst sit
To judge at distance of a thousand miles
With the short-sighted vision of a span?
To him, who subtilizes thus with me,
There would assuredly be room for doubt
Even to wonder, did not the safe word
Of Scripture hold supreme authority.

"O animals of clay! O spirits gross!
The primal will, that in itself is good,
Hath from itself, the chief Good, ne'er been moved.
Justice consists in consonance with it,

PARADISE

Derivable by no created good,
Whose very cause depends upon its beam."

As on her nest the stork, that turns about
Unto her young, whom lately she hath fed,
Whiles they with upward eyes do look on her;
So lifted I my gaze; and, bending so,
The ever-blessed image waved its wings,
Laboring with such deep counsel. Wheeling round
It warbled, and did say: "As are my notes
To thee, who understand'st them not; such is
The eternal judgment unto mortal ken."

Then still abiding in that ensign ranged,
Wherewith the Romans overawed the world,
Those burning splendors of the Holy Spirit
Took up the strain; and thus it spake again:
"None ever hath ascended to this realm,
Who hath not a believer been in Christ,
Either before or after the blest limbs
Were nail'd upon the wood. But lo! of those
Who call 'Christ! Christ!' there shall be many found,
In judgment, further off from him by far,
Than such to whom his name was never known.
Christians like these the Æthiop shall condemn:
When that the two assemblages shall part;
One rich eternally, the other poor.

"What may the Persians say unto your kings,
When they shall see that volume, in the which
All their dispraise is written, spread to view?
There amidst Albert's works shall that be read,
Which will give speedy motion to the pen,
When Prague shall mourn her desolated realm.
There shall be read the woe, that he doth work
With his adulterate money on the Seine,
Who by the tusk will perish: there be read
The thirsting pride, that maketh fool alike
The English and Scot, impatient of their bound.
There shall be seen the Spaniard's luxury;

[369]

THE DIVINE COMEDY

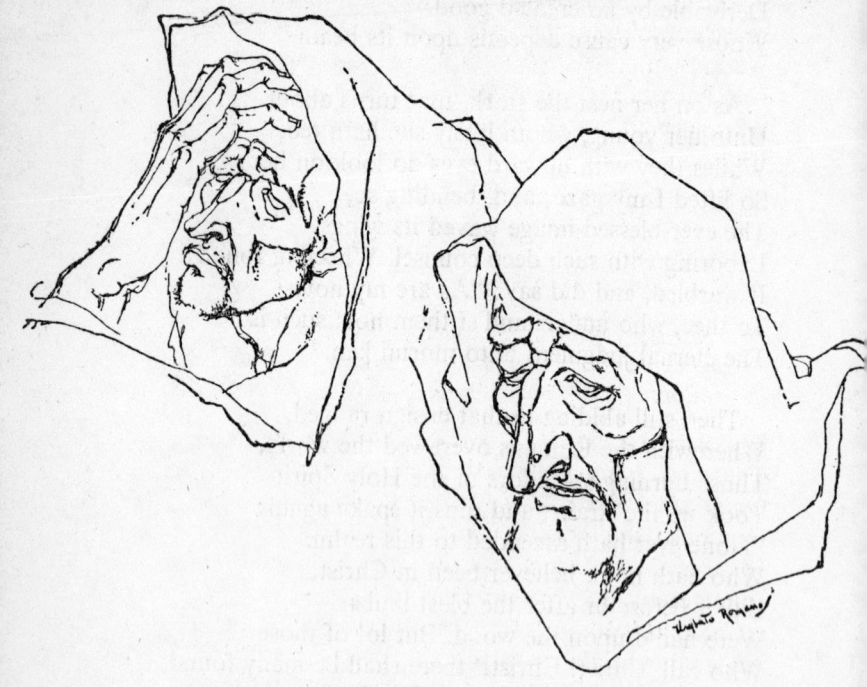

The delicate living there of the Bohemian,
Who still to worth has been a willing stranger.
The halter of Jerusalem shall see
A unit for his virtue; for his vices,
No less a mark than million. He, who guards
The isle of fire by old Anchises honor'd,
Shall find his avarice there and cowardice;
And better to denote his littleness,
The writing must be letters maim'd, that speak
Much in a narrow space. All there shall know
His uncle and his brother's filthy doings,
Who so renown'd a nation and two crowns
Have bastardized. And they, of Portugal
And Norway, there shall be exposed, with him
Of Ratza, who hath counterfeited ill
The coin of Venice. O blessed Hungary!
If thou no longer patiently abidest
Thy ill-entreating: and, O blest Navarre!

[370]

PARADISE

If with thy mountainous girdle thou wouldst arm thee.
In earnest of that day, e'en now are heard
Wailings and groans in Famagosta's streets
And Nicosia's, grudging at their beast,
Who keepeth even footing with the rest."

CANTO XX

*The eagle celebrates the praise of certain kings
and explains how the souls of those who had no
means of believing in Christ came to heaven.*

WHEN, disappearing from our hemisphere,
The world's enlightener vanishes, and day
On all sides wasteth; suddenly the sky,
Erewhile irradiate only with his beam,
Is yet again unfolded, putting forth
Innumerable lights wherein one shines.
Of such vicissitude in Heaven I thought;
As the great sign, that marshalleth the world
And the world's leaders, in the blessed beak
Was silent: for that all those living lights,
Waxing in splendor, burst forth into songs,
Such as from memory glide and fall away.

Sweet Love, that dost apparel thee in smiles!
How lustrous was thy semblance in those sparkles,
Which merely are from holy thoughts inspired.

After the precious and bright beaming stones,
That did ingem the sixth light, ceased the chiming
Of their angelic bells; methought I heard
The murmuring of a river, that doth fall
From rock to rock transpicuous, making known
The richness of his spring-head: and as sound
Of cittern, at the fret-board, or of pipe,
Is, at the wind-hole, modulate and tuned;
Thus up the neck, as it were hollow, rose

[371]

THE DIVINE COMEDY

That murmuring of the eagle; and forthwith
Voice there assumed; and thence along the beak
Issued in form of words, such as my heart
Did look for, on whose tables I inscribed them.

"The part in me, that sees and bears the sun
In mortal eagles," it began, "must now
Be noted steadfastly: for, of the fires,
That figure me, those, glittering in mine eye,
Are chief of all the greatest. This, that shines
Midmost for pupil, was the same who sang
The Holy Spirit's song, and bare about
The ark from town to town: now doth he know
The merit of his soul-impassion'd strains
By their well-fitted guerdon. Of the five,
That make the circle of the vision, he,
Who to the beak is nearest, comforted
The widow for her son: now doth he know,
How dear it costeth not to follow Christ;
Both from experience of this pleasant life,
And of its opposite. He next, who follows
In the circumference, for the over-arch,
By true repenting slack'd the pace of death:
Now knoweth he, that the decrees of heaven
Alter not, when, through pious prayer below,
To-day is made to-morrow's destiny.
The other following, with the laws and me,
To yield the shepherd room, pass'd o'er to Greece;
From good intent, producing evil fruit:
Now knoweth he, how all the ill, derived
From his well doing, doth not harm him aught;
Though it have brought destruction on the world.
That, which thou seest in the under bow,
Was William, whom that land bewails, which weeps
For Charles and Frederick living: now he knows,
How well is loved in heaven the righteous king;
Which he betokens by his radiant seeming.
Who, in the erring world beneath, would deem
That Trojan Ripheus, in this round, was set,
Fifth of the saintly splendors? now he knows

PARADISE

Enough of that, which the world cannot see;
The grace divine: albeit e'en his sight
Reach not its utmost depth." Like to the lark,
That warbling in the air expatiates long,
Then, trilling out his last sweet melody,
Drops, satiate with the sweetness; such appear'd
That image, stamped by the everlasting pleasure,
Which fashions, as they are, all things that be.

I, though my doubting were as manifest,
As is through glass the hue that mantles it,
In silence waited not; for to my lips
"What things are these?" involuntary rush'd,
And forced a passage out: whereat I mark'd
A sudden lightening and new revelry.
The eye was kindled; and the blessed sign,
No more to keep me wondering and suspense,
Replied: "I see that thou believest these things,
Because I tell them, but discern'st not how;
So that thy knowledge waits not on thy faith:
As one, who knows the name of thing by rote,
But is a stranger to its properties,
Till other's tongue reveal them. Fervent love,
And lively hope, with violence assail
The kingdom of the heavens, and overcome
The will of the Most High; not in such sort
As man prevails o'er man; but conquers it,
Because 'tis willing to be conquer'd; still,
Though conquer'd, by its mercy, conquering.

"Those, in the eye who live the first and fifth,
Cause thee to marvel, in that thou behold'st
The region of the angels deck'd with them.
They quitted not their bodies, as thou deem'st,
Gentiles, but Christians; in firm rooted faith,
This, of the feet in future to be pierced,
That, of feet nail'd already to the cross.
One from the barrier of the dark abyss,
Where never any with good-will returns,
Came back unto his bones. Of lively hope

THE DIVINE COMEDY

Such was the meed; of lively hope, that wing'd
The prayers sent up to God for his release,
And put power into them to bend His will.
The glorious Spirit, of whom I speak to thee,
A little while returning to the flesh,
Believed in him, who had the means to help;
And, in believing, nourish'd such a flame
Of holy love, that at the second death
He was made sharer in our gamesome mirth.
The other, through the riches of that grace,
Which from so deep a fountain doth distil,
As never eye created saw its rising,
Placed all his love below on just and right:
Wherefore, of grace, God oped in him the eye
To the redemption of mankind to come;
Wherein believing, he endured no more
The filth of Paganism, and for their ways
Rebuked the stubborn nations. The three nymphs,
Whom at the right wheel thou beheld'st advancing,
Were sponsors for him, more than thousand years
Before baptizing. O how far removed,
Predestination! is thy root from such
As see not the First Cause entire: and ye,
O mortal men! be wary how ye judge:
For we, who see our Maker, know not yet
The number of the chosen; and esteem
Such scantiness of knowledge our delight:
For all our good is, in that primal good,
Concentrate; and God's will and ours are one."

So, by that form divine, was given to me
Sweet medicine to clear and strengthen sight.
And, as one handling skilfully the harp,
Attendant on some skilful songster's voice,
Bids the chord vibrate; and therein the song
Acquires more pleasure: so the whilst it spake,
It doth remember me, that I beheld
The pair of blessed luminaries move,
Like the accordant twinkling of two eyes,
Their beamy circlets, dancing to the sounds.

CANTO XXI

Dante ascends to Saturn, the seventh heaven, for the souls of those who had passed their lives in holy retirement and contemplation.

AGAIN mine eyes were fix'd on Beatrice;
And, with mine eyes, my soul that in her looks
Found all contentment. Yet no smile she wore:
And, "Did I smile," quoth she, "thou wouldst be straight
Like Semele when into ashes turn'd:
For, mounting these eternal palace-stairs,
My beauty, which the loftier it climbs,
As thou hast noted, still doth kindle more,
So shines, that, were no tempering interposed,
Thy mortal puissance would from its rays
Shrink, as the leaf doth from the thunderbolt.
Into the seventh splendor are we wafted,
That, underneath the burning lion's breast,
Beams, in this hour, commingled with his might.
Thy mind be with thine eyes; and, in them, mirror'd
The shape, which in this mirror shall be shown."

Whoso can deem, how fondly I had fed
My sight upon her blissful countenance,
May know, when to new thoughts I changed, what joy
To do the bidding of my heavenly guide;
In equal balance, poising either weight.

Within the crystal, which records the name
(As its remoter circle girds the world)
Of that loved monarch, in whose happy reign
No ill had power to harm, I saw rear'd up,
In color like to sun-illumined gold,
A ladder, which my ken pursued in vain,
So lofty was the summit; down whose steps
I saw the splendors in such multitude
Descending, every light in heaven, methought,

[375]

Was shed thence. As the rooks, at dawn of day,
Bestirring them to dry their feathers chill,
Some speed their way a-field; and homeward some,
Returning, cross their flight; while some abide,
And wheel around their airy lodge: so seem'd
That glitterance, wafted on alternate wing,
As upon certain stair it came, and clash'd
Its shining. And one, lingering near us, wax'd
So bright, that in my thought I said: "The love,
Which this betokens me, admits no doubt."

Unwillingly from question I refrain;
To her, by whom my silence and my speech
Are order'd, looking for a sign: whence she,
Who in the sight of Him, that seeth all,
Saw wherefore I was silent, prompted me
To indulge the fervent wish; and I began:
"I am not worthy, of my own desert,
That thou shouldst answer me: but for her sake,
Who hath vouchsafed my asking, spirit blest,
That in thy joy are shrouded! say the cause,
Which bringeth thee so near: and wherefore, say,
Doth the sweet symphony of Paradise
Keep silence here, pervading with such sounds
Of rapt devotion every lower sphere?"
"Mortal art thou in hearing, as in sight";
Was the reply: "and what forbade the smile
Of Beatrice interrupts our song.
Only to yield thee gladness of my voice,
And of the light that vests me, I thus far
Descend these hallow'd steps; not that more love
Invites me; for, lo! there aloft, as much
Or more of love is witness'd in those flames:
But such my lot by charity assign'd,
That makes us ready servants, as thou seest,
To execute the counsel of the Highest."

"That in this court," said I, "O sacred lamp!
Love no compulsion needs, but follows free
The eternal Providence, I well discern:

PARADISE

This harder find to deem: why, of thy peers,
Thou only, to this office wert foredoom'd."

I had not ended, when, like rapid mill,
Upon its centre whirl'd the light; and then
The love that did inhabit there, replied:
"Splendor eternal, piercing through these folds,
Its virtue to my vision knits; and thus
Supported, lifts me so above myself,
That on the sovran essence, which it wells from,
I have the power to gaze: and hence the joy,
Wherewith I sparkle, equalling with my blaze
The keenness of my sight. But not the soul,
That is in heaven most lustrous, nor the seraph,
That hath his eyes most fix'd on God, shall solve
What thou hast ask'd: for in the abyss it lies
Of th' everlasting statute sunk so low,
That no created ken may fathom it.
And, to the mortal world when thou return'st,
Be this reported: that none henceforth dare
Direct his footsteps to so dread a bourn.
The mind, that here is radiant, on the earth
Is wrapt in mist. Look then if she may do
Below, what passeth her ability
When she is ta'en to heaven." By words like these
Admonish'd, I the question urged no more;
And of the spirit humbly sued alone
To instruct me of its state. " 'Twixt either shore
Of Italy, nor distant from thy land,
A stony ridge ariseth; in such sort,
The thunder doth not lift his voice so high.
They call it Catria: at whose foot, a cell
Is sacred to the lonely Eremite;
For worship set apart and holy rites."
A third time thus it spake; then added: "There
So firmly to God's service I adhered,
That with no costlier viands than the juice
Of olives, easily I pass'd the heats
Of summer and the winter frosts; content
In heaven-ward musings. Rich were the returns

THE DIVINE COMEDY

And fertile, which that cloister once was used
To render to these heavens: now 'tis fallen
Into a waste so empty, that ere long
Detection must lay bare its vanity.
Pietro Damiano there was I y-clept:
Pietro the sinner, when before I dwelt,
Beside the Adriatic, in the house
Of our blessed Lady. Near upon my close
Of mortal life, through much importuning
I was constrained to wear the hat, that still
From bad to worse is shifted.—Cephas came;
He came, who was the Holy Spirit's vessel;
Barefoot and lean; eating their bread, as chanced,
At the first table. Modern Shepherds need
Those who on either hand may prop and lead them,.
So burly are they grown; and from behind,
Others to hoist them. Down the palfrey's sides
Spread their broad mantles, so as both the beasts
Are cover'd with one skin. O patience! thou
That look'st on this, and dost endure so long."

I at those accents saw the splendors down
From step to step alight, and wheel, and wax,
Each circuiting, more beautiful. Round this
They came, and stay'd them; utter'd then a shout
So loud, it hath no likeness here: nor I
Wist what it spake, so deafening was the thunder.

CANTO XXII

*St. Benedict inveighs against the corruption of the monks.
Dante mounts to the eighth heaven; the fixed stars.*

ASTOUNDED, to the guardian of my steps
I turn'd me, like the child, who always runs
Thither for succor, where he trusteth most:
And she was like the mother, who her son
Beholding pale and breathless, with her voice

PARADISE

Soothes him, and he is cheer'd; for thus she spake,
Soothing me: "Know'st not thou, thou art in heaven?
And know'st not thou, whatever is in heaven,
Is holy; and that nothing there is done,
But is done zealously and well? Deem now,
What change in thee the song, and what my smile
Had wrought, since thus the shout had power to move thee;
In which, couldst thou have understood their prayers,
The vengeance were already known to thee,
Which thou must witness ere thy mortal hour.
The sword of heaven is not in haste to smite,
Nor yet doth linger; save unto his seeming,
Who, in desire or fear, doth look for it.
But elsewhere now I bid thee turn thy view;
So shalt thou many a famous spirit behold."

Mine eyes directing, as she will'd, I saw
A hundred little spheres, that fairer grew
By interchange of splendor. I remain'd,
As one, who fearful of o'er-much presuming,
Abates in him the keenness of desire,
Nor dares to question; when, amid those pearls,
One largest and most lustrous onward drew,
That it might yield contentment to my wish;
And, from within it, these the sounds I heard.

"If thou, like me, beheld'st the charity
That burns amongst us; what thy mind conceives,
Were utter'd. But that, ere the lofty bound
Thou reach, expectance may not weary thee;
I will make answer even to the thought,
Which thou hast such respect of. In old days,
That mountain, at whose side Cassino rests,
Was, on its height, frequented by a race
Deceived and ill-disposed: and I it was,
Who thither carried first the name of Him,
Who brought the soul-subliming truth to man.
And such a speeding grace shone over me,
That from their impious worship I reclaim'd
The dwellers round about, who with the world

[379]

Were in delusion lost. These other flames,
The spirits of men contemplative, were all
Enliven'd by that warmth, whose kindly force
Gives birth to flowers and fruits of holiness.
Here is Macarius; Romoaldo here;
And here my brethren, who their steps refrain'd
Within the cloisters, and held firm their heart."

I answering thus: "My gentle words and kind,
And this the cheerful semblance I behold,
Not unobservant, beaming in ye all,
Have raised assurance in me; wakening it
Full-blossom'd in my bosom, as a rose
Before the sun, when the consummate flower
Has spread to utmost amplitude. Of thee
Therefore intreat I, father, to declare
If I may gain such favor, as to gaze
Upon thine image by no covering veil'd."

"Brother!" he thus rejoin'd, "in the last sphere
Expect completion of thy lofty aim:
For there on each desire completion waits,
And there on mine; where every aim is found
Perfect, entire, and for fulfilment ripe.
There all things are as they have ever been:
For space is none to bound; nor pole divides.
Our ladder reaches even to that clime;
And so, at giddy distance, mocks thy view.
Thither the patriarch Jacob saw it stretch
Its topmost round; when it appear'd to him
With angels laden. But to mount it now
None lifts his foot from earth: and hence my rule
Is left a profitless stain upon the leaves;
The walls, for abbey rear'd, turn'd into dens;
The cowls, to sacks chok'd up with musty meal.
Foul usury doth not more lift itself
Against God's pleasure, than that fruit, which makes
The hearts of monks so wanton: for whate'er
Is in the Church's keeping, all pertains

PARADISE

To such, as sue for heaven's sweet sake; and not
To those, who in respect of kindred claim,
Or on more vile allowance. Mortal flesh
Is grown so dainty, good beginnings last not
From the oak's birth unto the acorn's setting.
His convent Peter founded without gold
Or silver; I, with prayers and fasting, mine;
And Francis, his in meek humility.
And if thou note the point, whence each proceeds,
Then look what it hath err'd to; thou shalt find
The white grown murky. Jordan was turn'd back.
And a less wonder, than the refluent sea,
May, at God's pleasure, work amendment here."

So saying, to his assembly back he drew:
And they together cluster'd into one;
Then all roll'd upward, like an eddying wind.

The sweet dame beckon'd me to follow them:
And, by that influence only, so prevail'd
Over my nature, that no natural motion,
Ascending or descending here below,
Had, as I mounted, with my pennon vied.

So, reader, as my hope is to return
Unto the holy triumph, for the which
I ofttimes wail my sins, and smite my breast;
Thou hadst been longer drawing out and thrusting
Thy finger in the fire, than I was, ere
The sign, that followeth Taurus, I beheld,
And enter'd its precinct. O glorious stars!
O light impregnate with exceeding virtue!
To whom whate'er of genius lifteth me
Above the vulgar, grateful I refer;
With ye the parent of all mortal life
Arose and set, when I did first inhale
The Tuscan air; and afterward, when grace
Vouchsafed me entrance to the lofty wheel
That in its orb impels ye, fate decreed

My passage at your clime. To you my soul
Devoutly sighs, for virtue, even now,
To meet the hard emprise that draws me on.

"Thou art so near the sum of blessedness,"
Said Beatrice, "that behoves thy ken
Be vigilant and clear. And, to this end,
Or ever thou advance thee further, hence
Look downward, and contemplate, what a world
Already stretch'd under our feet there lies:
So as thy heart may, in its blithest mood,
Present itself to the triumphal throng,
Which, through the ethereal concave, comes rejoicing."

I straight obey'd; and with mine eye return'd
Through all the seven spheres; and saw this globe
So pitiful of semblance, that perforce
It moved my smiles: and him in truth I hold
For wisest, who esteems it least; whose thoughts
Elsewhere are fix'd, him worthiest call and best.
I saw the daughter of Latona shine
Without the shadow, whereof late I deem'd
That dense and rare were cause. Here I sustain'd
The visage, Hyperion, of thy son;
And mark'd, how near him with their circles, round
Move Maia and Dione; here discern'd
Jove's tempering 'twixt his sire and son; and hence,
Their changes and their various aspects,
Distinctly scann'd. Nor might I not descry
Of all the seven, how bulky each, how swift;
Nor, of their several distances, not learn.
This petty area (o'er the which we stride
So fiercely), as along the eternal Twins
I wound my way, appear'd before me all,
Forth from the havens stretch'd unto the hills.
Then, to the beauteous eyes, mine eyes return'd.

CANTO XXIII

He sees Christ triumphing with his church. The Saviour ascends, followed by the Virgin Mother. The others remain with St. Peter.

E'EN as the bird, who midst the leafy bower
Has, in her nest, sat darkling through the night,
With her sweet brood; impatient to descry
Their wished looks, and to bring home their food,
In the fond quest unconscious of her toil:
She, of the time prevenient, on the spray,
That overhangs their couch, with wakeful gaze
Expects the sun; nor ever, till the dawn,
Removeth from the east her eager ken:
So stood the dame erect, and bent her glance
Wistfully on that region, where the sun
Abateth most his speed; that, seeing her
Suspense and wondering, I became as one,
In whom desire is waken'd, and the hope
Of somewhat new to come fills with delight.

Short space ensued; I was not held, I say,
Long in expectance, when I saw the heaven
Wax more and more resplendent; and, "Behold,"
Cried Beatrice, "the triumphal hosts
Of Christ, and all the harvest gather'd in,
Made ripe by these revolving spheres." Meseem'd,
That, while she spake, her image all did burn;
And in her eyes such fulness was of joy,
As I am fain to pass unconstrued by.

As in the calm full moon, when Trivia smiles,
In peerless beauty, 'mid the eternal nymphs,
That paint through all its gulfs the blue profound;
In bright pre-eminence so saw I there
O'er million lamps a sun, from whom all drew
Their radiance, as from ours the starry train:

THE DIVINE COMEDY

And, through the living light, so lustrous glow'd
The substance, that my ken endured it not.

O Beatrice! sweet and precious guide,
Who cheer'd me with her comfortable words:
"Against the virtue, that o'erpowereth thee,
Avails not to resist. Here is the Might,
And here the Wisdom, which did open lay
The path, that had been yearnèd for so long,
Betwixt the heaven and earth." Like to the fire,
That, in a cloud imprison'd, doth break out
Expansive, so that from its womb enlarged,
It falleth against nature to the ground;
Thus, in that heavenly banqueting, my soul
Outgrew herself; and, in the transport lost,
Holds now remembrance none of what she was.

"Ope thou thine eyes, and mark me: thou hast seen
Things that empower thee to sustain my smile."

I was as one, when a forgotten dream
Doth come across him, and he strives in vain
To shape it in his fantasy again:
Whenas that gracious boon was proffer'd me,
Which never may be cancel'd from the book
Wherein the past is written. Now were all
Those tongues to sound, that have, on sweetest milk
Of Polyhymnia and her sisters, fed
And fatten'd; not with all their help to boot,
Unto the thousandth parcel of the truth,
My song might shadow forth that saintly smile,
How merely, in her saintly looks, it wrought.
And, with such figuring of Paradise,
The sacred strain must leap, like one that meets
A sudden interruption to his road.
But he, who thinks how ponderous the theme,
And that 'tis laid upon a mortal shoulder,
May pardon, if it tremble with the burden.
The track, our venturous keel must furrow, brooks
No unribb'd pinnace, no self-sparing pilot.

[384]

PARADISE

"Why doth my face," said Beatrice, "thus
Enamour thee, as that thou dost not turn
Unto the beautiful garden, blossoming
Beneath the rays of Christ? Here is the rose,
Wherein the Word Divine was made incarnate;
And here the lilies, by whose odor known
The way of life was follow'd." Prompt I heard
Her bidding, and encounter'd once again
The strife of aching vision. As, erewhile,
Through glance of sun-light, stream'd through broken cloud,
Mine eyes a flower-besprinkled mead have seen;
Though veil'd themselves in shade: so saw I there
Legions of splendors, on whom burning rays
Shed lightnings from above; yet saw I not
The fountain whence they flow'd. O gracious virtue!
Thou, whose broad stamp is on them, higher up
Thou didst exalt thy glory, to give room
To my o'erlabor'd sight; when at the name
Of that fair flower, whom duly I invoke
Both morn and eve, my soul with all her might
Collected, on the goodliest ardor fix'd.
And, as the bright dimensions of the star
In heaven excelling, as once here on earth,
Were, in my eye-balls livelily portray'd;
Lo! from within the sky a cresset fell,
Circling in fashion of a diadem;
And girt the star; and, hovering, round it wheel'd.

Whatever melody sounds sweetest here,
And draws the spirit most unto itself,
Might seem a rent cloud, when it grates the thunder;
Compared unto the sounding of that lyre,
Wherewith the goodliest sapphire, that inlays
The floor of heaven, was crown'd. "Angelic Love
I am, who thus with hovering flight enwheel
The lofty rapture from that womb inspired,
Where our desire did dwell: and round thee so,
Lady of Heaven! will hover; long as thou
Thy Son shalt follow, and diviner joy
Shall from thy presence gild the highest sphere."

THE DIVINE COMEDY

Such close was to the circling melody:
And, as it ended, all the other lights
Took up the strain, and echoed Mary's name.

The robe, that with its regal folds enwraps
The world, and with the nearer breath of God
Doth burn and quiver, held so far retired
Its inner hem and skirting over us,
That yet no glimmer of its majesty
Had stream'd unto me: therefore were mine eyes
Unequal to pursue the crowned flame,
That towering rose, and sought the seed it bore.
And like to babe, that stretches forth its arms
For very eagerness toward the breast,
After the milk is taken; so outstretch'd
Their wavy summits all the fervent band,
Through zealous love to Mary: then, in view,
There halted; and "Regina Cœli" sang
So sweetly, the delight hath left me never.

Oh! what o'erflowing plenty is up-piled
In those rich-laden coffers, which below
Sow'd the good seed, whose harvest now they keep.
Here are the treasures tasted, that with tears
Were in the Babylonian exile won,
When gold had fail'd them. Here, in synod high
Of ancient council with the new convened,
Under the Son of Mary and of God,
Victorious he his mighty triumph holds,
To whom the keys of glory were assign'd.

CANTO XXIV

*St. Peter examines Dante touching Faith
and is contented with his answers.*

"O YE! in chosen fellowship advanced
To the great supper of the blessed Lamb,

[386]

PARADISE

Whereon who feeds hath every wish fulfill'd;
If to this man through God's grace be vouchsafed
Foretaste of that, which from your table falls,
Or ever death his fated term prescribe;
Be ye not heedless of his urgent will:
But may some influence of your sacred dews
Sprinkle him. Of the fount ye alway drink,
Whence flows what most he craves." Beatrice spake;
And the rejoicing spirits, like to spheres
On firm-set poles revolving, trail'd a blaze
Of comet splendor: and as wheels, that wind
Their circles in the horologe, so work
The stated rounds, that to the observant eye
The first seems still, and as it flew, the last;
E'en thus their carols weaving variously,
They, by the measure paced, or swift or slow,
Made me to rate the riches of their joy.

From that, which I did note in beauty most
Excelling, saw I issue forth a flame
So bright, as none was left more goodly there.
Round Beatrice thrice it wheel'd about,
With so divine a song, that fancy's ear
Records it not; and the pen passeth on,
And leaves a blank: for that our mortal speech,
Nor e'en the inward shaping of the brain,
Hath colors fine enough to trace such folds.

"O saintly sister mine! thy prayer devout
Is with so vehement affection urged,
Thou dost unbind me from that beauteous sphere."

Such were the accents toward my lady breathed
From that blest ardor, soon as it was stay'd;
To whom she thus: "O everlasting light
Of him, within whose mighty grasp our Lord
Did leave the keys, which of this wondrous bliss
He bare below! tent this man as thou wilt,
With lighter probe or deep, touching the faith,
By the which thou didst on the billows walk.

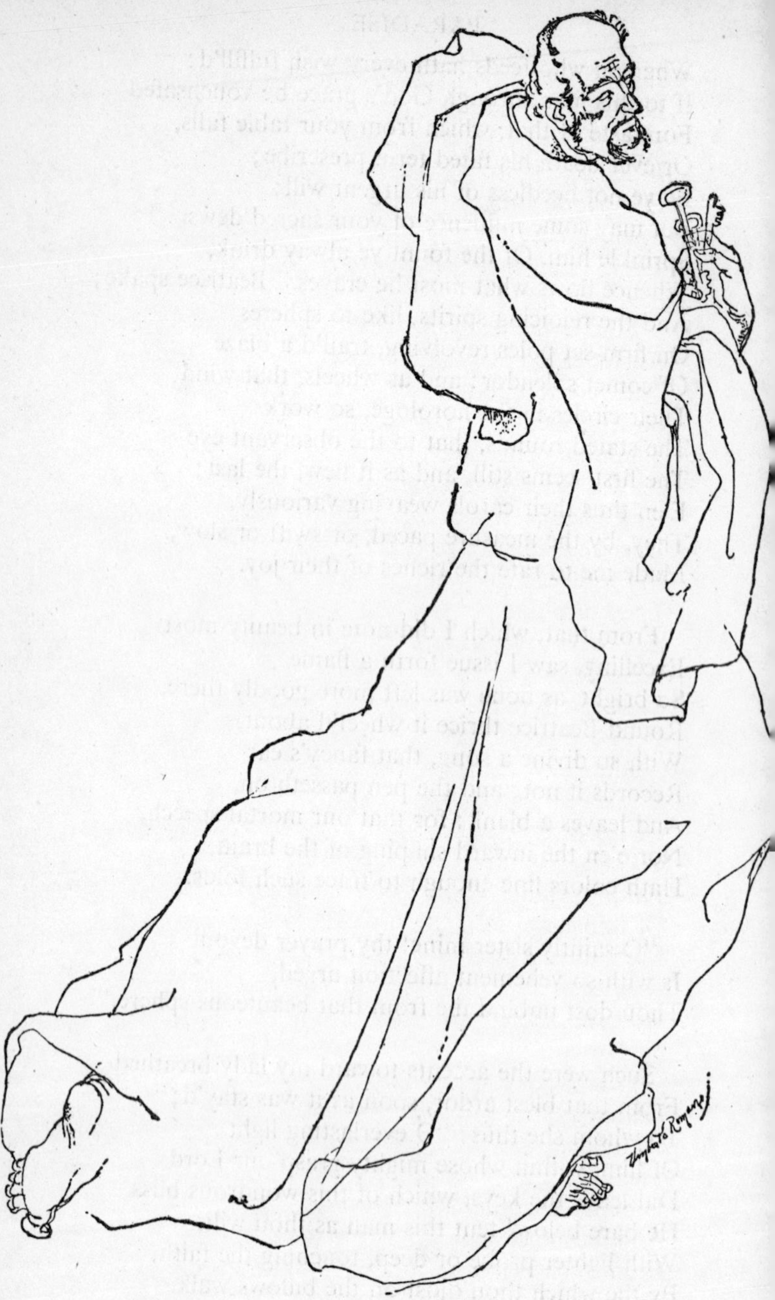
Umberto Romano

PARADISE

If he in love, in hope, and in belief,
Be steadfast, is not hid from thee: for thou
Hast there thy ken, where all things are beheld
In liveliest portraiture. But since true faith
Has peopled this fair realm with citizens;
Meet is, that to exalt its glory more,
Thou, in his audience, shouldst thereof discourse."

Like to the bachelor, who arms himself,
And speaks not, till the master have proposed
The question, to approve, and not to end it;
So I, in silence, arm'd me, while she spake,
Summoning up each argument to aid;
As was behoveful for such questioner,
And such profession: "As good Christian ought,
Declare thee, what is faith?" Whereat I raised
My forehead to the light, whence this had breathed;
Then turn'd to Beatrice; and in her looks
Approval met, that from their inmost fount
I should unlock the waters. "May the grace,
That giveth me the captain of the church
For confessor," said I, "vouchsafe to me
Apt utterance for my thoughts"; then added: "Sire,
E'en as set down by the unerring style
Of thy dear brother, who with thee conspired
To bring Rome in unto the way of life,
Faith of things hoped is substance, and the proof
Of things not seen; and herein doth consist
Methinks its essence." "Rightly hast thou deem'd,"
Was answer'd; "if thou well discern, why first
He hath defined it substance, and then proof."

"The deep things," I replied, "which here I scan
Distinctly, are below from mortal eye
So hidden, they have in belief alone
Their being; on which credence, hope sublime
Is built: and, therefore substance, it intends.
And inasmuch as we must needs infer
From such belief our reasoning, all respect
To other view excluded; hence of proof

THE DIVINE COMEDY

The intention is derived." Forthwith I heard:
"If thus, whate'er by learning men attain,
Were understood; the sophist would want room
To exercise his wit." So breathed the flame
Of love; then added: "Current is the coin
Thou utter'st, both in weight and in alloy.
But tell me, if thou hast it in thy purse."

"Even so glittering and so round," said I,
"I not a whit misdoubt of its assay."

Next issued from the deep-imbosom'd splendor:
"Say, whence the costly jewel, on the which
Is founded every virtue, came to thee."

"The flood," I answer'd, "from the Spirit of God
Rain'd down upon the ancient bond and new,—
Here is the reasoning, that convinceth me
So feelingly, each argument beside
Seems blunt, and forceless, in comparison."
Then heard I: "Wherefore holdest thou that each,
The elder proposition and the new,
Which so persuade thee, are the voice of heaven?"

"The works, that follow'd, evidence their truth";
I answer'd: "Nature did not make for these
The iron hot, or on her anvil mould them."

"Who voucheth to thee of the works themselves,"
Was the reply, "that they in very deed
Are that they purport? None hath sworn so to thee."

"That all the world," said I, "should have been turn'd
To Christian, and no miracle been wrought,
Would in itself be such a miracle,
The rest were not an hundredth part so great.
E'en thou went'st forth in poverty and hunger
To set the goodly plant, that, from the vine
It once was, now is grown unsightly bramble."

PARADISE

That ended, through the high celestial court
Resounded all the spheres, "Praise we one God!"
In song of most unearthly melody.
And when that Worthy thus, from branch to branch,
Examining, had led me, that we now
Approach'd the topmost bough; he straight resumed:
"The grace, that holds sweet dalliance with thy soul
So far discreetly hath thy lips unclosed;
That, whatsoe'er has passed them, I commend.
Behoves thee to express, what thou believest,
The next; and, whereon, thy belief hath grown."

"O saintly sire and spirit!" I began,
"Who seest that, which thou didst so believe,
As to outstrip feet younger than thine own,
Toward the sepulchre; thy will is here,
That I the tenor of my creed unfold;
And thou, the cause of it, hast likewise ask'd.
And I reply: I in one God believe;
One sole eternal Godhead, of whose love
All Heaven is moved, himself unmoved the while.
Nor demonstration physical alone,
Or more intelligential and abstruse,
Persuades me to this faith: but from that truth
It cometh to me rather, which is shed
Through Moses; the rapt Prophets; and the Psalms;
The Gospel; and what ye yourselves did write,
When ye were gifted of the Holy Ghost.
In three eternal Persons I believe;
Essence threefold and one; mysterious league
Of union absolute, which, many a time,
The word of gospel lore upon my mind
Imprints: and from this germ, this firstling spark
The lively flame dilates; and, like heaven's star,
Doth glitter in me." As the master hears,
Well pleased, and then enfoldeth in his arms
The servant, who hath joyful tidings brought,
And having told the errand keeps his peace;
Thus benediction uttering with song,
Soon as my peace I held, compass'd me thrice

The apostolic radiance, whose behest
Had oped my lips: so well their answer pleased.

CANTO XXV

*St. James questions the poet concerning Hope.
St. John informs him Christ and the Virgin
alone had come with their bodies into heaven.*

If e'er the sacred poem, that hath made
Both heaven and earth copartners in its toil,
And with lean abstinence, through many a year,
Faded my brow, be destined to prevail
Over the cruelty, which bars me forth
Of the fair sheep-fold, where, a sleeping lamb,
The wolves set on and fain had worried me;
With other voice, and fleece of other grain,
I shall forthwith return; and, standing up
At my baptismal font, shall claim the wreath
Due to the poet's temples: for I there
First enter'd on the faith, which maketh souls
Acceptable to God: and, for its sake,
Peter had then circled my forehead thus.

Next from the squadron, whence had issued forth
The first fruit of Christ's vicars on the earth,
Toward us moved a light, at view whereof
My Lady, full of gladness, spake to me:
"Lo! lo! behold the peer of mickle might,
That makes Galicia throng'd with visitants."

As when the ring-dove by his mate alights;
In circles, each about the other wheels,
And, murmuring, coos his fondness: thus saw I
One, of the other great and glorious prince,
With kindly greeting, hail'd; extolling, both,
Their heavenly banqueting: but when an end
Was to their gratulation, silent, each,

[392]

PARADISE

Before me sat they down, so burning bright,
I could not look upon them. Smiling then,
Beatrice spake: "O life in glory shrined!
Who didst the largess of our kingly court
Set down with faithful pen; let now thy voice,
Of hope the praises, in this height resound.
For well thou know'st, who figurest it as oft,
As Jesus, to ye three, more brightly shone."

"Lift up thy head; and be thou strong in trust:
For that, which hither from the mortal world
Arriveth, must be ripen'd in our beam."

Such cheering accents from the second flame
Assured me; and mine eyes I lifted up
Unto the mountains, that had bow'd them late
With over-heavy burden. "Sith our Liege
Wills of his grace, that thou, or e'er thy death,
In the most secret council with his lords
Shouldst be confronted, so that having view'd
The glories of our court, thou mayst therewith
Thyself, and all who hear, invigorate
With hope, that leads to blissful end; declare,
What is that hope? how it doth flourish in thee?
And whence thou hadst it?" Thus, proceeding still,
The second light: and she, whose gentle love
My soaring pennons in that lofty flight
Escorted, thus preventing me, rejoin'd:
"Among her sons, not one more full of hope,
Hath the church militant: so 'tis of him
Recorded in the sun, whose liberal orb
Enlighteneth all our tribe: and ere his term
Of warfare, hence permitted he is come,
From Egypt to Jerusalem, to see.
The other points, both which thou hast inquired,
Not for more knowledge, but that he may tell
How dear thou hold'st the virtue; these to him
Leave I: for he may answer thee with ease,
And without boasting, so God give him grace."

[393]

Like to the scholar, practised in his task,
Who, willing to give proof of diligence,
Seconds his teacher gladly; "Hope," said I,
"Is of the joy to come a sure expectance,
The effect of grace divine and merit preceding.
This light from many a star, visits my heart;
But flow'd to me, the first, from him who sang
The songs of the Supreme; himself supreme
Among his tuneful brethren. 'Let all hope
In thee,' so spake his anthem, 'who have known
Thy name'; and, with my faith, who know not that?
From thee, the next, distilling from his spring,
In thine epistle, fell on me the drops
So plenteously, that I on others shower
The influence of their dew." While as I spake,
A lamping, as of quick and volley'd lightning,
Within the bosom of that mighty sheen
Play'd tremulous; then forth these accents breathed:
"Love for the virtue, which attended me
E'en to the palm, and issuing from the field,
Glows vigorous yet within me; and inspires
To ask of thee, whom also it delights,
What promise thou from hope, in chief, dost win."

"Both scriptures, new and ancient," I replied,
"Propose the mark (which even now I view)
For souls beloved of God. Isaias saith,
'That, in their own land, each one must be clad
In twofold vesture'; and their proper land
Is this delicious life. In terms more full,
And clearer far, thy brother hath set forth
This revelation to us, where he tells
Of the white raiment destined to the saints."
And, as the words were ending, from above,
"They hope in thee!" first heard we cried: whereto
Answer'd the carols all. Amidst them next,
A light of so clear amplitude emerged,
That winter's month were but a single day,
Were such a crystal in the Cancer's sign.

PARADISE

Like as a virgin riseth up, and goes,
And enters on the mazes of the dance;
Though gay, yet innocent of worse intent,
Than to do fitting honor to the bride:
So I beheld the new effulgence come
Unto the other two, who in a ring
Wheel'd, as became their rapture. In the dance,
And in the song, it mingled. And the dame
Held on them fix'd her looks; e'en as the spouse,
Silent, and moveless. "This is he, who lay
Upon the bosom of our pelican:
This he, into whose keeping, from the cross,
The mighty charge was given." Thus she spake;
Yet therefore naught the more removed her sight
From marking them: or e'er her words began,
Or when they closed. As he, who looks intent,
And strives with searching ken, how he may see
The sun in his eclipse, and, through desire
Of seeing, loseth power of sight; so I
Peer'd on that last resplendence, while I heard:
"Why dazzlest thou thine eyes in seeking that,
Which here abides not? Earth my body is,
In earth; and shall be, with the rest, so long,
As till our number equal the decree
Of the Most High. The two that have ascended,
In this our blessed cloister, shine alone
With the two garments. So report below."

As when, for ease of labor, or to shun
Suspected peril, at a whistle's breath,
The oars, erewhile dash'd frequent in the wave,
All rest: the flamy circle at that voice
So rested; and the mingling sound was still,
Which from the trinal band, soft-breathing, rose.
I turn'd, but ah! how trembled in my thought,
When, looking at my side again to see
Beatrice, I descried her not; although,
Not distant, on the happy coast she stood.

CANTO XXVI

St. John examines Dante touching Charity, and tells him about Adam's creation, residence in Paradise, fall and admittance to heaven.

With dazzled eyes, whilst wondering I remain'd;
Forth of the beamy flame, which dazzled me,
Issued a breath, that in attention mute
Detain'd me; and these words it spake: " 'Twere well,
That, long as till thy vision, on my form
O'erspent, regain its virtue, with discourse
Thou compensate the brief delay. Say then,
Beginning, to what point thy soul aspires:
And meanwhile rest assured, that sight in thee
Is but o'erpower'd a space, not wholly quench'd;
Since thy fair guide and lovely, in her look
Hath potency, the like to that, which dwelt
In Ananias' hand." I answering thus:
"Be to mine eyes the remedy, or late
Or early, at her pleasure; for they were
The gates, at which she enter'd, and did light
Her never-dying fire. My wishes here
Are centred: in this palace is the weal,
That Alpha and Omega are, to all
The lessons love can read me." Yet again
The voice, which had dispersed my fear when dazed
With that excess, to converse urged, and spake:
"Behoves thee sift more narrowly thy terms;
And say, who level'd at this scope thy bow."

"Philosophy," said I, "hath arguments,
And this place hath authority enough,
To imprint in me such love: for, of constraint,
Good, inasmuch as we perceive the good,
Kindles our love; and in degree the more,
As it comprises more of goodness in 't.
The essence then, where such advantage is,

PARADISE

That each good, found without it, is naught else
But of his light the beam, must needs attract
The soul of each one, loving, who the truth
Discerns, on which this proof is built. Such truth
Learn I from him, who shows me the first love
Of all intelligential substances
Eternal: from his voice I learn, whose word
Is truth; that of himself to Moses saith,
'I will make all my good before thee pass':
Lastly, from thee I learn, who chief proclaim'st
E'en at the outset of thy heralding,
In mortal ears the mystery of heaven."

"Through human wisdom, and the authority
Therewith agreeing," heard I answer'd, "keep
The choicest of thy love for God. But say,
If thou yet other cords within thee feel'st,
That draw thee toward him; so that thou report
How many are the fangs, with which this love
Is grappled to thy soul." I did not miss,
To what intent the eagle of our Lord
Had pointed his demand; yea, noted well
The avowal which he led to; and resumed:
"All grappling bonds, that knit the heart to God,
Confederate to make fast our charity.
The being of the world; and mine own being;
The death which He endured, that I should live;
And that, which all the faithful hope, as I do;
To the foremention'd lively knowledge join'd;
Have from the sea of ill love saved my bark,
And on the coast secured it of the right.
As for the leaves, that in the garden bloom,
My love for them is great, as is the good
Dealt by the eternal hand, that tends them all."

I ended: and therewith a song most sweet
Rang through the spheres; and "Holy! Holy! Holy!"
Accordant with the rest, my lady sang.
And as a sleep is broken and dispersed
Through sharp encounter of the nimble light,

With the eye's spirit running forth to meet
The ray, from membrane on to membrane urged;
And the upstartled wight loathes that he sees;
So, at his sudden waking, he misdeems
Of all around him, till assurance waits
On better judgment: thus the saintly dame
Drove from before my eyes the motes away,
With the resplendence of her own, that cast
Their brightness downward, thousand miles below.
Whence I my vision, clearer than before,
Recover'd; and well-nigh astounded, ask'd
Of a fourth light, that now with us I saw.

   And Beatrice: "The first living soul,
That ever the first virtue framed, admires
Within these rays his Maker." Like the leaf,
That bows its lithe top till the blast is blown;
By its own virtue rear'd, then stands aloof:
So I, the whilst she said, awe-stricken bow'd.
Then eagerness to speak embolden'd me;
And I began: "O fruit! that wast alone
Mature, when first engender'd; ancient father!
That doubly seest in every wedded bride
Thy daughter, by affinity and blood;
Devoutly as I may, I pray thee hold
Converse with me: my will thou seest: and I,
More speedily to hear thee, tell it not."

   It chanceth oft some animal bewrays,
Through the sleek covering of his furry coat,
The fondness, that stirs in him, and conforms
His outside seeming to the cheer within:
And in like guise was Adam's spirit moved
To joyous mood, that through the covering shone,
Transparent, when to pleasure me it spake:
"No need thy will be told, which I untold
Better discern, than thou whatever thing
Thou hold'st most certain: for that will I see
In Him, who is truth's mirror; and Himself,
Parhelion unto all things, and naught else,

PARADISE

To Him. This wouldst thou hear: how long since, God
Placed me in that high garden, from whose bounds
She led me up this ladder, steep and long;
What space endured my season of delight;
Whence truly sprang the wrath that banish'd me;
And what the language, which I spake and framed.
Not that I tasted of the tree, my son,
Was in itself the cause of that exile,
But only my transgressing of the mark
Assign'd me. There, whence at thy lady's hest
The Mantuan moved him, still was I debarr'd
This council, till the sun had made complete,
Four thousand and three hundred rounds and twice,
His annual journey; and, through every light
In his broad pathway, saw I him return,
Thousand save seventy times, the whilst I dwelt
Upon the earth. The language I did use
Was worn away, or ever Nimrod's race
Their unaccomplishable work began.
For naught, that man inclines to, e'er was lasting;
Left by his reason free, and variable
As is the sky that sways him. That he speaks,
Is nature's prompting: whether thus, or thus,
She leaves to you, as ye do most affect it.
Ere I descended into hell's abyss,
El was the name on earth of the Chief Good,
Whose joy enfolds me: Eli then 'twas call'd.
And so beseemeth: for, in mortals, use
Is as the leaf upon the bough: that goes,
And other comes instead. Upon the mount
Most high above the waters, all my life,
Both innocent and guilty, did but reach
From the first hour, to that which cometh next
(As the sun changes quarter) to the sixth."

[399]

CANTO XXVII

St. Peter bitterly rebukes his successors in the apostolic see. Afterward, Dante is borne to the ninth heaven.

Then "Glory to the Father, to the Son,
And to the Holy Spirit," rang aloud
Throughout all Paradise; that with the song
My spirit reel'd, so passing sweet the strain.
And what I saw was equal ecstasy:
One universal smile it seem'd of all things;
Joy past compare; gladness unutterable;
Imperishable life of peace and love;
Exhaustless riches, and unmeasured bliss.

Before mine eyes stood the four torches lit:
And that, which first had come, began to wax
In brightness, and, in semblance, such became,
As Jove might be, if he and Mars were birds,
And interchanged their plumes. Silence ensued,
Through the blessed quire; by Him, who here appoints
Vicissitude of ministry, enjoin'd;
When thus I heard: "Wonder not, if my hue
Be changed; for, while I speak, these shalt thou see
All in like manner change with me. My place
He who usurps on earth (my place, ay, mine,
Which in the presence of the Son of God
Is void), the same hath made my cemetery
A common sewer of puddle and of blood:
The more below his triumph, who from hence
Malignant fell." Such color, as the sun,
At eve or morning, paints an adverse cloud,
Then saw I sprinkled over all the sky
And as the unblemish'd dame, who, in herself
Secure of censure, yet at bare report
Of other's failing, shrinks with maiden fear;
So Beatrice, in her semblance, changed:
And such eclipse in heaven, methinks, was seen,

PARADISE

When the Most Holy suffer'd. Then the words
Proceeded, with voice, alter'd from itself
So clean, the semblance did not alter more.
"Not to this end was Christ's spouse with my blood
With that of Linus, and of Cletus, fed;
That she might serve for purchase of base gold:
But for the purchase of this happy life,
Did Sextus, Pius, and Calixtus bleed,
And Urban; they, whose doom was not without
Much weeping seal'd. No purpose was of ours,
That on the right hand of our successors,
Part of the Christian people should be set,
And part upon their left; nor that the keys,
Which were vouchsafed me, should for ensign serve
Unto the banners, that do levy war
On the baptized: nor I, for sigil-mark,
Set upon sold and lying privileges:
Which makes me oft to bicker and turn red.
In shepherd's clothing, greedy wolves below
Range wide o'er all the pastures. Arm of God!
Why longer sleep'st thou? Cahorsines and Gascons
Prepare to quaff our blood. O good beginning!
To what a vile conclusion must thou stoop.
But the high providence, which did defend,
Through Scipio, the world's empery for Rome,
Will not delay its succor: and thou, son,
Who through thy mortal weight shalt yet again
Return below, open thy lips, nor hide
What is by me not hidden." As a flood
Of frozen vapors streams adown the air,
What time the she-goat with her skyey horn
Touches the sun; so saw I there stream wide
The vapors, who with us had linger'd late,
And with glad triumph deck the ethereal cope.
Onward my sight their semblances pursued;
So far pursued, as till the space between
From its reach sever'd them: whereat the guide
Celestial, marking me no more intent
On upward gazing, said, "Look down and see
What circuit thou hast compassed." From the hour

[401]

THE DIVINE COMEDY

When I before had cast my view beneath,
All the first region overpast I saw,
Which from the midmost to the boundary winds,
That onward, thence, from Gades, I beheld
The unwise passage of Laërtes' son;
And hitherward the shore, where thou, Europa,
Madest thee a joyful burden; and yet more
Of this dim spot had seen, but that the sun,
A constellation off and more, had ta'en
His progress in the zodiac underneath.

Then by the spirit, that doth never leave
Its amorous dalliance with my lady's looks,
Back with redoubled ardor were mine eyes
Led unto her: and from her radiant smiles,
Whenas I turn'd me, pleasure so divine
Did lighten on me, that whatever bait
Or art or nature in the human flesh,
Or in its limn'd resemblance, can combine
Through greedy eyes to take the soul withal,
Were, to her beauty, nothing. Its boon influence
From the fair nest of Leda rapt me forth,
And wafted on into the swiftest heaven.

What place for entrance Beatrice chose,
I may not say; so uniform was all,
Liveliest and loftiest. She my secret wish
Divined; and, with such gladness, that God's love
Seem'd from her visage shining, thus began:
"Here is the goal, whence motion on his race
Starts: motionless the centre, and the rest
All moved around. Except the soul divine,
Place in this heaven is none; the soul divine,
Wherein the love, which ruleth o'er its orb,
Is kindled, and the virtue, that it sheds:
One circle, light and love, enclasping it,
As this doth clasp the others; and to Him,
Who draws the bound, its limit only known.
Measured itself by none, it doth divide
Motion to all, counted unto them forth,

PARADISE

As by the fifth or half ye count forth ten.
The vase, wherein time's roots are plunged, thou seest
Look elsewhere for the leaves. O mortal lust!
That canst not lift thy head above the waves
Which whelm and sink thee down. The will in man
Bears goodly blossoms; but its ruddy promise
Is, by the dripping of perpetual rain,
Made mere abortion: faith and innocence
Are met with but in babes; each taking leave,
Ere cheeks with down are sprinkled: he, that fasts
While yet a stammerer, with his tongue let loose
Gluts every food alike in every moon:
One, yet a babbler, loves and listens to
His mother; but no sooner hath free use
Of speech, that he doth wish her in her grave.
So suddenly doth the fair child of him,
Whose welcome is the morn and eve his parting,
To negro blackness change her virgin white.

"Thou, to abate thy wonder, note, that none
Bears rule in earth; and its frail family
Are therefore wanderers. Yet before the date,
When through the hundredth in his reckoning dropped
Pale January must be shoved aside
From Winter's calendar, these heavenly spheres
Shall roar so loud, that fortune shall be fain
To turn the poop, where she hath now the prow;
So that the fleet run onward: and true fruit,
Expected long, shall crown at last the bloom."

CANTO XXVIII

*The poet is permitted to behold the divine essence,
and then sees nine choirs of angels.*

So she, who doth imparadise my soul,
Had drawn the veil from off our present life,
And bared the truth of poor mortality:

THE DIVINE COMEDY

When lo! as one who, in a mirror, spies
The shining of a flambeau at his back,
Lit sudden ere he deem of its approach,
And turneth to resolve him, if the glass
Have told him true, and sees the record faithful
As note is to its metre; even thus,
I well remember, did befall to me,
Looking upon the beauteous eyes, whence love
Had made the leash to take me. As I turn'd:
And that which none, who in that volume looks,
Can miss of, in itself apparent, struck
My view; a point I saw, that darted light
So sharp, no lid, unclosing, may bear up
Against its keenness. The least star we ken
From hence, had seem'd a moon; set by its side,
As star by side of star. And so far off,
Perchance, as is the halo from the light
Which paints it, when most dense the vapor spreads;
There wheel'd about the point a circle of fire,
More rapid than the motion which surrounds,
Speediest, the world. Another this enring'd;
And that a third; the third a fourth, and that
A fifth encompass'd; which a sixth next bound;
And over this, a seventh, following, reach'd
Circumference so ample, that its bow,
Within the span of Juno's messenger,
Had scarce been held entire. Beyond the seventh,
Ensued yet other two. And every one,
As more in number distant from the first,
Was tardier in motion: and that glow'd
With flame most pure, that to the sparkle of truth,
Was nearest; as partaking most, methinks,
Of its reality. The guide beloved
Saw me in anxious thought suspense, and spake:
"Heaven and all nature hangs upon that point
The circle thereto most conjoin'd observe;
And know, that by intenser love its course
Is, to this swiftness, wing'd." To whom I thus:
"It were enough; nor should I further seek,
Had I but witness'd order, in the world

PARADISE

Appointed, such as in these wheels is seen.
But in the sensible world such difference is,
That in each round shows more divinity,
As each is wider from the centre. Hence,
If in this wondrous and angelic temple,
That hath, for confine, only light and love,
My wish may have completion, I must know,
Wherefore such disagreement is between
The exemplar and its copy: for myself,
Contemplating, I fail to pierce the cause."

"It is no marvel, if thy fingers foil'd
Do leave the knot untied: so hard 'tis grown
For want of tenting." Thus she said: "But take,"
She added, "if thou wish thy cure, my words,
And entertain them subtly. Every orb,
Corporeal, doth proportion its extent
Unto the virtue through its parts diffused.
The greater blessedness preserves the more,
The greater is the body (if all parts
Share equally) the more is to preserve.
Therefore the circle, whose swift course enwheels
The universal frame, answers to that
Which is supreme in knowledge and in love.
Thus by the virtue, not the seeming breadth
Of substance, measuring, thou shalt see the heavens,
Each to the intelligence that ruleth it,
Greater to more, and smaller unto less,
Suited in strict and wondrous harmony."

As when the north blows from his milder cheek
A blast, that scours the sky, forthwith our air,
Clear'd of the rack that hung on it before,
Glitters; and, with his beauties all unveil'd,
The firmament looks forth serene, and smiles:
Such was my cheer, when Beatrice drove
With clear reply the shadows back, and truth
Was manifested, as a star in heaven.
And when the words were ended, not unlike
To iron in the furnace, every cirque,

Ebullient, shot forth scintillating fires:
And every sparkle shivering to new blaze,
In number did outmillion the account
Reduplicate upon the checker'd board.
Then heard I echoing on, from choir to choir,
"Hosanna," to the fixed point, that holds,
And shall forever hold them to their place,
From everlasting, irremovable.

   Musing awhile I stood: and she, who saw
My inward meditations, thus began:
"In the first circles, they, whom thou beheld'st
Are seraphim and cherubim. Thus swift
Follow their hoops, in likeness to the point,
Near as they can, approaching; and they can
The more, the loftier their vision. Those
That round them fleet, gazing the Godhead next,
Are thrones; in whom the first trine ends. And all
Are blessed, even as their sight descends
Deeper into the truth, wherein rest is
For every mind. Thus happiness hath root
In seeing, not in loving, which of sight
Is aftergrowth. And of the seeing such
The meed, as unto each, in due degree,
Grace and good-will their measure have assign'd.
The other trine, that with still opening buds
In this eternal springtide blossom fair,
Fearless of bruising from the nightly ram,
Breathe up in warbled melodies threefold
Hosannas, blending ever; from the three,
Transmitted, hierarchy of gods, for aye
Rejoicing; dominations first; next them,
Virtues; and powers the third; the next to whom
Are princedoms and archangels, with glad round
To tread their festal ring; and last, the band
Angelical, disporting in their sphere.
All, as they circle in their orders, look
Aloft; and, downward, with such sway prevail,
That all with mutual impulse tend to God.
These once a mortal view beheld. Desire,

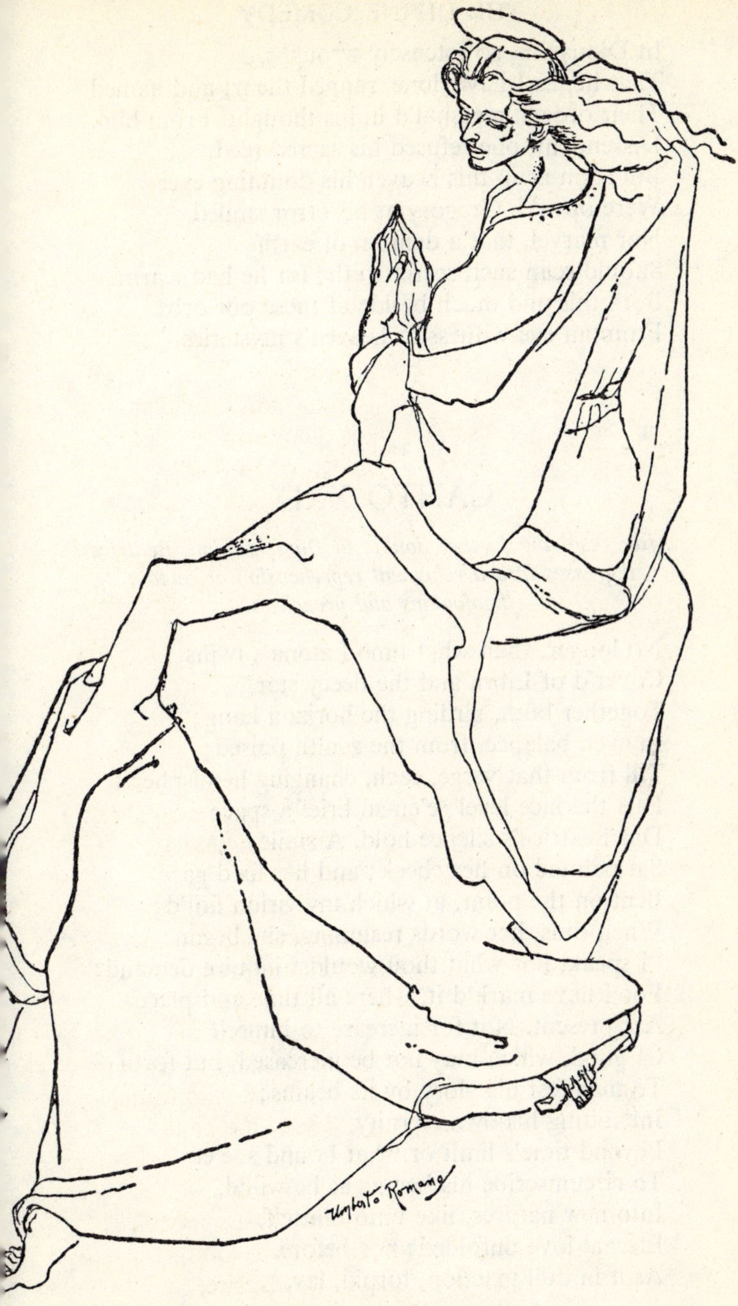
Umberto Romano

THE DIVINE COMEDY

In Dionysius, so intensely wrought,
That he, as I have done, ranged them; and named
Their orders, marshal'd in his thought. From him,
Dissentient, one refused his sacred reed.
But soon as in this heaven his doubting eyes
Were open'd, Gregory at his error smiled.
Nor marvel, that a denizen of earth
Should scan such secret truth; for he had learnt
Both this and much beside of these our orbs,
From an eye-witness to heaven's mysteries."

CANTO XXIX

After resolving further doubts in Dante's mind, Beatrice digresses into a vehement reprehension of certain theologians and preachers.

No longer, than what time Latona's twins
Cover'd of Libra and the fleecy star,
Together both, girding the horizon hang;
In even balance, from the zenith poised;
Till from that verge, each, changing hemisphere,
Part the nice level; e'en so brief a space
Did Beatrice's silence hold. A smile
Sat painted on her cheek; and her fix'd gaze
Bent on the point, at which my vision fail'd:
When thus, her words resuming, she began:
"I speak, nor what thou wouldst inquire demand;
For I have mark'd it, where all time and place
Are present. Not for increase to himself
Of good, which may not be increased, but forth
To manifest his glory by its beams;
Inhabiting his own eternity,
Beyond time's limit or what bound soe'er
To circumscribe his being; as he will'd,
Into new natures, like unto himself,
Eternal love unfolded: nor before,
As if in dull inaction, torpid, lay,

[408]

PARADISE

For, not in process of before or aft,
Upon these waters moved the Spirit of God.
Simple and mix'd, both form and substance, forth
To perfect being started, like three darts
Shot from a bow three-corded. And as ray
In crystal, glass, and amber, shines entire,
E'en at the moment of its issuing; thus
Did, from the eternal Sovran, beam entire
His threefold operation, at one act
Produced coeval. Yet, in order, each
Created his due station knew: those highest,
Who pure intelligence were made; mere power,
The lowest; in the midst, bound with strict league,
Intelligence and power, unsever'd bond.
Long tract of ages by the angels past,
Ere the creating of another world,
Described on Jerome's pages, thou hast seen.
But that what I disclose to thee is true,
Those penmen, whom the Holy Spirit moved
In many a passage of their sacred book,
Attest; as thou by diligent search shalt find:
And reason, in some sort, discerns the same,
Who scarce would grant the heavenly ministers,
Of their perfection void, so long a space.
Thus when and where these spirits of love were made,
Thou know'st, and how: and, knowing, hast allay'd
Thy thirst, which from the triple question rose.
Ere one had reckon'd twenty, e'en so soon,
Part of the angels fell: and in their fall,
Confusion to your elements ensued.
The others kept their station: and this task,
Whereon thou look'st, began, with such delight,
That they surcease not ever, day nor night,
Their circling. Of that fatal lapse the cause
Was the curst pride of him, whom thou hast seen
Pent with the world's incumbrance. Those, whom here
Thou seest, were lowly to confess themselves
Of his free bounty, who had made them apt
For ministries so high: therefore their views
Were, by enlightening grace and their own merit,

[409]

THE DIVINE COMEDY

Exalted; so that in their will confirm'd
They stand, nor fear to fall. For do not doubt,
But to receive the grace, which Heaven vouchsafes,
Is meritorious, even as the soul
With prompt affection welcometh the guest.
Now, without further help, if with good heed
My words thy mind have treasured, thou henceforth
This consistory round about mayst scan,
And gaze thy fill. But, since thou hast on earth
Heard vain disputers, reasoners in the schools,
Canvass the angelic nature, and dispute
Its powers of apprehension, memory, choice;
Therefore, 'tis well thou take from me the truth,
Pure and without disguise; which they below,
Equivocating, darken and perplex.

"Know thou, that, from the first, these substances,
Rejoicing in the countenance of God,
Have held unceasingly their view, intent
Upon the glorious vision, from the which
Naught absent is nor hid: where then no change
Of newness, with succession, interrupts,
Remembrance, there, needs none to gather up
Divided thought and images remote.

"So that men, thus at variance with the truth,
Dream, though their eyes be open; reckless some
Of error; others well aware they err,
To whom more guilt and shame are justly due.
Each the known track of sage philosophy
Deserts, and has a by-way of his own:
So much the restless eagerness to shine,
And love of singularity, prevail.
Yet this, offensive as it is, provokes
Heaven's anger less, than when the book of God
Is forced to yield to man's authority,
Or from its straightness warp'd: no reckoning made
What blood the sowing of it in the world
Has cost; what favor for himself he wins,
Who meekly clings to it. The aim of all

PARADISE

Is how to shine: e'en they, whose office is
To preach the gospel, let the gospel sleep,
And pass their own inventions off instead.
One tells, how at Christ's suffering the wan moon
Bent back her steps, and shadow'd o'er the sun
With intervenient disc, as she withdrew:
Another, how the light shrouded itself
Within its tabernacle, and left dark
The Spaniard, and the Indian, with the Jew.
Such fables Florence in her pulpit hears,
Bandied about more frequent, than the names
Of Bindi and of Lapi in her streets.
The sheep, meanwhile, poor witless ones, return
From pasture, fed with wind: and what avails
For their excuse, they do not see their harm?
Christ said not to his first conventicle,
'Go forth and preach impostures to the world,'
But gave them truth to build on; and the sound
Was mighty on their lips: nor needed they,
Beside the Gospel, other spear or shield,
To aid them in their warfare for the faith.
The preacher now provides himself with store
Of jests and gibes; and, so there be no lack
Of laughter, while he vents them, his big cowl
Distends, and he has won the meed he sought:
Could but the vulgar catch a glimpse the while
Of that dark bird which nestles in his hood,
They scarce would wait to hear the blessing said,
Which now the dotards hold in such esteem,
That every counterfeit, who spreads abroad
The hands of holy promise, finds a throng
Of credulous fools beneath. Saint Anthony
Fattens with this his swine, and others worse
Than swine, who diet at his lazy board,
Paying with unstamped metal for their fare.

"But (for we far have wander'd) let us seek
The forward path again; so as the way
Be shorten'd with the time. No mortal tongue,
Nor thought of man, hath ever reach'd so far,

That of these natures he might count the tribes.
What Daniel of their thousands hath reveal'd,
With finite number, infinite conceals.
The fountain, at whose source these drink their beams,
With light supplies them in as many modes,
As their are splendors that it shines on: each
According to the virtue it conceives,
Differing in love and sweet affection.
Look then how lofty and how huge in breadth
The eternal might, which, broken and dispersed
Over such countless mirrors, yet remains
Whole in itself and one, as at the first."

CANTO XXX

*Dante is taken to the empyrean and sees the triumph
of the angels and the souls of the blessed.*

Noon's fervid hour perchance six thousand miles
From hence is distant; and the shadowy cone
Almost to level on our earth declines;
When, from the midmost of this blue abyss,
By turns some star is to our vision lost,
And straightway as the handmaid of the sun
Puts forth her radiant brow, all, light by light,
Fade; and the spangled firmament shuts in,
E'en to the loveliest of the glittering throng;
Thus vanish'd gradually from my sight
The triumph, which plays ever round the point,
That overcame me, seeming (for it did)
Engirt by that it girdeth. Wherefore love,
With loss of other object, forced me bend
Mine eyes on Beatrice once again.

If all, that hitherto is told of her,
Were in one praise concluded, 'twere too weak
To furnish out this turn. Mine eyes did look
On beauty, such, as I believe in sooth,

[412]

PARADISE

Not merely to exceed our human; but,
That save its Maker, none can to the full
Enjoy it. At this point o'erpower'd I fail;
Unequal to my theme; as never bard
Of buskin or of sock hath fail'd before.
For as the sun doth to the feeblest sight,
E'en so remembrance of that witching smile
Hath dispossessed my spirit of itself.
Not from that day, when on this earth I first
Beheld her charms, up to that view of them,
Have I with song applausive ever ceased
To follow; but now follow them no more;
My course here bounded, as each artist's is,
When it doth touch the limit of his skill.

She (such as I bequeath her to the bruit
Of louder trump than mine, which hasteneth on
Urging its arduous matter to the close)
Her words resumed, in gesture and in voice
Resembling one accustom'd to command:
"Forth from the last corporeal are we come
Into the heaven, that is unbodied light;
Light intellectual, replete with love;
Love of true happiness, replete with joy;
Joy, that transcends all sweetness of delight.
Here shalt thou look on either mighty host
Of Paradise; and one in that array,
Which in the final judgment thou shalt see."
As when the lightning, in a sudden spleen
Unfolded, dashes from the blinding eyes
The visive spirits, dazzled and bedimm'd;
So, round about me, fulminating streams
Of living radiance play'd, and left me swathed
And veil'd in dense impenetrable blaze.
Such weal is in the love, that stills this heaven;
For its own flame the torch thus fitting ever.

No sooner to my listening ear had come
The brief assurance, than I understood
New virtue into me infused, and sight

Kindled afresh, with vigor to sustain
Excess of light however pure. I look'd;
And, in the likeness of a river, saw
Light flowing, from whose amber-seeming waves
Flash'd up effulgence, as they glided on
'Twixt banks, on either side, painted with spring,
Incredible how fair: and, from the tide,
There ever and anon, outstarting, flew
Sparkles instinct with life; and in the flowers
Did set them, like to rubies chased in gold:
Then, as if drunk with odors, plunged again
Into the wondrous flood; from which, as one
Re-enter'd, still another rose. "The thirst
Of knowledge high, whereby thou art inflamed,
To search the meaning of what here thou seest,
The more it warms thee, pleases me the more,
But first behoves thee of this water drink,
Or e'er that longing be allay'd." So spake
The day-star of mine eyes: then thus subjoin'd:
"This stream; and these, forth issuing from its gulf,
And dividing back, a living topaz each;
With all this laughter on its bloomy shores;
Are but a preface, shadowy of the truth
They emblem: not that, in themselves, the things
Are crude; but on thy part is the defect,
For that thy views not yet aspire so high."

Never did babe that had outslept his wont,
Rush, with such eager straining, to the milk,
As I toward the water; bending me,
To make the better mirrors of mine eyes
In the refining wave: and as the eaves
Of mine eyelids did drink of it, forthwith
Seem'd it unto me turn'd from length to round.
Then as a troop of maskers, when they put
Their vizors off, look other than before;
The counterfeited semblance thrown aside:
So into greater jubilee were changed
Those flowers and sparkles; and distinct I saw,
Before me, either court of heaven display'd.

PARADISE

O prime enlightener! thou who gavest me strength
On the high triumph of thy realm to gaze;
Grant virtue now to utter what I kenn'd.

There is in heaven a light, whose goodly shine
Makes the Creator visible to all
Created, that in seeing him alone
Have peace; and in a circle spreads so far,
That the circumference were too loose a zone
To girdle in the sun. All is one beam,
Reflected from the summit of the first,
That moves, which being hence and vigor takes.
And as some cliff, that from the bottom eyes
His image mirror'd in the crystal flood,
As if to admire his brave apparelling
Of verdure and of flowers; so, round about,
Eying the light, on more than million thrones,
Stood, eminent, whatever from our earth
Has to the skies return'd. How wide the leaves,
Extended to their utmost, of this rose,
Whose lowest step embosoms such a space
Of ample radiance! Yet, nor amplitude
Nor height impeded, but my view with ease
Took in the full dimensions of that joy.
Near or remote, what there avails, where God
Immediate rules, and Nature, awed, suspends
Her sway? Into the yellow of the rose
Perennial, which, in bright expansiveness,
Lays forth its gradual blooming, redolent
Of praises to the never-wintering sun,
As one, who fain would speak yet holds his peace,
Beatrice led me; and, "Behold," she said,
"This fair assemblage; stoles of snowy white,
How numberless. The city, where we dwell,
Behold how vast; and these our seats so throng'd,
Few now are wanting here. In that proud stall,
On which, the crown, already o'er its state
Suspended, holds thine eyes—or e'er thyself
Mayst at the wedding sup—shall rest the soul
Of the great Harry, he who, by the world

[415]

Augustus hail'd, to Italy must come,
Before her day be ripe. But ye are sick,
And in your tetchy wantonness as blind,
As is the bantling, that of hunger dies,
And drives away the nurse. Nor may it be,
That he, who in the sacred forum sways,
Openly or in secret, shall with him
Accordant walk: whom God will not endure
I' the holy office long; but thrust him down
To Simon Magus, where Alagna's priest
Will sink beneath him: such will be his meed."

CANTO XXXI

Beatrice disappears, and Dante finds at his side an old man, St. Bernard, who tells him she has returned to her throne.

IN fashion, as a snow white rose, lay then
Before my view the saintly multitude,
Which in his own blood Christ espoused. Meanwhile,
That other host, that soar aloft to gaze
And celebrate his glory, whom they love,
Hover'd around; and, like a troop of bees,
Amid the vernal sweets alighting now,
Now, clustering, where their fragrant labor glows,
Flew downward to the mighty flower, or rose
From the redundant petals, streaming back
Unto the steadfast dwelling of their joy,
Faces had they of flame, and wings of gold:
The rest was whiter than the driven snow;
And, as they flitted down into the flower,
From range to range, fanning their plumy loins,
Whisper'd the peace and ardor, which they won
From that soft winnowing. Shadow none, the vast
Interposition of such numerous flight
Cast, from above, upon the flower, or view
Obstructed aught. For, through the universe,

PARADISE

Wherever merited, celestial light
Glides freely, and no obstacle prevents.

   All there, who reign in safety and in bliss,
Ages long past or new, on one sole mark
Their love and vision fix'd. O trinal beam
Of individual star, that charm'st them thus!
Vouchsafe one glance to gild our storm below.

   If the grim brood, from Arctic shores that roam'd
(Where Helice forever, as she wheels,
Sparkles a mother's fondness on her son),
Stood in mute wonder 'mid the works of Rome,
When to their view the Lateran arose
In greatness more than earthly; I, who then
From human to divine had passed, from time
Unto eternity, and out of Florence
To justice and to truth, how might I chuse
But marvel too? 'Twixt gladness and amaze,
In sooth no will had I to utter aught,
Or hear. And, as a pilgrim, when he rests
Within the temple of his vow, looks round
In breathless awe, and hopes some time to tell
Of all its goodly state; e'en so mine eyes
Coursed up and down along the living light,
Now low, and now aloft, and now around,
Visiting every step. Looks I beheld,
Where charity in soft persuasion sat;
Smiles from within, and radiance from above;
And, in each gesture, grace and honor high.

   So roved my ken, and in its general form
All Paradise survey'd: when round I turn'd
With purpose of my lady to inquire
Once more of things, that held my thought suspense,
But answer found from other than I ween'd;
For, Beatrice, when I thought to see,
I saw instead a senior, at my side,
Robed, as the rest, in glory. Joy benign

[417]

THE DIVINE COMEDY

Glow'd in his eye, and o'er his cheek diffused,
With gestures such as spake a father's love.
And, "Whither is she vanish'd?" straight I ask'd.

"By Beatrice summon'd," he replied,
"I come to aid thy wish. Looking aloft
To the third circle from the highest, there
Behold her on the throne, wherein her merit
Hath placed her." Answering not, mine eyes I raised,
And saw her, where aloof she sat, her brow
A wreath reflecting of eternal beams.
Not from the centre of the sea so far
Unto the region of the highest thunder,
As was my ken from hers; and yet the form
Came through that medium down, unmix'd and pure.

"O lady! thou in whom my hopes have rest;
Who, for my safety, hast not scorn'd, in hell
To leave the traces of thy footsteps mark'd;
For all mine eyes have seen, I to thy power
And goodness, virtue owe and grace. Of slave
Thou hast to freedom brought me: and no means,
For my deliverance apt, hast left untried.
Thy liberal bounty still toward me keep:
That, when my spirit, which thou madest whole,
Is loosen'd from this body, it may find
Favor with thee." So I my suit preferr'd:
And she, so distant, as appear'd, look'd down,
And smiled; then toward the eternal fountain turn'd.

And thus the senior, holy and revered:
"That thou at length mayst happily conclude
Thy voyage (to which end I was despatch'd,
By supplication moved and holy love),
Let thy upsoaring vision range, at large,
This garden through: for so, by ray divine
Kindled, thy ken a higher flight shall mount;
And from heaven's queen, whom fervent I adore,
All gracious aid befriend us; for that I
Am her own faithful Bernard." Like a wight,

[418]

PARADISE

Who haply from Croatia wends to see
Our Veronica; and the while 'tis shown,
Hangs over it with never-sated gaze,
And, all that he hath heard revolving, saith
Unto himself in thought: "And didst thou look
E'en thus, O Jesus, my true Lord and God?
And was this semblance thine?" So gazed I then
Adoring; for the charity of him,
Who musing, in this world that peace enjoy'd,
Stood livelily before me. "Child of grace!"
Thus he began: "thou shalt not knowledge gain
Of this glad being, if thine eyes are held
Still in this depth below. But search around
The circles, to the furthest, till thou spy
Seated in state, the queen, that of this realm
Is sovran." Straight mine eyes I raised; and bright,
As, at the birth of morn, the eastern clime
Above the horizon, where the sun declines;
So to mine eyes, that upward, as from vale
To mountain sped, at the extreme bound, a part
Excell'd in lustre all the front opposed.
And as the glow burns ruddiest o'er the wave,
That waits the ascending team, which Phaëton
Ill knew to guide, and on each part the light
Diminish'd fades, intensest in the midst;
So burn'd the peaceful oriflamb, and slack'd
On every side the living flame decay'd.
And in that midst their sportive pennons waved
Thousands of angels; in resplendence each
Distinct, and quaint adornment. At their glee
And carol, smiled the Lovely One of Heaven,
That joy was in the eyes of all the blessed.

Had I a tongue in eloquence as rich,
As is the coloring in fancy's loom,
'Twere all too poor to utter the least part
Of that enchantment. When he saw mine eyes
Intent on her, that charm'd him; Bernard gazed
With so exceeding fondness, as infused
Ardor into my breast, unfelt before.

[419]

CANTO XXXII

St. Bernard shows Dante blessed souls of the New and Old Testaments and explains that their places are assigned by grace and not according to merit.

FREELY the sage, though wrapt in musings high,
Assumed the teacher's part, and mild began:
"The wound, that Mary closed, she open'd first,
Who sits so beautiful at Mary's feet.
The third in order, underneath her, lo!
Rachel with Beatrice: Sarah next;
Judith; Rebecca; and the gleaner-maid,
Meek ancestress of him, who sang the songs
Of sore repentance in his sorrowful mood.
All, as I name them, down from leaf to leaf,
Are, in gradation, throned on the rose.
And from the seventh step, successively,
Adown the breathing tresses of the flower,
Still doth the file of Hebrew dames proceed.
For these are a partition wall, whereby
The sacred stairs are sever'd, as the faith
In Christ divides them. On this part, where bloom
Each leaf in full maturity, are set
Such as in Christ, or e'er he came, believed.
On the other, where an intersected space
Yet shows the semicircle void, abide
All they, who look'd to Christ already come
And as our Lady on her glorious stool,
And they who on their stools beneath her sit,
This way distinction make; e'en so on his,
The mighty Baptist that way marks the line
(He who endured the desert, and the pains
Of martyrdom, and, for two years, of hell,
Yet still continued holy), and beneath,
Augustin; Francis; Benedict; and the rest,
Thus far from round to round. So Heaven's decree
Forecasts, this garden equally to fill,

PARADISE

With faith in either view, past or to come.
Learn too, that downward from the step, which cleaves,
Midway, the twain compartments, none there are
Who place obtain for merit of their own,
But have through others' merit been advanced,
On set conditions; spirits all released,
Ere for themselves they had the power to chuse.
And, if thou mark and listen to them well,
Their childish looks and voice declare as much.

"Here, silent as thou art, I know thy doubt;
And gladly will I loose the knot, wherein
Thy subtile thoughts have bound thee. From this realm
Excluded, chance no entrance here may find;
No more than hunger, thirst, or sorrow can.
A law immutable hath stablish'd all;
Nor is there aught thou seest, that doth not fit,
Exactly, as the finger to the ring.
It is not, therefore, without cause, that these
O'erspeedy comers to immortal life,
Are different in their shares of excellence.
Our Sovran Lord, that settleth this estate
In love and in delight so absolute,
That wish can dare no further, every soul,
Created in his joyous sight to dwell,
With grace, at pleasure, variously endows.
And for a proof the effect may well suffice.
And 'tis moreover most expressly mark'd
In holy Scripture, where the twins are said
To have struggled in the womb. Therefore, as grace
Inweaves the coronet, so every brow
Weareth its proper hue of orient light.
And merely in respect to his prime gift,
Not in reward of meritorious deed,
Hath each his several degree assign'd.
In early times with their own innocence
More was not wanting, than the parents' faith,
To save them: those first ages past, behoved
That circumcision in the males should imp
The flight of innocent wings: but since the day

[421]

Of grace hath come, without baptismal rites
In Christ accomplish'd, innocence herself
Must linger yet below. Now raise thy view
Unto the visage most resembling Christ:
For, in her splendor only, shalt thou win
The power to look on him." Forthwith I saw
Such floods of gladness on her visage shower'd,
From holy spirits, winging that profound;
That, whatsoever I had yet beheld,
Had not so much suspended me with wonder,
Or shown me such similitude of God.
And he, who had to her descended, once,
On earth, now hail'd in heaven; and on poised wing,
"Ave, Maria! Gratia Plena!" sang:
To whose sweet anthem all the blissful court,
From all parts answering, rang: that holier joy
Brooded the deep serene. "Father revered!
Who deign'st, for me, to quit the pleasant place
Wherein thou sittest, by eternal lot;
Say, who that angel is, that with such glee
Beholds our queen, and so enamour'd glows
Of her high beauty, that all fire he seems."

   So I again resorted to the lore
Of my wise teacher, he, whom Mary's charms
Embellish'd, as the sun the morning star;
Who thus in answer spake: "In him are summ'd,
Whate'er of buxomness and free delight
May be in spirit, or in angel, met:
And so beseems: for that he bare the palm
Down unto Mary, when the Son of God
Vouchsafed to clothe him in terrestrial weeds.
Now let thine eyes wait heedful on my words;
And note thou of this just and pious realm
The chiefest nobles. Those, highest in bliss,
The twain, on each hand next our empress throned,
Are as it were two roots unto this rose:
He to the left, the parent, whose rash taste
Proves bitter to this seed; and, on the right,
That ancient father of the holy church,

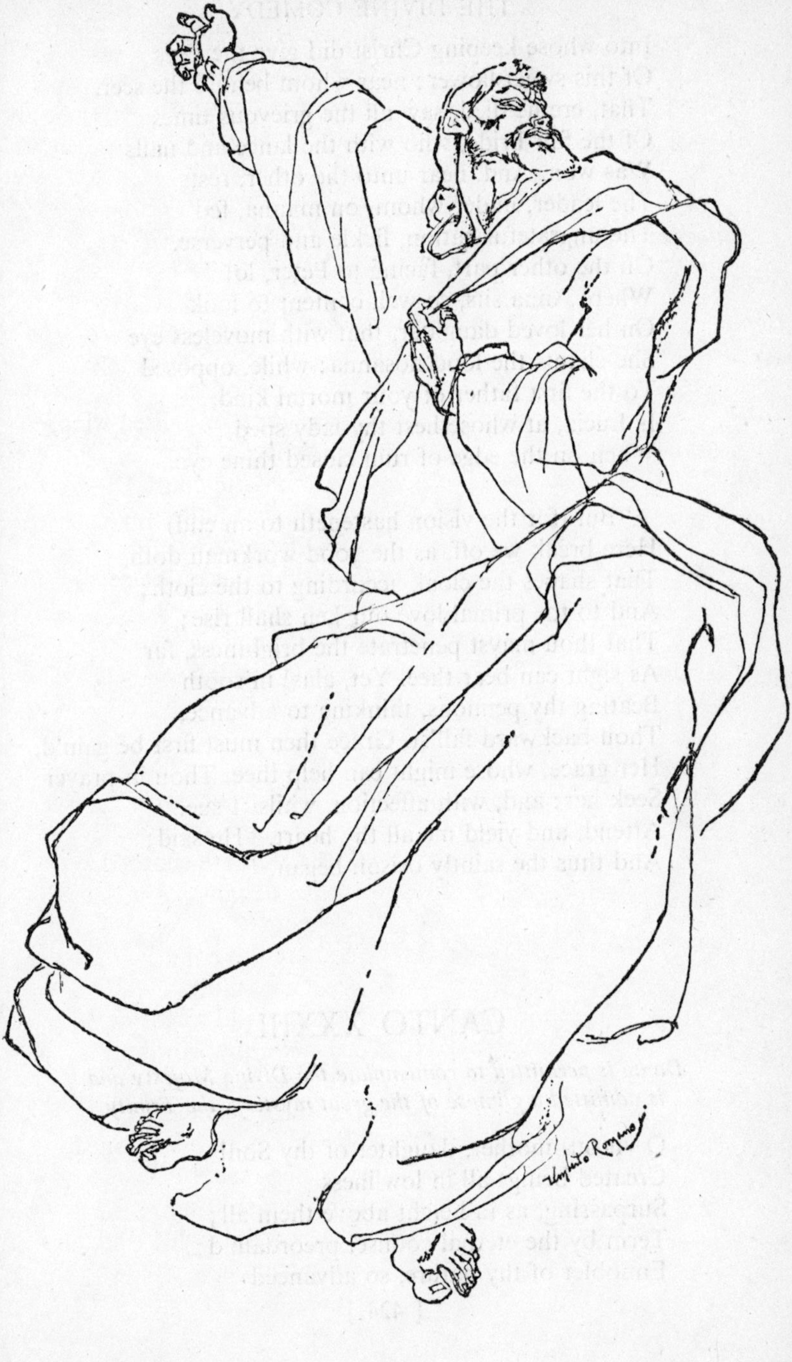
Umberto Romano

THE DIVINE COMEDY

Into whose keeping Christ did give the keys
Of this sweet flower; near whom behold the seer,
That, ere he died, saw all the grievous times
Of the fair bride, who with the lance and nails
Was won. And, near unto the other, rests
The leader, under whom, on manna, fed
The ungrateful nation, fickle and perverse.
On the other part, facing to Peter, lo!
Where Anna sits, so well content to look
On her loved daughter, that with moveless eye
She chants the loud hosanna: while, opposed
To the first father of your mortal kind,
Is Lucia, at whose hest thy lady sped,
When on the edge of ruin closed thine eye.

"But (for the vision hasteneth to an end)
Here break we off, as the good workman doth,
That shapes the cloak according to the cloth;
And to the primal love our ken shall rise;
That thou mayst penetrate the brightness, far
As sight can bear thee. Yet, alas! in sooth
Beating thy pennons, thinking to advance,
Thou backward fall'st. Grace then must first be gain'd,
Her grace, whose might can help thee. Thou in prayer
Seek her: and, with affection, whilst I sue,
Attend, and yield me all thy heart." He said;
And thus the saintly orison began.

CANTO XXXIII

Dante is permitted to contemplate the Divine Majesty and is admitted a glimpse of the great mystery, the Trinity.

O VIRGIN mother, daughter of thy Son!
Created beings all in lowliness
Surpassing, as in height above them all;
Term by the eternal counsel preordain'd;
Ennobler of thy nature, so advanced

[424]

PARADISE

In thee, that its great Maker did not scorn,
To make himself his own creation;
For in thy womb rekindling shone the love
Reveal'd, whose genial influence makes now
This flower to germin in eternal peace:
Here thou to us, of charity and love,
Art, as the noon-day torch; and art, beneath,
To mortal men, of hope a living spring.
So mighty art thou, lady, and so great,
That he, who grace desireth, and comes not
To thee for aidance, fain would have desire
Fly without wings. Not only him, who asks,
Thy bounty succors; but doth freely oft
Forerun the asking. Whatsoe'er may be
Of excellence in creature, pity mild,
Relenting mercy, large munificence,
Are all combined in thee. Here kneeleth one,
Who of all spirits hath review'd the state,
From the world's lowest gap unto this height.
Suppliant to thee he kneels, imploring grace
For virtue yet more high, to lift his ken
Toward the bliss supreme. And I, who ne'er
Coveted sight, more fondly, for myself,
Than now for him, my prayers to thee prefer.
(And pray they be not scant), that thou wouldst drive
Each cloud of his mortality away,
Through thine own prayers, that on the sovran joy
Unveil'd he gaze. This yet, I pray thee, Queen,
Who canst do what thou wilt; that in him thou
Wouldst, after all he hath beheld, preserve
Affection sound, and human passions quell.
Lo! where, with Beatrice, many a saint
Stretch their clasp'd hands, in furtherance of my suit.

The eyes, that heaven with love and awe regards,
Fix'd on the suitor, witness'd, how benign
She looks on pious prayers: then fasten'd they
On the everlasting light, wherein no eye
Of creature, as may well be thought, so far
Can travel inward. I, meanwhile, who drew

[425]

THE DIVINE COMEDY

Near to the limit, where all wishes end,
The ardor of my wish (for so behoved),
Ended within me. Beckoning smiled the sage,
That I should look aloft: but, ere he bade,
Already of myself aloft I look'd;
For visual strength, refining more and more,
Bare me into the ray authentical
Of sovran light. Thenceforward, what I saw,
Was not for words to speak, nor memory's self
To stand against such outrage on her skill.

As one, who from a dream awaken'd, straight,
All he hath seen forgets; yet still retains
Impression of the feeling in his dream;
E'en such am I: for all the vision dies,
As 'twere, away; and yet the sense of sweet,
That sprang from it, still trickles in my heart.
Thus in the sun-thaw is the snow unseal'd;
Thus in the winds on flitting leaves was lost
The Sibyl's sentence. O eternal beam!
(Whose height what reach of mortal thought may soar?)
Yield me again some little particle
Of what thou then appearedst; give my tongue
Power, but to leave one sparkle of thy glory,
Unto the race to come, that shall not lose
Thy triumph wholly, if thou waken aught
Of memory in me, and endure to hear
The record sound in this unequal strain.

Such keenness from the living ray I met,
That, if mine eyes had turn'd away, methinks,
I had been lost; but, so embolden'd, on
I pass'd, as I remember, till my view
Hover'd the brink of dread infinitude.

O grace, unenvying of thy boon! that gavest
Boldness to fix so earnestly my ken
On the everlasting splendor, that I look'd,
While sight was unconsumed; and, in that depth,
Saw in one volume clasp'd of love, whate'er

PARADISE

The universe unfolds; all properties
Of substance and of accident, beheld,
Compounded, yet one individual light
The whole. And of such bond methinks I saw
The universal form; for that whene'er
I do but speak of it, my soul dilates
Beyond her proper self; and, till I speak,
One moment seems a longer lethargy,
Than five-and-twenty ages had appear'd
To that emprise, that first made Neptune wonder
At Argo's shadow darkening on his flood.

With fixed heed, suspense and motionless,
Wondering I gazed; and admiration still
Was kindled as I gazed. It may not be,
That one, who looks upon that light, can turn
To other object, willingly, his view.
For all the good, that will may covet, there
Is summ'd; and all, elsewhere defective found,
Complete. My tongue shall utter now, no more
E'en what remembrance keeps, than could the babe's
That yet is moisten'd at his mother's breast.
Not that the semblance of the living light
Was changed (that ever as at first remain'd),
But that my vision quickening, in that sole
Appearance, still new miracles descried,
And toil'd me with the change. In that abyss
Of radiance, clear and lofty, seem'd, methought,
Three orbs of triple hue, clipped in one bound:
And, from another, one reflected seem'd,
As rainbow is from rainbow: and the third
Seem'd fire, breathed equally from both. O speech!
How feeble and how faint art thou, to give
Conception birth. Yet this to what I saw
Is less than little. O eternal light!
Sole in thyself that dwell'st; and of thyself
Sole understood, past, present, or to come;
Thou smiledst, on that circling, which in thee
Seem'd as reflected splendor, while I mused
For I therein, methought, in its own hue

[427]

THE DIVINE COMEDY

Beheld our image painted: steadfastly
I therefore pored upon the view. As one,
Who versed in geometric lore, would fain
Measure the circle; and, though pondering long
And deeply, that beginning, which he needs,
Finds not: e'en such was I, intent to scan
The novel wonder, and trace out the form,
How to the circle fitted, and therein
How placed: but the flight was not for my wing;
Had not a flash darted athwart my mind,
And, in the spleen, unfolded what I sought.

Here vigor fail'd the towering fantasy:
But yet the will roll'd onward, like a wheel
In even motion, by the love impell'd,
That moves the sun in heaven and all the stars.

Notes

HELL

CANTO I

In the midway. The thirty-fifth year of the poet, 1300 A.D. — *Line 1, p. 3*

Which to remember. "Even when I remember I am afraid and trembling taketh hold on my flesh." *Job* xxi. 6. — *Line 6, p. 3*

A mountain's foot. The mountain of salvation. — *Line 13, p. 3*

That planet's beam. The sun. — *Line 16, p. 3*

A panther. Pleasure or luxury. — *Line 30, p. 4*

With those stars. The sun was in Aries, the sign in which it is supposed to have begun its course at the creation. — *Line 36, p. 4*

The sweet season. Spring according to the terminology of the Middle Ages. — *Line 41, p. 4*

A lion. Pride or ambition. — *Line 43, p. 4*

A she-wolf. Avarice. — *Line 45, p. 4*

Mantuans. Virgil was born in Andes, today Pietola, a village near Mantua, twenty-five years before Julius Cæsar assumed dictatorial power. — *Line 64, p. 5*

That greyhound. Commonly understood to be Can Grande della Scala, Lord of Verona. — *Line 98, p. 5*

'Twixt either Feltro. Verona was situated between Feltro and Monte Feltro. — *Line 102, p. 6*

Camilla, etc. Characters in *The Aeneid* which ended with the death of Turnus. — *Line 104, p. 6*

A second death. "And in these days men shall seek death and shall not find it; and shall desire to die and death shall flee from them." *Rev.* ix. 6. — *Line 114, p. 6*

Content in fire. The spirits in Purgatory. — *Line 115, p. 6*

A spirit worthier. Beatrice who conducts Dante through Paradise and represents Divine Wisdom while Virgil represents Earthly Wisdom. — *Line 118, p. 6*

Saint Peter's gate. The gate of Purgatory which the poet pretends is guarded by an angel placed there by St. Peter. — *Line 130, p. 6*

CANTO II

Silvius' sire. Aeneas. — *Line 14, p. 7*

High effect. Founding of Rome. — *Line 19, p. 7*

Peter's sacred chair. The papal throne. — *Line 26, p. 7*

The chosen vessel. St. Paul; *Acts* ix. 15. — *Line 30, p. 7*

Who rest suspended. The spirits in Limbo who are not admitted to a state of glory nor doomed to punishment. — *Line 54, p. 8*

Beatrice. The daughter of Folco Portinari who is invested in the poem with the character of celestial wisdom or theology. — *Line 71, p. 8*

NOTES

Whatever is contained. Everything within the lunar heaven which is the lowest of all and has the smallest circle.
Line 77, p. 9

This centre. The earth is the centre of the heavenly spheres and Hell extends to the centre of the earth.
Line 84, p. 9

A blessed dame. The Divine Mercy.
Line 93, p. 9

Lucia. The enlightening Grace of Heaven.
Line 97, p. 9

Three maids. The Divine Mercy, Lucia and Beatrice.
Line 124, p. 10

CANTO III

A flag. Those who in life were blown about by every wind of doctrine.
Line 50, p. 12

... Who to base fear
Yielding, abjured his high estate. Commonly understood to be Celestine V who abdicated as pope in 1294 and made way for Boniface VIII.
Line 56, p. 12

A great stream. The Acheron.
Line 66, p. 13

A nimbler boat. Perhaps the bark "swift and light" (*Purg.*, ii, 40) in which the Angel conducts the spirits to Purgatory; the saved souls go to the mouth of the Tiber and are carried over the ocean to Purgatory. *Line 87, p. 13*

CANTO IV

The first circle. Limbo containing the souls of unbaptized children and the virtuous adults who lived before Christ.
Line 23, p. 16

New to that estate. Virgil died in 19 B.C., and had been in Limbo fifty years when Christ came to free the virtuous of the old dispensation.
Line 49, p. 17

A puissant one. Christ.
Line 50, p. 17

The monarch of sublimest song. Homer.
Line 90, p. 18

A magnificent castle. Human knowledge symbolized.
Line 101, p. 18

With lofty walls. The seven cardinal virtues.
Line 102, p. 18

Seven gates. The seven liberal arts.
Line 104, p. 18

Electra. The daughter of Atlas and mother of Dardanus, the founder of Troy.
Line 117, p. 19

Camilla. Also mentioned in *Hell*, i, 104.
Line 120, p. 19

Penthesilea. Queen of the Amazons who fell fighting for the Trojans in Asia.
Line 121, p. 19

Latinus. Father-in-law of Aeneas.
Line 122, p. 19

Brutus. Junius Brutus, the first consul.
Line 123, p. 19

Julia. Daughter of Julius Cæsar and wife of Pompey.
Line 125, p. 19

Cornelia. Daughter of Scipio Africanus and mother of the Gracchi.
Line 125, p. 19

The Soldan fierce. Saladin, sultan of Egypt and Syria, the rival of Richard the Lion-Hearted; died 1193.
Line 126, p. 19

The master of the sapient throng. Aristotle.
Line 128, p. 19

Democritus. Who maintained the world had been formed by the fortuitous concourse of atoms.
Line 132, p. 19

Thales sage. Thales of Miletus, the founder of the Ionic school.
Line 135, p. 19

Zeno. Chief of the Stoics.
Line 136, p. 19

Dioscorides. Who wrote a treatise on properties of plants and stone.
Line 136, p. 19

Linus. Possibly the son of Apollo who was fabled as a singer.
Line 138, p. 19

Tully. Marcus Tullius Cicero.
Line 138, p. 19

Avicen. Avicenna, the Arab physician whom Dante presents with two other famous physicians of antiquity.
Line 140, p. 19

Averroes. An Arab philosopher who wrote a celebrated commentary on Aristotle.
Line 141, p. 19

CANTO V

Minos. King of Crete whom Virgil made one of the judges in Hell.
Line 4, p. 20

HELL

Semiramis. Queen of Assyria famous for her licentiousness. *Line 57, p. 21*

Soldan. The Sultan of Egypt was also called the Sultan of Babylon in Dante's time. *Line 59, p. 21*

With love fought to the end. Polyxena whom Achilles loved; her brother, Paris, killed Achilles while the marriage was taking place. *Line 65, p. 21*

The land. Ravenna. *Line 96, p. 22*

Caïna. The place to which murderers are doomed. *Line 105, p. 22*

Francesca. Francesca da Rimini who was given by her father, lord of Ravenna, in marriage to Lanciotto, son of the lord of Rimini; she fell in love with Lanciotto's brother, Paolo, and with him was put to death for adultery by the enraged Lanciotto. *Line 113, p. 23*

CANTO VI

Ciacco. In Italian, signifying pig. *Line 52, p. 25*

The divided city. Florence, divided into the Bianchi and Neri factions. *Line 61, p. 25*

The wild party from the woods. So called because it was headed by Veri de' Cerchi whose family had come from the woody country of the Val di Nievole. *Line 65, p. 25*

The other. The opposite party of the Neri, headed by Corso Donati. *Line 66, p. 26*

This must fall. The Bianchi. *Line 67, p. 26*

Three solar circles. Within three years; the Bianchi were banished in 1302, and so was Dante. *Line 68, p. 26*

... of one, who under shore Now rests. Charles of Valois by whom the Neri were replaced. *Line 69, p. 26*

The just are two in number. Unknown. *Line 73, p. 26*

Of Farinata and Tegghiaio. See notes to *Hell*, x, 32 and xvi, 42. *Line 79, p. 26*

Giacopo. Giacopo Rusticucci. See notes to *Hell*, xvi, 45. *Line 80, p. 26*

Arrigo. Of Arrigo who, commentators say, came from the noble family of Fifanti. *Line 81, p. 26*

Mosca. Mosca degli Uberti is introduced in Canto xxviii. *Line 81, p. 26*

Plutus. Following his custom with mythological characters, Dante makes Plutus, the god of riches, a demon. *Line 117, p. 27*

CANTO VII

The first adulterer proud. Satan; the word is here used in the sense of one who experiences a revolt of affections from God, and appears often in this way in the Bible. See *Rev.* xii, 7–9. *Line 12, p. 27*

Each part. Each hemisphere of the heavens shines upon the hemisphere of the earth placed under it. *Line 75, p. 30*

Each star is falling now. From the zenith so that it is past midnight. *Line 101, p. 31*

CANTO VIII

Phlegyas. Who was so incensed against Apollo for violating his daughter, Coronis, that he set fire to Apollo's temple, and was cast into Tartarus. See Virg. *Aen.*, I, vi, 618. *Line 18, p. 32*

Filippo Argenti. According to Boccaccio, "a man remarkable for the large proportions and extraordinary vigor of his bodily frame and the extreme waywardness and irascibility of his temper." *Line 59, p. 34*

Dis. The city of Dis which forms the sixth circle of Hell and was fortified with walls, moats and towers. *Line 66, p. 34*

Seven times. Reckoning the beasts in the first canto as one, and adding Charon, Minos, Cerberus, Plutus, Phlegyas and Filippo Argenti as the rest, the number is seven; but Dante may have put a definite number for an indeterminate number. *Line 94, p. 35*

This their insolence, not new. These spirits had shown the same insolence when Christ descended into Hell. *Line 122, p. 35*

CANTO IX

Erictho. A Thessalian sorceress employed by Sextus, son of Pompey the Great, to conjure up a spirit who would inform him of the outcome of the civil wars between his father and Cæsar. This may refer to some other incident or be an anachronism because Sextus died thirty years before Virgil's death. *Line 24, p. 36*

Lowest place of all. Hell's lowest circle where arch-traitors are punished; see *Hell*, xxxiv. *Line 28, p. 36*

NOTES

All-circling orb. The primum mobile, or outermost of the Nine Spheres.   *Line* 30, *p.* 36

Erynnis. The female divinities who were the avengers of iniquity in Greek mythology.   *Line* 46, *p.* 37

Your Cerberus. When Cerberus tried to oppose his entrance to Hell, Hercules bound him with a threefold chain and dragged him out of the gate.   *Line* 97, *p.* 39

Arles. The Roman antiquities there include a theatre, a forum and a cemetery.   *Line* 111, *p.* 40

Pola. Also contains Roman antiquities.   *Line* 112, *p.* 40

CANTO X

Josaphat. A common opinion among Jews as well as Christians was that the final judgment would be held in the valley of Josaphat, or Jehoshaphat; see *Joel* iii, 2.   *Line* 12, *p.* 41

Farinata. Farinata degli Uberti, a noble Florentine, leader of the Ghibelline faction; exiled from Florence, he regained the city with the help of Manfred, king of the Two Sicilies, in 1260. He saved Florence when his party wished to burn it to the ground.   *Line* 32, *p.* 41

Twice. The first time in 1248 when they were driven out by Frederick II and the second in 1260, after the battle of Montaperti.   *Line* 47, *p.* 42

Return'd. Dante's ancestors returned to Florence in 1251 after the defeat of the Ghibellines at Figlione, and in 1266 after the death of Manfred.   *Line* 49, *p.* 42

A shade. The spirit of Cavalcante Cavalcanti, a noble Florentine, of the Guelph party.   *Line* 52, *p.* 42

My son. Guido, the son of Cavalcante Cavalcanti, whom Dante calls "the first of my friends" in the *Vita Nuova*; he died either in exile in Serrazana or soon after his return to Florence in December, 1300, during the spring of which year the action of this poem is supposed to be taking place.   *Line* 59, *p.* 42

Had in contempt. Guido, more given to philosophy than poetry, may not have been an admirer of Virgil.   *Line* 63, *p.* 42

Not yet fifty times. Fifty months will not pass before Dante will learn the difficulty of returning to his native city from banishment.   *Line* 77, *p.* 42

Queen of this realm. The moon, who bore the title of Proserpine, queen of the shades below, in heathen mythology.   *Line* 78, *p.* 42

The slaughter. By means of Farinata degli Uberti, the Guelphs were conquered by the army of Manfred near the river Arbia with so great a slaughter that those who escaped took refuge in Lucca; they considered Florence was lost.   *Line* 83, *p.* 43

Such orisons. May refer to prayers in the churches of Florence for the deliverance from the Uberti; or perhaps public counsels were held in the churches, and the speeches were called "orisons."   *Line* 86, *p.* 43

Singly there I stood. Guido Novello assembled a council of the Ghibellines at Empoli where it was agreed that in order to maintain the ascendency of the Ghibelline party in Tuscany, it was necessary to destroy Florence. This cruel sentence, passed upon so noble a city, met with no opposition from any of its citizens or friends, except Farinata degli Uberti.   *Line* 90, *p.* 43

We view. The departed spirits know things of the past and future, but are ignorant of present things.   *Line* 98, *p.* 43

Frederick. The Emperor Frederick II who died in 1250.   *Line* 120, *p.* 44

The Lord Cardinal. Ottaviano Ubaldini, a Florentine, made cardinal in 1245, and deceased about 1273. On account of his great influence, he was generally known as "the Cardinal." It is reported of him, that he declared, if there were any such thing as a human soul, he had lost his for the Ghibellini.   *Line* 121, *p.* 44

Her gracious beam. Beatrice.   *Line* 132, *p.* 44

CANTO XI

Anastasius. Anastasius II, made pope in 496, died in 498.   *Line* 9, *p.* 45

Photinus. Bishop of Sirmio, condemned as a heretic by the synod of Antioch in 351; Dante confuses him with Photinus, deacon of Thessalonica and follower of Acacius.   *Line* 9, *p.* 45

Cahors. A city in France which had the name of being frequented by usurers in the Middle Ages.   *Line* 53, *p.* 46

Dis. Lucifer.   *Line* 68, *p.* 46

Whom the rain beats, etc. The gluttonous and licentious.   *Line* 74, *p.* 46

With tongues. Misers and prodigals.   *Line* 75, *p.* 46

Thy ethic page. Aristotle's *Ethics.*   *Line* 83, *p.* 46

HELL

Fell spirits. The violent, fraudulent and traitorous.   *Line 91, p. 47*

Her laws. Aristotle's *Physics.*   *Line 104, p. 47*

Creation's holy book. Genesis ii. 15.   *Line 111, p. 47*

Pisces. Pisces is already above the horizon, and the sun, in Aries, will rise shortly.   *Line 118, p. 47*

The Wain. The constellation Boötes, called Charles's Wain.   *Line 119, p. 47*

CANTO XII

The infamy of Crete. The Minotaur.   *Line 13, p. 48*

The feign'd heifer. Pasiphaë, the mother of the Minotaur, by a bull sent by Poseidon.   *Line 14, p. 48*

The king of Athens. Theseus who was able to destroy the Minotaur by the instruction of Ariadne, his sister.   *Line 17, p. 48*

He arrived. Christ who, according to Dante, carried with him the souls of the Patriarchs and other just men from the first circle when he ascended from Hell; see *Hell,* iv.   *Line 36, p. 49*

Been into chaos turn'd. This opinion is attributed to Empedocles.   *Line 42, p. 49*

Chiron. Son of Saturn and Philyra, pupil of Apollo, instructor of Achilles, friend of Peleus; renowned for his wisdom and skill in medicine, hunting and music.   *Line 62, p. 49*

And wrought himself revenge. Nessus, when dying by the hand of Hercules, charged Deianira to preserve the gore from his wound; if the affections of Hercules should at any time be estranged from her, he said it would act as a charm, and recall them. Deianira had occasion to try the experiment, and the venom caused Hercules to expire in torments.   *Line 66, p. 49*

Pholus. A Centaur who threatened the wives of the Lapithae at the wedding of Pirithous when he was overheated with wine.   *Line 69, p. 50*

Dionysius. Tyrant of Syracuse, died 367 B.C.   *Line 107, p. 52*

Azzolino. Or Ezzolino di Romano, a noted Ghibelline leader, notorious for his cruelty, who died 1260; he was lord of Padua, Vicenza, Verona and Brescia, and the subject of a Latin tragedy, *Eccerinis,* by Albertino Mussato, a contemporary of Dante.   *Line 110, p. 52*

Obizzo of Este. Marquis of Ferrara and of Marca d'Ancona murdered by his own son for the sake of the wealth he had amassed by his rapacity.   *Line 111, p. 52*

He. Henry, nephew of Henry III of England, was slain at Viterbo, Italy, by Guy de Montfort, the son of Simon de Montfort, Earl of Leicester, in revenge for his father's death. Henry's heart was reputedly put in a golden cup and placed on a pillar of the London Bridge.   *Line 119, p. 52*

Attila. King of Huns who began his reign in 433.   *Line 134, p. 52*

On Sextus and on Pyrrhus. Sextus was the son either of Pompey the Great or Tarquin the Proud; Pyrrhus was king of Epirus.   *Line 135, p. 52*

... the Rinieri, of Corneto this,
Pazzo, the other named. Two noted marauders who preyed on the public ways of Italy. The latter was of the noble family of Pazzi in Florence.   *Line 137, p. 52*

CANTO XIII

Betwixt Corneto and Cecina's stream. A wild and woody tract of country abounding in deer, goats and wild boars.   *Line 10, p. 53*

I it was. Piero delle Vigne, a native of Capua who raised himself to the office of Chancellor to Emperor Frederick II who had great confidence in him. Courtiers by means of forged letters convinced Frederick that he held a secret and traitorous intercourse with the Pope, then at odds with the Emperor. Piero was condemned to lose his eyes, and driven to despair, dashed out his brains against the walls of a church in 1245.   *Line 60, p. 54*

The harlot. Envy.   *Line 67, p. 54*

The fierce soul. A suicide.   *Line 97, p. 55*

Lano. A Siennese who was reduced by prodigality to a state of extreme want and took the opportunity of exposing himself to sure death in the military expedition which the Siennese sent to assist the Florentines against the Aretini.   *Line 122, p. 56*

O Giacomo of Sant' Andrea! Iacopo da Sant' Andrea, a Paduan who killed himself after he had wasted his property in the most wanton acts of profusion.   *Line 133, p. 56*

In that city. Florence who changed her first patron, Mars, for St. John.   *Line 144, p. 57*

NOTES

Ashes left by Attila. According to the tradition of Dante's time, Attila destroyed Florence and Charlemagne rebuilt it.
Line 150, p. 57

CANTO XIV

By Cato's foot. The Libyan desert where Cato led the remnant of Pompey's army to Juba, the king of Numidia.
Line 15, p. 57

As, in the torrid Indian clime. A reference to Alexander the Great's supposed account to Aristotle of the falling of snow, then fire, upon his soldiers. Dante has apparently confused the story.
Line 28, p. 58

Yon huge spirit. Capaneus, one of the seven kings besieging Thebes, who defied Jupiter to help the city and was destroyed for his presumption.
Line 43, p. 58

Mongibello. Mt. Aetna.
Line 53, p. 58

Little brook. Phlegethon.
Line 74, p. 59

Bulicame. Warm, medicinal spring near Viterbo which passed by a place of ill fame.
Line 76, p. 59

Under whose monarch. Saturn's reign, regarded as the golden age.
Line 91, p. 59

At Rome. Rome was ordained by God as the centre of spiritual and temporal power.
Line 100, p. 60

The red seething wave. Phlegethon.
Line 130, p. 60

Whither. The other side of Purgatory.
Line 133, p. 61

CANTO XV

Chiarentana. A part of the Alps where the river Brenta rises.
Line 10, p. 61

Brunetto. Brunetto Latini, born in 1220 of a noble family, a noted scholar of his day, and Dante's teacher; he wrote *Il Tesoretto*, an allegorical didactic poem in Italian, and *Li Tresors*, a variety of encyclopedia, in French.
Line 28, p. 62

Fesole. The first city built in Europe, according to Florentine tradition; destroyed by J. Cæsar, a new city, called Florence, was built on its foundations by the Romans.
Line 62, p. 63

Either party. The Bianchi and Neri parties.
Line 71, p. 63

Priscian. There was a grammarian by that name, but most commentators believe Dante here uses an individual name for the species because he wishes to imply the frequency of the crime among those who abused their opportunities in educating youth.
Line 110, p. 64

Francesco. Accorso, a Florentine, who interpreted the Roman law at Bologna, and died in 1229.
Line 111, p. 64

Him. Andrea de' Mozzi, who was translated by Pope Nicholas III or Pope Boniface VIII from the see of Florence to Vicenza so that his scandalous life would be less exposed to observation.
Line 113, p. 64

I commend my Treasure to thee. Brunetto's great work.
Line 121, p. 64

CANTO XVI

Gualdrada. Daughter of Bellincione Berti whom Emperor Otho IV married because he was so impressed with her modesty and loveliness; Guidoguerra was her grandson, a man of great military skill and prowess who led four hundred Florentines of the Guelph party in the victory of Charles of Anjou over Manfred, King of Naples, in 1266. By this victory, the Ghibellines were expelled from Florence, and the Guelphs reestablished there.
Line 38, p. 66

Aldobrandi. Tegghiaio Aldobrandi of the noble family of Adimari; the rejection of his advice caused the memorable defeat of the Florentines at the hands of the Siennese at Montaperto, and the consequent banishment of the Guelphs from Florence.
Line 42, p. 66

Rusticucci. Giacopo Rusticucci, a Florentine, noted for his opulence and generous spirit.
Line 45, p. 66

Borsiere. Guglielmo Borsiere, another Florentine, whom Boccaccio calls "a man of courteous and elegant manners, and of great readiness in conversation."
Line 70, p. 67

E'en as the river. The fall of Phlegethon is likened to that of Montone in the Apennines above the Abbey of St. Benedict.
Line 94, p. 67

At Forli. Because there it loses the name of Acquacheta and takes that of Montone.
Line 99, p. 67

Where space. Either because the abbey was capable of containing more than those who occupied it or because the lords of that territory intended to build a castle near the waterfall and collect within its walls the population of surrounding villages.
Line 102, p. 67

A cord. It is believed that Dante entered the order of St. Francis in an earlier part of his life. By observing the rules of that order, he had wanted to mortify his carnal appetites or "take the painted leopard," repre-

HELL

senting Pleasure. "with his cord," the rope Franciscans wore around their waists as a symbol for this purpose.
Line 106, p. 68

CANTO XVII
The fell monster. Fraud. *Line 1, p. 69*

A pouch. A purse bearing the armorial bearings of each. *Line 53, p. 70*

A yellow purse. The arms of the Gianfigliazzi of Florence. *Line 57, p. 70*

Another. Those of the Ubbriachi, another Florentine family of high distinction. *Line 60, p. 70*

A fat and azure swine. The arms of the Scrovigni, a noble family of Padua. *Line 62, p. 70*

Vitaliano. Vitaliano del Dente, a Paduan. *Line 66, p. 70*

That noble knight. Giovanni Bujamonti, a Florentine usurer, the most infamous of his time. *Line 69, p. 71*

CANTO XVIII
With us beyond. Beyond the middle point they went the same way with us, but their pace was quicker than ours. *Line 28, p. 73*

E'en thus the Romans. In the year 1300, Pope Boniface VIII, to remedy the inconvenience occasioned by the press of people who were passing over the bridge of St. Angelo during the time of the Jubilee, caused it to be divided lengthwise by a partition; and ordered that all those who were going to St. Peter's should keep one side, and those returning the other. *Line 29, p. 73*

The castle. Sant' Angelo, originally the mausoleum of Adrian, and made a citadel in the Middle Ages.
Line 33, p. 74

Venedico. Venedico Caccianimico, a Bolognese, who prevailed on his sister, Ghisola, to prostitute herself to Obizzo da Este, Marquis of Ferrara, who appeared in Canto xii. *Line 50, p. 74*

To answer Sipa. He denotes Bologna by its situation between the rivers Savena and Reno and by a peculiarity of dialect which uses the affirmative *sipa* instead of *si* or *sia*. *Line 62, p. 74*

Hypsipyle. She deceived the other women of Lemnos by concealing her father, Thoas, when they had agreed to put all their males to death. *Line 90, p. 75*

Alessio. Of an ancient and considerable family in Lucca, called the Interminei. *Line 120, p. 76*

CANTO XIX
Saint John's fair dome. The fonts of St. John the Baptist in Florence. *Line 18, p. 78*

O Boniface. The spirit mistakes Dante for Boniface VIII who was then alive and whom he did not expect to arrive so soon because of a prophecy predicting his death at a later period. Boniface died in 1303.
Line 55, p. 79

In guile. He means that he arrived at papal power by fraudulent means and afterwards abused it.
Line 58, p. 79

In the mighty mantle I was robed. Nicholas III of the Orsini family whom Dante therefore calls "figliuol dell' orsa," son of the she-bear. He died in 1281. *Line 71, p. 80*

From forth the west, a shepherd without law. Bertrand de Got, Archbishop of Bordeaux, who succeeded to the pontificate in 1305 under the name of Clement V. He transferred the holy see to Avignon in 1308 where it remained until 1376. He died in 1314. *Line 86, p. 80*

A new Jason. Son of Simon the High Priest, who offered King Antiochus a huge sum for the high-priesthood. See 2 Maccab., iv. *Line 88, p. 80*

Of France's monarch. Philip IV of France. *Line 91, p. 80*

Nor Peter. Acts of the Apostles i, 26. *Line 97, p. 80*

The condemned soul. Judas. *Line 100, p. 81*

Against Charles. Nicholas III was enraged against Charles I, King of Sicily, because he rejected with scorn a proposition made by that pope for an alliance between their families. *Line 103, p. 81*

The Evangelist. Rev. xvii, 1-3. *Line 109, p. 81*

Ah, Constantine. Reference to the pretended gift of the Lateran by Constantine to Sylvester. *Line 118, p. 81*

CANTO XX
When she is dead. A play on the words "pity" and "piety." *Line 27, p. 82*

Before whose eyes. Amphiaraus, a soothsayer and one of the seven kings against Thebes, who is said to have been swallowed up by an opening of the earth. *Line 30, p. 82*

[437]

NOTES

Tiresias. The Theban soothsayer who went to Troy with the Greeks. By striking two serpents entwined together, he changed to woman's shape, and only regained the figure of a man at the end of seven years.
Line 37, p. 83

Aruns. Etruscan diviner who foretold the victory of Cæsar over Pompey.
Line 43, p. 83

Manto. The daughter of Tiresias of Thebes, a city dedicated to Bacchus. She founded Mantua, the country of Virgil.
Line 50, p. 83

Camonica. Large valley of Lombardy.
Line 62, p. 83

There is a spot, Prato di Fame, where the dioceses of Trento, Verona and Brescia meet.
Line 63, p. 83

Peschiera. A garrison situated to the south of the lake where it empties to form the Mincius; owned by the Scala family against whom the Bergamese and Brescians banded together.
Line 69, p. 83

Casalodi's madness. Alberto da Casalodi, who had got possession of Mantua, was persuaded, by Pinamonte Buonacossi, that he might ingratiate himself with the people, by banishing to their own castles the nobles, obnoxious to them. No sooner was this done than Pinamonte put himself at the head of the populace, drove out Casalodi and his adherents, and obtained the sovereignty for himself.
Line 94, p. 84

Michael Scot. A Scottish scholar who flourished in the thirteenth century and gained the name of being a great necromancer after his death; he superintended the translation of Aristotle at the invitation of Frederick II and wrote several treatises on natural philosophy.
Line 114, p. 85

Guido Bonatti. An astrologer of Forli on whose skill Guido da Montefeltro, lord of Forli, so much relied that he is reported never to have gone into battle except at the hour recommended by Bonatti as fortunate.
Line 116, p. 85

Asdente. A shoemaker of Padua who deserted his business to practice divination and attracted much public notice at the time.
Line 116, p. 85

Cain with fork of thorns. The moon designated by a phrase comparable to "the man in the moon."
Line 123, p. 85

CANTO XXI

One of Santa Zita's elders. The elders or chief magistrates of Lucca where Santa Zita was held in special veneration. This sinner is supposed to have been named Martino Botaio.
Line 37, p. 86

Except Bonturo, barterers. Said ironically of Bonturo de' Dati. By "barterers" are meant peculators of every description, all who traffic the interests of the public for their own private advantage.
Line 40, p. 86

The hallow'd visage. A representation of the head of Christ, worshipped at Lucca.
Line 47, p. 87

Is other swimming than in Serchio's wave. The river that flows by Lucca.
Line 48, p. 87

From Caprona. The surrender of the castle of Caprona to the combined forces of Florence and Lucca on the condition that the garrison should march out in safety; Dante was a witness of this event which took place in 1290.
Line 92, p. 88

Yesterday. This passage fixes the time of Dante's descent at Good Friday of the year 1300, and at the thirty-fifth year of the poet's life. At Christ's death, the convulsion which shook the earth reached even to Hell and the bridge over the pits of the hypocrites was destroyed.
Line 109, p. 88

CANTO XXII

Scouring thy plains. Probably reference to the battle of Camaldino when the Guelphs of Florence defeated the Ghibellines of Arezzo; Dante took part.
Line 6, p. 89

Born in Navarre's domain. The name of this peculator is said to have been Ciampolo.
Line 47, p. 91

The good King Thibault. Thibault I, King of Navarre, whom the historian Mariana commends for his desire to aid in the war in the Holy Land and reprehends for oppressing the rights and privileges of the church; died in 1233.
Line 51, p. 91

Their chief. Barbariccia, head of the ten sent to escort the two poets.
Line 73, p. 91

The friar Gomita. Entrusted by Nino de' Viconti with the government of Gallura, one of the four jurisdictions into which Sardinia is divided. He took a bribe from Nino's enemies whom he had in his power and allowed them to escape.
Line 80, p. 91

Michel Zanche. The president of Logodoro, another of the four Sardinian jurisdictions.
Line 88, p. 92

CANTO XXIII

Aesop's fable. Reference to a fable, not in Aesop, about the frog who offered to carry the mouse across a ditch with the intention of drowning him, but who was carried off, with his victim, by a kite.
Line 5, p. 95

Monks in Cologne. They wore their cowls unusually large.
Line 63, p. 96

HELL

Fvederick's. The Emperor Frederick II is said to have punished those who were guilty of high treason by wrapping them in lead and casting them into a furnace. *Line 66, p. 97*

Joyous friars. Two knights, M. Catalano de' Malavolti, a Guelph, and M. Loderingo degli Andalò, a Ghibelline, who were imported by the Ghibelline rulers of Florence to pacify the discontented people; they were of the order of *Joyous Friars*, called Knights of St. Mary, and were supposed to act in this situation as mediators and helpers of the people, and save the commonwealth unnecessary expense, but they connived with each other and promoted their own advantage rather than that of the public. *Line 104, p. 98*

Gardingo's vicinage. The name of that part of the city which was inhabited by the powerful Ghibelline family of the Uberti, and destroyed under the partial and iniquitous administration of Catalano and Loderingo. *Line 110, p. 98*

That pierced spirit. Calaphas. *Line 117, p. 98*

The father of his consort. Annas, father-in-law to Calaphas. *Line 124, p. 98*

He is a liar. John viii. 44. *Line 146, p. 99*

CANTO XXIV

In the year's early nonage. The latter part of January when the sun enters Aquarius and the equinox is drawing near, when the hoar-frosts often wear the appearance of snow in the morning, but are melted by the rising sun. *Line 1, p. 99*

A longer ladder. Purgatory. *Line 55, p. 101*

Vanni Fucci. Said to have been an illegitimate offspring of the family of Lazari in Pistoia, who robbed the sacristy of the church of St. James in Pistoia and charged Vanni della Nona with the sacrilege for which he was put to death. *Line 120, p. 102*

Pistoia. In May, 1301, the Bianchi party of Pistoia, with the assistance of the Bianchi, who ruled Florence, drove out the Neri from the former place, destroying their houses, palaces, and farms. *Line 142, p. 103*

Then Florence. Soon after the Bianchi will be expelled from Florence, the Neri will prevail, and the laws and people will be changed. *Line 143, p. 103*

From Valdimagra. The commentators explain this prophetical threat as alluding to the victory by the Marquis Morello Malaspina of Valdimagra who put himself at the head of the Neri and defeated the Bianchi at Campo Piceno near Pistoia. *Line 144, p. 103*

CANTO XXV

Thy seed. Thy ancestry. *Line 12, p. 104*

Not him. Capaneus. See Canto xiv. *Line 15, p. 104*

On Maremma's marsh. An extensive tract near the seashore of Tuscany. *Line 18, p. 104*

Cacus. Son of Vulcan who stole from Hercules some of Geryon's cattle and dragged them to his cave under the Aventine. *Line 24, p. 104*

A hundred blows. Less than ten blows out of the hundred Hercules gave him had deprived him of feeling. *Line 31, p. 104*

Cianfa. Said to have been of the family of Donati, Florence. *Line 39, p. 104*

Agnello. Agnello Brunelleschi. *Line 61, p. 105*

In that part. The navel. *Line 77, p. 105*

Sabellus. With Nasidius, soldier in Cato's army; both met horrible deaths from the bite of animals. *Line 86, p. 105*

Cadmus and Arethusa. The first was changed to a snake, the second, to a fountain. *Line 89, p. 107*

Buoso. Said by some to have been of the Donati family, but by others, of the Abbati. *Line 131, p. 108*

Sciancato. Puccio Sciancato, a noted robber. *Line 138, p. 108*

Gaville. Francesco Guercio Cavalcante was killed at Gaville near Florence and in revenge for his death several inhabitants of the district were put to death. *Line 140, p. 108*

CANTO XXVI

Shalt feel what Prato. A prophecy of the calamities soon to befall Florence which, Dante says, even her nearest neighbor, Prato, would wish her. *Line 9, p. 108*

As he whose wrongs. II Kings ii. *Line 35, p. 109*

Ascending from that funeral pile. The flame is said to have divided on the funeral piles of Eteocles and Polynices, as if conscious of the enmity that actuated them while living. *Line 54, p. 110*

[439]

NOTES

The ambush of the horse. The ambush of the wooden horse, that caused Aeneas to quit the city of Troy and seek his fortune in Italy, where his descendants founded the Roman empire. *Line 60, p. 110*

Deïdamia. Daughter of Lycomedes, king of Sciros, to whom Achilles was sent by his mother to save him from the fate awaiting him at Troy. *Line 64, p. 110*

Her Palladium. Ulysses and Diomedes, disguised as beggars, stole the Palladium from the temple of Minerva. *Line 65, p. 110*

Caieta. Virgil, *Aeneid*, vii, 1. *Line 91, p. 111*

The strait pass. The straits of Gibraltar. *Line 106, p. 111*

Ceuta. African city on Strait of Gibraltar. *Line 109, p. 111*

A mountain dim. Purgatory, supposedly separated by a long space of sea or land from regions inhabited by men and placed in the ocean reaching as far as the lunar circle so that the waters of the deluge did not reach it. *Line 128, p. 112*

CANTO XXVII

The Sicilian bull. The engine of torture invented by Perillus for the tyrant Phalaris. *Line 6, p. 112*

Romagna. A territorial division of Italy which now stretches over the provinces of Bologna, Ferrara, Ravenna and Forlì. *Line 25, p. 113*

Of the mountains there. Montefeltro. *Line 26, p. 113*

Polenta's eagle. The arms of Guido Novello da Polenta, Dante's last and most munificent patron; Guido made himself master of Ravenna in 1265, but was deprived of his sovereignty in 1322 and died in Bologna. During his supremacy, he extended his rule over Cervia, a small maritime city about fifteen miles south of Ravenna. *Line 38, p. 113*

The land. The inhabitants of the territory of Forlì in 1282 were able to defeat the French army besieging them through a stratagem of Guido da Montefeltro, their governor. Dante informs the former ruler that Forlì is now in possession of Sinibalde Ordolaffi, or Ardelaffi, whom he designates by his coat of arms, a lion vert. *Line 41, p. 113*

The old mastiff of Verruchio and the young. Malatesta and Malatestino, his son, lords of Rimini; Verruchio was the name of their castle. Malatestino was perhaps the husband of Francesca, see note, Canto v, 113. *Line 43, p. 113*

Montagna. Montagna de' Parcitati, a noble knight and leader of the Ghibelline party at Rimini, murdered by Malatestino. *Line 44, p. 113*

Lamone's city and Santerno's. Lamone is the river at Faenza, and Santerno at Imola. *Line 46, p. 113*

The lion of the snowy lair. Machinardo Pagano whose arms were a lion azure on a field argent. *Line 47, p. 113*

Whose flank is wash'd of Savio's wave. Cesena, situated at the foot of a mountain and washed by the river Savio which often descends with rapidity from the Apennines. *Line 50, p. 113*

A man of arms. Guido da Montefeltro. *Line 64, p. 114*

The high priest. Boniface VIII. *Line 68, p. 114*

The chief of the new Pharisees. Boniface VIII, whose enmity to the family of Colonna prompted him to destroy their houses near the Lateran. Wishing to obtain possession of their other seat, Penestrino, he consulted with Guido da Montefeltro and offered him absolution for his past sins, and for that which he was then tempting him to commit. Guido's advice was that kind words and fair promises would put his enemies into his power, and they accordingly soon afterwards fell into the snare laid for them. A.D. 1298. *Line 81, p. 114*

Nor against Acre. Allusion to the renegade Christians who assisted the Saracens in 1291 to recover St. John d'Acre, the last possession of the Christians in the Holy Land and a valuable trading centre. *Line 84, p. 114*

Constantine. Sylvester had to flee from Constantine's persecution according to the legend, but when Constantine contracted leprosy, he sent for Sylvester who healed him. *Line 89, p. 114*

My predecessor. Celestine V. *Line 101, p. 115*

With performance scant. Boniface VIII broke his promise of restoring to them the estates and dignities of the Colonnas. *Line 106, p. 115*

CANTO XXVIII

In that long war. The war of Hannibal in Italy. "When Mago brought news of his victories to Carthage, in order to make his successes more easily credited, he commanded the golden rings to be poured out in the senate-house, which made so large a heap, that, as some relate, they filled three *modii* and a half." Livy, *Hist.*, xxiii. 12. *Line 8, p. 116*

HELL

Guiscard's Norman steel. Robert Guiscard, who conquered the kingdom of Naples, and died in 1110. He is introduced in *Paradise,* xviii. *Line 12, p. 116*

And those the rest. The army of Manfred through the treachery of the Apulian troops was overcome by Charles of Anjou in 1265 and fell in such numbers that the bones of the slain were still gathered near Ceperano. See *Purg.,* iii. *Line 13, p. 116*

O Tagliacozzo. Reference to the victory which Charles gained in 1268 over Conradino by the sage advice of Sieur de Valeri. *Line 16, p. 116*

Ali. The disciple of Mahomet who later founded his own sect. *Line 32, p. 117*

Dolcino. In 1305, a friar called Dolcino who belonged to no regular order raised in Novara, Lombardy, a large company of the meaner sort of people, declared himself a true apostle of Christ, and promulgated a community of property and wives and many other heretical doctrines. His more than three thousand followers lived promiscuously in the mountains, but after about two years, the sect diminished, and Dolcino was taken by the people of Novara and burnt with Margarita, his companion, and many others of his followers. *Line 53, p. 117*

Medicina. A place in the territory of Bologna. Piero fomented dissensions there and among the leaders of neighboring states. *Line 69, p. 117*

The pleasant land. Lombardy. *Line 70, p. 117*

Vercelli . . . Mercabò. A city and castle marking the beginning of Lombardy. *Line 71, p. 118*

The twain. Guido del Cassero and Angiolello da Cagnano, two of the worthiest and most distinguished citizens of Fano; invited by Malatestino da Rimini to an entertainment on the pretence that he had some important business to transact with them, they were drowned according to Malatestino's instructions as they crossed the river near Cattolica. *Line 72, p. 118*

Focara's wind. Focara is a mountain from which blows a wind peculiarly dangerous to navigators. *Line 85, p. 118*

The doubt in Cæsar's mind. Curio, whose speech determined Julius Cæsar to proceed when he had arrived at Rimini (Ariminum) and doubted whether he should prosecute the civil war. *Line 94, p. 118*

Mosca. Buondelmonte was engaged to marry a lady of the Amidei family, but broke his promise and married one of the Donati. At a meeting of the Amidei to consider the best means of revenging the insult, Mosca degli Uberti urged the assassination of Buondelmonte. This advice was the source of many terrible calamities that happened to Florence and was the beginning of the Guelph and Ghibelline parties there. *Line 102, p. 118*

Bertrand. Bertrand de Born, Vicomte de Hautefort, near Perigueux in Guienne, who incited John to rebel against his father, Henry II of England. *Line 130, p. 120*

CANTO XXIX

The time. A little after mid-day. *Line 11, p. 120*

Geri of Bello. A kinsman of Dante's, murdered by one of the Sacchetti family; he was the son of Bello, the poet's great-uncle. *Line 26, p. 121*

Of Valdichiana. Stagnation of water made this valley unwholesome in the heat of autumn until the Emperor Leopold II had the valley drained. *Line 45, p. 121*

Maremma's pestilent fen. See note, xxv, 18. *Line 47, p. 121*

In Aegina. The fable of the ants changed into Myrmidons. *Line 58, p. 122*

Arezzo was my dwelling. Grifolino of Arezzo. *Line 104, p. 123*

Albero of Sienna. The son of the Bishop of Sienna who put Grifolino to death at Albero's request. *Line 105, p. 123*

*. . . was ever race
Light as Sienna's?* See also *Purg.,* xiii. 141. *Line 117, p. 123*

Stricca. This is said ironically. Stricca, Niccolo Salimbeni, Caccia of Asciano, and Abbagliato, or Meo de' Folcacchieri, belonged to a company of prodigal and luxurious young men in Sienna. Niccolo was the inventor of a new manner of using cloves. Out of the sum raised from the sale of their estates, they built in common a palace designed for luxurious enjoyment. *Line 121, p. 123*

In that garden. Sienna. *Line 125, p. 124*

Capocchio's ghost. Said to have been a fellow-student of Dante's in natural philosophy. *Line 134, p. 124*

CANTO XXX

Athamas. King of Thebes, husband of Semele's sister, Ino. *Line 4, p. 124*

[441]

NOTES

Polyxena. Sacrificed by demand of the spirit of Achilles when the Greeks landed at Thrace. *Line 18, p. 125*

Polydorus. Hecuba's only remaining son whom she found murdered by the king of Thrace as she returned from seeking water to wash the dead Polyxena's wounds. *Line 19, p. 125*

Schicchi. Gianni Schicchi of the family of Cavalcanti impersonated others so well that he was employed by Simon Donati to pretend to be Buoso Donati, recently deceased, and to make up a will leaving Simon his heir; Schicchi's reward was a mare of great value called "the lady of the herd." *Line 33, p. 125*

Myrrha. See Ovid, *Metam.*, x. *Line 39, p. 125*

Adamo's woe. Adamo of Brescia, at the instigation of Guido, Alessandro, and their brother Aghinulfo, lords of Romena, counterfeited the coin of Florence and was burnt for the crime. *Line 60, p. 126*

Casentino. Romena is a part of Casentino. *Line 64, p. 126*

Romena. Castle near the source of the Arno. *Line 72, p. 126*

Branda's limpid spring. Fountain in Sienna. *Line 77, p. 126*

Three carats of alloy. The florin was a coin that ought to have had twenty-four carats of pure gold.
Line 88, p. 126

The false accuser. Potiphar's wife. *Line 96, p. 127*

Sinon. Who persuaded the Trojans to admit the wooden horse into the city. *Line 97, p. 127*

CANTO XXXI

His father's javelin. Telephos, king of Mysia, was wounded by Achilles' spear and could only be healed by its rust; he had inherited the spear from his father. *Line 4, p. 128*

Orlando. Or Roland, Charlemagne's famous knight, who won this horn from the giant Jatmund; the horn was magical and could be heard twenty miles away. *Line 14, p. 129*

Montereggion. Castle near Sienna. *Line 36, p. 129*

The pine. A large pine made of bronze which decorated the top of the belfry of St. Peter. *Line 53, p. 130*

Raphel, etc. These unmeaning sounds are meant to express the confusion of languages at the building of the tower of Babel. *Line 61, p. 130*

Ephialtes. Son of Neptune, brother of Otus. *Line 85, p. 131*

Briareus. Son of Neptune and Terra. *Line 90, p. 131*

Antæus. Son of same. *Line 92, p. 131*

The fortunate vale. Country near Carthage, where Scipio conquered Hannibal. *Line 105, p. 131*

Tityus. Son of Jupiter slain by Apollo for attempted assault on Latona. *Line 115, p. 131*

Typhon. A giant destroyed by Jupiter and buried under Mt. Aetna. *Line 115, p. 131*

Alcides. Hercules. *Line 123, p. 131*

The tower of Carisenda. Leaning tower of Bologna. *Line 128, p. 132*

CANTO XXXII

Amphion. Induced the rocks to form a wall around Thebes by charming them with his lyre. *Line 10, p. 132*

Tabernich or Pietrapana. The one a mountain in Solavonia, the other in that tract of country called the Garfagnana, not far from Lucca. *Line 29, p. 133*

To where modest shame appears. As high as the face. *Line 33, p. 133*

Who are these two. Alessandro and Napoleone, sons of Alberto Alberti, who murdered each other. They were proprietors of the valley of Falterona, where the Bisenzio has its source, a river that falls into the Arno about six miles from Florence. *Line 53, p. 133*

Not him. Mordrec, son of King Arthur. In the romance of Lancelot of the Lake, Arthur, having discovered the traitorous intentions of his son, pierces him through with the stroke of his lance so that the sunbeam passes through the body of Mordrec. *Line 59, p. 135*

Focaccia. Focaccia of Cancellieri (the Pistoian family) whose atrocious act of revenge against his uncle is said to have given rise to the parties of the Bianchi and Neri, in the year 1300. *Line 60, p. 135*

Mascheroni. Sasso Mascheroni, a Florentine, who also murdered his uncle. *Line 63, p. 135*

Camiccione. Camiccione de' Pazzi of Valdarno who treacherously put to death his kinsman Ubertino.
Line 66, p. 135

HELL

Carlino. Of the same family, he betrayed the Castel di Piano Travigne in Valdarno to the Florentines after the refugees of the Bianca and Ghibelline party had defended it against a siege for 29 days in the summer of 1302.   *Line 67, p. 135*

Montaperto. The defeat of the Guelphs here was caused by the treachery of Bocca degli Abbati who, during the engagement, cut off the hand of Giacopo del Vacca de' Pazzi, the Florentine standard-bearer.   *Line 81, p. 135*

Antenora. So-called from Antenor who betrayed Troy, his country.   *Line 89, p. 135*

Him of Duera. Buoso of Cremona, who was bribed by Guy de Montfort to leave a pass he was supposed to defend for the Ghibellines open to the army of Charles of Anjou in 1265; the people of Cremona were so enraged they extirpated the whole family.   *Line 113, p. 136*

Beccaria. Abbot of Vallombrosa, the Pope's Legate at Florence where he was beheaded on the discovery of his intrigues for the Ghibellines.   *Line 116, p. 136*

Soldanieri. Gianni Soldanieri put himself at the head of the people of Florence and thereby brought mischief to the Ghibelline party and his own ruin.   *Line 118, p. 136*

Ganellon. Betrayer of Charlemagne.   *Line 119, p. 136*

Tribaldello. Trobaldello de' Manfredi, bribed to betray the city of Faenza, 1282.   *Line 119, p. 136*

Tydeus. One of the seven kings at Thebes who called for the head of the killed Menalippus and gnawed on it before he expired himself.   *Line 128, p. 136*

CANTO XXXIII

Count Ugolino. During the factional strife between the Guelphs and the Ghibellines in Pisa in 1288, the Pisan people, enraged against this man for many treacheries, imprisoned him with two sons and two grandchildren in a tower on the Piazza of the Anziani; the tower was locked, the key thrown into the Arno and all food was withheld from them so that they died of hunger in a few days. The Archbishop Ruggiero degli Ubaldini of the Ghibelline faction was instrumental in turning the people against Count Ugolino. Judge Nino di Gallura de' Visconti of the Guelph faction was one of those betrayed by Ugolino; he is mentioned in *Purgatory,* vii, 53.   *Line 14, p. 137*

Unto the mountain. S. Giuliano between Pisa and Lucca.   *Line 29, p. 138*

Lanfranchi, etc. Members of the Archbishop's party.   *Line 32, p. 138*

Capraia and Gorgona. Small islands near the mouth of the Arno.   *Line 82, p. 139*

The friar Alberigo. Alberigo de' Manfredi of Faenza, one of the *Joyous Friars* who quarrelled with some of his brotherhood, and, under the pretense of wishing to be reconciled, invited them to a banquet where, at the signal of his calling for the fruit, assassins rushed in and murdered them.   *Line 116, p. 140*

Ptolomea. Named for Ptolemy, son of Abubus, by whom Simon and his sons were murdered at a great banquet he had for them; see *Maccab.,* xvi. Or from Ptolemy, king of Egypt, the betrayer of Pompey the Great.   *Line 123, p. 140*

Branca Doria. The family of Doria possessed great influence in Genoa. Branca is said to have murdered his father-in-law, Michel Zanche, introduced in Canto xxii.   *Line 136, p. 140*

Romagna's darkest spirit. The friar Alberigo.   *Line 152, p. 141*

CANTO XXXIV

Three faces. The first is anger, signified by red; the second, envy, signified by being between pale and yellow; the third, melancholy signified by black.   *Line 37, p. 142*

Brutus. Commentators explain the presence of Brutus and Cassius in the same place of punishment as Judas as the result of the belief that Julius Cæsar whom they betrayed was the founder of the Roman Empire; since the Empire is the temporal arm of God's authority, its betrayers would go to the same place as the betrayer of Christ, the founder of the Church.   *Line 61, p. 143*

NOTES

PURGATORY

CANTO I

Birds of chattering note. The daughters of Pierus challenged the muses to sing and were changed by them into magpies.
Line 11, p. 149

Planet. Venus.
Line 19, p. 149

The Pisces' light. The constellation of the Fish veiled by the more luminous body of Venus, then a morning star.
Line 21, p. 149

Four stars. Perhaps personifying the four cardinal virtues of Justice, Fortitude, Prudence and Temperance.
Line 24, p. 150

Our first parents. Adam and Eve could see the four stars mentioned here from Paradise, which was on the top of Mt. Purgatory, which is placed in the Southern hemisphere.
Line 25, p. 150

The wain. Charles's Wain or Boötes.
Line 30, p. 150

An old man. Cato.
Line 31, p. 150

A Dame from heaven. Beatrice.
Line 53, p. 150

Leave those weeds. Cato retired to Utica in North Africa where he committed suicide in 46 B.C. on hearing of the victory of Cæsar at Thapsus.
Line 74, p. 151

Through thy seven regions. The seven rounds of Purgatory in which the seven capital sins are punished.
Line 82, p. 151

A slender reed. Simplicity and patience.
Line 94, p. 151

CANTO II

Now had the sun. Dante was now antipodal to Jerusalem; while the sun was setting in that place which he takes as being the middle of the inhabited earth, it was rising where he was.
Line 1, p. 153

The scales. The constellation Libra.
Line 6, p. 153

When she reigns highest. When the autumnal equinox is past.
Line 7, p. 153

In Exitu. "When Israel came out of Egypt." Psalms cxiv.
Line 45, p. 154

Had chased Capricorn. Since Capricorn is 90 degrees from the sun now in Aries, it must have left the zenith when the sun rose above the horizon; it is after sunrise, therefore.
Line 55, p. 154

My Casella. A Florentine celebrated for his skill in music, in whose company Dante refreshed his spirits.
Line 88, p. 155

If he. The conducting angel.
Line 91, p. 155

These three months past. Since the time of the Jubilee of Boniface VIII, Christmas 1299; even the dead seem to have had special privileges at that time.
Line 94, p. 155

The shore. Ostia.
Line 96, p. 155

CANTO III

To Naples. Virgil died at Brundisium from which his body is said to have been removed to Naples.
Line 26, p. 157

'Twixt Lerice and Turbia. The two extremities of the Genoese republic of the time.
Line 49, p. 158

Manfredi. King of Naples and Sicily and natural son of Frederick II, lovely and agreeable in his manners and fond of poetry, music and dancing, but ambitious and without religion. He fell in the battle with Charles of Anjou in 1265 (see *Hell*, xxviii, 13). Dying excommunicated, he was not allowed to be buried in sacred ground by King Charles, and he was interred near the bridge of Benevento where each soldier in the army cast a stone on his grave; his body was finally removed by order of the Pope from there because it was church land, and buried by the river Verde near Campagna.
Line 110, p. 161

My fair daughter. Costanza, the daughter of Manfredi, and wife of Peter III, king of Aragon, by whom she was mother to Frederick, king of Sicily, and James, king of Aragon. With the latter of these she was at Rome 1296.
Line 112, p. 161

Clement. Clement IV.
Line 122, p. 161

[444]

PURGATORY

The stream of Verde. A river near Ascoli, that falls into the Tronto. The "extinguished lights" formed part of the ceremony at the interment of one excommunicated. *Line 127, p. 161*

CANTO IV

Full fifty steps. Three hours and twenty minutes, fifteen degrees reckoned to the hour. *Line 14, p. 162*

Sanleo. A fortress on the summit of Montefeltro. *Line 23, p. 162*

Noli. In the Genoese territory between Finale and Savona. *Line 24, p. 162*

Bismantua. A steep mountain in Reggio. *Line 25, p. 162*

Amazed. Dante does not remember he is antipodal to Europe where the sun took an opposite course. *Line 57, p. 163*

Were Leda's offspring. The constellation of the Gemini is nearer the Bears than Aries. If the sun, instead of being in Aries, had been in Gemini, both the sun and that portion of the Zodiac made "ruddy" by the sun would have been seen to "wheel nearer to the Bears," and Dante would see the sun still farther north. *Line 59, p. 163*

The path. The ecliptic. *Line 68, p. 164*

Thou wilt see. Since Purgatory and Sion are antipodal, the sun must rise on opposite sides of their respective eminences. *Line 69, p. 164*

That the mid orb. The sun recedes from this mountain toward the north at the time when the Jews on Mount Sion see it depart for the south. *Line 75, p. 164*

Belacqua. An excellent master of the harp and lute, but negligent in his affairs, both spiritual and temporal. *Line 119, p. 165*

Behoves so long. Those who have put off repentance until late in life. *Line 126, p. 165*

CANTO V

. . . as if the light not shone
From the left hand. The sun was now on their right; before, when seated and looking to the east on their ascent, the sun was on their left. They are ascending the mountain from east to west. *Line 4, p. 166*

"Miserere." The class of negligent who deferred repentance until overtaken by violent death. *Line 24, p. 166*

That land. The Marca d'Ancona between Romagna and Apulia, the kingdom of Charles of Anjou. *Line 67, p. 168*

From thence I came. Giacopo del Cassero, a citizen of Fano who spoke ill of Azzo da Este, Marquis of Ferrara, and was slain by assassins sent by the latter at Oriaco. *Line 73, p. 168*

The blood. Supposed to be the seat of life. *Line 74, p. 168*

Antenor's land. Padua, said to have been founded by Antenor, the Trojan prince. *Line 75, p. 168*

Of Montefeltro I. Buonconte, son of Guido da Montefeltro (see *Hell*, xxxii, 89) who fell in the battle of Campaldino, fighting on the side of the Aretini. *Line 87, p. 168*

Giovanna. His wife. *Line 88, p. 168*

Casentino's foot. In upper Arno valley. *Line 92, p. 168*

The hermit's seat. Hermitage of Camaldoli. *Line 94, p. 168*

Where its name is cancel'd. Between Bibbiena and Poppi where the Archiano falls into the Arno. *Line 95, p. 168*

From Pratomagno to the mountain range. Pratomagno which divides the Valdarno from Casentino to the Apennines. *Line 115, p. 169*

Pia. A Siennese lady of the family of Tolommei whose husband, Nello della Pietra, did away with her by having her thrown out of a window of his castle at Maremma. *Line 131, p. 169*

CANTO VI

Of Arezzo him. Benincasa of Arezzo, an eminent judge, who condemned to death the brother of Ghino di Tacco for his robberies in Maremma and was murdered by Ghino, also a violent man and robber. *Line 14, p. 170*

Him beside. Cione or Ciacco de' Tarlatti of Arezzo, said to have been carried by his horse into the Arno and there drowned while he was pursuing his enemies. *Line 15, p. 170*

Frederic Novello. Son of the Conte Guido da Battifolle slain by one of the Bostoli. *Line 17, p. 170*

[445]

NOTES

Of Pisa he. Farinata, son of Marzuco degli Scornigiani of Pisa; all commentators agree that Farinata was murdered but there is a good deal of difference in the opinions on what his father did about it.
Line 18, p. 170

Count Orso. Son of Napoleone da Cerbaia slain by Albert da Mangona, his uncle.
Line 20, p. 170

Peter de la Brosse. Secretary of Philip III of France; the courtiers, envying his high place in the king's favor, prevailed on Mary of Brabant to charge him falsely with an attempt upon her person, for which supposed crime he suffered death. Another story has it that he accused Mary of having poisoned her stepson to secure the throne for her own son.
Line 23, p. 170

In thy text. Virgil, *Aeneid*, vi, 376.
Line 30, p. 170

The hill. It was now past noon.
Line 51, p. 171

Sordello. A Provençal poet, flourishing in the 13th century, to whom feats of military prowess, as well as poetry, are attributed.
Line 75, p. 172

Justinian's hand. Justinian's reform of Italy's laws.
Line 89, p. 172

That which God commands. "Render unto Cæsar the things which are Cæsar's."
Line 94, p. 172

O German Albert! The Emperor Albert I, who succeeded Adolphus in 1298 and was murdered in 1308, neglected Italy.
Line 98, p. 172

Thy successor. Henry of Luxembourg who Dante hoped would deliver Italy.
Line 103, p. 172

Thy sire. Emperor Rudolph who was so intent on increasing his power in Germany that he also neglected Italy.
Line 104, p. 172

Capulets and Montagues. Mentioned as examples of feuding families; Verona is their city. Line 107, p. 173

Filippeschi and Monaldi. Rival families in Orvieto.
Line 108, p. 173

What safety Santafiore can supply. A place between Pisa and Sienna; this may be a reference to the robbers infesting the region or to the losses of the counts of Santafiore.
Line 113, p. 173

Marcellus. Probably the one who opposed Julius Cæsar.
Line 127, p. 173

Many refuse. The Florentines, on the contrary, are eager for public office.
Line 135, p. 173

CANTO VII

By Octavius' care. Which saw to it that Virgil's remains were transferred to Naples from Brundisium.
Line 5, p. 174

There is a place. Limbo. See *Hell*, iv, 24.
Line 27, p. 175

The three holy virtues. Faith, Hope and Charity.
Line 34, p. 175

The rest. Prudence, Justice, Fortitude and Temperance.
Line 35, p. 175

Only this line. "Walk while ye have the light, lest darkness come upon you; for he that walketh in darkness, knoweth not whither he goeth." *John* xii, 35.
Line 53, p. 175

Salve Regina. The beginning of a prayer to the Virgin.
Line 82, p. 176

The Emperor Rodolph. See last canto, v. 104. He died in 1291.
Line 94, p. 177

That country. Bohemia.
Line 98, p. 177

Ottocar. King of Bohemia, killed in the battle of Marchfield, fought with Rudolph, 1278. Winceslaus II, his son, who succeeded him, died in 1305.
Line 100, p. 177

That one with the nose deprest. Philip III of France, father of Philip IV, died in 1285, at Perpignan, in his retreat from Aragon.
Line 104, p. 177

Him of gentle look. Henry of Navarre, father of Jane married to Philip IV of France.
Line 105, p. 177

Gallia's bane. Philip IV of France ordered the seizure of all Italians in his country and realm under the pretence of arresting the money-lenders, but many good merchants were included in this round-up, and those of Florence suffered great losses.
Line 111, p. 177

He, so robust of limb. Peter III, King of Aragon, who died in 1285, leaving four sons, Alonzo, James, Frederick, and Peter. The two former succeeded him in the kingdom of Aragon, and Frederick in that of Sicily.
Line 113, p. 177

Him of feature prominent. Charles I, King of Naples, Count of Anjou, and brother of St. Louis. He died in 1284.
Line 114, p. 177

That stripling. Either Alonzo III, King of Aragon, the eldest son of Peter III, who died in 1291 at the age of twenty-seven, or Alonzo's youngest son, Peter.
Line 116, p. 177

PURGATORY

To Charles. Charles II, King of Naples, is no less inferior to his father Charles I than James and Frederick to theirs, Peter III. See Canto xx, 78, and *Paradise*, xix, 125.
Line 125, p. 177

Beatrix and Margaret. The two wives of Charles I of Naples.
Line 129, p. 177

Costanza. Widow of Peter III.
Line 130, p. 177

Better issue. Edward I of whose glory Dante was perhaps a witness on his visit to England.
Line 133, p. 178

William, that brave Marquis. William, Marquis of Montferrat, was treacherously seized by his own subjects at Alessandria in Lombardy, A.D. 1290, and ended his life in prison.
Line 136, p. 178

CANTO VIII

Te Lucis Ante. First verse of the hymn sung by the church at the last service of the day.
Line 13, p. 178

Here, reader. Dante points out the allegory intended in the previous passage to the effect that the soul is still exposed to sin while striving to cleanse itself and that God will send help if prayers ask it.
Line 19, p. 179

Nino, thou courteous judge. Nino di Gallura de' Visconti, judge at Sardinia and later, Pisa, where his uncle, Count Ugolino de' Gherardeschi, betrayed him in the strife between the Guelphs and Ghibellines in 1288. See *Hell*, xxxiii, 14.
Line 53, p. 179

Conrad. Currado, father to Marcello Malaspina.
Line 65, p. 180

My Giovanna. Only daughter of Nino.
Line 71, p. 180

Her mother. Beatrice, Marchioness of Este, wife of Nino, and after his death married to Galeazzo de' Visconti of Milan.
Line 73, p. 180

The white and wimpled folds. Weeds of widowhood.
Line 74, p. 180

The viper. Arms of Galeazzo and the ensign of the Milanese.
Line 80, p. 180

Shrill Gallura's bird. The cock was the ensign of Gallura, Nino's province in Sardinia.
Line 81, p. 180

The three torches. The three evangelical virtues, Faith, Hope and Charity.
Line 89, p. 180

Conrad Malaspina. Son of Frederick I, Marquis of Villafranca; died about 1294.
Line 117, p. 181

That old one. Grandfather of the speaker.
Line 118, p. 181

Seven times the tired sun. Dante was hospitably received by the family of Malaspina during his banishment in 1307.
Line 133, p. 182

CANTO IX

Now the fair consort. An obscure passage; some scholars think Dante means the time was morning, some, evening.
Line 1, p. 182

All five. Virgil, Dante, Sordello, Nino and Currado Malaspina.
Line 11, p. 182

Remembering haply ancient grief. Progne was changed into a swallow after she and her sister had served her son, Itys, to her husband to eat.
Line 13, p. 182

Young Ganymede. Ganymede was snatched by the eagle at Mount Ida, and carried to Zeus to become his cup-bearer.
Line 21, p. 183

To the fire. Sphere of fire between the atmosphere and heaven of the moon.
Line 28, p. 183

There. Thetis, Achilles' mother, carried him from Thessaly to Scyros where Ulysses persuaded him to accompany the Greek army to Troy.
Line 36, p. 183

Lucia. Who symbolizes the Enlightening Grace of Heaven.
Line 51, p. 183

And one. The angel who guards the entrance to Purgatory and holds the sword of justice.
Line 71, p. 184

The lowest stair. The white step represents the distinctness with which the conscience of the penitent reflects his offences; the burnt and cracked one, his contrition on their account; the one of porphyry, the fervor with which he resolves on the future pursuit of piety and virtue.
Line 86, p. 184

Seven times. Seven P's, to denote the seven sins, *Peccata*, of which Dante is to to be cleansed in his passage through Purgatory.
Line 101, p. 186

One is more precious. The golden key denotes divine authority by which the priest absolves the sinner, and is the more precious because it was bought by the death of Christ; the silver key expresses the learning and judgment requisite in discharging this office.
Line 116, p. 186

Metellus. The guardian of the public treasure kept in Saturn's temple on the Tarpeian rock which Julius Cæsar seized to pay his soldiers.
Line 130, p. 186

[447]

NOTES

CANTO X

"Hail!" The Virgin Mary.
Line 37, p. 188

That from unbidden office awes mankind. Uzzah was smitten down by the Lord for touching the ark. 2 *Sam.* vi, 7.
Line 52, p. 188

Preceding. "And David danced before the Lord with all his might, and David was girded with a linen ephod." 2 *Sam.* vi, 14.
Line 58, p. 188

Michol. Daughter of Saul, wife of David, cursed with sterility as a punishment of her pride.
Line 63, p. 189

Gregory. St. Gregory's prayers were supposed to have delivered Trajan from hell. See *Paradise,* xx, 40.
Line 68, p. 189

The winged insect. The butterfly was an ancient and well-known symbol of the human soul.
Line 114, p. 190

Abortive. Man's development is arrested by sin.
Line 117, p. 190

CANTO XI

I was of Latium. Omberto, the son of Guglielmo Aldobrandesco, Count of Santafiore, of Sienna. His arrogance so provoked his countrymen that they murdered him.
Line 58, p. 192

The common mother. The earth.
Line 63, p. 192

Oderigi. The illuminator or miniature painter, a friend of Giotto and Dante.
Line 79, p. 193

Bolognian Franco. Said to have been a pupil of Oderigi.
Line 83, p. 193

The cry is Giotto's. Discovered by Cimabue, Giotto was afterwards patronized by Pope Benedict XI and Robert King of Naples; he was a friend of Dante and did a portrait of him still extant. He died in 1337.
Line 95, p. 193

One Guido from the other. Guido Cavalcanti, the friend of Dante (see *Hell,* Canto x, 59), had eclipsed the literary fame of Guido Guinicelli of a noble family in Bologna (Canto xxvi). Guinicelli died in 1276, and Cavalcanti, in 1301.
Line 96, p. 193

Heaven's slowest orb. That of the fixed stars which was supposed to move one degree in 100 years.
Line 108, p. 193

He, there. Provenzano Salvani, the head of the Siennese municipal government at the time of the defeat of the Florentine Guelphs at Montaperti, 1260.
Line 108, p. 193

A suitor. Provenzano personally begged the people to contribute the sum demanded by Charles I of Sicily for the ransom of one of his friends.
Line 136, p. 194

Thy neighbors soon. Dante was soon to be banished from Florence and would learn the difficulty of asking charity.
Line 140, p. 194

CANTO XII

Briareus. A hundred-headed monster who was knocked down by a thunderbolt in the war of the Titans against the gods; he was buried at Mt. Aetna.
Line 25, p. 195

The Thymbræan god. Apollo.
Line 26, p. 195

Stupendous work. The tower of Babel.
Line 30, p. 195

O Rehoboam. I *Kings* xii, 18.
Line 42, p. 196

Alcmæon. Killed his mother, Eriphyle, for betraying the hiding place of Amphiaraus who was forced to go to the Theban wars and was slain.
Line 46, p. 196

Sennacherib. II *Kings* xix, 37.
Line 48, p. 196

Tomyris. Queen of Scythians who had the head of Cyrus cut off after his defeat and death and plunged into blood.
Line 51, p. 196

The sixth handmaid. Noon.
Line 74, p. 198

Against my front. One of the P's, the sin of pride, was erased from Dante's forehead.
Line 91, p. 198

The chapel stands. The church of San Miniato in Florence, situated on a height that overlooks the Arno, where it is crossed by the bridge Rubaconte.
Line 94, p. 198

The registry. Reference to certain instances of fraud in the public accounts and measures.
Line 99, p. 198

Sin's broad characters. The six P's still left on Dante's forehead.
Line 113, p. 199

CANTO XIII

Spirits invisible. Who tell of charity, the opposite of envy.
Line 23, p. 200

PURGATORY

"They have no wine." John ii, 3, the words of the Virgin are referred to as an instance of charity. *Line 26, p. 200*

Orestes. Pylades said this to save Orestes from death. *Line 29, p. 201*

"Love ye those have wronged you." Matt. v. 44. *Line 32, p. 201*

"Blessed Mary!" The litany of the saints. *Line 45, p. 201*

Haggard hawk. A wild hawk was tamed by temporarily blinding him with wires fastening his eyelids together. *Line 65, p. 201*

Citizens of one true city. "For here have we no continuing city, but we seek one to come." Heb. xiii, 14. *Line 87, p. 202*

Sapia. A lady of Sienna in exile at Colle who was so overjoyed at a defeat of her countrymen near there that she declared nothing more was wanting to make her die contented. *Line 101, p. 203*

The merlin. Induced by a gleam of fine weather in the winter to escape from his master, he soon discovered the cold weather was not over. *Line 114, p. 203*

The hermit Piero. Piero Pettinagno, a holy hermit of Florence who died in 1289. *Line 119, p. 203*

That vain multitude. The Siennese whose acquisition of Telamone, a seaport on the confines of the Maremma, led them into hopes of rivalling Pisa and Genoa as a naval power. *Line 141, p. 204*

They, who lead. Those who were to command the fleets of the Siennese. *Line 144, p. 204*

CANTO XIV

Say. The two spirits who speak to each other are Guido del Duca of Brettinoro and Rinieri da Calboli of Romagna. *Line 1, p. 204*

The one. Guido del Duca. *Line 11, p. 204*

A brooklet. The Arno rises in Falterona, a mountain in the Apennines, and runs a course of 120 miles. *Line 18, p. 204*

The other. Rinieri. *Line 27, p. 205*

From the source. From the rise of the Arno in the Apennines, from which Pelorus in Sicily was torn by a convulsion of the earth, to the point where the same river unites its waters to the ocean, Virtue is persecuted by all. *Line 32, p. 205*

'Midst brute swine. The people of Casentino. *Line 45, p. 205*

Curs. The people of Arezzo. *Line 49, p. 205*

Wolves. The Florentines. *Line 53, p. 205*

Foxes. The Pisans. *Line 55, p. 205*

My words are heard. Guido is still addressing Rinieri. *Line 57, p. 205*

Thy grandson. Fulcieri da Calboli, grandson of Rinieri, who was twice podestà of Florence and persecuted the Bianchi in 1302. *Line 61, p. 206*

'Twixt Po, the mount, the Reno, and the shore. The boundaries of Romagna. *Line 95, p. 206*

Lizio. Lizio da Valbona, lord of Ravenna, famous for his generosity and courtesy. *Line 99, p. 207*

Manardi, Traversaro, and Carpigna. From Brettinoro, Ravenna and Montefeltro, respectively, and all praised for liberality. *Line 100, p. 207*

In Bologna the low artisan. One named Lambertaccia who had been a mechanic and arrived at almost supreme power at Bologna. *Line 102, p. 207*

Yon Bernardin. Bernardin di Fosco, a man of low origin but great talents, who governed Pisa in 1249. *Line 103, p. 207*

Prata. A place between Faenza and Ravenna. *Line 107, p. 207*

Of Azzo him. Ugolino of the Ubaldini family in Tuscany. *Line 107, p. 207*

Tignoso. Federigo Tignoso of Rimini. *Line 108, p. 207*

Traversaro's house and Anastagio's. Two noble families of Ravenna. *Line 109, p. 207*

O Brettinoro. A beautifully situated castle in Romagna, the hospitable residence of Guido del Duca, who is here speaking. *Line 114, p. 207*

Bagnacavallo. Castle between Imola and Ravenna. *Line 118, p. 207*

Castracaro ... Conio. Both of Romagna. *Line 118, p. 207*

NOTES

Pagani. The Pagani were lords of Faenza and Imola. One of them, Machinardo, was named *the Demon*, from his treachery.
Line 121, p. 207

Hugolin. Ugolino Ubaldini, a noble and virtuous person in Faenza, who, on account of his age probably, was not likely to leave any offspring behind him.
Line 124, p. 207

"... *whosoever finds*
Will slay me." The words of Cain, *Gen.* iv., 14.
Line 136, p. 208

Aglauros. Ovid, *Met.* ii, fab. 12.
Line 142, p. 208

CANTO XV

As much. It wanted three hours of sunset.
Line 1, p. 208

"*Blessed the merciful.*" Matt. v. 7.
Line 38, p. 209

Romagna's spirit. Guido del Duca of Brettinoro, mentioned in the last canto.
Line 43, p. 209

A dame. Luke ii, 48.
Line 87, p. 210

Over this city. Athens, named after Minerva because she had produced a more valuable gift for it in the olive than Neptune had in the horse.
Line 96, p. 211

How shall we those requite. The answer of Pisistratus the tyrant to his wife when she urged him to punish by death a young man who had snatched a kiss from his daughter in public.
Line 101, p. 211

A stripling youth. The protomartyr Stephen.
Line 105, p. 211

CANTO XVI

As thou. As if thou wert still living.
Line 24, p. 213

I was of Lombardy, and Marco call'd. A Venetian gentleman whose surname was Lombardo to denote the country from which he had come. There are many stories about him.
Line 46, p. 214

Elsewhere. What Guido del Duca had said in the fourteenth canto concerning the degeneracy of his countrymen.
Line 58, p. 214

The fortress. Justice, the most necessary virtue in the chief magistrate.
Line 99, p. 215

Who. He compares the Pope, on account of the union of the temporal with the spiritual power in his person, to an unclean beast in the Levitical law.
Line 103, p. 216

Two suns. The spiritual and temporal power represented by the Pope and Emperor.
Line 110, p. 216

That land. Lombardy.
Line 117, p. 216

Ere the day. Before the Emperor Frederick II was defeated at Parma in 1248.
Line 119, p. 216

The good Gherardo. Gherardo di Camino of Trevigi died in 1306.
Line 126, p. 216

Conrad. Currado da Palazzo, a gentleman of Brescia.
Line 127, p. 216

Guido of Castello. Of Reggio. All Italians were called Lombards by the French.
Line 127, p. 216

His daughter Gaïa. A lady admired for her modesty, beauty and talents; the first Italian lady to cultivate vernacular poetry.
Line 144, p. 217

CANTO XVII

On an Alpine height. All high mountains are termed Alps in Tuscan phraseology.
Line 2, p. 217

... the bird, that most
Delights itself in song. Probably an allusion to the story of Philomela, who by mistake slew her own son, Itylus, and for her punishment was transformed by Jupiter into a nightingale.
Line 21, p. 218

One crucified. Haman. See *Esther* vii.
Line 26, p. 218

A damsel. Lavinia, mourning for her mother Amata, who, filled with grief and indignation for the supposed death of Turnus, destroyed herself. *Aeneid,* lib. xii, 595.
Line 34, p. 218

That fann'd my face. The third P, for anger, is erased from Dante's brow.
Line 67, p. 219

The peace-makers. Matt. v. 9.
Line 68, p. 219

The primal blessings. Spiritual good.
Line 94, p. 220

The inferior. Temporal good.
Line 95, p. 220

There is. The proud.
Line 111, p. 220

There is. The envious.
Line 114, p. 220

There is he. The resentful; the four remaining sins are punished on the terraces to come.
Line 117, p. 220

PURGATORY

CANTO XVIII

Your apprehension. It is literally: "your apprehensive faculty derives intension from a thing really existing, and displays that intension within you, so that it makes the soul turn to it." *Line 23, p. 221*

Perhaps. Dante uses the language of the Peripatetics, which denominates the *kind* of things, as determinable by many differences, *matter*. Love, then, in kind, perhaps, appears good; and it is said *perhaps*, because, strictly speaking, *in kind* there is neither good nor bad, neither praiseworthy nor blameable. *Line 35, p. 222*

Spirit. The human soul though united with the body has a separate existence of its own. *Line 47, p. 222*

Up the vault. With a motion opposite that of the heavens when the sun is in Scorpion, it appears to set between the isles of Corsica and Sardinia to those in Rome. *Line 78, p. 223*

Andes. Now Pietola, the birthplace of Virgil. *Line 84, p. 223*

Mary. "And Mary arose in those days, and went into the hill-country with haste, into a city of Juda; and entered into the house of Zacharias, and saluted Elisabeth." Luke i, 39, 40. *Line 98, p. 223*

Cæsar. Cæsar left Brutus to complete the siege of Marseilles, and hastened on to the attack of Afranius and Petreius, the generals of Pompey, at Ilerda (Lerida) in Spain. *Line 99, p. 223*

Abbot. Alberto, abbot of San Zeno in Verona when Emperor Frederick I reduced Milan to ashes in 1162. *Line 118, p. 224*

There is he. Alberto della Scala, Lord of Verona, the natural father of the above-mentioned Albert, whom he made abbot. *Line 121, p. 224*

CANTO XIX

The hour. Near the dawn. *Line 1, p. 225*

The geomancer. Who drew a figure consisting of 16 marks named from stars and called one of them the greater fortune. *Line 4, p. 225*

A woman's shape. Symbol of avarice, gluttony and licentiousness. *Line 7, p. 225*

Ulysses. It is not easy to determine why Ulysses, contrary to the authority of Homer, is said to have been drawn aside from his course by the song of the Syren. *Line 21, p. 225*

A dame. Philosophy or perhaps Truth. *Line 26, p. 225*

Who mourn. Matt. v, 4. *Line 49, p. 226*

Lure. A decoy used by falconers to recall their hawks. *Line 62, p. 226*

My soul. Psalms cxix, 25. *Line 72, p. 227*

The successor of Peter. Ottobuono, of the family of Fieschi, Counts of Lavagno, died thirty-nine days after he became Pope, with the title of Adrian V, in 1276. *Line 97, p. 227*

That stream. The river Lavagno in the Genoese territory; to the east are situated Siestri and Chiaveri. *Line 98, p. 227*

Err not. Rev. xix, 10. *Line 132, p 229*

"Nor shall be given in marriage." Matt. xxii, 30. *Line 135, p. 229*

A kinswoman. Alagia, the wife of the Marchese Marcello Malaspina, one of the poet's protectors during his exile. See Canto viii, 133. *Line 140, p. 230*

CANTO XX

I drew the sponge. I did not persevere in my inquiries from the spirit though anxious to learn more. *Line 3, p. 230*

Wolf. Avarice. *Line 11, p. 230*

Of his appearing. Can Grande della Scala. See *Hell*, i, 98. *Line 16, p. 230*

Fabricius. Caius Fabricius, a Roman general and consul who refused bribes from Pyrrhus, king of Epirus. *Line 25, p. 231*

Nicholas. Bishop of Mira, said to have lived in the fourth century; he is supposed to have saved three maidens from shame by throwing three bags of gold for their dowry into the window of their house. *Line 30, p. 231*

Root. Hugh Capet, ancestor of Philip IV. *Line 42, p. 231*

Had Ghent and Douay, Lille and Bruges power. These cities had lately been seized by Philip IV; the spirit intimates the approaching defeat of the French army by the Flemings at the battle of Courtrai, 1302. *Line 46, p. 231*

[451]

NOTES

The slaughterer's trade. This reflection on the birth of his ancestor led Francis I to forbid the reading of Dante in his dominions.
Line 51, p. 231

All save one. The posterity of Charlemagne with the exception possibly of Charles of Lorraine who is said to have always clothed himself in black on account of his melancholy disposition.
Line 52, p. 231

My son. Hugh Capet had his son, Robert, crowned at Orleans in 988.
Line 57, p. 231

The great dower of Provence. Louis IX and his brother, Charles of Anjou, married two of the four daughters of Raymond Berenger, Count of Provence. Hugh's descendants had little power until that time.
Line 59, p. 231

Young Conradine. Charles of Anjou put Conradino, last of the House of Suabia, to death in 1268 and made himself King of Naples.
Line 66, p. 231

The angelic teacher. Thomas Aquinas, reported to have been poisoned by a physician who wished to ingratiate himself with Charles of Anjou.
Line 67, p. 232

Another Charles. Charles of Valois, brother of Philip IV, was sent by Pope Boniface VIII to settle the disturbed state of Florence. He drove Dante and the Bianchi from the city.
Line 69, p. 232

The other. Charles, King of Naples, the eldest son of Charles of Anjou. In a naval battle with Ruggier de Lauria, the admiral of Peter of Aragon, he was made prisoner and was carried into Sicily in 1284. For a large sum of money, he married his daughter to Azzo VIII, Marquis of Ferrara.
Line 78, p. 232

The flower-de-luce. The arms of France; Boniface VIII was seized at Alagna in Campagna by the order of Philip IV in 1303 and soon afterward died of grief.
Line 85, p. 232

Into the temple. Reference to the destruction of the order of the Templars in 1312 by Philip IV.
Line 94, p. 232

Pygmalion. Brother of Dido who killed Sichaeus for his money.
Line 103, p. 233

Achan. Joshua vii.
Line 107, p. 233

Heliodorus. "For there appeared unto them an horse, with a terrible rider upon him, and adorned with a very fair covering, and he ran fiercely and smote at Heliodorus with his fore feet." 2 *Maccabees* iii, 25.
Line 111, p. 233

Thracia's king. Polymnestor, the murderer of Polydorus, who had been entrusted to him by his father, Priam of Troy.
Line 112, p. 233

Crassus. Marcus Crassus, famous for his riches, who fell miserably in the Parthian war; his head was carried to the Parthian king who had molten gold poured into his mouth.
Line 114, p. 233

Delos. A floating island which became stationary after the birth of Apollo and Diana.
Line 126, p. 233

CANTO XXI

The well. "The woman saith unto him, Sir, give me this water, that I thirst not." *John* iv, 15.
Line 1, p. 234

Luke. Chapter xxiv, 13.
Line 6, p. 234

The tokens. The three P's remaining on Dante's forehead.
Line 22, p. 234

She. Lachesis, one of the three fates.
Line 25, p. 234

Thaumantian. Iris, daughter of Thaumus, was the personification of the rainbow.
Line 49, p. 235

Highest of the trinal stairs. The gate of Purgatory.
Line 52, p. 235

Through wind. The ancients believed subterranean winds caused earthquakes.
Line 55, p. 235

Five hundred years. Statius died in 96 A.D. He had spent five hundred years on the fifth terrace, and been in Purgatory for nearly twelve hundred years.
Line 69, p. 236

When the good Titus. Titus by the destruction of Jerusalem in 70 A.D. avenged the death of Christ on the Jews.
Line 83, p. 236

The name. Of poet.
Line 85, p. 236

From Tolosa. Dante confuses Statius the poet, who was a Neapolitan, with the rhetorician of the same name, who was from Toulouse.
Line 89, p. 236

Fell. Statius lived to write only a small part of the *Achilleid*.
Line 94, p. 236

CANTO XXII

Blessed. "Blessed are they which do hunger and thirst after righteousness, for they shall be filled." *Matt.* v, 6.
Line 5, p. 238

PURGATORY

Aquinum's bard. Juvenal had celebrated his contemporary, Statius, though some critics imagine that there is a secret derision couched under his praise. *Line 14, p. 238*

The fierce encounter. The punishment of the Prodigal Son; see *Hell,* vii, 26. *Line 41, p. 239*

With shorn locks. See *Hell,* vii, where the prodigals are so symbolized. *Line 46, p. 239*

Sov'reign of the pastoral song. Virgil. *Line 55, p. 239*

The twin sorrow of Jocasta's womb. Eteocles and Polynices. *Line 57, p. 239*

And follow. St. Peter. *Line 63, p. 239*

Before. I had composed the *Thebaid.* *Line 87, p. 240*

Our old Terence. Roman comic poet, born at Carthage 185 B.C. *Line 96, p. 240*

Cæcilius. Cæcilius Statius, a Latin comic poet, of whose works some fragments only remain. *Line 97, p. 240*

Plautus. Another comic poet, died in 184 B.C. *Line 97, p. 240*

Varro. Probably P. Terentius Varro, author of two epic poems. *Line 97, p. 240*

Persius. Satiric poet, born in 34 B.C. *Line 99, p. 240*

That Greek. Homer. *Line 100, p. 240*

In the first ward. Limbo. *Line 102, p. 240*

Of Pella. Euripides. *Line 105, p. 240*

The Teian. Anacreon or possibly Antiphon. *Line 105, p. 240*

Agatho. Tragic poet, contemporary of Euripides. *Line 105, p. 240*

Simonides. Greek lyric poet, born 559 B.C. *Line 106, p. 240*

Of thy train. Of those celebrated in thy poem. *Line 107, p. 240*

Who show'd Langia's wave. Hypsipile showed the spring Langia to Adrastus' soldiers. *Line 110, p. 241*

Tiresias' daughter. Manto; see *Hell,* xx. *Line 112, p. 241*

. . . the bride
Sea-born of Peleus. Thetis. *Line 112, p. 241*

Four handmaids. Four hours; it was now after 10 A.M. *Line 116, p. 241*

Mary took more thought. The blessed virgin, who answers for you now in heaven, when she said to Jesus, at the marriage in Cana of Galilee, "they have no wine," regarded not the gratification of her own taste, but the honor of the nuptial banquet. *Line 139, p. 241*

Daniel. See *Dan.* i, 11-12, 16-17. *Line 143, p. 241*

CANTO XXIII

My lips. "O Lord, open thou my lips; and my mouth shall show forth thy praise." *Psalms* li, 15.
Line 9, p. 242

Erisichthon. As punishment for coveting the grove of Ceres, he was inflicted with such an insatiable hunger that he bit his own limbs. *Line 23, p. 242*

When Mary. During the Roman siege of Jerusalem, Mary ate half of her child and offered the other half to soldiers demanding food. *Line 26, p. 242*

Who reads the name. In the Middle Ages, it was a popular belief that the word OMO had been written on man's face by God, the O's being formed by the eyes, and the M by the nose and eye-sockets. *Line 28, p. 243*

Forese. Brother of Corso Donati and of Piccarda; see next canto and *Paradise,* iii. *Line 44, p. 243*

To call on Eli. Matt. xxvii, 46. *Line 68, p. 244*

Lower. In the Ante-Purgatory. See Canto ii. *Line 76, p. 244*

My Nella. The wife of Forese. *Line 80, p. 244*

The tract, most barbarous. The *Barbagia* is part of Sardinia, so named because of the uncivilized state of its inhabitants. *Line 87, p. 244*

Saracens. This word during the Middle Ages was indiscriminately applied to Pagans, Mahometans, and all but Christians and Jews. *Line 97, p. 244*

That shade. Statius. *Line 127, p. 245*

[453]

NOTES

CANTO XXIV

He journeys. The soul of Statius perhaps proceeds more slowly so that he may enjoy the company of Virgil.
Line 8, p. 246

Piccarda. See *Paradise*, iii.
Line 11, p. 246

Buonaggiunta. Buonaggiunta Urbiciani of Lucca who lived toward the end of the thirteenth century; he was a poet who imitated the Troubadours.
Line 20, p. 246

He was of Tours. Simon of Tours became Pope with the title of Martin IV in 1281.
Line 23, p. 246

Ubaldino. Ubaldino degli Ubaldini of Pila, brother of Cardinal Ottaviano (*Hell*, x) and of Ugolino d'Azzo (*Purg.*, xiv) and father of Archbishop Ruggieri (*Hell*, xxxiii).
Line 29, p. 246

Boniface. Archbishop of Ravenna; died in 1295.
Line 30, p. 246

The Marquis. The Marchese de' Rigogliosi, of Forli. When his butler told him it was commonly reported in the city that he did nothing but drink, he is said to have answered: "And do you tell them that I am always thirsty."
Line 32, p. 246

Him of Lucca. Buonaggiunta.
Line 36, p. 246

Gentucca. It is thought Dante became enamored of this lady during his exile.
Line 38, p. 246

There. In the throat, where the torment inflicted by divine justice was felt.
Line 39, p. 246

Whose brow no wimple shades yet. Who has not yet assumed the dress of a married woman.
Line 45, p. 247

"Ladies, ye that con the lore of love." The first verse of a canzone in Dante's *Vita Nuova*.
Line 51, p. 247

The notary. Jacopo da Lentino, called the Notary, a poet of these times.
Line 56, p. 247

Guittone. Fra Guittone of Arezzo holds a distinguished place in Italian literature; died in 1294.
Line 56, p. 247

That new and sweeter style. The style introduced in our poet's time.
Line 57, p. 247

The place. Florence.
Line 78, p. 248

He. Corso Donati, the brother of Forese and chief of the Neri. He was suspected of trying to aim at the sovereignty of Florence, and to escape the fury of his fellow-citizens he fled on horseback, but was overtaken and slain in 1308.
Line 81, p. 248

Creatures of the clouds. The Centaurs.
Line 120, p. 249

The Hebrews. Judges vii; the story of Gideon.
Line 123, p. 249

CANTO XXV

The sun. The sun was two hours past the meridian now occupied by Taurus and its opposite, Scorpion, was consequently at the meridian of night.
Line 2, p. 250

How there can leanness come. How can spirits not subject to corporeal nourishment be subject to leanness?
Line 19, p. 250

Meleager. As Meleager was wasted away by the decree of the Fates, so by the divine appointment there may be leanness where there is no need of nourishment.
Line 22, p. 250

From whence it came. From the heart.
Line 50, p. 251

As sea-sponge. The foetus is in this stage a zoophyte.
Line 58, p. 251

. . . more wise,
Than thou, has erred. Averroes is here meant.
Line 65, p. 252

Mark the sun's heat. From Cicero's *De Senectute*.
Line 79, p. 252

When Lachesis hath spun the thread. When a man's life on earth is ended.
Line 81, p. 252

To one strand. The damned go to the river Acheron, the saved to the mouth of the Tiber.
Line 86, p. 252

"O God of mercy." The beginning of the hymn sung on the Sabbath at matins as it stands in the ancient breviaries.
Line 118, p. 254

Callisto. Driven from Diana's band and changed to a bear by Juno after she had been seduced by Jupiter, she was transferred to the sky to become the constellation, Ursa Major.
Line 126, p. 254

CANTO XXVI

Thus spake one. Guido Guinicelli.
Line 22, p. 255

Emmets. Ants.
Line 29, p. 255

PURGATORY

Pasiphaë. Wife of Minos and mother of the Minotaur.   *Line 36, p. 256*

Their first song. "O God of Mercy"; see last canto, 118 and 123.   *Line 42, p. 256*

A dame on high. The Virgin Mary.   *Line 52, p. 256*

Orb of heaven. The Empyrean.   *Line 55, p. 256*

Cæsar. For the opprobrium cast on Cæsar's effeminacy, see Suetonius, *Julius Cæsar*, chapter 49.   *Line 70, p. 257*

Guinicelli. A celebrated poet of Bologna who died in exile in 1276. See Canto xi, 96.   *Line 83, p. 257*

Lycurgus. When she went to show the Greek the river of Langia, Hypsipile had left her infant charge, the son of Lycurgus, on a bank where it was destroyed by a serpent; when she escaped the effects of Lycurgus' resentment, the joy her own children felt on seeing her matched Dante's on beholding Guinicelli.   *Line 87, p. 257*

He. Dante and Petrarch place Arnault Daniel at the head of the Provençal poets; Arnault lived in the twelfth century.   *Line 111, p. 258*

The songster of Limoges. Giraud de Borneil, of Sideuil, a castle in Limoges. He was a Troubadour of the twelfth and thirteenth centuries much admired and caressed in his day, in favor with the monarchs of Castile, Leon Navarre, and Aragon.   *Line 113, p. 258*

Guittone. From Arezzo, see Canto xxiv, 56.   *Line 118, p. 258*

Thy courtesy. Arnault here speaks in Provençal, his own tongue.   *Line 132, p. 258*

CANTO XXVII
Libra. The opposite sign of Aries in which sign the sun is.   *Line 3, p. 259*

Ebro. Spanish river.   *Line 4, p. 259*

Blessed. Matt. v, 8.   *Line 10, p. 259*

While vermeil dyed the mulberry. Ovid, *Metam.*, iv, 55: the story of Thisbe and Pyramus.   *Line 40, p. 260*

The name. Beatrice.   *Line 42, p. 260*

Come. Matt. xxv, 34.   *Line 58, p. 260*

I am Leah. The active life as Rachel personifies the contemplative.   *Line 102, p. 261*

She. Her delight is in admiring in her mirror, that is, in the Supreme Being, the light, or knowledge, that He vouchsafes her.   *Line 105, p. 261*

CANTO XXVIII
To that part. The west.   *Line 11, p. 263*

Chiassi. A large pine forest on the Adriatic near Ravenna.   *Line 20, p. 263*

A lady. According to some, the Countess Matilda who endowed the Holy See with estates called the Patrimony of St. Peter; she died in 1115. Believed to represent either love for the church or the active life.   *Line 41, p. 264*

Cytherea. Venus was accidentally wounded by Cupid and fell passionately in love with Adonis.   *Line 63, p. 264*

A curb for ever to the pride of man. Because Xerxes had been so humbled, when he was compelled to repass the Hellespont in one small bark, after having a little before crossed with a prodigious army, in the hopes of subduing Greece.   *Line 71, p. 265*

The circumambient air. An explanation of the origin of the breeze: the earth is fixed, the heavens revolve with the Primum Mobile and the *aer viva* from east to west; the revolution causes the breeze which bends the trees of the Earthly Paradise westward.   *Line 106, p. 265*

The other land. The continent inhabited by the living and separated from Purgatory by the ocean.   *Line 116, p. 266*

Eunoë. Lethe brings forgetfulness of sin; Eunoë, joyful consciousness of God's forgiveness.   *Line 138, p. 266*

CANTO XXIX
Blessed they. Psalms xxxii, 1.   *Line 2, p. 267*

Helicon. Boeotian mountain range, abode of the muses, containing the fountains of Aganippe and Hippocrene.   *Line 38, p. 268*

Urania. Muse of Astronomy.   *Line 39, p. 268*

[455]

NOTES

Tapers of gold. See *Rev.* i, 12. In his *Convito*, our author says: "Because these gifts proceed from ineffable charity, and divine charity is appropriated to the Holy Spirit, hence, also, it is that they are called gifts of the Holy Spirit, the which, as Isaiah distinguishes them, are seven."
Line 49, p. 268

Listed colors. Colors of the rainbow.
Line 76, p. 269

Four and twenty elders. Rev. iv, 4.
Line 81, p. 269

Blessed be thou. "Blessed art thou among women, and blessed is the fruit of thy womb." *Luke* i, 42.
Line 83, p. 269

Four. The four evangelists.
Line 89, p. 269

Ezekiel. Ezekiel i, 4–6.
Line 96, p. 269

John. St. John gives the four beasts six wings apiece (*Rev.* iv, 8) but Ezekiel gave them only four wings; Dante perhaps agrees with St. John because he lived in the sixth age of man along with St. John while Ezekiel lived in the fourth.
Line 101, p. 270

A car triumphal. The Christian church; the two wheels symbolize the Old and New Testaments and the Griffon, the double nature of Christ who is both human and divine.
Line 103, p. 270

Tellus' prayer. Jupiter answered his prayer by hurling thunderbolts at Phaëton when the latter drove the sun's chariot out of its course.
Line 115, p. 270

Three nymphs. The three evangelical virtues: the first Charity, the next Hope, and the third Faith.
Line 116, p. 271

A band quaternion. The four moral or cardinal virtues in which Prudence is the director.
Line 125, p. 271

The rest conducted. Prudence, described with three eyes, regards past, present and future.
Line 127, p. 271

Two old men. Saint Luke, the physician, characterized as the writer of the Acts of the Apostles, and Saint Paul, represented with the sword, on account, as it should seem, of the power of his style.
Line 129, p. 271

Of the great Coan. Hippocrates, born in Cos about 460 B.C. "whom nature made for the benefit of her favorite creature, man."
Line 133, p. 271

Four others. Authorities differ as to whether these are the four evangelists, the four principal doctors of the church, or a personification of the Minor Epistles.
Line 138, p. 271

One single old man. Some say St. John in his character as author of the Apocalypse, some say Moses.
Line 140, p. 271

Roses. Symbolic of love.
Line 144, p. 271

CANTO XXX

That polar light. The seven candlesticks of gold, which he calls the polar light of heaven itself, because they perform the same office for Christians that the polar star does for mariners, in guiding them to their port.
Line 1, p. 272

Come. "Come with me from Lebanon, my spouse, with me, from Lebanon." Song of Solomon iv, 8.
Line 12, p. 272

Blessed. Matt. xxi, 9.
Line 19, p. 272

A virgin. Beatrice; the olive symbolizes peace and wisdom and the color she wears Faith, Hope and Charity.
Line 32, p. 272

But. They sang the thirty-first Psalm, to the end of the eighth verse. What follows in that Psalm would not have suited the place or the occasion.
Line 84, p. 274

The land whereon no shadow falls. When the wind is south.
Line 89, p. 274

Those bright semblances. The angels.
Line 103, p. 274

The threshold of my second age. As she neared twenty-five; according to Dante's divisions of the human life into four ages.
Line 126, p. 275

CANTO XXXI

Counter to the edge. The weapons of divine justice are blunted by the confession and sorrow of the offender.
Line 39, p. 277

For a slight girl. Commentators differ on the identity; suggestions include Gentucca of Lucca (Canto xiv) or a woman named "Pargoletta," or possibly Gemma de' Donati whom Dante married.
Line 56, p. 277

From Iarbas' land. The south.
Line 69, p. 278

PURGATORY

The beard. A severe reflection was implied on Dante's want of the wisdom which should accompany the age of manhood. *Line 71, p. 278*

The stream. Lethe. *Line 94, p. 278*

"Tu asperges me." "Purge me with hyssop, and I shall be clean; wash me, and I shall be whiter than snow." *Ps.* li, 7. Sung by the choir, while the priest is sprinkling the people with holy water. *Line 98, p. 278*

Should drench me. The immersion meant God's forgiveness of Dante's sins and the swallowing of the water, Dante's oblivion of his sins. *Line 102, p. 278*

Those yonder three. Faith, Hope and Charity. *Line 111, p. 279*

The emeralds. The eyes of Beatrice. *Line 116, p. 279*

Twofold being. The divine and human nature of Christ symbolized by the Griffon. *Line 122, p. 279*

CANTO XXXII

Their ten years' thirst. Beatrice had been dead ten years. *Line 2, p. 280*

But soon. As soon as his sight was recovered, so as to bear the view of that glorious procession, which, splendid as it was, was yet less so than Beatrice, by whom his vision had been overpowered, &c. *Line 12, p. 280*

A plant. The tree of knowledge of good and evil, also symbolizing the Empire the way the chariot symbolizes the Church; the leafless state of the tree represents the depravity of Rome before Christ. *Line 37, p. 281*

Gryphon. Our Saviour's submission to the Roman empire appears to be intended, and particularly his injunction, "to render unto Cæsar the things that are Cæsar's." *Line 42, p. 281*

There, left unto the stock. By his suffering under the sentence of Pilate, the delegate of the Roman emperor, Christ acknowledged and confirmed the supremacy of that emperor over the whole world; he thereby joined the Church to the Empire. *Line 50, p. 281*

When large floods of radiance. When the sun enters into Aries, the next constellation to Pisces. *Line 51, p. 281*

The unpitying eyes. Argus, guardian of Io; Mercury killed him after he had put Argus to sleep with the story of Syrinx and Pan. *Line 63, p. 281*

Chosen three. Peter, James and John. *Line 72, p. 282*

Deeper sleeps. The sleep of death, in the instance of the ruler of the Synagogue's daughter and of Lazarus. *Line 77, p. 282*

Quire. Seven virtues. *Line 86, p. 282*

To that place. The earth. *Line 104, p. 282*

The bird of Jove. This imitated from *Ezekiel* xvii, 3, 4, is typical of the persecutions of the church by the Roman emperors. *Line 110, p. 284*

A fox. Probably the treachery of the heretics is meant. *Line 118, p. 284*

With his feathers lined. Reference to the donations of Constantine to the church. *Line 124, p. 284*

A dragon. Mahomet, or Satan according to those who believe this to be a reference to the great schism of the ninth century. *Line 130, p. 284*

Heads. By the seven heads are meant the seven capital sins: by the three with two horns, pride, anger, and avarice, injurious both to man himself and to his neighbor; by the four with one horn, gluttony, gloominess, concupiscence, and envy, hurtful, at least in their primary effects, chiefly to him who is guilty of them. Compare *Rev.* xvii. *Line 142, p. 284*

O'er it. The harlot is thought to be the state of the church under Boniface VIII and the giant to be Philip IV of France who brought the Pope's residence to Avignon. *Line 146, p. 285*

CANTO XXXIII

The heathen. Psalms lxxix, 1. *Line 1, p. 285*

Yet a little while. John xvi, 16. *Line 10, p. 285*

Was, and is not. Dante did not consider the church at Avignon the true church. *Line 35, p. 286*

Hope not to scare God's vengeance with a sop. In Dante's time, a murderer at Florence imagined himself secure from vengeance if he ate a sop of bread in wine upon the grave of the person murdered, within the space of nine days. *Line 36, p. 286*

That eagle. He prognosticates that the Emperor of Germany will not always submit to the usurpations of the

[457]

NOTES

Pope, and foretells the coming of Henry VII, Duke of Luxemburgh, signified by the numerical figures DVX, or of Can Grande della Scala, appointed the leader of the Ghibelline forces.   *Line 38, p. 286*

Themis. Noted for obscurity of her oracles; the Sphinx tore to pieces the travellers who could not solve the riddles he gave them.   *Line 47, p. 286*

Naïads. Dante should have used Laïades (son of Laius).   *Line 50, p. 286*

Twice. First by the eagle and next by the giant.   *Line 57, p. 286*

Elsa's numbing waters. The Elsa, a little stream, which flows into the Arno about twenty miles below Florence, is said to possess a petrifying quality.   *Line 67, p. 286*

That one brings home his staff inwreathed with palm. "For the same cause that the *palmer*, returning from Palestine, brings home his staff, or bourdon, bound with palm," that is, to show where he has been.   *Line 78, p. 286*

PARADISE

CANTO I
Heaven. The empyrean, seat of God.   *Line 3, p. 293*

Thus far. One of the peaks of Parnassus was sacred to the Muses, one to Apollo.   *Line 15, p. 293*

Marsyas. Who challenged Apollo to a musical contest in which the victor could do as he wished with the loser. Apollo flayed Marsyas alive.   *Line 19, p. 293*

Penean foliage. From Daphne, daughter of Peneus, who was changed to a laurel.   *Line 31, p. 294*

Through that. Where the four circles, the horizon, the zodiac, the equator, and the equinoctial colure join; the last three intersect each other so as to form three crosses in the spring equinox.   *Line 37, p. 294*

In happiest constellation. Aries.   *Line 39, p. 294*

Eternal wheels. The heavens eternal and ever circling.   *Line 62, p. 294*

Glaucus. Who saw a fish he had caught recovering life by eating grass; he ate some himself and became immortal.   *Line 66, p. 295*

So much of heaven. The sphere of fire.   *Line 77, p. 295*

The heaven. The empyrean, always motionless.   *Line 118, p. 297*

The substance, that hath greatest speed. The primum mobile.   *Line 119, p. 297*

CANTO II
The increate perpetual thirst. The desire for celestial beatitude natural for the soul.   *Line 20, p. 298*

This first star. The moon.   *Line 30, p. 298*

By bodies dense or rare. Spots on the moon.   *Line 60, p. 299*

Numberless lights. The fixed stars which differ in bulk and splendor.   *Line 65, p. 299*

Save one. Except that principle of rarity and denseness. By "formal principles" are meant constituent or essential causes.   *Line 71, p. 300*

Change the leaves. Like leaves of parchment, darker in some parts than others.   *Line 78, p. 300*

Within the heaven. According to the poet's system, there are ten heavens. The heaven where peace divine inhabits is the empyrean; the body within it that circles round is the primum mobile; the following heaven, that of the fixed stars; and the other orbs, the seven lower heavens, are Saturn, Jupiter, Mars, the Sun, Venus, Mercury and the Moon.   *Line 111, p. 301*

By blessed movers. Angels.   *Line 129, p. 301*

The deep spirit. The moving angel.   *Line 131, p. 301*

Different virtue. "There is one glory of the sun, and another glory of the moon, and another glory of the stars for one star differeth from another star in glory." 1 *Cor.* xv, 41.   *Line 139, p. 301*

CANTO III
Delusion. Narcissus mistook a shadow for substance, and Dante, substance for a shadow.   *Line 16, p. 302*

[458]

PARADISE

She. Charity, the divine love of God. *Line 44, p. 303*

Piccarda. Sister of Corso Donati and of Forese (*Purg.*, xxiii). *Line 50, p. 303*

The Lady. St. Clare, founder of the order called after her; she was born of opulent, noble parents at Assisi in 1193. *Line 99, p. 304*

God knows. Her brother Corso, inflamed with rage against his virgin sister, gathered Farinata, an infamous assassin, and twelve other abandoned ruffians, entered the monastery by a ladder, and carried away his sister forcibly to his own house; and then tearing off her religious habit, compelled her to go in a secular garment to her nuptials. Before the spouse of Christ came together with her new husband, she knelt down before a crucifix and recommended her virginity to Christ. Soon after her whole body was smitten with leprosy and in a few days, through divine disposal, she passed with a palm of virginity to the Lord. According to Rodolfo da Tossignano. *Line 110, p. 305*

Constance. Daughter of Ruggieri, king of Sicily, wife of Emperor VI and mother of Frederick II. She was supposed to have been taken from a nunnery by force after she was fifty, and her son was supposedly born after that. *Line 121, p. 305*

The second, Henry VI, son of Frederick I, was the second emperor of the house of Suabia, and his son Frederick II, "the third and last." *Line 122, p. 305*

CANTO IV

Daniel. See *Daniel* ii. Beatrice did for Dante what Daniel did for Nebuchadnezzar, when he freed the king from the uncertainty respecting his dream, which had enraged him against the Chaldeans. *Line 13, p. 306*

Plato. Plato, Timæus, ix. "The Creator, when he had framed the universe, distributed to the stars an equal number of souls, appointing to each soul its several star." *Line 24, p. 306*

Of Seraphim. Angels and beatified spirits dwell all and eternally together, only partaking more or less of the divine glory, in the empyrean; although, in condescension to human understanding, they appear to have different spheres allotted to them. *Line 28, p. 306*

The first circle. The empyrean. *Line 34, p. 307*

... him who made Tobias whole. The Archangel Raphael. *Line 48, p. 307*

Timæus. Reference to the work of Plato. *Line 50, p. 307*

Laurence. Who suffered martyrdom in the third century. *Line 82, p. 308*

Scævola. Mucius Scævola (died 82 B.C.) whose story is told in Livy, *Hist.*, ii, 12. *Line 82, p. 308*

His father's. Amphiaraus. *Line 100, p. 308*

His own mother. Eriphyle. *Line 101, p. 308*

Of will. Piccarda speaks absolutely and without relation to circumstances, while Beatrice speaks conditionally and respectively. *Line 107, p. 309*

That truth. The light of divine truth. *Line 119, p. 309*

CANTO V

Thou wouldst of theft. A thief's gift of stolen goods to a poor man should not be called almsgiving. *Line 32, p. 311*

It was enjoin'd the Israelites. Lev. xii, xxvii. *Line 48, p. 311*

Either key. The authority of the Church; see Canto ix, 108. *Line 56, p. 311*

Jephthah. Who sacrificed his daughter in order to keep the vow made to God that he would offer up the first thing that came within his sight. *Judges* xi, xii. *Line 64, p. 311*

Leader of the Greeks. Agamemnon who sacrificed his daughter, Iphigenia, in order to obtain favorable winds to speed his ships from Aulis. *Line 69, p. 311*

That region. The east, the equinoctial line, or the empyrean, according to various commentators. *Line 86, p. 312*

The orb. Mercury which holds the spirits of those who strove for honor and glory on earth. *Line 93, p. 312*

This sphere. Mercury, nearest to the sun, is often hidden by it. *Line 124, p. 314*

The lustre. Justinian. *Line 126, p. 314*

CANTO VI

After that Constantine the eagle turn'd. Constantine, in transferring the seat of empire from Rome to Byzan-

NOTES

tium, carried the eagle, the Imperial ensign, from the west to the east. Aeneas, on the contrary, had, with better augury, moved along with the sun's course, when he passed from Troy to Italy. *Line 1, p. 314*

A hundred years twice told and more. The Emperor Constantine entered Byzantium in 324; and Justinian began his reign in 527.
Line 5, p. 315

At Europe's extreme point. Constantinople situated at the extreme of Europe, not far from the mountains near Troy from which the founders of Rome came.
Line 6, p. 315

Prime love. Holy Ghost.
Line 12, p. 315

In Christ one nature only. Justinian is said to have been a follower of the heretical opinions held by Eutyches, "who taught that in Christ there was but one nature, viz. that of the incarnate word."
Line 15, p. 315

Agapete. Bishop of Rome whose *Scheda Regia* addressed to Justinian won him a place among the wisest and most judicious writers of his century.
Line 16, p. 315

Belisarius. General of Justinian who reconquered Italy from the Goths.
Line 25, p. 315

Who pretend its power. The Ghibellines; the Guelphs are referred to in the following line.
Line 33, p. 315

Pallas. Son of Evander, King of Latium, killed in battle by Turnus; Dante implies that Aeneas inherited his rights to Latium.
Line 34, p. 315

Alba. Alba Longa built by the son of Aeneas, Ascanius.
Line 38, p. 315

The rival three. The Horatii and the Curiatii.
Line 39, p. 315

Brennus. Leader of the Senonian Gauls, and reputed conqueror of Rome in 390 B.C.
Line 44, p. 316

The Epirot prince. Pyrrhus, King of Epirus.
Line 44, p. 316

Torquatus. Titus Manlius Torquatus, leader of Roman armies; he killed his son for disobeying his commands.
Line 46, p. 316

Quintius. Quintius Cincinnatus, so called for his long hair; named dictator in 458 B.C., he defeated the Aequians, and laid down his extraordinary powers after sixteen days.
Line 47, p. 316

Arab hordes. Barbarians in general.
Line 50, p. 316

What then it wrought. The exploits of Julius Cæsar.
Line 59, p. 316

In its next bearer's gripe. Augustus Cæsar.
Line 75, p. 316

The third Cæsar. The eagle in the hand of Tiberius, the third of the Cæsars, outdid all its achievements, both past and future, by becoming the instrument of that mighty and mysterious act of satisfaction made to the divine justice in the crucifixion of our Lord.
Line 89, p. 317

Vengeance for vengeance. Destruction of Jerusalem by Titus.
Line 95, p. 317

Charlemain. Pope Adrian I asked his aid against Desiderius, last king of the Lombards, in 773.
Line 98, p. 317

The one. The Guelphs.
Line 102, p. 317

The yellow lilies. The French ensign.
Line 104, p. 317

The other. The Ghibellines.
Line 105, p. 317

Charles. Charles II of Anjou, head of the Guelphs opposing the Emperor.
Line 110, p. 317

Romeo's light. Romeo of Villeneuve (1170–1250), prime minister of Raymond Berenger, Count of Provence; his history is uncertain, but the legend is that he rose high in the service of the Count, and when jealousy of the courtiers forced his dismissal, he took up the pilgrim's staff which he had had when he entered the Count's service.
Line 131, p. 318

Four daughters. The four kings they married were: Louis IX of France; Henry III of England; Richard, King of the Romans; and Charles I, King of Naples and Sicily.
Line 135, p. 318

CANTO VII

Hosanna. Hosanna holy God of Sabaoth, abundantly illumining with thy brightness the blessed fires of these kingdoms.
Line 1, p. 318

That substance bright. Justinian.
Line 4, p. 318

That man. Adam.
Line 25, p. 319

Different effects. The death of Christ was pleasing to God, inasmuch as it satisfied the divine justice; and to the Jews, because it gratified their malignity; and while heaven opened for joy at the ransom of man, the earth trembled through compassion for its Maker.
Line 44, p. 319

[460]

PARADISE

A just vengeance. The punishment of Christ by the Jews, although just as far as regarded the human nature assumed by him, and so a righteous vengeance of sin, yet being unjust as it regarded the divine nature, was itself justly revenged on the Jews by the destruction of Jerusalem. *Line* 48, p. 320

What distils. The things directly created by God without the intervention of secondary causes are immortal. *Line* 63, p. 320

These tokens of pre-eminence. The gifts of immediate creation: freedom, immortality and likeness to God. *Line* 72, p. 320

By both his ways. Either by mercy and justice united or by mercy alone. *Line* 102, p. 321

By created virtue inform'd. Matter is first created and afterward the "informing virtue," residing in the stars, produces plants, animals, etc., which are secondary forms. *Line* 132, p. 322

Our resurrection certain. Adam and Eve, directly created by God, are immortal; their descendants are also immortal because the death of Christ restored them to their former privileges. *Line* 142, p. 322

CANTO VIII

The world. In heathen days, sensual love proceeded from the star Venus who along with her mother, Dione, and son, Cupid, was worshipped as a divinity. *Line* 1, p. 322

Epicycle. A little sphere revolving by itself in the heavens. *Line* 4, p. 322

Now obvious. Venus is a morning star at one part of the year, and an evening star at another. *Line* 14, p. 323

Lofty seraphim. Who preside over the primum mobile, the source of all heavenly motion. *Line* 31, p. 323

Had the time been more. The spirit now speaking is Charles Martel, crowned King of Hungary and son of Charles II, King of Naples and Sicily; born in 1271, he died before he could succeed his father in Naples, and thus left that kingdom to his brother Robert who resisted Emperor Henry VII. *Line* 53, p. 324

Thou lovedst me well. Charles Martel came to Florence in 1295 and may have known Dante there.
Line 57, p. 324

The left bank. Provence. *Line* 60, p. 324

*... that horn
Of fair Ausonia.* The kingdom of Naples. *Line* 62, p. 324

The land. Hungary. *Line* 68, p. 324

The beautiful Trinacria. Sicily so called from its three mountains, two of which are Pachynus and Pelorus. *Line* 73, p. 324

Typhoëus. The giant whom Jupiter overwhelmed under Mt. Aetna where he vomited forth smoke and flame. *Line* 74, p. 324

Sprung through me from Charles and Rodolph. Sicily would still be ruled by the descendants of these two. *Line* 77, p. 324

Had not ill-lording. The ill-conduct of the governors of Sicily had roused the people to the uprising at Palermo in 1282 called the Sicilian Vespers; as a result, the kingdom fell to Peter III of Aragon. *Line* 78, p. 324

My brother's foresight. His brother Robert was a hostage in Catalonia from 1288 to 1295, and when he became king surrounded himself with many Catalonians. *Line* 81, p. 325

Consult your teacher. Aristotle. *Line* 125, p. 326

Solon, etc. Civil life demands different occupations as represented by Solon, a law-giver, Xerxes, a warrior, and Melchisedec, a priest. *Line* 129, p. 326

Quirinus. Romulus was born of so obscure a father that his parentage was attributed to Mars. *Line* 137, p. 326

CANTO IX
O fair Clemenza. Daughter of Charles Martel, and second wife of Louis X of France. *Line* 2, p. 327

The treachery. The occupation of the Sicilian throne by Robert to the exclusion of his brother's son, Carobert, the rightful heir. *Line* 2, p. 327

In that part. Between Rialto in the Venetian territory and the sources of the rivers Brenta and Piava, is situated a castle called Romano, the birthplace of the famous tyrant Ezzolino or Azzolino, the brother of Cunizza, who is now speaking. The tyrant we have seen in "the river of blood." *Hell,* Canto xii, 110. *Line* 25, p. 327

Cunizza. Who was overcome by the influence of her star Venus; she lived from about 1198 to 1279, was married three times and had many lovers including Sordello. *Line* 32, p. 328

[461]

NOTES

This. Folco of Genoa or Marseilles, a noted Provençal poet, who became Bishop of Toulouse in 1205 and persecuted the Albigensians.
Line 34, p. 328

By Adice and Tagliamento. Two rivers, the first to the west and the second to the east.
Line 44, p. 328

The hour is near. For the defeat of Giacopo da Carrara and the Paduans by Can Grande at Vicenza, in 1314.
Line 45, p. 328

One. Riccardo da Camino, murdered at Trevigi where the Cagnano and Sile meet.
Line 48, p. 328

Feltro. The Bishop of Feltro who received a number of Ghibelline refugees from Ferrara with a promise of protection and afterward gave them up; they were taken back to Ferrara where many of them were put to death.
Line 50, p. 328

Malta's. A tower, either in the citadel of Padua, which under the tyranny of Ezzolino had been "with many a foul and midnight murder fed"; or (as some say) near a river of the same name, that falls into the lake of Bolsena, in which the Pope was accustomed to imprison those guilty of irremissible sin.
Line 53, p. 328

Six shadowing wings. "Above it stood the seraphims: each one had six wings." Isaiah vi, 2.
Line 76, p. 329

The valley of waters. The Mediterranean; some commentators believe Dante is describing Marseilles, others, Genoa.
Line 80, p. 329

Discordant shores. Europe and Africa.
Line 82, p. 329

Meridian. Extending to the east, the Mediterranean reaches the coast of Palestine which is on its horizon when it enters the Straits of Gibraltar.
Line 83, p. 329

... Ebro's stream And Macra's. According to those who believe Dante is describing Genoa, these are two streams west and east of Genoa; the believers in the Marseilles theory say the Ebro here mentioned is the Spanish river.
Line 85, p. 329

Begga. In Africa, opposite Genoa in Europe.
Line 88, p. 329

Whose haven. A reference either to the terrible slaughter of the Genoese by the Saracens in 936, or by Julius Cæsar; if Dante is referring to Marseilles, he probably means here the slaughter of the Marseillais under Nasidius by Brutus in command of J. Cæsar's fleet.
Line 89, p. 329

Belus' daughter. Dido who wronged her husband, Sichaeus, and Aeneas' wife, Creusa, through her love for Aeneas.
Line 93, p. 329

She of Rhodope. Phyllis who hanged herself when Demophon did not come to marry her on the promised day.
Line 96, p. 329

Jove's son. Hercules whose wife, Dejanira, was jealous of Hercules' love for Iole.
Line 98, p. 329

Rahab. Heb. xi, 31.
Line 112, p. 330

This heaven. Venus where the shadow of the earth ends, according to Ptolemy.
Line 115, p. 330

First, in Christ's triumph. She was the first saved when Christ released from Hell the spirits of the prophets and patriarchs of the old dispensation.
Line 117, p. 330

With either palm. By both hands nailed to the cross.
Line 120, p. 330

The Pope. Who does not care that the Holy Land is in the possession of the Saracens.
Line 123, p. 330

The cursed flower. The coin of Florence—the florin; the covetous desire of the Pope has caused much evil.
Line 126, p. 330

The decretals. The canon law.
Line 130, p. 330

The Vatican. Allusion either to the death of Boniface VIII in 1303, the coming of Henry VII into Italy, or the removal of the papacy to Avignon under Clement V.
Line 134, p. 330

CANTO X

The point. At the intersection of the equinoctial circle and the zodiac where the common motion of the heavens from east to west strikes with greatest force the motion of the planets; according to Dante's system, the force is greatest here because the velocity of each is increased by its distance from the poles.
Line 7, p. 331

Oblique. The zodiac.
Line 11, p. 331

In heaven above. The planets would not receive or transmit their influences if they did not keep their order of motion and if the zodiac were not oblique.
Line 14, p. 331

Minister. The sun.
Line 26, p. 331

Along the spires. According to Dante's system, the earth is motionless and the sun passes in spiral motion from one tropic to the other.
Line 30, p. 331

PARADISE

As a man. He was quite insensible of it. — Line 32, p. 331

Fourth family. Inhabitants of the sun, the fourth planet. — Line 45, p. 332

Of his spirit and of his offspring. Who manifest the mystery of the Trinity to those studying divine things; the sun is the heaven of the doctors of theology. — Line 46, p. 332

Latona's daughter. The moon. — Line 64, p. 332

Such was the song. Of the ineffable spirits. — Line 70, p. 332

I, then, was of the lambs. The Dominican order. — Line 91, p. 333

Albert of Cologne. Albertus Magnus, born at Lauingen in Thuringia in 1193; he entered the Dominican order and taught theology in Germany, particularly in Cologne: Thomas Aquinas was his pupil; in 1260, he accepted the bishopric of Ratisbon, but resigned after two years to return to his cell in Cologne where he superintended the school and composed his voluminous works on divinity and natural science. — Line 95, p. 333

Of Aquinum, Thomas. Thomas Aquinas, born of noble parents at Rocca Secca, in 1224, studied under Albertus Magnus in Paris and Cologne, wrote many religious treatises, the most famous of which, his *Summa Theologiae*, is followed closely by Dante. — Line 96, p. 333

Gratian. A Benedictine monk, author of *Decretum Gratiani*, a compendium and correlation of civil and church law. — Line 101, p. 333

Peter. Bishop of Paris, 1155, author of *Liber Sententiarum*, which contained the most complete system of theology that had yet appeared at the time. — Line 104, p. 333

The fifth light. Solomon. — Line 105, p. 333

His doom. It was a common question whether Solomon was saved. — Line 107, p. 333

That taper's radiance. St. Dionysius the Areopagite, a disciple of St. Paul, supposed to have suffered martyrdom, and to have written a book about the different orders of angels and their functions called *De Coelesti Hierarchia*. — Line 112, p. 334

That pleader. Paulus Orosius, a Spanish priest of the fifth century, who wrote a history of the world to refute the charges that the misfortunes of Rome were the result of the introduction of Christianity. — Line 116, p. 334

The eighth. Boetius whose *De Consolatione Philosophiae* was much appreciated in the Middle Ages; he was a senator, and under the suspicion of treason was put in prison by Theodoric and perhaps killed by him in 524. — Line 119, p. 334

Cieldauro. Boetius was buried at Pavia in the monastery of St. Pietro called Ciel d'Oro. — Line 124, p. 334

Isidore. Archbishop of Seville, died 636. — Line 126, p. 334

Bede. The Venerable Bede, a well-known English church historian, who was born in 672. — Line 127, p. 334

Richard. Of St. Victor, a native of Scotland or Ireland; he was canon and prior of St. Victor in Paris, and a noted mystic of his day. — Line 127, p. 334

Sigebert. Sigier of Brabant, died about 1283. — Line 132, p. 334

The straw-litter'd street. The Rue de Fouarre, *street of straw*, on which the University of Paris stands. — Line 134, p. 334

The spouse of God. The Church. — Line 135, p. 334

CANTO XI

Aphorisms. The study of medicine. — Line 4, p. 335

The lustre. The spirit of Thomas Aquinas. — Line 17, p. 335

She. The Church. Her "well-beloved" is Christ. — Line 29, p. 335

One. Saint Francis; "the other" is Saint Dominic. — Line 34, p. 336

Tupino. Description of the birthplace of Saint Francis between Tupino, a rivulet near Assisi where the saint was born in 1182, and Chiasciò, a stream rising in a mountain near Agobbio which was chosen by Saint Ubaldo for the place of his retirement. — Line 40, p. 336

Nocera with Gualdo. Two cities near Assisi whose heavy yoke might be the taxes of Robert of Naples. — Line 44, p. 336

A dame. Personification of the vow of poverty taken by Saint Francis. — Line 54, p. 336

[463]

NOTES

Before the spiritual court. He made the vow of poverty in the presence of the bishop and his natural father.
Line 57, p. 336

Her first husband. Christ.
Line 60, p. 336

Amyclas. A poor fisherman who opened his door to Christ without fear because he knew his poverty protected him.
Line 63, p. 336

Bernard. Of Quintavalle, one of the first followers of the saint.
Line 72, p. 337

Egidius. The third of his disciples, who died in 1262. His work, entitled *Verba Aurea*, was published in 1534 at Antwerp.
Line 76, p. 337

Sylvester. Another of his earliest associates.
Line 76, p. 337

Whom now the cord. Saint Francis bound his body with a cord, in sign that he considered it as a beast, and that it required, like a beast, to be led by a halter.
Line 80, p. 337

Pietro Bernardone. A man in a humble station at Assisi.
Line 83, p. 337

Innocent. Pope Innocent III who first approved the order in 1210.
Line 85, p. 337

Honorius. His successor, Honorius III, who granted certain privileges to the Franciscans and gave the order formal confirmation in 1223.
Line 90, p. 337

In the proud Soldan's presence. Saint Francis is said to have preached before the Sultan of Egypt.
Line 94, p. 337

On the hard rock. The mountain Alverna in the Apennines.
Line 98, p. 337

The last signet. The stigmata or marks resembling the wounds of Christ, said to have been found on the saint's body.
Line 100, p. 337

His dearest lady. Poverty.
Line 106, p. 337

Our Patriarch. Saint Dominic to whose order Thomas Aquinas belonged.
Line 113, p. 338

CANTO XII
The blessed flame. Thomas Aquinas.
Line 1, p. 338

The holy mill. The circle of spirits.
Line 2, p. 338

Handmaid. Iris, the rainbow.
Line 9, p. 339

In manner of that voice. One rainbow giving back the image of the other, as sound is reflected by Echo, that nymph who was melted away by her fondness for Narcissus, as vapor is melted by the sun.
Line 12, p. 339

One. Saint Bonaventura, a famous churchman of his day; he was made general of the Franciscan order in 1256, Bishop of Albano and a cardinal in 1272; he was born in Bagnoregio, Tuscany, in 1221.
Line 25, p. 339

The love. Out of courtesy, Bonaventura, a Franciscan, praises the founder of the Dominicans, and Thomas Aquinas, a Dominican, praises the founder of the Franciscans.
Line 28, p. 339

The army of Christ. The Church, in a low state at this time.
Line 35, p. 339

In that clime. Spain.
Line 42, p. 339

Those billows. The Atlantic.
Line 45, p. 339

Sometimes. During the summer solstice.
Line 47, p. 339

Callaroga. Between Osma and Aranda in Old Castile, designated by the royal coat of arms.
Line 48, p. 339

The loving minion of the Christian faith. Dominic, born in 1170 in Callorga.
Line 51, p. 340

In the mother's womb. His mother is said to have dreamed that she should bring forth a white and black dog with a lighted torch in his mouth, which were signs of the habit to be worn by his order, and of his fervent zeal.
Line 55, p. 340

The dame. His godmother's dream was that he had one star in his forehead, and another in the nape of his neck, from which he communicated light to the east and the west.
Line 59, p. 340

After the first counsel. "Jesus said unto him, If thou wilt be perfect, go and sell that thou hast, and give to the poor, and thou shalt have treasure in heaven; and come and follow me." *Matt. xix*, 21.
Line 69, p. 340

As men interpret it. Gift of grace of the Lord.
Line 75, p. 340

Ostiense. Henry of Susa, cardinal of Ostia and Velletri, who was celebrated for his lectures on the five books of the Decretals; lived around 1250.
Line 77, p. 340

PARADISE

Taddeo. Either Taddeo d'Alderotto, a Florentine, called the Hippocratean, who translated the ethics of Aristotle into Latin, and died at an advanced age about the end of the thirteenth century; or Taddeo of Bologna, noted for his legal knowledge, who left no writings behind him. *Line 77, p. 340*

No dispensation. Dominic did not ask license to compound for the use of unjust acquisitions by dedicating part of them to pious uses. *Line 85, p. 340*

Nor the first vacant fortune. Not the first benefice that fell vacant. *Line 86, p. 340*

In favor of that seed. For that seed of the divine word, from which have sprung up these four-and-twenty plants, these holy spirits now surrounding Beatrice and Dante. *Line 89, p. 341*

One wheel. Dominic; the other wheel is Francis. *Line 99, p. 341*

Thomas. Aquinas. *Line 103, p. 341*

Rejected tares. Matt. xiii, 30. The tares were burned and the wheat gathered into the barn. *Line 110, p. 341*

I question not. At Casale, in Monferrat, the discipline had been enforced by Uberto with unnecessary rigor; and at Acquasparta, in the territory of Todi, it had been equally relaxed by the Cardinal Matteo, general of the order. *Line 111, p. 341*

One, who, in discharge. Bonaventura; see xii, 25, note. *Line 119, p. 341*

Illuminato . . . Agostino. Two of Saint Francis' earliest followers. *Line 121, p. 341*

Hugues of St. Victor. A mystic and theologian who spent most of his life at the monastery of St. Victor in Paris where he wrote ten books illustrating the celestial hierarchy of Dionysius the Areopagite; he died in 1142. *Line 125, p. 341*

Pietro Mangiadore. Or Petrus Comestor, the Eater, born at Troyes, canon and dean of the church there and later chancellor of the University of Paris; best known for his *Historia Scolastica*; he retired to St. Victor's where he died in the late twelfth century. *Line 125, p. 341*

He of Spain. John XXI, born about 1226, Pope in 1276; he wrote a famous book on logic and others on medicine. *Line 126, p. 341*

Chrysostom. John of Antioch, called "Chrysostom," or golden-mouthed, on account of his eloquence, was born in 347, and died in 407 in Cappadocia where he lived as an exile. *Line 128, p. 342*

Anselmo. Anselm, born in Aosta in 1034, prior and later abbot of the monastery of Bec, Normandy, Archbishop of Canterbury in 1093. *Line 128, p. 342*

Donatus. Ælius Donatus, the grammarian, in the fourth century, one of the preceptors of St. Jerome. *Line 129, p. 342*

Raban. Born in Mentz in 766, abbot of the monastery of Fulda, Archbishop of Mentz in 847. *Line 130, p. 342*

Joachim. Abbot of Flora in Calabria; died 1202. *Line 131, p. 342*

A peer. Saint Dominic. *Line 134, p. 342*

CANTO XIII

Who would conceive. Dante imagines the double circle formed by the twenty-four theologians as if the seven stars of Ursa Major, the two largest stars of Ursa Minor and fifteen of the brightest stars in the heavens were arranged in two circles like the crown of Ariadne and revolved in opposite directions. The "wain" is Ursa Major, "that horn," Ursa Minor and "the swiftest heaven," the primum mobile. *Line 1, p. 342*

The Chiana. River in Tuscany near Arezzo. *Line 21, p. 342*

That luminary. Thomas Aquinas. *Line 29, p. 343*

The meek man of God. Saint Francis. *Line 30, p. 343*

In the bosom. Eve was created from Adam's rib. *Line 34, p. 343*

By the keen lance. Christ's suffering redeems man from the original sin. *Line 37, p. 343*

Light. The Word; the Son of God. *Line 51, p. 343*

His love triune with them. The Holy Ghost. *Line 53, p. 343*

New existences. Angels and human souls. *Line 55, p. 343*

The lowest powers. Irrational life and brute matter. *Line 57, p. 343*

Their wax, and that which moulds it. Matter and the virtue or energy acting on it. *Line 62, p. 344*

The heaven. The influence of the planetary bodies. *Line 69, p. 344*

[465]

NOTES

The brightness of the seal. The divine idea.
Line 70, p. 344

Therefore. A brief description of the Trinity; the primal virtue is the Father, the lustrous image, the Son, and the fervent love, the Holy Ghost.
Line 74, p. 344

The clay. Adam.
Line 77, p. 344

Burden. Christ.
Line 78, p. 344

Who ask'd. Solomon.
Line 88, p. 344

If necessary. If a necessary conclusion must be drawn from two premises of which one is not necessary.
Line 92, p. 344

That first motion. If one must admit a primal motion that is not the effect of the other motion.
Line 94, p. 344

Of the mid-circle. If a triangle one side of which is the diameter of the semi-circle can be drawn in the semi-circle without forming a right angle.
Line 95, p. 344

... Parmenides,
Melissus, Bryso. The first two are of the Eleatic school, and the last, a mathematician who claimed he squared the circle; all are examples of false reasoning.
Line 120, p. 345

Sabellius, Arius. Well-known heretics.
Line 123, p. 345

Dame Birtha and Sir Martin. Names for anybody with more curiosity than discretion.
Line 135, p. 346

CANTO XIV

The goodliest light. Solomon.
Line 31, p. 347

Gleed. White-hot coal glowing in the centre of a flame.
Line 47, p. 347

To more lofty bliss. The planet Mars.
Line 78, p. 348

A holocaust. Thanksgiving sacrifice.
Line 82, p. 348

Its pathway. Reference to the galaxy which philosophers explain in different ways.
Line 92, p. 348

The venerable sign. The cross placed in the planet of Mars to denote the glory of those who fought in the crusades.
Line 94, p. 348

The atomies of bodies. Motes.
Line 106, p. 350

He. The heavens or "living seals" become more resplendent the higher Dante goes; and so do the eyes of Beatrice.
Line 125, p. 350

CANTO XV

Our greater muse. Virgil, *Aeneid,* vi, 684.
Line 24, p. 351

I am thy root. Cacciaguida was the father of Alighieri, Dante's great-grandfather, who began the name of Alighieri and who has been in the first round of Purgatory for more than one hundred years.
Line 84, p. 353

Which calls her still. The public clock was still within the circuit of the ancient walls in the Benedictine church, La Badia.
Line 93, p. 353

Sardanapalus. The luxurious monarch of Assyria, noted for his effeminacy.
Line 102, p. 353

Montemalo. Either an elevated spot between Rome and Viterbo; or Monte Mario, the site of the villa Mellini, commanding a view of Rome.
Line 103, p. 353

Our suburban turret. Uccellatojo near Florence which had a commanding view of the city; Florence had not yet vied with Rome in the grandeur of her public buildings.
Line 104, p. 353

Of Nerli, and of Vecchio. Two of the most opulent families of Florence.
Line 110, p. 354

Each. None fearful either of dying in banishment, or of being deserted by her husband on a scheme of traffic in France.
Line 113, p. 354

A Salterello and Cianghella. The latter a shameless woman of the family of Tosa, married to Lito degli Alidosi of Imola; the former Lapo Salterello, a lawyer, with whom Dante was at variance.
Line 120, p. 354

Mary. The Virgin was invoked in the pains of childbirth.
Line 125, p. 354

Valdipado. Cacciaguida's wife, whose family name was Alighieri, came from Ferrara, called Val di Pado, from its being watered by the Po.
Line 130, p. 354

Conrad. Emperor Conrad III who died in 1152.
Line 132, p. 354

Whose people. The Mahometans who were left in possession of the Holy Land through the supineness of the Pope.
Line 136, p. 354

[466]

PARADISE

CANTO XVI

With greeting. Dante shows his respect by addressing his ancestor with the ceremonious "you."
Line 10, p. 355

Guenever. Beatrice's smile reminded him of the female servant who, by her coughing, emboldened Queen Guenever to admit the freedoms of Lancelot.
Line 15, p. 355

The fold. Florence whose patron saint was John the Baptist.
Line 23, p. 355

From the day. From the incarnation of our Lord to the birth of Cacciaguida, the planet Mars had returned five hundred and eighty times to the constellation of Leo, with which it is supposed to have a congenial influence. As Mars then completes his revolution in a period forty-three days short of two years, Cacciaguida was born about 1090.
Line 31, p. 356

The last. The city was divided into four compartments. The Elisei, the ancestors of Dante, resided near the entrance of that, named from the Porta S. Piero, which was the last reached by the competitor in the annual race at Florence.
Line 38, p. 356

Mars. The limits of the city were marked by the statue of Mars on Ponte Vecchio and the baptistery of St. John.
Line 45, p. 356

Campi and Certaldo and Fighine. Country places near Florence.
Line 48, p. 356

That these people. That the inhabitants of the above-mentioned places had not been mixed with the citizens; nor the limits of Florence extended beyond Galluzzo and Trespiano.
Line 50, p. 356

Aguglione's hind, and Signa's. Baldo of Aguglione and Bonifazio of Signa, a small town near Florence.
Line 54, p. 356

Had not the people. If Rome had continued her allegiance to the Emperor and the Guelph and Ghibelline factions had thus been prevented, Florence would not have been polluted by a race of upstarts and lost the most respectable of her old families.
Line 56, p. 356

Simifonte. A castle dismantled by the Florentines.
Line 61, p. 356

Montemurlo. The Conti Guidi sold their castle to the state of Florence when they were unable to defend it from the Pistoians.
Line 63, p. 356

The Cerchi. Chiefs of the Bianchi party who had risen from humble origins in Acone to riches and power through trade.
Line 63, p. 356

Valdigreve. Site in southern France of the castle of the Buondelmonti.
Line 65, p. 356

Luni; Urbisaglia. Formerly important cities now fallen to decay.
Line 72, p. 357

Chiusi and Sinigaglia. Same as Luni, etc.
Line 74, p. 357

Ughi. Well-known Florentine families of Cacciaguida's time.
Line 86, p. 357

At the poop. The Cerchi, Dante's enemies, had succeeded to the houses over the gate of Saint Peter, formerly inhabited by the Ravignani and the Count Guido.
Line 91, p. 357

The gilded hilt and pommel. Symbols of knighthood.
Line 99, p. 357

The column, clothed with verrey. Arms of the Pigli, also called Billi.
Line 100, p. 357

With them. Either the Chiaramontesi, or the Tosinghi, one of which had committed a fraud in measuring out the wheat from the public granary.
Line 103, p. 357

Sizii and Arriguccí. Families which still held magisterial offices.
Line 106, p. 357

Them. The Uberti.
Line 107, p. 357

The bullets of bright gold. Arms of the Abbati or Lamberti.
Line 109, p. 357

The sires of those. The Visdomini, the Tosinghi and the Cortigiani sprung from the founders of the bishopric of Florence and now curators of its revenues which they use to their own purposes.
Line 110, p. 357

The o'erweening brood. This family was so little esteemed that Ubertino Donato, who had married a daughter of Bellincion Berti, himself derived from the same stock, was offended with his father-in-law for giving another of his daughters in marriage to one of them.
Line 113, p. 358

Caponsacco. The family of Caponsacchi, who had removed from Fesole, lived at Florence in the Mercato Vecchio.
Line 120, p. 358

Giuda and Infangato. Guida Guidi and the family of Infangati.
Line 121, p. 358

The great Baron. The Marchese Ugo, who lived at Florence as a lieutenant of Emperor Otho III and gave many of the chief families their license to bear his arms; according to one story, he had a vision in which he heard he was to suffer the fate of the condemned souls, and thereupon he sold all his possessions in Germany

[467]

NOTES

and founded seven abbeys with the proceeds. His memory was celebrated in Florence on St. Thomas's Day.
Line 127, p. 358

One. Giano della Bella who belonged to one of the families bearing Ugo's arms which were bordered with gold, but who no longer retained his place among the nobility.
Line 130, p. 358

Gualterotti dwelt, and Importuni. Two families in the compartment of the city called Borgo. *Line 132, p. 358*

Newer neighborhood. The Bardi, or the Buondelmonti. *Line 134, p. 358*

The house. The Amidei, a reference to the murder of Buondelmonti and the division of the city into Guelphs and Ghibellines. See *Hell*, xxviii, 102, note.
Line 135, p. 358

To Ema. It had been well for the city if your ancestor had been drowned in the Ema, when he crossed that stream on his way from Montebuono to Florence.
Line 142, p. 358

On that maim'd stone. Near the remains of the statue of Mars, Buondelmonti was slain, as if he had been a victim to the god; and Florence had not since known the blessing of peace.
Line 144, p. 358

The lily. The arms of Florence had never hung reversed on the spear of her enemies in token of her defeat, nor been changed from argent to gules; they afterwards were, when the Guelfi gained the predominance.
Line 150, p. 359

CANTO XVII

The youth. Phaëton, who came to his mother Clymene, to inquire of her if he were indeed the son of Apollo.
Line 1, p. 359

That saintly lamp. Cacciaguida. *Line 6, p. 359*

Contingency. That which may or may not be. *Line 37, p. 360*

Necessity. The evidence with which we see casual events portrayed in the source of all truth no more necessitates those events than does the image, reflected in the sight by a ship sailing down a stream, necessitate the motion of the vessel.
Line 40, p. 360

From thence. From the eternal sight or the view of the Deity himself. *Line 43, p. 360*

His cruel stepdame. Phaedra by false accusations drove Hippolytus from Athens. *Line 46, p. 360*

There. At Rome where the expulsion of Dante's party from Florence was being plotted in 1300.
Line 49, p. 360

The common cry. The multitude will, as usual, be ready to blame those who are sufferers, whose cause will at last be vindicated by the overthrow of their enemies.
Line 51, p. 360

The great Lombard. Either Bartolommeo della Scala, or Alboino, his brother; their coat of arms was a ladder and an eagle.
Line 69, p. 361

That mortal. Can Grande della Scala, born under the influence of Mars, but at this time only nine years old. He was, as the other two, a son of Alberto della Scala.
Line 75, p. 361

The Gascon. Pope Clement V. *Line 80, p. 361*

Great Harry. Emperor Henry VII of Luxembourg. *Line 80, p. 361*

The treasure. Cacciaguida. *Line 117, p. 362*

CANTO XVIII

The hallow'd light. In which the spirit of Cacciaguida was enclosed. *Line 22, p. 363*

On this fifth lodgment of the tree. Mars, the fifth of the heavens. *Line 25, p. 363*

The great Maccabee. Judas Maccabeus who delivered his people from the tyranny of the King of Syria; see 1 *Maccabeus*, iii.
Line 37, p. 364

Orlando. Roland, hero of the battle of Roncesvalles, and nephew of Charlemagne. *Line 40, p. 364*

William. Of Orange, hero of the southern cycle of French romances. *Line 43, p. 364*

Renard. Subject of a long episode in the William cycle; a heathen, ignorant of his high birth, who took service with William.
Line 43, p. 364

Duke Godfrey. Of Bouillon, leader of the first crusade and King of Jerusalem. *Line 43, p. 364*

Robert Gutscard. A Norman knight who fought the Saracens in Sicily and Lower Italy, defended Gregory VII, and founded the kingdom of Naples; see *Hell*, xxviii, 12.
Line 44, p. 364

Through silvery. "The heaven of Jupiter may be compared to geometry, for two properties: the one is, that it moves between two heavens repugnant to its temperature, as that of Mars and that of Saturn; whence

PARADISE

Ptolemy, in the above-cited book, says that Jupiter is a star of temperate complexion, between the coldness of Saturn and the heat of Mars; the other is, that, among all the stars, it shows itself white, as it were silvered." *Convito*, ii, 14.   *Line 63, p. 364*

O nymph divine. Urania.   *Line 75, p. 365*

Beatitude. The band of spirits; "beatitudo" in its original meaning of multitude.   *Line 105, p. 365*

Taking the bread away. Excommunication or interdiction of the Eucharist now used as a weapon of warfare.   *Line 124, p. 366*

That writest but to cancel. Boniface VIII, John XXII or the Popes in general.   *Line 126, p. 366*

To him. The coin of Florence was stamped with the impression of John the Baptist; and for this the avaricious Pope is made to declare that he felt more devotion than for either Peter or Paul.   *Line 130, p. 366*

CANTO XIX

The beauteous image. The eagle.   *Line 2, p. 366*

Who turn'd his compass. When he prepared the heavens.   *Line 38, p. 367*

The Word. God's word is still greater than the power of his creatures to understand.   *Line 42, p. 367*

The primal will. The divine will.   *Line 83, p. 368*

Who call "Christ! Christ!" "Not every one that saith unto me, Lord, Lord, shall enter into the kingdom of heaven." *Matt.* vii, 21.   *Line 105, p. 369*

The Aethiop. "The men of Nineveh shall rise in judgment with this generation, and shall condemn it." *Matt.* xii, 41.   *Line 108, p. 369*

That volume. "And I saw the dead, small and great, stand before God; and the books were opened, and another book was opened, which is the book of life, and the dead were judged out of those things which were written in the books, according to their works." *Rev.* xx, 12.   *Line 112, p. 369*

Albert. See *Purgatory*, vi, 98.   *Line 114, p. 369*

Prague. The eagle predicts the devastation of Bohemia in 1304 by Albert of Austria.   *Line 116, p. 369*

He. Philip IV of France, after the battle of Courtrai, 1302, in which the French were defeated by the Flemings, raised the nominal value of the coin. This king died after his horse was thrown to the ground by a wild boar, in 1314.   *Line 117, p. 369*

The English and Scot. The disputes between Edward I and Robert Bruce or John Baliol.   *Line 121, p. 369*

The Spaniard's luxury. Alonzo X of Spain or Ferdinand IV, King of Castile, who died supposedly as a result of extreme intemperance, in 1312.   *Line 122, p. 369*

The Bohemian. Winceslaus II, died 1305; see *Purgatory*, vii, 99.   *Line 123, p. 370*

The halter of Jerusalem. Charles II of Naples and Jerusalem who was lame; see *Purgatory*, vii, 122, and xx, 78, notes.   *Line 125, p. 370*

He. Frederick of Sicily, son of Peter III of Aragon; see *Purgatory*, vii, 117. The isle of fire is Sicily where the tomb of Anchises is located.   *Line 127, p. 370*

His uncle. James, King of Majorca and Minorca, brother of Peter III.   *Line 133, p. 370*

His brother. James II of Aragon who died in 1327; see *Purgatory*, vii, 117.   *Line 133, p. 370*

Crowns. Majorca and Aragon.   *Line 134, p. 370*

Of Portugal. Denis was King of Portugal in Dante's time; Denis died in 1325 after a reign of nearly forty-six years and does not seem to have deserved the stigma here cast on him.   *Line 135, p. 370*

Norway. Haakon, King of Norway, is probably meant; in 1288, he gave refuge to the murderers of Eric VII, King of Denmark, and started a nine-year war against Eric VIII, his successor, which almost ruined both kingdoms.   *Line 136, p. 370*

Him of Ratza. Possibly Ouros I of Servia, 1275–1307, who debased the coinage of Venice.   *Line 136, p. 370*

Hungary. The kingdom of Hungary was about this time disputed by Carobert, son of Charles Martel, and Winceslaus, prince of Bohemia, son of Winceslaus II.   *Line 138, p. 370*

Navarre. Navarre was now under the yoke of France. It soon after (in 1328) followed the advice of Dante, and had a monarch of its own.   *Line 140, p. 370*

Mountainous girdle. The Pyrenees.   *Line 141, p. 371*

Famagosta's streets and Nicosia's. Cities in the kingdom of Cyprus at that time ruled by Henry II, a pusillanimous prince.   *Line 143, p. 371*

NOTES

CANTO XX

The great sign. The eagle, the Imperial ensign. — Line 8, p. 371

After. After the spirits in the sixth planet, Jupiter, had stopped singing. — Line 16, p. 371

The part. The eyes; the highest spirits are those forming the eye. — Line 29, p. 372

Who. David. — Line 34, p. 372

He. Trajan knows the difference between heaven and hell by experience because he was in the latter until the prayers of Pope Gregory released him; see *Purgatory*, x, 68. — Line 41, p. 372

He next. Hezekiah who delayed his death by fifteen years at his own request; II *Kings* xx. — Line 44, p. 372

The other following. Constantine who removed the Empire to Byzantium and left Rome to the Pope. — Line 50, p. 372

William. William II, King of Sicily in the latter part of the twelfth century; of the Norman line of sovereigns; his loss was as much a subject of regret in his dominions as the presence of Charles II of Anjou and Frederick of Aragon was of sorrow and complaint. — Line 57, p. 372

Trojan Ripheus. Unknown except for some praise by Virgil. — Line 62, p. 372

This. Ripheus. — Line 97, p. 373

That. Trajan who lived after the crucifixion. — Line 98, p. 373

The prayers. Of St. Gregory. — Line 103, p. 374

The three nymphs. Faith, Hope and Charity; see *Purgatory*, xxix, 116. — Line 119, p. 374

The pair. Ripheus and Trajan. — Line 138, p. 374

CANTO XXI

Semele. Who wished to see her lover, Jupiter, in all his glory and was reduced to ashes by the lightning surrounding him. — Line 5, p. 375

The seventh splendor. Saturn, the planet. — Line 12, p. 375

The burning lion's breast. The constellation of Leo. — Line 13, p. 375

In them, mirror'd. Let the form of Saturn, later called the Crystal, be reflected in the mirror of thy sight. — Line 15, p. 375

Of that loved monarch. Saturn; see *Hell*, xiv, 91—the reign of Saturn was the golden age. — Line 24, p. 375

That glitterance. The multitude of shining spirits. — Line 36, p. 376

What forbade the smile. It would have overcome him. — Line 56, p. 376

Thou only. You only bring up the question of predestination. — Line 70, p. 377

Catria. Now the abbey of Santa Croce, in the duchy of Urbino, about half way between Gubbio and La Pergola. Dante is said to have resided here for some time. — Line 99, p. 377

Pietro Damiano. St. Peter Damiano, supposedly born in Ravenna about 1007; entered the monastery of Fonte Avellano on the side of the mountain Catria; known for his learning and holiness, he was made a cardinal and Bishop of Ostia in 1058. — Line 112, p. 378

Cephas. St. Peter. — Line 118, p. 378

The Holy Spirit's vessel. St. Paul; see *Hell*, ii, 30. — Line 119, p. 378

Round this. The spirit of Pietro Damiano. — Line 130, p. 378

CANTO XXII

The vengeance. Reference to captivity of the Popes at Avignon, *Purgatory*, xxxii, 155, or to the capture of Boniface VIII at Agnani, *Purgatory*, xx, 86, or to the messenger of God who was to kill a giant, *Purgatory*, xxxiii, 40. — Line 14, p. 379

One largest and most lustrous. St. Benedict, founder of the Benedictine order; born in 480 in Norcia, Umbria, he became a hermit in a cave near Subiaco, and went in 528 to Monte Cassino where he founded his monastery on the site of a temple of Apollo which he destroyed. — Line 27, p. 379

Macarius. Either an Egyptian monk who was an eminent practical writer of the time, or an anchorite from Alexandria who lived in the desert between the Nile and the Red Sea. — Line 48, p. 380

Romoaldo. S. Romoaldo, a native of Ravenna, and the founder of the order of Camaldoli, died in 1027. He was the author of a commentary on the Psalms. — Line 48, p. 380

PARADISE

In the last sphere. The empyrean, where he afterwards sees Saint Benedict, Canto xxxii, 30. Beatified spirits, though they have different heavens allotted them, have all their seat in that higher sphere.   *Line 61, p. 380*

The patriarch Jacob. "And he dreamed, and behold a ladder set up on the earth, and the top of it reached to heaven: and behold the angels of God ascending and descending on it." Gen. xxviii, 12.   *Line 70, p. 380*

The sign. Of the constellation Gemini.   *Line 107, p. 381*

The parent. The sun was in the constellation of the Twins at the time of Dante's birth.   *Line 112, p. 381*

The lofty wheel. The eighth heaven, that of the fixed stars.   *Line 115, p. 381*

Daughter of Latona. The moon.   *Line 135, p. 382*

Without the shadow. Spots on the moon.   *Line 136, p. 382*

Of thy son. The sun.   *Line 138, p. 382*

Maia and Dione. Maia was the mother of Mercury, and Dione, of Venus.   *Line 140, p. 382*

'Twixt his sire and son. Between Saturn and Mars.   *Line 141, p. 382*

CANTO XXIII
Prevenient. Anticipating or going before.   *Line 6, p. 383*

That region. Towards the south, where the course of the sun appears less rapid than when he is in the east or the west.   *Line 11, p. 383*

Trivia. A name of Diana.   *Line 25, p. 383*

The eternal nymphs. The stars.   *Line 26, p. 383*

The Might. Christ.   *Line 36, p. 384*

Of Polyhymnia. Muse of lyric poetry.   *Line 55, p. 384*

The rose. The Virgin Mary, who is termed by the church Rosa Mystica. "I was exalted like a palm-tree in Engaddi, and as a rose-plant in Jericho." Ecclesiasticus, xxiv, 14.   *Line 71, p. 385*

The lilies. The Apostles: "And give ye a sweet savor as frankincense, and flourish as a lily." *Ecclesiasticus,* xxxix, 14.   *Line 73, p. 385*

Of that fair flower. The Virgin.   *Line 86, p. 385*

A cresset. The angel Gabriel.   *Line 92, p. 385*

That lyre. By synecdoche, the lyre is put for the angel.   *Line 98, p. 385*

The goodliest sapphire. The Virgin.   *Line 99, p. 385*

The robe. The ninth heaven, the primum mobile, which enfolds and moves the eight lower heavens.   *Line 110, p. 386*

The crowned flame. The Virgin with the angel hovering over her.   *Line 116, p. 386*

The seed. Christ.   *Line 117, p. 386*

"Regina Cœli." Beginning of an anthem sung by the Church at Easter in honor of our Lady.   *Line 123, p. 386*

Those rich-laden coffers. The spirits who sowed the seed of good works on earth and now contain the fruit of their pious endeavors.   *Line 126, p. 386*

In the Babylonian exile. During their abode on earth.   *Line 129, p. 386*

He. St. Peter with the other holy men of the Old and New Testaments   *Line 133, p. 386*

CANTO XXIV
From that. St. Peter.   *Line 20, p. 387*

Tent. Try, examine.   *Line 37, p. 387*

Bachelor. Scholar.   *Line 47, p. 389*

Faith. Reference to St. Paul's Epistle to the Hebrews xi, 1.   *Line 65, p. 389*

The ancient bond and new. Old and New Testaments.   *Line 91, p. 390*

That Worthy. St. Peter.   *Line 114, p. 391*

CANTO XXV
The fair sheep-fold. Florence from which Dante was banished.   *Line 6, p. 392*

[471]

NOTES

Peer of mickle might. The Apostle James, brother of St. John; he was reputedly buried at Compostella, Galicia, Spain, and his shrine was the destination of many a pilgrimage in the Middle Ages. *Line* 19, p. 392

One, of the other. St. Peter and St. James. *Line* 24, p. 392

Largess. Apparently an allusion to the Epistle of James i, 5. "If any of you lack wisdom, let him ask of God that giveth to all men liberally and upbraideth not, and it shall be given him." Or, to 17: "Every good gift and every perfect gift is from above, and cometh down from the Father of lights." *Line* 31, p. 393

I lifted up. "I will lift up mine eyes unto the hills, from whence cometh my help." *Psalms* cxxi, 1. *Line* 40, p. 393

From Egypt to Jerusalem. From the lower world to heaven. *Line* 59, p. 393

His anthem. "They that know thy name will put their trust in thee." *Psalms* ix, 10. Dante got the answer to this question from David, and the following from St. James. *Line* 74, p. 394

That mighty sheen. The spirit of St. James. *Line* 81, p. 394

Palm. Of martyrdom. *Line* 84, p. 394

Isaias. "He hath clothed me with the garments of salvation, he hath covered me with the robe of righteousness." *Isaiah* lxi, 10. *Line* 90, p. 394

Thy brother. St. John in *Rev.* vii, 9. *Line* 94, p. 394

Winter's month. If a star as bright as the sun were in the constellation of Cancer during the winter month it is above the horizon, night would become day for a whole month. *Line* 101, p. 394

This. St. John; see *Gospel of St. John* xiii, 23, and xxi, 20. *Line* 112, p. 395

Pelican. Christ; see *Psalms* cii, 6. *Line* 113, p. 395

Our number. The Elect; see *Rev.* vi, 2. *Line* 126, p. 395

The two. Christ and Mary. *Line* 127, p. 395

Two garments. Body and soul. *Line* 129, p. 395

Trinal band. Peter, James and John. *Line* 135, p. 395

CANTO XXVI

The beamy flame. St. John. *Line* 2, p. 396

Ananias' hand. Ananias restored St. Paul's sight by putting his hand on him; see *Acts* ix, 17. *Line* 13, p. 396

From him. Plato, Aristotle or Dionysius the Areopagite. *Line* 36, p. 397

I will make. Exodus xxxiii, 19. *Line* 40, p. 397

At the outset. John i, 1. *Line* 42, p. 397

The eagle of our Lord. St. John. *Line* 51, p. 397

The leaves. Created beings who live in the world or "garden." *Line* 62, p. 397

By affinity and blood. Daughter and daughter-in-law. *Line* 92, p. 398

Parhelion. Who enlightens and comprehends all things, but is himself enlightened and comprehended by none. *Line* 107, p. 398

Whence. Limbo. Adam says that 5232 years elapsed from his creation to the time of his deliverance, which followed the death of Christ. *Line* 117, p. 399

All my life. I remained in the terrestrial Paradise only to the seventh hour. *Line* 138, p. 399

CANTO XXVII

Four torches. St. Peter, St. James, St. John and Adam. *Line* 10, p. 400

That. St. Peter who looked as the planet Jupiter would if he assumed the sanguine appearance of Mars; he became red with indignation. *Line* 11, p. 400

He. Boniface VIII who is not Pope in the eyes of God. *Line* 20, p. 400

Christ's spouse. The Church. *Line* 36, p. 401

Of Linus, and of Cletus. Bishops of Rome in the first century. *Line* 37, p. 401

Did Sextus, Pius and Calixtus bleed And Urban. The first two were Bishops of Rome in the second century, and the last two, in the fourth; all were persecuted or martyred. *Line* 40, p. 401

[472]

PARADISE

No purpose was of ours. They did not intend that their successors should take part in the political divisions among Christians like the Guelphs and Ghibellines, or that the seal, "sigil-mark," of St. Peter should be used to authorize iniquitous grants and privileges, or that the Church should make war as Boniface VIII did against the Colonnas. *Line* 42, *p.* 401

Cahorsines and Gascons. Jacques d'Ossa, a native of Cahors, who became Pope in 1316 as John XXII; and Clement V, a Gascon, for whom see *Hell*, xix, 86. *Line* 53, *p.* 401

The she-goat. Capricorn. *Line* 63, *p.* 401

From the hour. Since he had last looked (Canto xxii), Dante had passed from the meridian of Jerusalem to the Atlantic Ocean beyond Gibraltar. *Line* 72, *p.* 401

From Gades. Spain. *Line* 76, *p.* 402

Passage of Laërtes' son. Ulysses' journey through the Straits of Gibraltar; see *Hell*, xxvi, 106. *Line* 77, *p.* 402

The shore. Phoenicia where Europa was carried off by Jupiter in the shape of a bull. *Line* 78, *p.* 402

The sun. Dante was in the constellation Gemini, and the sun was in Aries; part of those two constellations and the whole of Taurus lay between them. *Line* 80, *p.* 402

The fair nest of Leda. Gemini; Leda was the mother of the twins, Castor and Pollux. *Line* 93, *p.* 402

Swiftest heaven. The primum mobile which contains all other heavens and gives motion to the others revolving around the motionless earth. *Line* 94, *p.* 402

One circle. The empyrean. *Line* 106, *p.* 402

Vase. The primum mobile which is the root of all heavenly motion. *Line* 112, *p.* 403

Before the date. Reference to the error in Cæsar's calendar which would eventually have made January come in the spring; Gregory XIII corrected it. *Line* 131, *p.* 403

CANTO XXVIII

That volume. The ninth heaven according to some; the empyrean, to others. *Line* 13, *p.* 404

A circle of fire. Seraphim around whom in turn revolve the nine orders of the celestial hierarchy. *Line* 22, *p.* 404

And that a third, etc. The primum mobile is surrounded by Cherubim, Thrones, Dominations, Virtues, and Powers. *Line* 25, *p.* 404

A seventh, etc. Principalities and finally Archangels and Angels. *Line* 27, *p.* 404

Heaven, and all nature, hangs upon that point. "From that beginning depend heaven and nature." Aristotle, *Metaph.*, xii, 7. *Line* 38, *p.* 404

The circle. Seraphim. *Line* 39, *p.* 404

Exemplar. Revolution of the nine orders of angels around God which is so different from the revolution of the nine heavens around the earth. *Line* 52, *p.* 405

That. The Seraphim to which the primum mobile answers; the measure of both angelic orders and heavens is the "ruling intelligence" or degree of divine virtue rather than the size. *Line* 65, *p.* 405

In number. The sparkles exceeded the number which would be produced by the sixty-four squares of a chessboard, if for the first we reckoned one; for the next, two; for the third, four; and so went on doubling to the end of the account. *Line* 84, *p.* 406

Fearless of bruising from the nightly ram. Not injured, like the productions of our spring, by the influence of autumn, when the constellation Aries rises at sunset. *Line* 108, *p.* 406

Dionysius. The Areopagite in his book *De Coelesti Hierarchia*. *Line* 121, *p.* 408

Gregory. Gregory the Great who learned it from St. Paul, the eyewitness; see II *Cor.* xii, 2. *Line* 126, *p.* 408

CANTO XXIX

No longer. As short a space as the sun and moon are in changing hemispheres when they are opposite to each other in Aries and Libra; they both hang for a moment poised at the zenith. *Line* 1, *p.* 408

For, not in process of before or aft. There was no distinction in time until the creation of the world. *Line* 22, *p.* 409

Simple and mix'd, both form and substance. Dante says there are three kinds of creation: the simple and unmixed *form* is the highest, "the pure intelligence" or pure form; simple and unmixed *substance* is the lowest, "mere power," or natural phenomena; mixed form and substance is in between, the league of "intelligence and power," or man. *Line* 24, *p.* 409

NOTES

His threefold operation. He means that spiritual beings, brute matter, and the intermediate part of the creation which participates both of spirit and matter, were produced at once.
Line 30, *p.* 409

On Jerome's pages. St. Jerome had described the angels as created long before the rest of the universe, an opinion which Thomas Aquinas controverted; the latter, as Dante thinks, had scripture on his side.
Line 38, *p.* 409

Those penmen. As in *Genesis* i, 1, and *Ecclesiasticus*, xviii, 1.
Line 40, *p.* 409

The triple question. Where, when and how the angels had been created.
Line 48, *p.* 409

Of Bindi and of Lapi. Common names of men at Florence.
Line 111, *p.* 411

. . . Saint Anthony
Fattens with this his swine. The brothers of St. Anthony supported their paramours on the sale of these blessings; Dante may here mean priests in general.
Line 131, *p.* 411

With unstamped metal. With false indulgences.
Line 134, *p.* 411

Daniel. "Thousand thousands ministered unto him, and ten thousand times ten thousand stood before him." *Daniel* vii, 10.
Line 140, *p.* 412

CANTO XXX
Six thousand miles. He compares the vanishing of the vision to the fading away of the stars at dawn, when it is noonday six thousand miles off, and the shadow formed by the earth over the part of it inhabited by the poet is about to disappear.
Line 1, *p.* 412

Engirt. Appearing to be encompassed by these angelic bands who really are encompassed by it.
Line 13, *p.* 412

The last corporeal. From the primum mobile, the limit of the material universe, to the empyrean, the purely spiritual world.
Line 39, *p.* 413

Either mighty host. Of angels that remained faithful or of beatified souls in the form they will have at the last day.
Line 44, *p.* 413

Topaz. Angel.
Line 78, *p.* 414

In heaven a light. The Lake of Light around which sit the Blessed; its circumference is larger than the sun.
Line 100, *p.* 415

Into the yellow. The Lake which is like the yellow heart of a rose.
Line 122, *p.* 415

Of the great Harry. Emperor Henry VII, who came to Italy to redress wrongs; Italy was not yet prepared for reform.
Line 135, *p.* 415

He. Pope Clement V who opposed Henry.
Line 141, *p.* 416

Alagna's priest. Boniface VIII; see *Hell*, xix, 79.
Line 145, *p.* 416

CANTO XXXI
The saintly multitude. Human souls advanced to the state of glory through the mediation of Christ.
Line 2, *p.* 416

That other host. The angels.
Line 4, *p.* 416

Trinal beam. God, one and triune.
Line 25, *p.* 416

If the grim brood. The northern hordes who invaded Rome.
Line 28, *p.* 416

Helice. Callisto and her son Arcas changed into the constellations of the Great Bear, or Ursa Major, and of Boötes.
Line 29, *p.* 416

Senior. St. Bernard, the abbot of Clairvaux and the great promoter of the second crusade; he is here the symbol of contemplation by which men attain knowledge of God.
Line 55, *p.* 417

The third circle. The Virgin is the highest, Eve is the second and Rachel next with Beatrice beside her.
Line 62, *p.* 418

The queen. The Virgin Mary.
Line 108, *p.* 419

CANTO XXXII
She. Eve.
Line 3, *p.* 420

Ancestress. Ruth, the ancestress of David.
Line 8, *p.* 420

Two years. The time between the death of John the Baptist and his redemption by the death of Christ.
Line 28, *p.* 420

PARADISE

Augustin. Bishop of Hippo in the fourth century, and a celebrated writer; see Canto x, 117.   *Line* 30, p. 420

In holy Scripture. Jacob and Esau; see *Genesis* xxv, 22.   *Line* 60, p. 421

Palm. Symbol of Annunciation.   *Line* 100, p. 422

The seer. St. John the Revelator.   *Line* 112, p. 424

Of the fair bride. The Church.   *Line* 114, p. 424

The leader. Moses.   *Line* 116, p. 424

Anna. Mother of Mary.   *Line* 119, p. 424

Lucia. See *Hell*, ii, 97, and *Purgatory*, ix, 50.   *Line* 123, p. 424

CANTO XXXIII

Ended within me. The soul has attained its end when it is granted the vision of God.   *Line* 47, p. 426

Dread infinitude. Infinite virtue.   *Line* 76, p. 426

All properties. The substance is that which exists in itself, and the accident is that which is inherent in the substance but not of the essence.   *Line* 82, p. 427

Argo's shadow. The first known event was the expedition of the Argonauts, the shadow of whose vessel astonished Neptune.   *Line* 92, p. 427

Three orbs of triple hue, clipped in one bound. The Trinity.   *Line* 109, p. 427

One reflected. Christ.   *Line* 110, p. 427

The third. Holy Spirit.   *Line* 111, p. 427

That circling. Second of the circle, or "Light of Light," in which he dimly beheld the mystery of the incarnation.   *Line* 118, p. 427